Belonging

Belonging

A Relationship-Based Approach for Trauma-Informed Education

Sian Phillips
Deni Melim
Daniel A. Hughes

ROWMAN & LITTLEFIELD
Lanham • Boulder • New York • London

Published by Rowman & Littlefield
An imprint of The Rowman & Littlefield Publishing Group, Inc.
4501 Forbes Boulevard, Suite 200, Lanham, Maryland 20706
www.rowman.com

6 Tinworth Street, London, SE11 5AL, United Kingdom

British Library Cataloguing in Publication Information Available

Library of Congress Cataloging-in-Publication Data

Names: Phillips, Sian, 1964- author. | Hughes, Daniel, 1945- author. | Melim, Deni, 1970- author.
Title: Belonging : a relationship-based approach for trauma-informed education / Sian Phillips, Daniel Hughes, Deni Melim.
Description: Lanham : Rowman & Littlefield, [2020] | Includes bibliographical references and index. | Summary: "This book focuses on three important and comprehensive areas of theory and research that provide a theoretical, clinical, and integrated intervention model for developing the relationships and a sense of safety for children with developmental trauma need"—Provided by publisher.
Identifiers: LCCN 2019059537 (print) | LCCN 2019059538 (ebook) | ISBN 9781538135983 (cloth) | ISBN 9781538135990 (paperback) | ISBN 9781538136003 (epub)
Subjects: LCSH: Affective education. | Attachment disorder in children.
Classification: LCC LB1072 .P55 2020 (print) | LCC LB1072 (ebook) | DDC 370.15/34—dc23
LC record available at https://lccn.loc.gov/2019059537
LC ebook record available at https://lccn.loc.gov/2019059538

♾️™ The paper used in this publication meets the minimum requirements of American National Standard for Information Sciences—Permanence of Paper for Printed Library Materials, ANSI/NISO Z39.48-1992.

Contents

Acknowledgments

I am a huge fan of the term "Ubuntu." Writing this book has highlighted its meaning—I am because we are. This journey has allowed me to work with colleagues who are passionate, skilled, and generous with time and spirit and my family who are generous with patience and love. None of what I have been able to do would have been possible alone.

Thank you, Dan, for introducing me to DDP, providing mentorship, and encouraging me to write this book. Jon Baylin, thank you too for your encouragement. My DDP family is large and I am lucky to be part of such a supportive community.

Deni, thank you for your wisdom, passion, and insight and for your remarkable ability to embody PACE in all that you do. You are a gifted teacher. Doug and Gerry, thank you for being such kind and caring men. Your obvious delight in the children, and your deep caring and courage to be vulnerable have allowed our boys to have new possibilities for what it means to be a man and for our girls to know that relationships with men don't have to hurt. Thank you to each student who comes into our classroom for teaching us to listen better and see what you need. The Belong classroom is supported by many behind the scenes. Karen Shannon, Alison McDonnell, Lisa Bickerstaffe, Stephanie Palmer, Sonia Gentile, and now The Maltby Center, thanks for having our back. Throughout the Limestone and Algonquin & Lakeshore Catholic boards, there are so many professionals who strive every day to make connections with our most vulnerable children. Thank you for all you do. Thank you especially to Wendy Fisher, Mike Blackburn, Jen Ramsay, Rob Lloyd, Alison Fraser, Nicola Dillard, Ean Patterson, Kelly Maracle, and Mike Payne for your energy and commitment and company on this journey.

Thank you Mark Kerr for giving us the opportunity to share our work. Your positivity and exuberance make me believe that anything is possible! Thank you to my mentor Vince Caccamo who died in April 2017. Whenever I get stuck, I ask myself, "What would Vince say?" I am so thankful for his influence and unwavering belief in me.

None of what I would have been able to accomplish in my work life would be possible without my family. Thank you to my mother, Hefina, whose passion for education has long been part of my world. To my husband, Chris, who has waited patiently for me to come up for air over the past few months of writing—you make me a better person. Thank you, Alastair and Megan for teaching me the power of loving you no matter what.

Sian

I would like to thank all the families who have trusted their children to my care, and who have worked alongside our team with open hearts and open minds. Thank you to my students for they are the true teachers. They are willing to shake off their protective armor and allow me to really know who they are rather than to just know the stories that brought them to Belong. For kids who have been hurt by relationships, they bravely step into forging new ones, and in doing so, they reveal what beautiful people they are inside and out.

Thank you, Jerry and Doug—you have taught me the importance of laughing together as often as possible and of leaning on each other whenever needed. I am in awe of your expertise, kindness, and genuine connection with our kids. These past six years would not have been possible without the two of you.

To my principal and friend, Lisa—you have been by our side with a smile and a secret door knock since the classroom opened. To Colin—our outstanding custodian who never hesitates to stop and talk with our students, who always makes sure we are included, and who tirelessly tosses our tennis balls back down to us from the roof! To my superintendent Karen—you have provided our classroom team with a sense of security in an ever-changing education climate and always put our families and students first.

Thank you to my family, Paul, Mackenzie, and Jake—I always seem to have something on the go and this book is no different. Your love, encouragement, and willingness to wait "just five more minutes" make this your accomplishment too.

Finally, to my mentor and friend, Dr. Sian Phillips—our journey together began seven years ago, and I am a better teacher because of you. As we like to say when we describe our beginning to others, "the stars aligned" and Belong came to be with the right people at the right time and in the right place. Your devotion to our students, their families, and to our classroom team is unwavering. It is your voice, your patient teaching, and your energy that keep us moving forward and create different possibilities for our kids. You have brought all of us together to truly understand the power of relationships.

Deni

I would like to acknowledge the incredible Belong program that Sian and Deni and others created and continue to develop year by year to serve children who face significant challenges along with their parents. It has been my great pleasure to see how they have brought to life principles of attachment and trauma in meeting the complex social, emotional, and cognitive needs of these children. This program has been able to demonstrate how to provide safe, nurturing, and transforming relationships for children who do not trust relationships. DDP has been a model of treatment and care for these children, and Belong has brought these therapeutic principles into the classroom.

At the same time, I would like to acknowledge the individuals who engage in the ongoing psychological and neurobiological research that demonstrate how our important relationships develop and are maintained, and how they are crucial for assisting children in healing and attaining their optimal developmental milestones.

Dan

Preface

There once was a boy named Lucas. For those of you who don't know him, he is a boy with the most magical brown eyes. They have this little twinkle to them that makes you think you're looking at stars! And . . . he has a smile to match! Lucas is a curious kid, a scientist in the making. He can tell you all about the Titanic and how blood pumps through your body. He can give you advice on how to build a world in Minecraft or how to create a masterpiece from Lego pieces. He even has these feet that have little springs in them that make him jump so high that he's as tall as his teacher! And he's probably the only kid you'll meet that can tell you what the W.I.P. standard is.

We didn't always know Lucas this way. The day he walked into our classroom for the first time was memorable. He and his foster parent were visiting the week before school started. He wandered around looking at everything as quickly as he could. As he moved from item to item, his face and his hands communicated his uncertainty. His eyes grew wider, and his hands started to fidget with items he picked up as he paced around. He wanted to leave just as quickly as he had arrived. He returned about five minutes later and asked, "Where is my desk? There aren't any desks. This is supposed to be a classroom!" Such a simple change in what he expected in a classroom created such anxiety for him. This became a common pattern of interaction with Lucas. He would have a preconceived expectation, something would be different from his expectation, and panic and anxiety would settle in, fueling a verbal and/or physical reaction (hyperarousal). At other times, he seemed sad and withdrawn, his face lacked expression, and he would avoid any attempts to engage him socially (hypo-arousal). We knew that we had a lot of work ahead of us to help Lucas feel safe and begin to learn.

Lucas is a young boy who had experienced both neglect and physical abuse as a young child. He was removed from his birth parent's care and placed in foster care. Unfortunately, multiple changes in caregivers reinforced his lack of trust in adults.

At the age of 8 years, his behavior made it too challenging for him to access a regular classroom environment, and he was referred to us at the Belong program, a specialized school program for children with attachment and trauma difficulties.

When children like Lucas are hurt repeatedly by the relationships that are supposed to keep them safe, their development becomes impaired in predictable ways. Cook et al. (2005) and van der Kolk (2005) use the term "developmental trauma" to describe impairment across seven different domains. Children who have been hurt by those who were supposed to keep them safe, struggle to be in relationships, identify and regulate their physical states, identify and regulate their emotional states, and dissociate in the presence of stress—which limits their memory. They have difficulty regulating their behavior and cognition, and have such difficulty developing a coherent and confident sense of self (see textbox 1.1).

TEXTBOX 1.1. DEVELOPMENTAL DOMAINS IMPACTED BY DEVELOPMENTAL TRAUMA

1. ATTACHMENT: Difficulties with trusting others, perspective taking, social isolation, empathy.
2. BIOLOGY: Difficulties identifying and regulating physical states, somatic problems, problems with balance and coordination.
3. AFFECT REGULATION: Difficulties identifying, regulating, and communicating emotional states.
4. DISSOCIATION: Variable access to states of consciousness, impaired memory for events occurring in particular states.
5. BEHAVIORAL CONTROL: Poor impulse control, self-destructive, difficulty self-soothing, oppositional behaviors, reenactments of past traumas.
6. COGNITION: Difficulties in attention, lack of curiosity, learning difficulties, speech/language problems, processing novel information, reflective functioning.
7. SELF-CONCEPT: Lack of continuity in sense of self, negative self-concept and high level of shame, poor body image.

Lucas is one of many students who struggle to manage in a regular school environment, given his developmental trauma. Students with developmental trauma demand a high level of limited resources, but they don't seem to benefit enough from them. They are the students who cause many sleepless nights for teachers who creatively and persistently try to teach them, but are met repeatedly with aggression, stealing, lying, social difficulties, defiance, attention difficulties, inability to learn from consequences, lack of remorse, or other forms of rejecting behavior.

One of the challenges for educators has been how to manage these highly disruptive behaviors in the classroom. Many school cultures reflect fundamental beliefs that students have the power to choose their behavior. If educators hold tight to these beliefs, then behavioral or cognitive behavioral strategies such as removal from class, withdrawal of privileges, or other forms of exclusion follow with the understanding that strong discipline—a more powerful incentive—is necessary to get students to "choose" an alternative or more appropriate behavior (Howard, 2013).

If you are interested in trauma-informed education, you have probably already realized that reward and punishment approaches are not successful with students who have experienced developmental trauma. Given the profound impairment across developmental domains, they do not yet have the neurological circuitry that allows them to be aware of their feelings and thoughts, and so have no way of modifying them. Neither do they have the self-regulation required to stop and think, make informed decisions, or ask for help from adults if needed. Self-awareness and self-regulation are skills that are built through the experience of safe, attuned relationships with adults and impaired in the absence of good care.

Students who have experienced safe and trusting relationships will do well when we outline clear goals, make choices clear, and combine those choices with appropriate consequences. Students with developmental trauma need first to experience adults who can create emotional safety for them, who accurately mirror and organize their internal experiences, and who can co-regulate their affective states. Without this experience of co-regulation of their affect, they will not be able to develop the self-regulation and self-reflection skills that they so desperately need if they are able to "choose" a better alternative behavior or a better life.

Psychological meta-analysis studies repeatedly show that the greatest predictor of change is through the development of safe relationships. Our dilemma is how to establish these safe relationships with our students who have given up trusting adults. Merely being kind and "nice" is not enough. Being kind, empathic, and nice can actually be a sign of danger for our children who have experienced abuse and neglect, causing increased arousal rather than the soothing we hope for leaving us feeling frustrated, rejected and perhaps wondering if we have the skills to work with this group of vulnerable children.

Dyadic Developmental Practice is the extension of Dyadic Developmental Psychotherapy (DDP), a model of therapy founded by Dan Hughes for children who experienced neglect and abuse and for the parents who care for them. The DDP framework and the practice of its principles provides us with a way to provide the necessary safety for our students and to facilitate the journey from mistrust to trust. It guides us to provide interventions and development of school cultures that can meet the needs of some of our most vulnerable children. This book focuses mainly on children who have experienced relational trauma. However, we also want the reader to be aware that inequity such as racism, poverty, homophobia and other forms of discrimination, lower expectations, and micro-aggressions also compromise a student's sense of safety and impede learning. Dyadic Developmental Practice provides a framework that allows us to recognize and talk about all aspects of our student's experiences. It also helps us be aware of how we might be exacerbating the lack of safety for our students in the way we structure our policies, schools, curriculum, and practices.

This book focuses on three important and comprehensive areas of theory and research that provide a theoretical, clinical, and integrated intervention model for developing the felt sense of safety children with developmental trauma need. These are attachment, intersubjectivity, and interpersonal neurobiology.

Attachment theory and research originated in the 1950s with John Bowlby and Mary Ainsworth. They made it clear that human infants form an attachment with their primary caregiver who will place the needs of the infant first in order to insure their safety and development. Subsequently, extensive research over the years has demonstrated that a secure attachment is a protective factor against the development of mental health problems and it facilitates the child's emotional, cognitive, psychological, and social development. Children with secure attachment have a template for relating with others that includes the readiness to rely on trusted others for guidance, comfort, and a knowledge of how best to learn and to live. Children without a secure attachment—especially children who have no organized pattern of attachment behaviors—have great difficulty managing routine stresses in their lives and also have difficulty with both regulating their emotional lives and being able to make sense of the meaning of what is happening in their lives. Children like Lucas carry the mistrust of adults into the classroom. They do not rely on adults, so they do not follow their guidance nor "respect their authority." For these children to begin to accept the influence of their teachers, they need to first learn to trust them, be comforted by them, and allow them to take the lead.

Intersubjectivity theory and research began to emerge in the 1960s and the 1970s when infant researchers discovered a pattern of synchronized movements occurring between parents and their infants. These movements involved their affective states, focus of attention, and intentional states. Within these synchronized, nonverbal (bodily) states, the parent and infant were communicating their experiences of each other. In this way, the infant most often discovered that she was interesting, delightful, lovable, and enjoyable because her parents communicated interest, delight, love, and joy when with her. She also learned that her parents listened to her wishes so that when she communicated that her parents were not relating in a way that she liked, her parents would change how they related. They would repair the relationship so that it would provide the safety and positive reciprocal engagement that the infant needed. Lucas, and other children like him, have had too few of these positive intersubjective experiences. Lucas learned from his early abusive and neglectful relationship that he was not interesting, lovable, or enjoyable. He also learned that he could not influence his parents to provide the kind of interaction that he needed. As a result, he began to avoid intersubjective experiences from all adults—anticipating that they would lead to the same negative relationship experiences and information about himself that he originally experienced with his first caregivers. His avoidance then made it very hard for his teachers to influence him. His avoidance was not a cognitive choice, but a deeply rooted, unconscious survival strategy.

In the last twenty to 30 years, the theories and research involving neurobiology and neuropsychology have corroborated what we have learned from attachment and intersubjectivity research. The field of interpersonal neurobiology identifies clearly how safety is essential if the brain is to develop well and function in a coherent and integrated manner, and that our sense of self is developed from our sense of the other. Without safety, our brains become preoccupied with how to find safety. The neural circuitry that then develops is that which facilitates defensive and protective behavior—fight, flight, or freeze. Our subcortex becomes specialized to deal with threat and to ensure survival. Children like Lucas are constantly in a state of alarm, making it difficult to develop the neural circuitry that will integrate his cortex, the thinking part of his brain that will help him be a good student. Without enough safety, children cannot develop the skills of self-regulation, problem-solving, controlling impulses, delaying gratification, or pursuing learning goals.

Safety, therefore, is crucial for any learning, but is essential for students with developmental trauma. Although it is relationships that have hurt our students who have experienced abuse and neglect, it is through relationships that they will begin to heal and learn. In order for them to benefit from the many opportunities that education has to offer, we must first find a way to facilitate secure attachment to teachers and to encourage them to engage in repetitive, synchronized, reciprocal interactions that will foster healthier brain development.

Our book focuses on Dyadic Developmental Practice as the means whereby we bring the findings of attachment, intersubjectivity, and neuropsychological research into the classroom. The framework and the practice of its principles provide us with a way to provide safety for our students and to facilitate the journey from mistrust to trust. It guides us to provide interventions and development of school cultures that can meet the needs of some of our most vulnerable children.

The first part of this book presents in some detail what we have learned from the interpersonal neurobiology, attachment, and intersubjectivity research about why students with developmental trauma have such a hard time learning. Lucas is a young boy who experienced abuse, neglect, and had multiple transitions. For all of the examples in this book we have changed names and ages and have sometimes created students that are an amalgam of students we have worked with to ensure confidentiality. We hope that you will come to understand our students' behavior, intentions, motivations, hopes, and struggles in ways that help you understand your own students. We will then introduce you to Dyadic Developmental Practice as a powerful framework for the development of safe relationships and interventions in the classroom.

In the second part of this book, we will introduce to you the Belong program. The Belong program in Kingston, Ontario, is the first classroom in North America to be built explicitly upon the Dyadic Developmental Practice principles. We will outline our program and the successes and challenges that the team face as they help students settle their arousal systems in preparation for developing relationships and learning. Our classroom is specifically for students who have experienced developmental trauma. We offer many examples of how to respond to challenging behaviors with the hope that it gives others a language to address these issues with their own students.

The third part of the book will describe the work of four schools in the Kingston area—three elementary and one alternative high school—who work with highly complex children and families, and where a high percentage of students have experienced developmental trauma. The teachers in these four schools have received training in Dyadic Developmental Practice and receive ongoing consultation to bring the principles into the development of school culture, their teaching, and classroom management. Unlike the Belong program, these schools do not have the luxury of such high teacher to student ratios or the possibility of being so flexible with structure and programming. Nevertheless, the understanding of how trauma impacts development and the use of Dyadic Developmental Practice are helping students be more settled to learn. We will leave you with what our journey has taught us about what it means for us to become truly trauma-informed and the subsequent implications for policies, school and classroom structure, curriculum, and day-to-day interactions.

Sian, Deni, and Dan

I

You Ask Why I Act As I Do

You ask why I act as I do—
My screaming, throwing hitting—
I think that I should know, but I don't know.

My actions—they call them
Compulsive, impulsive, repulsive—keep bursting out
Of some nameless, chaotic, broken
place that you call my "self"

You say that they are intentional,
Though I don't know if I have ever had an intention,
If you mean a clear motive that follows from my own interwoven
Thoughts and feelings.

You talk about thoughts and feelings as if I
Had any idea what you are talking about.
I guess I have them since you say so, but
I just cannot find words—
Or even pictures—for them.

If you want to help me . . .
Help me stop what I'm doing,
You will have to go with me into
The inner place that is me.
You will have to join your thoughts with mine,
Your feelings with mine.
Give me words for those moving forms within me.

If I let you discover and name those inner places in me
I will feel terror
*   that you might name them disgusting or "evil."*
Understand why I hesitate.

If you can accept what you find in me and believe it to be of value
I may learn to do the same.
If you join me inside
And help me to arrange the parts in side—
Name, understand, and
Even be proud of them—
We will know why I do what I do
And we will discover what
I now can begin to do.

Daniel, A. Hughes, 2012

1

Lessons from Polyvagal Theory

If a Child Could Do Better, He or She Would

SAFETY

The key to survival is relationships. Stephen Porges speaks of connection to others as a biological imperative. We are wired to connect. Clinical research and the literature on trauma-informed education have long identified relationships as a key ingredient in the therapy office or classroom. However, the ability to engage in relationships is determined by how our autonomic nervous system "feels" in the presence of another person. If we feel safe, we can approach; if we don't feel safe, we find ways to avoid connection.

Our brain's job is to keep us alive. To do so, it has developed particular neural circuits that specialize in deciding whether we are safe, in danger, or are in a life-threatening situation. Stephen Porges coined the term *neuroception* to describe how our autonomic nervous system can instantaneously shift our physiological state to respond to safety or danger. This neural evaluation of risk is unconscious and reflexive (Porges, 2004). If we are in immediate danger, we don't have time to think. Imagine if you came face-to-face with a bear while on a hike. It would not be prudent to be curious about its size, the shape of its nose, or its hair color. Such perception is a much slower process that involves more integration of brain regions and is an option only when we are sure that we are not going to get eaten by the bear.

The difference between neuroception and perception is one of the challenges for us in the classroom. We ask children to perceive or think about the ways they are safe when their neuroception has already communicated to their autonomic nervous system that they are unsafe and their neural circuits have already organized many biological systems to mobilize or immobilize. We have no control over our bodies once neuroception communicates danger. Breathing is the only function of the autonomic nervous system that we have any control over. This is why breathing is such a fundamental part of therapies, meditation, yoga, or tai chi that have been developed to help us calm our minds. So many of our students desperately want to be good students and to have friends, but are puzzled by their enormous fight, flight, or freeze reactions. They don't know why they behave the way they do. They are hijacked by their autonomic nervous system that is convinced, based on early negative experiences, that all adults are bears and that all environments have hidden threats.

Being told that we are safe or receiving reassurance that there is no risk rarely, if ever, makes us feel better. Safety is a sensory or physiological experience, not a cognitive one. In order to relax, learn, or approach others, we must "feel" safe. Many foster parents and teachers struggle to understand why children, despite months in a safe environment and many repetitions of being told that they will not be left alone or punished harshly, continue to behave in ways that reflect such a deep experience of mistrust and lack of safety. Their brain circuitry cannot yet offer them a different sensory experience.

Neuroception unfortunately can't be changed by thinking. To feel safe, we require from others repetitive signaling of safety from their voices, faces, and body language. Those safety signals bypass our consciousness and target primitive areas of our brain, allowing us to put a brake on our defense systems and find connection with others. Feeling safe is crucial for us to develop properly. A sense of safety makes others like us better, allows us to use our brains optimally, allows our organs and bodies to work as they should, influences what we hear, and even alters our sense of smell (Porges, 2011). When relationships hurt, there is huge impact on brain development, our immune system, hormonal systems, and even the way our DNA is read and transcribed (Siegel, 2012). Those who cannot find safety in relationships are more likely to die 20 years earlier and are more than seven times more likely to have heart, lung, and other organ diseases than those of us who can (Felitti et al., 1998).

When Lucas entered the classroom for the first time, he neurocepted a lack of safety, despite all intentions to place him at ease. The classroom and the people in it were unfamiliar to him, and the signals his brain then received were to be mobilized for a flight response. The neural circuits in his subcortex knew how to take care of him and produced the cortisol and adrenaline required to activate his large muscles, so he could run out of the classroom. This was not something he had any conscious control over. It was an adaptive immediate coping strategy. Given its unconscious origin, conscious intervention, such as provision of consequences or a program of incentives, would not be effective. We would first need to develop Lucas's ability to neurocept safety. Once his nervous system could relax, he would then be able to "think" about what might happen if he turned over his desk, swore at his friends, or tore up his work.

During his first few weeks with us, Lucas maintained a hypervigilance for threat. Our soft eye contact, calm voices, and attempts to communicate safety with smiles and relaxed body language could not be neurocepted as they were intended. He couldn't trust them and saw them as manipulation. He was completely unaware of what was happening to him, but because he needed to make sense of his behavior, he typically blamed others for the way he was feeling. He didn't know he was scared; he believed he was angry and that others had made him angry by walking too close to him, moving his work, not letting him play the game he wanted, and so on.

Predictability in the routines made him most settled, yet he walked around fearing that things could change at any moment, so he could never truly relax. This constant state of hypervigilance must have felt like walking a tightrope with no net below and no hand on the side to catch him if he fell. He always felt as if he was in danger. Anticipation of harm kept him in his sympathetic nervous system. He was angry and reactive, and frequently yelled at staff or peers, sometimes over-tipping a desk or throwing something that was close to him. Any indication of alarm from adults or peers would confirm to him that others were going to give him trouble or were going to reject him, reinforcing his need for hypervigilance and defense. If things didn't go his way in those first few weeks, there would be anger and tears that communicated his underlying sense of panic. Peers were wary of him and gave him a wide berth. Lucas was so obviously unhappy and had no insight into why he behaved the way he did or why others were behaving the way they did. His behavior was not a choice. If he could do better, he would.

When driven by his sympathetic nervous system, Lucas heard others' tone of voice as threatening and frequently misinterpreted facial expressions as communicating anger. If we could have measured his heart rate, it would have been rapid, and we could certainly see a more shallow and quick breathing pattern. His behavior was limited to two options: fight or flight. His thinking was concrete and focused on the present danger. All of the internal and external signals to his brain were ones of danger.

Although he was typically angry and reactive, after several weeks we started to experience times when he was anxious and clingy. His fight responses were less present, and his desire for connection started to be less ambiguous. Relationships created so much anxiety for him that although he wanted to be near the staff, he was still so wary that they might not like him or might hurt him in other ways. His solution was to be demanding and controlling. He resisted direction and authority. In this way, there was less possibility for uncertainty. He wanted full attention, and when the staff had competing obligations, he fell back into his angry and rejecting solutions. Their momentary disconnection felt dangerous to him—he wasn't important any more, he wasn't liked—and his sympathetic nervous system provided him with protection from the painful feelings. Again, trying to make sense of his feelings and behavior, he typically blamed others for his feeling upset.

Occasionally, he would be quiet. His face would appear flat, his eyes, in contrast to the hypervigilant scanning, would be downcast, and when he could talk, his voice lacked richness or variability. The staff experienced these moments as Lucas somehow being far away from them. His mobilization responses were not enough for him in these moments, and he fell out of connection into a more hypo-aroused or immobilized state. These states typically followed peer conflicts or interactions with staff where the staff member used a firm tone for limit setting. Lucas, when he was in this physiological state, made sense of his behavior by saying that he was "dumb" or "a bad kid." He withdrew from others, not understanding why anyone would want to be near him.

This hypo-aroused state was facilitated by the dorsal branch of the parasympathetic nervous system. The parasympathetic nervous system is typically associated with relaxation and social engagement. However, when danger is very high, this second parasympathetic system, driven by the unmyelinated dorsal vagal nerve, offers us a last-chance solution: a freeze response. This freeze response is like having a foot on the brake and gas at the same time. Although highly aroused, our dorsal vagal system lowers our heart rate dramatically, and our breathing slows right down. Oxygen to our brain and organs is limited, and we could faint. We share this ancient immobilization system with all vertebrates, and it originates low down in the brain stem—the oldest part of our brain in terms of our evolution (Porges, 2018). In humans, the freeze response is thought to be the mechanism that underlies dissociation often experienced as emotional numbing, difficulty thinking, or articulating our thoughts, a sense of speechlessness, de-personalization, or losing touch with our surroundings.

Lucas found it impossible to negotiate a safe interpersonal connection. Angry and rejecting didn't feel safe. Anxious and clingy didn't feel safe. Dissociation didn't feel safe. Without the operation of the social engagement system, Lucas could not accurately read the safety signals coming from the staff and could not engage with others in a way that calmed him. His physiology was primed for getting him out of a dangerous situation, and others were seen as an obstacle to survival rather than a support. The muscles in his inner ear were tuned to frequencies of sound that communicated danger. Visually, he misread our faces, seeing calm or neutral faces as angry faces, and his high heart rate and breathing fed back to his brain that he was about to be eaten by an angry bear. He could not think about what might happen if he behaved in a particular way, nor did he have the cortical resources to help him recognize that what was making him anxious was something he could manage. His deep mistrust of interpersonal connection made it very difficult for us to provide the reciprocal safety signals he needed to calm his nervous system and prove that we were not bears.

Lucas's early years were so full of danger, given neglect and abuse, that his physiology had become trained to keep him alive through various fight, flight, or freeze strategies. Trauma prevents the capacity for close relationships and the ability to play—two crucial opportunities for social, emotional, and cognitive learning (Porges, 2018). If we are constantly neurocepting danger, our only objective is to find safety. We don't have the luxury of listening to others' ideas, engaging in imaginative play, or sharing physical space. A vicious cycle emerges; the less capacity for intimacy and play, the less opportunity to develop the social engagement system, and the less capacity for intimacy and play—unfortunately, a clear example of the aphorism—"the rich get richer and the poor get poorer." Lucas and other students with developmental trauma are locked into this negative feedback cycle where easy, mutually enjoyable social relationships are elusive.

Typical classroom management strategies rely on asking students to think ahead about what will happen if they choose to behave negatively and on asking them to choose an alternative strategy if they would like to avoid punishment. If we believe that a child is "choosing" to behave in one way, then we assume they *can* choose to behave in more socially acceptable ways. A child who is mobilized by his or her sympathetic nervous system or the dorsal vagal system has neurocepted danger or life threat and is in no position to think into the future or to evaluate the implications of one behavior versus another until their arousal levels decrease and the threat of danger has passed. Unfortunately, adults tend to get irritated or angry at a child who is not complying or who is responding with aggression. Their eyes, muscles around their mouth, tone of voice, and body posture, all communicate signs of threat, thus reinforcing the need for a defensive response rather than influencing different behavioral outcomes.

Keeping safety as a priority does not mean that we never provide limits or consequences. It just reminds us about *how* we do so. In fact, the predictability of structure and adult responses is part of what contributes to that felt sense of safety. Understanding our body's innate responses to safety and danger reminds us that big behavioral reactions are often outside of our student's control and, therefore, require us to co-regulate their underlying emotions—be it fear, anxiety, or anger—so that their nervous system can relax and be open to other behavioral possibilities.

For us to provide our students with a felt sense of safety, we as adults have to be in our social engagement system where we can communicate with our eyes, voices, gestures, and body language that there is nothing to fear. We need to be able to co-regulate our children's emotional experiences to initiate that felt sense of safety. The minute we become fearful, angry, defensive, critical, or judgmental, we communicate that there is an interpersonal threat and reinforce the very behaviors that we find troubling. To feel safe ourselves in the presence of aggression or high-risk behaviors is not easy. We must always put our own oxygen mask on first if we are to be of help to our students. It is our hope as we continue to offer you insights into what is happening in our student's brains that you can use this knowledge to recognize that their behavior is driven by fear and if they could do better they would. This knowledge in combination with Dyadic Developmental Practice provides us with a way to have safe interactions and conversations with our students.

For Lucas, we started by arranging the physical environment to optimize his sense of safety. We brought a desk in and allowed him to place it where he wanted. He put it near the back of the room, closest to where the teacher kept her own materials. He initially worked at his desk and ensured that no one worked behind him. It was important that he could see who might approach him from every angle. Our hope was that if we could give Lucas a sense of control over his physical environment, he could be less activated physiologically. His brain then could neurocept less danger and there was a chance that he could be more open to social engagement.

In combination with providing a physical space that allowed him to feel safer, we used the DDP principles of acceptance and empathy liberally to communicate emotional safety. We reminded ourselves that his hyper- or hypo-aroused behavior was not pleasurable or deliberately chosen. It represented a fundamental fear of harm. If he could do better, he would. Having this understanding helped us from moving ourselves into reactive and defensive responses. Although we were clear that hurting himself or others was not permitted in the classroom, we accepted his underlying emotional experiences of fear, anger, shame, and confusion without judgment. We used our voices at a frequency and with prosody that communicated safety. We made sure our faces were clear and unambiguous in the communication of acceptance and empathy and that we were attuned to any possibility that he needed a break from our attempts to engage him. Social engagement was new for him, and his brain was trained to view novelty with alarm rather than with interest. He could initially only manage limited interactions with us. Following upsets, our focus was to help Lucas understand what had made him fearful and organize his experience, and then, importantly, how to repair with staff and peers. With many repetitions, we hoped to move him from the more primitive defense systems to a ventral vagal organization where he would be able to engage with others, collaborate, negotiate, and experience reciprocal pleasure.

THE SHAPING OF OUR NERVOUS SYSTEM AND IMPLICATIONS FOR THE CLASSROOM

Porges's Polyvagal theory helps us to understand our student's challenging behavior as adaptations for survival, as well as giving us ways to understand why the establishment of safety is such a crucial first step to any intervention. From Porges's work, we know that we have a hierarchy of three defense systems. The most recently evolved is the social engagement system, facilitated by a myelinated (smart) branch of the vagus nerve that links our heart and lungs with pathways that regulate the muscles of the face and head. When we feel safe, a branch of the myelinated vagus nerve influences the heart and lungs to allow for slower, regulated breathing. Our stress response system that produces adrenaline and cortisol is turned down. Our facial muscles coordinate expressions that communicate warmth and allow for eye contact that is soft and maintained. The muscles of our inner ear are tuned to frequencies of sound that feel safe, and our larynx promotes vocalizations that are likewise experienced as nonthreatening communication. The information that is then being read from our visceral organs, as well as our social environment, is communicating that there is nothing to fear and that we can lean into our relationships. In a positive feedback cycle, the pleasure we receive from being in safe reciprocal relationships supports higher vagal tone and social engagement. Our vagal circuit, when working from this organization, allows for optimal health, a dampening of stress-related physiological states, and a support of growth and restoration for our body's organs (Porges, 2018). This social engagement system is unique to mammals and evolved as we recognized the need for collaboration and caring for our young as a way to maximize our survival.

In the classroom, students who are in their social engagement system appear relaxed. They manage distractions and slight upsets smoothly using negotiation or collaboration to solve interpersonal problems. They are open to new learning are adaptive, creative, intuitive, and engaged. These are the students who know how to ask for help from adults when they have reached their limits of independence and expect that help will be forthcoming.

When we feel safe, the social engagement system inhibits older more primitive defense systems. Humans share with vertebrates two primary defense systems. The fight-flight system, which is facilitated through the sympathetic nervous system, allows a rapid access to physiological resources so we have enough power to defend through aggression or running away. When we are being organized for defense by our sympathetic nervous system, our breathing is more rapid, our heart rate is faster, and the muscles of our inner ear are tuned for lower frequency, more threatening sounds. We communicate with our faces and voices alarm, fear, and anger that communicate danger for others. We also become highly attuned to the nonverbal expressions of others that communicate danger. We are not connected in that warm, easy way that the social engagement system allows.

Students who are driven by their sympathetic nervous system are typically quick to upset. They become verbally and sometimes physically aggressive, blame others, and fail to see their role in a situation. They are impulsive and have difficulty paying attention. They may be demanding, controlling, intimidating, and argumentative. Challenges often precipitate anger, followed by running out of the room, or angry refusal to comply. They are often the students labeled with attention deficit disorder or oppositional defiant disorder.

When mobilization responses can't provide safety, our autonomic nervous system facilitates a shift to the dorsal vagal pathway of the parasympathetic nervous system. We share this survival mechanism with vertebrates, and it is the oldest one in terms of our evolution. The greater the danger, the older the system we use for survival. When in this state, we play dead in the hope that danger will pass us by. We have chemicals in our brain that protect us from feeling pain. We become numb, spacey, unfocused, and desolate. The vagus nerve, in addition to slowing our heart rate, changes the function of our organs below the diaphragm. When we are in life threat, we may urinate or defecate. If we spend a lot of time in immobilized organization, we may develop gut problems, stomach problems, diabetes, and chronic fatigue as those organs no longer receive the oxygen and chemical nutrients required to rest and restore function.

At school, we may not immediately recognize the student who is immobilized. They are not the squeaky wheel that demands immediate attention. However, as we begin to know them, they are often the students who seem to miss much of our instruction because they are daydreaming. They may seem depressed or to have low energy. They don't seem to be able to initiate work or social interactions. They have difficulty looking you in the eye and may be hard to hear when they talk to you. You may feel that connection with them is elusive and that they seem very far away from you.

To maximize our chances of survival, our brain must be able to neurocept accurately and to move between the three hierarchies of defense as needed. To learn this skill, we require an environment that is predominately safe and where, if there is danger, that danger is infrequent and does not last long. We also need adults to co-regulate our arousal—adults who can accurately read our distress and provide comfort, and who are constantly reading our nonverbal responses about whether they are responding in a way that is right for us. Children who have experienced developmental trauma have experienced danger that was frequent, prolonged, and often life-threatening, requiring their alarm system to be in constant operation and limiting the opportunity for relaxed social engagement. The adults in their world typically increased distress rather than calmed it.

The neural circuitry that develops in the face of persistent danger is not that which allows for accurate neuroception and social engagement. Children who have experienced abuse and neglect become skilled at using fight and flight responses, freeze responses, or both in order to survive. Even when the danger is removed, they are constantly neurocepting danger either because they now have a faulty neuroception and perception system or because they believe that although there may be no danger in that moment, there soon will be and to relax would be foolish. Fight, flight, or freeze responses remain in place because our brain's job is to keep us alive and it is better to overprotect than to under-protect.

When we don't have safety, we don't have choice. Our biology takes over. Our students may be confused by their behavior. Their conscious awareness may tell them that they want to be a good student, make friends, and be liked, and yet they behave in ways that makes that impossible. The story they come to tell themselves is that they are just stupid or bad kids and they carry a backpack of shame with them to school each day.

Establishing safety and trust for Lucas was a long and difficult path. Staff had to be so creative in the ways that they facilitated connection. What worked one day did not work the next. The closer we came, the more nervous he became about how that felt. It was definitely a two steps forward, three steps back kind of dance. He wanted to trust us, but tolerating the vulnerability that came with needing someone and the potential harm that could come from adults easily frightened him. Acceptance of that struggle, empathy for it, and letting him know that we noticed his dilemma helped us all stay on the path.

Before we outline how attachment theory and intersubjectivity theory guide us to establishing safe relationships, let's delve a little further into what we have learned about interpersonal neurobiology to help us understand these behavioral responses. The constant experience of stress involved with not feeling safe causes structural alterations in our student's brain akin to acquired brain injuries.

2

Lessons from Interpersonal Neurobiology

The brain develops from the bottom up and the inside out. Higher or more external brain regions reflect the health and organization of these lower, internal brain regions (Siegel, 2012). The way the brain develops is greatly dependent on the type of caregiving it receives. When we receive the kind of caregiving that allows us to feel safe, then our brain organizes neural circuits that allow us to think flexibly, be adaptive when we encounter difficulties, process information coherently, have the right kind of energy for whatever environment we are in, and behave in ways that are predictable and stable. Dan Siegel (2012) provides the acronym FACES to describe the functions available to a healthy mind: a healthy mind is one that is Flexible, Adaptive, Coherent, Energized and Stable, characteristics that are associated with being a good student.

Many of our students who have developmental trauma are very inflexible, often insisting on control, and are very unpracticed at the give and take of healthy relationships. They are also not adaptive, are easily overwhelmed by stress and unable to find strategies to make things better. Information is not perceived or communicated in a coherent fashion, which makes communication challenging and leads to frustrations in relationships. Energy levels are either too high or too low, again making it difficult to engage in a comfortable and socially engaged manner. Instability of emotions and behavior is characteristic of interactions with others, making it difficult for us to predict what student we will have on any given day or in any given moment. These behaviors are not chosen but are a direct result of brain regions and neuronal connectivity that are impaired by chronic levels of stress.

To be in our social engagement or ventral vagal system, which provides us with the ideal state of flexibility, adaptability, coherence, energy, and stability, the brain has to differentiate and integrate neurobiological systems. Using the metaphor of

11

islands and bridges is a helpful one to understand the necessary processes of differentiation and integration as our brains grow. Differentiation can be thought of as the development of islands. Each island has its particular resource that we can use to tackle problems that we encounter. Having a heavily resourced island is of benefit, but only if the problems we encounter require that resource. Although we used to understand brain function as a simplistic one—resourced island for one function—we have known for a long time that human functions are complex and they typically require the resources from an archipelago or from islands much further afield. Awareness of what resources lie on other islands and a way to get them and bring them back to the problem at hand are necessary. Bridges, therefore, are essential and represent integration in brain function. Having bridges is crucial because all regulation comes from this process of integration (Siegel, 2012). Neural integration in turn depends on our felt sense of safety

For students with developmental trauma, the lack of interpersonal safety impairs both the resourcing of islands as well as the bridges to connect them. Given the tremendous advances in neuroscience over the last decade, several disciplines are making a paradigm shift to the focus on building bridges or integration, rather than focusing purely on the resourcing of the islands. This is a difficult shift for the education system that has traditionally relied so heavily on providing knowledge or resourcing as many islands as possible to facilitate learning and vocational success.

THE VERTICAL BRIDGE

We often refer to the brain as a triune brain (Maclean, 1960), organizing it into three main islands, although in reality, each of those three regions is an archipelago with bridges within and between regions that need to be constructed and maintained in order to help a student learn (figure 2.1). We depend on the vertical bridge to coordinate our unconscious experiencing (reptilian brain), feeling (limbic system), and thinking (cortex).

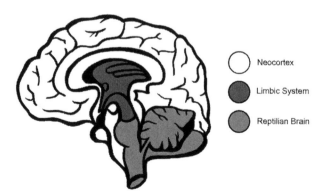

Figure 2.1   The Triune Brain. Jackson Morse.

The Reptilian Brain

The brain stem is often referred to as the reptilian or "lizard" brain as it is the oldest phylogenetically and is the first part of the brain to develop in utero. All information between the body and the brain passes through the brain stem. Information about our body's position, any pain we may have, how hot or cold we feel, how awake or sleepy we feel is registered by the brain stem and then conveyed higher up the brain for a decision. Do we need to sleep, move, put a sweater on, and so on? Our brain stem also controls a number of homeostatic functions such as our heart rate, breathing, and sleeping. Reflexive actions such as coughing, sneezing, and vomiting are also controlled by the lower part of the brain stem. Our motor functions, sensory functions, and hearing and taste, as well as our reflexes and automatic homeostatic functions, are all regulated by the brain stem. It is the area of our brain that facilitates our freeze response when we feel that our life is threatened—an adaptive response we share with vertebrates.

Lucas's behavior suggested that the islands and bridges in the brain stem were operating in a way that were consistently sending him signals that he was in danger. Lucas struggled with sensory integration, a function mediated by the brain stem. Sensory problems are often present in children who have experienced abuse, as are dysregulated eating and sleeping. Neglected children may have even more difficulties as they have had poor movement experiences early in life. Their bodies and central nervous systems fail to read or organize their own body cues well. Students may be over or under-reactive to touch, sounds, light, colors, and smells. The level of distress associated with these uncomfortable sensory experiences communicates to the higher regions of the limbic system that there is a problem, and the stress response is activated. Once his stress response was activated, Lucas's bridge to his cortex washed away. He could not then use logic and knowledge to argue against the message that he was in danger.

Many of the behavioral challenges in a classroom may stem from the failure of building islands and bridges. We may all have witnessed the distress of a youngster whose socks don't *feel right,* and no learning can occur until they are discarded or fixed. Other students who can't manage crowds or noise struggle at recess time or other transitions. Some struggle to sit still at a desk or to move their bodies around the classroom, or they constantly chew their pencils, shirts, or fingers or shy away from any physical touch as they struggle to regulate their proprioceptive system. So often we label these behaviors as willful, and we are irritated with the child who can't wear those particular pants or is screaming at his sister to stop singing or who has banged his way through the classroom upsetting all his classmates. But if we can see this as a function of a failure of differentiation and integration in the brain stem, we may be better placed to offer comfort and modify our expectations or environment to make things more comfortable for the child's brain.

Lucas struggled with touch in particular. The texture of certain clothes, the sharpness of a tag at his neck, or the discomfort of having his socks bunch up in his shoes could all send him into a tailspin. He certainly couldn't tolerate any staff member touching him, whether on purpose or by accident. This made the classroom, the school yard, and a simple walk down the hallway places of potential threat for him. His body was extremely rigid, and all movements toward him were perceived as dangerous. Touch is such an important means of co-regulating another's emotional experience, so we knew we would have to find a way to help Lucas tolerate touch in a safe way. Staff avoided touching him until he could manage the sensation. We first started by communicating our intent to touch, for example, high fiving the air. This nonverbal action was paired with a verbal explanation of what was happening *("I'm so excited with Lucas's courage to try his work today that I wish to high five him, but I know that he's not ready to high five me back yet!")*. This total acceptance eventually led to enough safety that he moved from air high fives to real high fives with hand to hand contact. It took a lot longer to allow him to feel safe enough to tolerate more intimate and comforting touch, but this was an exciting beginning.

He experienced other sensory challenges that needed to be addressed within the classroom. Noise was overwhelming to him. The scratching of a pencil that for other people was outside of awareness was for him loud and abrasive. The ambient sound of others laughing, talking, and playing would also overwhelm him. For Lucas, these were signals that he was in danger, and the islands and bridges required for mobilization would come into action. At times he would run out of the room. At other times, he would scream at his classmates to shut up. To reduce the signals of danger, we made noise buffering headphones available. When wearing them, Lucas could then concentrate on his reading or work rather than on the danger signals. Since the functioning of our higher regions of our brain will depend on the functioning of the lower regions, we consistently worked to help Lucas's physical body and environment feel more comfortable. Without a better functioning brain stem, we would not expect him to feel safe enough to use the higher regions of his brain to help him stay regulated.

The Limbic System

Higher up the brain is the limbic system, the second part of the triune brain. Within the limbic system is the group of islands and bridges that deal with emotions, memories, and levels of arousal. Crudely, it decides the emotional relevance of the information from the brain stem and connects with the higher-order resources of the cortex for a behavioral response. If we feel too cold or too hungry, there is relevance for comfort and survival; the limbic system flags these problems a priority and communicates to higher up in the brain that the problem needs to be rectified and we put another sweater on or have a snack.

Limbic System Bridges

There are a number of islands and bridges in the limbic system that become compromised when we are not safe. Many of our students' challenging behaviors are a direct

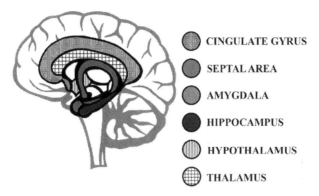

Figure 2.2   Limbic System. Jackson Morse.

result of poorly resourced islands and of the lack of bridges within the limbic system and between the limbic system and the higher regions of the brain.

The primary structures within the limbic system include the amygdala, hippocampus, thalamus, hypothalamus, basal ganglia, and cingulate gyrus (figure 2.2). The amygdala is like a fire alarm and is fundamental to our fear and stress response. It receives information from our brain stem about whether we are safe or unsafe and it communicates a response through a system of chemicals and hormones: stay in our social engagement system and use what we know to manage the threat or mobilize and avoid. Our amygdala is a major player in whether we develop trust and can lean into our relationships or mistrust and avoid them. If we think about Lucas, his amygdala was constantly receiving messages from within his body and from his environment that he was not safe. As a consequence, he could not learn to trust others or his environment. His amygdala worked in concert with other islands in his limbic system, in particular the thalamus and hypothalamus, to produce stress hormones that kept him alert and ready to cope with danger.

When we have too many stress hormones for prolonged periods of time, we become expert at preparing for battle and poor at exploration, discovery, and new learning. The hippocampus is another important island within the limbic system and its job is to help us learn new things, help us place our experiences in a context of time and place, and organize our memory. It is an area of our brain that continues to produce new neurons and synaptic connections throughout our lifetime to help us learn. However, the hippocampus is very sensitive to the chemical impact of stress, and if stress remains high, new neurons don't get generated. The hippocampus actually shrinks and loses its connections with other areas of the brain. Both the island and the bridges from it are compromised. Children with developmental trauma so often have difficulties with learning as their hippocampus has fewer neuronal pathways. The island is poorly resourced. Bridges from the hippocampus to other limbic areas are also impaired.

The bridge between the amygdala and the hippocampus is an important one for regulating fear. If we can rely on our memory that things have worked out in the past or that we have skills to handle the situation, the amygdala can be convinced that all is ok and it doesn't need to send out an alarm. If we are open to new learning, then we can understand that this moment is different to the one that was harmful. If the amygdala is overactive, however, the bridge to the hippocampus is less reliable and the hippocampus itself becomes compromised.

The failure of differentiation and integration between the amygdala and hippocampus helps us understand why children who have been hurt struggle so much to learn from new experiences. Cortisol and adrenaline, two powerful stress hormones, can temporarily shut down the functioning of the hippocampus. When scared, a hurt child can't actually feel, hear, or see how their new teacher, foster parent, or gains in their biological parent are different. They cannot effectively compare the present to the past, sense the disparity and learn from the difference (Baylin & Hughes, 2016). Without a healthy hippocampus, our memories are not coded explicitly. Our autobiographical memory can't develop properly then: we can't see ourselves in time. When we recall something, it is if it is happening in the present, and we can't make use of new learning. So often when we ask our students why they got upset they can't find an answer. Their implicit memory has not been integrated with the explicit memory system. Implicit fear-based memories rapidly signaled a need for mobilization or immobilization. The student is often puzzled at their behavior because they can't access those implicit memories. They don't know they are frightened. Many will then create a story to explain their behavior to themselves and to us. Most of those stories are shame-based—"I am a bad, stupid, crazy kid"—or blaming "you are a bad, stupid or crazy teacher!"

The lack of empathy or remorse that many of our students have at times is also a function of poorly built bridges within the limbic system and to the cortex. The bridges between the amygdala, hippocampus, insula, and the right supramarginal gyrus help us have empathy. The right supramarginal gyrus is an island toward the front of the brain, at the junction between the temporal, parietal, and frontal lobes in the cortex. Its job is to distinguish our own emotional state from that of others and facilitates empathy and compassion (Silani, Lamm, Ruff, & Singer, 2013).

Research shows that when this specific part of the brain doesn't work well or when we have to make fast decisions regarding safety, the capacity for empathy is drastically reduced (Silani, 2013). It is easy then to see that our children who are stuck in their limbic system or brain stem responses find it difficult to have empathy. They have not yet constructed a reliable bridge to their prefrontal cortex. That bridge develops only in the context of caregiving that is safe and nurturing. Given their constant neuroception of danger, they are also making quick decisions about survival. Empathy is really a luxury of feeling safe enough. We often see that children with developmental trauma can have empathy toward younger children, animals, or peers when they don't feel threatened. However, as soon as they believe that trouble is coming, they behave in non-empathic or unremorseful ways. Their job in that moment is to keep themselves safe, and not to worry about others.

Empathy also requires us to feel the pain of others and to differentiate it from our own emotional experiences. Children with developmental trauma have found ways to chemically manage the physical and social pain that they have experienced so that they can function day to day (Baylin & Hughes, 2016). The production of a group of opioids called dynorphins helps them do this. Dynorphins essentially stop the conscious experience of pain. If we can't feel our own pain, then we will also not read other people's pain and recognize that empathy or compassion is needed. As we can increase our children's felt sense of safety, we can unblock the ability to show empathy.

The Cortex

As we have mentioned, our lower brain systems are the biological tutors of our later developing regions. Paying attention to subcortical regions is, therefore, essential if we are to become good problem-solvers and to manage successfully in school. The cortex, however, has a huge capacity to develop resource-rich islands that help us know things and problem-solve effectively when we don't know.

The cortex is the most plastic region of our brain, which means that it is constantly developing new islands and bridges. It requires a lot of energy to make it work, and it tends to work effectively for only short periods of time before it needs to re-energize. Jim Coan's work from the University of Virginia is particularly exciting as he has shown that the cortex works longer and more efficiently in the presence of a safe attachment figure (Coan, 2016). Obstacles that feel insurmountable are less so when in the presence of a positive attachment figure (Conner et al., 2012). The opposite is also true: things become more distressing if in the presence of another person with whom you don't feel safe (Coan et al., 2017). This has huge implications for our delivery of education, which is heavily biased toward resourcing islands in the cortex. Without a sense of safety in relationships, we will not achieve our goal of creating good students.

In the second part of this book, we will look at how teachers "lend" students their brains to help them be more effective in learning. For now, the idea that relationships with safe adults will help children learn probably validates what you already know and highlights the need to prioritize relationships for learning, especially in those children who have difficulty accessing or staying in their cortex.

Lucas had great difficulty accessing his cortex, despite him being a very bright and capable student. Sensory integration difficulties as well as faulty neuroception of interpersonal cues constantly communicated that he was in danger. His limbic system then became organized to manage that problem. His amygdala was constantly sending out alarm signals. His hippocampus responded by communicating to his pituitary gland to generate cortisol and adrenaline. The bridges to his thalamus and hypothalamus that help turn down the production of stress hormones had not, given his constant state of alarm, been built well, so stress hormones could not recede to allow him a way to travel the bridge to his islands in his cortex for a more relaxed or thoughtful way to solve his problem. The adrenaline and cortisol prepared him to yell at others, throw things, hit out, or to use the energy diverted to his large muscles to run away. Lucas was not able to access the higher, more frontal regions of his brain no matter how hard he tried. When alarmed in this way, Lucas's bridge to the cortex was inaccessible. He also couldn't use the bridges in the limbic system to turn off his alarm system. As a result, he was often hypervigilant, highly reactive, and exhausted.

One of the frustrations in the classroom is the variability of a student's ability to manage behavioral or academic expectations: "He could do this yesterday, why not today?" This variability may reflect the impact of stress on the bridges required for regulation. Many of us have witnessed a child with developmental trauma outline to us the many steps he or she would use for a particular problem. If we asked Lucas when he was calm what he was going to do to cope with social challenges at recess time he could tell us, "*First I am going to breathe deeply in through my nose and out through my mouth three times*," and he could add "*if that doesn't work I am going to count to 10 slowly, imagine myself on a beach with the sun on my face and the sound of the water, ask for help, walk away*." We might be impressed by his knowledge of coping strategies and feel confident that he could successfully negotiate recess. However, five minutes later someone takes his basketball and he becomes an angry, raging, aggressive young boy who refuses to listen to the yard monitor and runs to the farthest end of the playground. Once calm, Lucas could again list the various strategies that he *should* have used. So why couldn't he use them?

If we continue to use the analogy of islands and bridges, the cognitive behavioral skills of breathing, counting to 10, and visual imaging are resources on various islands in the cortex. They are fully accessible to knowledge when the student is calm and there are no challenges in front of him. However, as soon as there is an actual or perceived threat, the brake comes off the social engagement system and the student becomes mobilized. The lower and internal regions of our brain send out alarm signals that quickly cause the bridge to the cortex to be washed out and the resources housed there to be beyond knowledge or access. The student can only use the resources available to the stress response system, fight, flight, or freeze. It is not until the arousal levels, or floodwaters, recede that the bridges are re-instated and the islands become available again. Again, the strength of this bridge is determined greatly by the type of care we receive during our first year of life. For our students with developmental trauma, that bridge to the cortex, particularly the prefrontal cortex, is poorly built at the best of times and easily flooded and washed out by even small amounts of stress. Our students know what they should do and what they should have done, but they can't access the resources when needed. Their neuroception of the classroom or interactions with others will influence how accessible those bridges are at any given time.

This then can also help us understand why for the population of children who have experienced abuse and neglect, behavioral and cognitive behavioral strategies have very little success. The brains of children who have experienced chronic stress have fewer islands and bridges, and the bridges tend to be much more susceptible to being nonfunctional. Mary Dozier and her colleagues (2014) suggest that purely behavioral or cognitive behavioral strategies are relevant only for those of us who are lucky enough to have developed a healthy brain with an effective system of islands and bridges built within a secure attachment. Using cognitive behavioral techniques well is also predicated on reading internal cues, which is very difficult for children who have had toxic levels of stress. If there is a constant state of danger, we learn to be hypervigilant to our environment. Being curious about our internal states is not conducive to staying alive. If you are face-to-face with that bear, your attention needs to be on the bear not on your own somatic experiences. If we don't know we are starting to feel anxious, we don't know to call on the resources that we may have. If you ask a child with developmental trauma how they feel or what they think, the number one answer is "I don't know." How can we then expect them to use behavioral strategies that are predicated upon knowing?

The stress associated with the different forms of abuse prevents the development of islands and bridges associated with learning. Neglect has an even more profoundly damaging impact on the developing brain. We cannot survive on our own. Babies have all kinds of ways to engage others to ensure they are not left alone, but if no one responds to these attempts to engage, the baby feels intolerable pain and does not have another person to co-regulate that pain and ensure a felt sense of safety. The development of islands and bridges in all three regions of the triune brain are severely impacted (figure 2.3).

Brains that have too few interactions with adults, and where those interactions are perfunctory, have much less neuronal connectivity (Siegel, 2007). Functional images of the brain show clear impairment in connectivity in the areas of the brain that develops the system of islands and bridges that allows for effective attention and emotion regulation as well as the ability to connect with others without fear. Being able to pass information to our prefrontal cortex for analyzing and problem-solving is the essence of self-regulation. When we have too much stress, the many synapses that are available in this area of the brain dwindle, making it harder for children to learn, remember, or figure things out. When we don't feel safe, a different set of islands and bridges are fortified, those that take us to the back and lower down in our brain where the fight, flight, or freeze responses are mediated (figure 2.4).

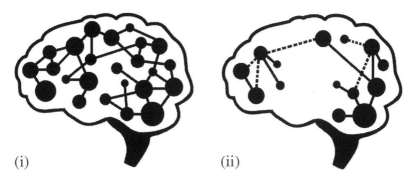

(i)   (ii)

Figure 2.3   Representation of neuronal connectivity normal development (i) and in the absence of safe relationships (ii). Jackson Morse.

Imagine the difficulty a child with circuitry primed toward survival behavior will have when we ask him to manage kindergarten or grade one. He or she will have no ability to manage the stresses that come with following routines and rules, and managing the frustrations of learning and sharing a physical space. Although normatively the islands and bridges in this area of the brain take longer to develop, the neglected child is very far behind. Such a child will require an education that is focused on creating interpersonal safety and the developing of these islands and bridges further down in the brain before we expect retention of knowledge related to literacy or social conventions.

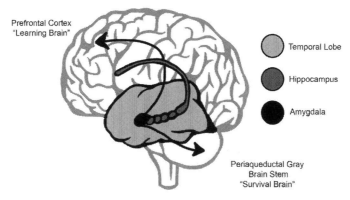

Figure 2.4   Different Neuronal Circuitry Provides Different Options for Behavioral Response. Jackson Morse.

Thankfully, most of our students will not have suffered the degree of neglect and poor connectivity that figure 2.3 represents. However, any degree of relational trauma will impact the development of islands and bridges. Badenoch (2017) posits that the essence of trauma is actually the felt sense of aloneness in times of fear and pain rather than the event itself. Recognizing the impact that being alone has on our brain helps us recognize that we are mistaken if we believe that a child is "choosing" to act impulsively, aggressively, or thoughtlessly. They don't yet have the neural circuitry to support regulation. If our students with developmental trauma could do better, they would.

HORIZONTAL BRIDGE

Good self-regulation skills require a strong vertical bridge, but also a strong horizontal bridge. We have two hemispheres—or perhaps continents—in our brain, and each becomes specialized for different functions. The right brain is the first area of our brain to develop during our first two years but is dominant for all of us in times of stress. It has the resources for recognizing nonverbal signals such as facial expressions, body language, and tone of voice, and is primarily relational. It holds our implicit memories and is specialized to act quickly to ensure that we stay alive. Our right brain is concerned with all things that we *experience,* and it becomes specialized for harm avoidance. In contrast, our left hemisphere develops later, is resourced for problem-solving, language, and metacognitive functions, and is concerned with what is *known*. Its resources are slower developing, starting around the age of three years, with some skills requiring 25 years to develop. In contrast to the harm avoidance bias of the right brain, the left is specialized for social approach.

It is easy to understand why a bridge between these hemispheres is necessary. For those stranded in the right hemisphere, they will be specialized to see harm everywhere, avoid people and situations, and organize their neural circuits to promote fight, flight, or freeze responses to maximize the chance of survival. Those stranded on the right tend to be quite anxious, pessimistic, and suspicious of taking risks or taking advantage of new learning. Decisions tend to be made on how the individual feels rather than on what they think if they are right-brain dominant. Without a bridge to our left hemisphere, we are at the mercy of our emotional experiences without a context, knowledge or understanding of those experiences or access to a solution. So often we ask our students to use their "skills." When calm, they can articulate what they will do. When emotionally aroused, they don't use their skills. When they return to a calm state, they tell us what they should have done.

A bridge between the hemispheres allows the brain to balance the adaptive abilities to avoid harm with the necessary requirement to approach others if we are to be in the relationships that will support our growth. For our students with trauma, this is one of the bridges that is rickety. Most of our students remain in a state of high alarm and social avoidance as they have learned to anticipate threat is everywhere. Chronic stress interferes both with the development of left-brain resources or islands as well as the bridge to access them. It is often our clinical experience when working with older children that developmentally they feel like three-year-olds, the age where left hemisphere functions such as language and episodic memory are starting to develop. The poor foundation of the bridge leaves our hurt children at the mercy of what they experience and not what they know.

As Lucas started to feel safe, he started to build this bridge between his right and left hemispheres. He no longer was quite as reactive. We could sometimes see him take the time to think his way through what was happening around him. He began to be more aware of his somatic experiences and have words for them. He could describe how he felt like his body was wobbly and how his voice sounded different to his ears. As his bridge became stronger, he could say to us that his amygdala was firing, telling him something was dangerous, but maybe his amygdala was wrong—information he was learning from discussions and lessons in school. As he began to learn to use what he knew to calm his amygdala, he also began to have better social interactions with his peers.

Most of our students with developmental trauma have a difficult time socially. This is because trauma impairs the neural networks that allow for reciprocal sharing of information and experiences. Somewhere toward the middle of his second year with us, Lucas was being much more successful in his interactions. The following example illustrates a temporary loss of his horizontal bridge.

Lucas and Josey had been playing beautifully together all week. We had all noticed how they seemed to be negotiating what they played and how both of their ideas could be incorporated into their play. Both children seemed to be organized by their social engagement system and we could see their mutual enjoyment. One morning, all of the students were out skating on our newly flooded skating rink. Lucas and Josey came bursting back into the classroom, obviously upset. Josey was yelling that Lucas had pushed her down. Lucas was angry that his friend had called him a "fat head." Our staff member was calm and reported that he was trying to help them both figure out what had happened. For both students, the bridge to their prefrontal cortex was washed out and they were being fueled by adrenaline and cortisol. Heart rates were high, eye contact poor or fierce in the case of Josey, and they were not able to access their social engagement system. Lucas and Josey sat on chairs waiting for some help to take off their skates, Josey adamantly protesting that she had not called Lucas names and Lucas just as adamantly insisting that she did. Deni calmly placed herself between the two of them and asked them with energy in her voice if this fight felt like the ones they had with their respective siblings. Both acknowledged that it did, which suggested that the bridge that linked experience and knowing was coming back online. As the staff strengthened the bridge with acceptance and curiosity, we discovered that the fight occurred because of a failure of this integration.

Here is how the conversation went:

Josey: "I did not call him fat head! He pushed me down twice!"

Lucas: "Yes you did!"

Deni: "Wow! It seems like the two of you have had a really tough moment. I can understand that you would both be upset. Lucas, you probably don't like being called a name and Josey, you don't like being pushed down."

Josey: "I didn't call him a name."

Deni: "Ok, but if Lucas thinks you called him a name, I can understand why he might be upset. I wonder too Josey if your feelings were hurt when Lucas pushed you down. You and Lucas have played together all week. I've heard you both laughing all week and I've watched you smiling and playing. How confusing then to have him push you down!"

Both children became quieter as their skates were being removed and the teacher was helping to organize their experiences. As they discarded their snow pants and jackets, they were both offered a snack and a drink. After about 5 minutes, Josey admitted to the staff member sitting with them that she had indeed called Lucas a name and that he had then pushed her down. She added that she was only joking and that she had been smiling when she said it so she didn't understand why he was angry. She could say that her feelings were hurt when he pushed her and that she retaliated with anger. Lucas responded that he did see her smile, but thought it was a mean smile because sometimes Josey would be mean to people even though she was smiling.

Lucas had neurocepted Josey's smile as one that communicated threat based on his past experience of seeing her be mean to others with a smile on her face as well as his own attachment history where he had needed to be hypervigilant to adult's faces so that he could predict when domestic violence or rejection may occur. In this moment, he could not discern her socially engaged, nonthreatening smile from her more defensive, less relaxed smile, and her teasing was then interpreted as being mean. His right brain, which was primed to be hypervigilant for facial expressions that might be harmful, organized his defensive response. His amygdala sent out alarm signals, and he became mobilized through his sympathetic nervous system, pushing her to avoid further perceived harm. He could not access his left brain's resources that could organize that experience differently and draw upon their positive friendship experience until his teachers helped him to return to a sense of emotional safety.

In the classroom, this bridge between hemispheres is essential for so many aspects of learning. We need both the facts as well as the emotional and social implications of those facts to be the most effective problem-solvers. Learning involves intense emotional states, curiosity, excitement, frustration, despair, hopelessness when things feel too hard to understand, euphoria when things go right, and the need for connection. We need optimal hemispheric integration to manage what we know and what we feel, and this can only occur when we feel safe.

The horizontal bridge may explain our own behavior in response to challenging students. Our North American culture tends to be quite left hemisphere-centric. When not integrated with the right hemisphere, we are drawn to focus on tasks and behaviors, on autonomy and self-reliance, and on getting specific results from particular techniques with less regard for the individuality and emerging experience of our students. Professionals create protocols and treatment plans that require students to behave differently, but without attention to what their experience is that is driving that behavior. Then when our treatment plans don't work, we are prone to judge our students negatively (they are not trying hard enough, they don't care) or ourselves (we are not adequate)—judgments that will bring on feelings of shame rather than feelings of safety (Badenoch, 2017).

Safety Is the Engineer

Bridges that support optimal integration can only be built when we feel safe and have repeated experiences of co-regulation that *whisper* (Baylin & Hughes, 2016) to the amygdala that there is nothing to fear. As we learned from Porges's Polyvalgal theory, co-regulation of affect from a safe trusted adult must precede self-regulation. Imagine telling a five-week-old baby to pull themselves together! The baby can only become calm if we rock, sing, soothe, feed, change, and communicate a sense of safety through our own social engagement system. A baby who is left alone may eventually stop crying, but will have no felt sense of safety and is likely to end up in the dorsal vagal mediated response of collapse and exhaustion, a state that will not be conducive to building the bridges between the limbic system and the prefrontal cortex that is so necessary for self-regulation.

INTERPERSONAL BRIDGE

The field of interpersonal neurobiology also teaches us that the regulation in one person is dependent on the regulation of the other. This makes sense given what we have learned from Porges's work. We neurocept safety or danger from another's face, voice, or body language, and are constantly responding to the other to maintain a connection that feels good. A child who has been well cared for can usually maintain the bridge to their cortex when their parent is upset, knowing that the relationship will not be damaged and that their parent will return soon to a better-feeling connection. The child who has not had adequate care, however, will immediately neurocept an adult's upset as dangerous and life-threatening. They do not have the ability to access thinking that can guide them to understand that the adult is upset about something that has nothing to do with them, or can manage their upset, or can be upset with the child without any intent to harm. So many of our hurt children cannot hold on to a sense of being liked or loved when an adult is upset.

The interpersonal bridge allows us to both remain in our social engagement systems and weather upsets. The bridge informs our desire to behave in ways that ensure that connection remains solid. We usually comply because we want those we like and love to be happy with us. We do nice things for other people because we like the feeling of praise and delight in that person's eyes. Our children who have come to fear others do not have a solid interpersonal bridge. They tend to be self-reliant and don't have a sense that turning to another person for help is a possibility. Both the child and the adult feel distant and wary of one another. At times it feels like there is a bridge, but a poorly constructed bridge. Some of our students have a one-way system rather than a reciprocal flow of traffic. They may be willing to have a connection as long as everything is going their way and they are getting what they want. As soon as an adult asserts their own needs or wishes, the bridge washes away. Reciprocal interaction is too dangerous.

Dyadic Developmental Practice will give us ways to create emotional safety, to whisper to the amygdala that there is a different possibility. It offers a framework where we can use our voices, and our facial expressions and gestures with our students, much as how we might to that five-week-old baby, to soothe them and allow for a different set of islands and bridges to develop. What we have learned from interpersonal neurobiology confirms what attachment theory has told us for decades: safe relationships are crucial to survival.

3

Lessons from Attachment Theory

In developing his theory of attachment, John Bowlby observed that infants are not able to provide for their own safety and they have what he described as an innate motivating factor to seek the aid of another when in distress. Bowlby believed that attachment behavior—seeking proximity with someone who will keep you safe—was necessary for the survival of our species. Originally seen as a central feature of infancy, attachment is now seen as a fundamental motivating factor throughout the lifespan. When in distress, most people want to be "home" and with people who make them feel better. When infants are responded to in helpful ways, they learn to trust that attachment figures will meet the need for safety and comfort. Adults must co-regulate their infant's distress because infants cannot regulate themselves. The experience of having their distress be co-regulated by their parent is the precursor to learning self-regulation. Co-regulation must precede self-regulation.

Children who have experienced developmental trauma are so often lacking in the ability to regulate their emotions because they have not had adults first co-regulate their emotional states. Their fears become terror, sadness becomes despair, and anger becomes rage. Even positive emotions of joy and excitement are very difficult for them to regulate and often create anxiety leading to dysregulation of their behavior. These children are not only delayed in their development of self-regulation skills, they are slow to learn these skills. To learn, they must experience co-regulation of their emotions by safe adults but they don't have the trust to let adults soothe them in this way. Providing these children with self-regulation coping skills before they have significant experiences of co-regulation is likely to lead to failure and frustration for both student and teacher.

As we will see in the next chapter on intersubjectivity, the young child is also ready to turn to the parent for learning about himself and the world. Another of Bowlby's insights was that to grow up healthy, the infant and young child should experience a warm, intimate, and ongoing relationship with his mother (or permanent mother substitute) in which both find satisfaction and enjoyment. If he is to develop his own skills of self-reliance, he needs his caregivers to teach him that he is lovable and worthy and teach him how to handle objects, talk, cooperate, and successfully engage in the activities of his family and community. The child is ready to learn a great many things from his attachment figures, being confident that learning is both interesting and in his best interest. Being a social mammal, the child is very motivated to learn how to relate with others, including learning how to experience reciprocal joy, shared interests, and love with others. Relationship with others is at the heart of what he wants to learn and what he needs in order to be able to learn.

We have already described how habitual distress over threats to basic safety impairs islands and bridges so that the child will not have much psychological or neurological readiness to learn these skills. He will focus on trying to survive on his own, not trusting that others will want to teach him. Or he believes they will teach him what is best for them, not for him. Children experiencing developmental trauma try to get by on their own. Self-reliance is a poor substitute for being protected by adults, but it is adaptive. Relying on yourself reduces the actual or anticipated psychological or physical pain caused by adults. The attachment system weakens. The child stops looking to others for comfort or learning.

BLOCKED TRUST

If we have brains that only see signs of danger and that cannot neurocept signs of safety, then other people remain a source of threat. Children develop what Jon Baylin and Dan Hughes term "blocked trust." In their book *The Neurobiology of Attachment-Focused Therapy*, they outline the typical presentation of children who have lost trust in their adult support system to provide the necessary care. The following characteristics are familiar to teachers because they make it very difficult for children to settle to learn (table 3.1).

These behavioral adaptations to not feeling safe were so noticeable for Lucas. The difficulty was that Lucas's expectation of rejection was now a self-fulfilling prophecy. He would behave in such a way that made it difficult for others to remain in connection with him. He was too clingy, too angry, or too far away. Since he was not able to recognize cues his body was giving him, he was certainly not aware of his underlying intrinsic fears that led to such ambivalence in his relationships. Our first goal was to help Lucas have more awareness of his behavior and his body. With awareness comes the ability to "override" the usual response and to use higher-order brain circuits to inhibit old strategies and develop new ones. When you read later about our Belong program, you can see why it is a two-year program. Safety takes a long time to develop when you have had as much hurt and rejection as Lucas (table 3.1).

Table 3.1   Characteristics of Blocked Trust

Hypervigilance	Chronic mistrust requires a strong negativity bias, and students with mistrust have an exquisitely tuned early detection system so that they can appraise harm and act accordingly.
Over-the-top reactions	Implicit memories of rejection, abuse, and neglect can trigger false alarms in current interactions. Rage, running, or freezing can appear out of the blue.
Safety blindness	The negativity bias keeps children hyper-focused on harm and away from recognizing signs of safety such as a kind face or a gentle tone of voice.
Need for control	The brain does not do well with uncertainty or ambiguity. Children who have lost trust have learned to control other people's emotions and actions as much as possible so as not to be taken by surprise. Being in control is the child's way of feeling safer.
Resisting authority	Mistrusting adults means no trust that rules or authority may be good or in the interest of safety. Students do not trust our intentions, and automatically resist until they can be sure that they are safe. Baylin talks about "connection lite," the ability to stay close enough to others to get basic needs met while avoiding any chance that the adult will exert authority. Teachers may be familiar with that automatic resistance as soon as their tone of voice signals that it is time to stop play and get back to work.
Immediate gratification	Children with good enough parents learn that adults will provide what they need. Abused children learn that they must get what they need for themselves and fast.
Suppression of social emotions	A hurt child needs to suppress social emotions because they are associated with needing others.
Blocked empathy	Baylin and Hughes introduce the concept of blocked empathy rather than having no empathy. Having empathy requires us to "feel" the distress or pain of another. If a child has already learned to suppress the pain associated with abuse and neglect, then not only do they not feel their own pain but they also don't feel other people's pain as their defense system won't let them. Pain is pain and must be avoided at all costs to survive.
High levels of shame	Children's behavior may not immediately be interpretable as shame. It is typically defended against with anger and rage. Shame is an inherent part of abuse and neglect, and if it is not co-regulated by a comforting adult, it becomes a persistent sense of not being good enough, lovable enough, pretty enough, and so on. It is a very painful emotion, and we are programmed to distance from that toxic state. Many of our students will use blame (it wasn't me it was someone else's fault), minimization (it wasn't so bad why are you making a fuss), lie (I didn't do it), or rage when they fear that they have made a mistake and trouble is coming.

(Continued)

Table 3.1   Characteristics of Blocked Trust (*Continued*)

Suppression of curiosity	If a child has learned to be on high alert for danger, they are not able to spend any time paying attention to their own thoughts or daydreams, or to other's intentions or motivations, or how the world works. "I don't know" is a familiar answer when we ask hurt students a question. Sometimes it is a way to keep distance, but most often our students really don't know why they or others behave the way they do. When on the alert for danger, thinking is concrete, black or white, and focused on the here and now. They do not yet have the safety that allows them to wonder, think abstractly, integrate information, or make connections in their learning.
Suppression of reality testing	Lying is a great way of removing oneself from trouble: if my brother took the cookie I may avoid being yelled at. So many of our hurt students use lying as a habitual way of avoiding shame and the chance of people being angry with them. Unfortunately, lying is one of those things that most adults find very difficult, and trouble comes anyway, reinforcing the child's need to use it for self-protection. As well as the habitual use of lying, hurt children may learn to construct alternative realities, a dissociated response that allows them relief from their actual pain-filled reality.

BLOCKED CARE

When children resist our attempts to connect or actively sabotage those attempts, it becomes hard for us to remain open and engaged with them. Children who have learned not to trust adults, given their previous history of harm, are notoriously poor at reciprocity. They tend to be very controlling and have little or no experience of a mutually enjoyable relationship. Their sense of self is one of being unlovable or unlikeable, and they work so hard to get us to see them in that light—and unfortunately, often with some success. As caregivers, having a reciprocal and pleasurable experience with our charges greatly aids us in our efforts to keep going. Parenting or teaching is hard work. When we are faced with children who reject our every move to care, whether passively through quiet avoidance or resistance to authority, or loudly with angry, raging destructive outbursts, our brains will start to protect us from the social rejection that we experience. In the same way that hurt children develop a defense system to distance from the pain of others not caring, adults too develop a system to manage the pain of children not responding to our cues. Baylin and Hughes call this "blocked care." In their book *Brain-Based Parenting: How Neuroscience Can Foster Healthy Relationships with Kids* (2012), they outline five caretaking systems: approach, reward, child-reading, meaning-making, and executive function. When we are engaged in reciprocal relationships, these systems work to keep us connected with one another. In blocked care, the first four of those five systems tend to begin to break down.

The first inkling we get that our caregiving systems are breaking down may be that we don't want to approach our student. We find ways to avoid interacting with them and when we do it feels like hard work. Without enjoyable, reciprocal interactions we don't get the release of oxytocin and dopamine that keeps us feeling warm and motivated to engage. We may continue to do our job, but our heart is no longer there.

When Sian's daughter Megan hit the teenage years, she became fully aware of how the processes of blocked care can co-opt what she liked to think of as a healthy brain. As a young child, Megan was delightfully reciprocal; she loved to be with her parents and didn't like to be too far away from them. As she hit puberty, her room and her friends became her world, and her parents suddenly knew nothing, dressed in all the wrong clothing, said all the wrong things, and, in her mind, were intentionally out to embarrass her. This sudden and strong rejection started to impact the integrative functioning of Sian's brain. As much as her cortex and left brain "knew" this was a normal developmental process, her right brain and limbic system informed her that she didn't feel good. Sian was sad at the loss of her younger daughter and would feel pain every time her attempts to reconnect were met with rejection. She desperately wanted the return to the easygoing, mutually enjoyable relationship that they had had and felt out of sorts. Teenage years can be long, and the many repetitions of rejection started to make it harder to be with her.

As Sian returned from work at the end of the day, her cortex and left brain that held knowledge about teenagers told her that she needed to go into her daughter's room and ask her how her day was. Her right brain would caution her against such a move and her amygdala warned of the danger in being met with derision and disdain. Some days her cortex won, some days it didn't. Oxytocin became in short supply as did the dopamine. Dopamine comes with enjoyment, and enjoying each other was difficult. Invariably Sian and Megan would spend some time together and Megan would ask a question to which "No" was the obvious answer. As you can imagine, that was the end of spending time together and as the years went by it became harder and harder for Sian to ask her to hang out. Her approach system and reward system were wearing down.

Next to go were child-reading and meaning-making systems. One of the hallmarks of adolescence is a rapid shifting of emotional states. From time to time, Megan would come out of her room and be pleasant and engaged, even occasionally offering to help with dinner. Rather than be in her smart-vagal system that could keep her socially engaged with Megan at those times, Sian confessed that if she was tired or preoccupied, she operated from her dorsal vagal system that was mistrusting of her motives, expecting a hurtful comment or a request for money when the two had had days or sometimes weeks of Megan being a difficult person to live with. Given her nature of being emotionally very attuned, Megan would perceive Sian's reticence to engage, and her defense system met Sian's, usually with a storming back to her room yelling that she wanted a different set of parents.

Thankfully, Sian's executive function system remained intact. It is this system that allows the bridge to the cortex to remain sturdy, so we can keep our processing to the top and to the front of the brain rather than to the reactive and defensive stance of the Amygdala to PAG to brain stem highway. Parents or teachers who lose their executive function system will typically move into shaming, abuse, and neglect in service of protecting their own experience of rejection and pain. Parent and child are left as isolated islands without a bridge for connection.

If we have a child in our classroom with blocked trust and we move ourselves into blocked care, it will not be possible to offer the felt sense of safety that is needed to move them from blocked trust toward engagement and learning. They will constantly sense signs of danger from our voice tone, facial expressions, and nonverbal gestures, reinforcing the need to avoid relationships rather than finding a way toward them. It is for this reason that putting our own oxygen mask on first is essential. If we are not doing well, our children and students will not do well.

Baylin and Hughes describe how blocked care is best ameliorated by being in a safe relationship ourselves. If we have a partner, friend, mentor, or therapist who doesn't judge us and who responds to us in an attuned, synchronized, and responsive way, then our caring brain can come back online. When starting the process of becoming a trauma-informed classroom or school, caring for the educators and the provision of a felt sense of safety for them was an essential and necessary ingredient. We will talk more about how we take care of teachers and encourage teachers to put on their own oxygen mask first when we describe our DDP-informed programs.

ATTACHMENT PATTERNS

There are four classifications of attachment patterns that children develop based on their parents' abilities to respond to their immediate needs. Because, as Stephen Porges states, connection is a biological imperative, we must find a way to remain close to our caregivers even if they are not able to provide good enough care. The majority of students are likely to be securely attached, and our customary educational programs tend to be sufficient for them. The three attachment patterns that are considered to be insecure all present special challenges to educators and will be described in more detail. The greatest challenge is the insecure pattern that is disorganized. This pattern is the most closely associated with developmental trauma.

Secure

Luckily, our children don't need us to be perfect to feel safe. Attachment researchers talk about being a "good enough parent." Tronick (2003), a researcher who studies the reciprocal interactions of mother-infant dyads discovered that good enough parents were able to build secure attachment for their children when they were able to respond accurately to their children's needs for resonance and reflection about 33 percent of the time. This does not mean that they were absent 67 percent of the time. What Tronick and his colleagues discovered was that those parents recognized immediately when they lost the connection and synchronicity in their interactions with their infant, and would work to repair the rupture, seeking again how to engage their infant and return to the comfort of the mutually responsive connection. When parents are able to repair in this way, the child learns to tolerate the breaks in connection because they have anticipated that it will be short-lived, and they will not be left in the stress of disconnection for long. This connect-break-repair cycle reinforced that adults could be trusted to comfort and bring them back into a state of physiological well-being. This trust is the base of a secure attachment. The infant is aware that when they signal that the parent is not relating in a manner that the infant finds enjoyable, the parent notices the signal and changes their behavior. The infant's wishes matter!

When an infant or young child trusts their parent's availability and responsiveness, they can build the bridges to their prefrontal cortex. They can get on with the business of exploring, learning, and being curious about their world as well as being in a physiological state that is consistent with growth and restoration. Their social engagement system can be reinforced and their vagal tone strengthened because their parents buffer them and whisper to the amygdala that there is no cause for alarm. As securely attached infants mature, they are able to use their social engagement system to negotiate and collaborate to get their needs met. They learn to put a brake on their sympathetic nervous system that operates defensively, instead using sympathetic activation for large muscle activities that bring them pleasure, such as running, dancing, turning cartwheels. They also learn to organize their parasympathetic nervous system for rest and quiet rather than freeze or shut-down (Porges, 2018). Because they have experienced co-regulation of their emotions, they are now able to self-regulate.

With this base of trust, securely attached children balance the competing needs for independence and dependence, learn to know when they need more of one than the other, and trust that their parent will not be upset with them for moving further away from them in exploration or toward them in their need for comfort. Because they are not always alarmed, the vertical and horizontal bridges in their brains, as well as the important limbic system bridges, can be built in ways that allow them to process information in flexible, adaptive, coherent, energized, and stable ways. Feeling safe with their parents, they begin to explore their inner world of thoughts, feelings, and wishes and their outer world of other people, objects, and events. They can use what they know to help them with the things they don't know and can become resilient in the face of day-to-day challenges. Resilient children tend to be children who have a trusting relationship with at least one attachment figure.

In the classroom, children with secure attachments are those who can move between independent exploration or play and activities within relationships that are enjoyable or reciprocal. They work well when asked to do independent work and are equally successful when asked to work in groups. They are the students who know how to ask for help because they trust that adults will give them an answer and be helpful. They tend to be popular with their peers because they are skilled at collaborating, and can be empathic to others because they do not have to block the pain of disconnection and don't get dysregulated by challenges. They are the students who will respond well when given positive incentives or consequences to influence their learning or behavior.

Insecure Patterns of Attachment

Given that we must be in relationships to survive, infants develop strategies to maintain connection with parents who may not be as responsive, attuned, and trustworthy as we would like them to be. Even if a parent is not particularly good at comforting, children must still ensure that they are fed, clothed, and have some form of interaction so that they do not perish. In addition to the secure pattern of attachment, Mary Ainsworth and her colleagues (1971, 1978) who furthered Bowlby's work, initially identified two patterns of insecure attachment: avoidant and ambivalent.

Avoidant

Those children who are described as avoidantly attached have had to learn to keep caregivers close by downplaying both their own needs for relationships and emotions. They have learned from repeated experiences that their parents cannot meet either their need for exploration or their need for comfort, or both. Expressing their needs jeopardizes the connection with the parent. The parent becomes angry and rejecting in response to the child's expressed relationship and emotional needs or else ignores or moves further away from the child in a tired, depressed withdrawn manner. The child is left alone with their feelings of distress and does not experience their parent's buffering or soothing of their distress. The child is also without an attuned adult to help them learn about themselves and the world. In comparison to the securely attached child where connection was unconditional, connection for the avoidantly attached child is conditional on not upsetting their parent.

Since they cannot rely on their parent's availability and comfort, avoidantly attached children become very self-reliant. They learn to believe that their own needs are bad or too much for other people and by extension they themselves are bad and too much for people. Behaviorally, they can look very independent for their age. They may rarely show signs of distress as they have learned to uncouple signals that they need comfort from their experience of distress to ensure they don't risk that tenuous connection. They tend to adopt a distant and rational approach to situations. They may react with rage, but never vulnerability. It can then be difficult for adults to recognize that these children are in great need of comfort or care. Adults may misinterpret the self-reliance as resilience, perpetuating the child's sense that adults cannot be relied upon to notice and that it must somehow be related to them being unlovable or undeserving of attention.

Often parents of avoidantly attached children have substance abuse issues, depression, or other mental health difficulties that cause them to withdraw from their relationships when they find them challenging. Children with this attachment pattern have learned to minimize their own needs and take care of parents' needs. The less fuss they make and the better they take care of the parent, the more likely it is that their parent will respond to them, feed them, and remember that they are there.

Physiologically, avoidantly attached individuals tend to overuse the dorsal vagus nerve, activating the parasympathetic branch of their autonomic nervous system to manage life experiences. Defenses such as denial, suppression, dissociation, and blocking of affect are typically employed to avoid experiencing more highly arousing emotions. The bridges that are being strengthened are the ones that connect the amygdala to the periaqueductal gray and the amygdala to the hypothalamus, weakening the bridges to the hippocampus and prefrontal cortex. The lack of trust in adults doesn't allow for the social engagement system to operate fully. Their neuroception communicates that their own or other's emotions are dangerous. The use of fight or flight responses feel too risky as they involve sympathetic arousal that will broadcast distress signals loudly. The best option for survival then is to use the dorsal vagal organization that uncouples communication of distress and shuts down the need for connection.

In the classroom, avoidantly attached children may be hard to spot as they are often highly responsible and effective problem-solvers. They are the students who like to please you and are compliant, sometimes excessively so. They don't signal that they don't understand something and are not disruptive or disrespectful. Externally, these students may appear strong, however internally, they are quite anxious. They suppress the pain of their loneliness and shame but remain vigilant that others might see it and reject them for it. That anxiety may translate into the need for perfectionism, anxiety disorders, somatic complaints or vulnerability to abusive relationships. Children may be highly controlling to ensure that others don't get too close to "know" them. They strive to control their environments to assuage the anxiety that threatens to overwhelm them. Given the enormous energy it takes to suppress their anxiety, from time to time, the avoidantly attached child may "crack" under the pressure and display uncharacteristic emotional displays of intense anger or defiance.

Lucy was a student who was new to the grade three classroom. She had recently moved to the area after following a disruption in her foster placement. Despite joining the class 4 months into the school year, Lucy bounced into the classroom that first day with a big smile on her face. Her teacher introduced her to the class and placed her in a group of students working on their science project. She immediately settled into the group, offering to sharpen pencils and share her markers. She asked the others questions about what their favorite color was and when their birthdays were, what their favorite thing to eat was. She complimented them on what they were wearing or how she liked their hair. The teacher thought how resilient she seemed to enter a strange classroom with such well-developed social skills.

As Lucy settled in, her teacher started to notice that she was the first to offer help to others but had a difficult time completing her own work. When directed to focus on her own work at her own desk, Lucy would smile and return to her desk where she would look like she was working hard. Her teacher noticed that she erased her work repeatedly even when just rough notes were required. When her teacher would sit beside her to try to assess her knowledge, Lucy would engage her in a conversation about anything other than the work she was to complete. The more insistent the teacher became, the more talkative and distracting Lucy became. Frustrated, her teacher stated sharply to Lucy that she must do her work and that she would not be able to join the others for free time until she had completed the assignment. Lucy's demeanor changed immediately. Her body stilled, her eyes were cast downward, and the muscles around her eyes flattened. Her voice lost its energy and volume as she whispered "OK."

Her teacher immediately felt badly and tried to repair with Lucy offering to help her with the math questions. It felt to her that Lucy was on the other side of a high wall. Her attempt to repair was not accepted.

Lucy had learned to engage with others in a precocious and pleasing manner. She showed none of the anxiety that most children would have shown in their demeanor if asked to walk into a classroom full of strangers where the routines and expectations were unfamiliar. Her anxiety was hidden behind a sunny smile and bouncy presentation. It seemed to others like she had no difficulty settling in until she was faced with conflict. Her teacher was irritated with her lack of focus. Lucy instantly dissociated and seemed far away. She did not have access to her emotions nor to a readiness to turn to another person to manage the distress that she was experiencing. She needed to make it go away on her own, and psychological withdrawal and physical passivity were her primary defenses.

Lucy had neurocepted that there was threat to her (e.g., more irritation or the potential of outright rejection) by her teacher's face and tone of voice. Her amygdala sensed danger, and anxiety spiked, increasing her heart rate and communicating to the bridges in the limbic system to generate cortisol and adrenaline. Simultaneously, the dorsal branch of her vagus nerve organized her parasympathetic nervous system to shut her down. She looked away, lost any vagal tone, and her teacher felt that she had "disappeared" from their interaction, which in essence she had. Lucy couldn't stay in her social engagement system. The bridge between the hippocampus and amygdala became nonfunctional, and she couldn't hold onto the knowledge that her teacher was different to her primary attachment figures.

Ambivalent

Children in this category differ from avoidantly attached students in that they find it extremely difficult to be independent. They are so concerned about the loss of relationship that they are unable to turn their attention toward developing their own self-reliance and independent interests in the world. They have learned that they can't rely on their parent for consistent delight and emotional availability. Their parents may sometimes be in synchronous connection, but they drop away from the reciprocal dance without warning and are poor at facilitating repair of ruptures and returning to relationship. These children can't trust that their parents will come back, so they adapt by not letting them leave. They intensify their emotions as signals for comfort, learning that their parents can't ignore them this way. They effectively coerce their parent into staying close by whining and clinging. If these fail, they have big emotions or outrageous behavior. Negative attention is better than no attention.

Although their signals for comfort may be loud and clear, the ability to receive comfort and be soothed is poor. They may effectively bring their parents closer to them, but that proximity is also anxiety provoking. What attention or comfort that they receive never seems to be enough. The parents of ambivalently attached children may have been inconsistent in their responses to their child's need for comfort. They may have sometimes been responsive and nurturing, but at other times harsh and rejecting. Although they may have intended to soothe their child, the parent may have found it hard to figure out the child's unique rhythm. Being misattuned in this way left the child in distress. The child then could not develop the trust that their parents could comfort them and, rather than being soothed by their presence, remained anxious or upset. For the parents, not being able to get their child to soothe increases feelings of inadequacy, shame, or upset as the experience is one of rejection. The parent becomes increasingly ambivalent in relating with their child with an ambivalent attachment. Their manner of relating tends toward becoming conflictual and unpredictable, holding little comfort and joy for either parent or child.

The child with an ambivalent attachment pattern can't trust that they will be comforted in a way that brings them into connection. If their parent is too far away, they are anxious, and if their parent is close, they are anxious—either that their parent will disappear again or that they will be angry and punitive. The anxiety for these children remains high, and they become organized by their sympathetic nervous system using strategies of fight and flight to figure out how to stay in relationships. Blocked trust and blocked care are likely to increase, creating a relationship that holds much dissatisfaction for both.

In the classroom, ambivalently attached children tend to be the students who are disruptive, reactive, and have great difficulty settling their bodies to sit, listen, or learn. They may have a diagnosis of attention deficit disorder, oppositional defiant disorder, or intermittent explosive disorder as they find ever more creative ways to keep people attending to them. They are the students who try to feel safe by being intimidating to adults and peers. They use refusal, defiance, or running out of the classroom to avoid the challenge of learning that threatens to overwhelm them. They do best in one-on-one teaching situations where an adult can co-regulate their anxiety, helping them down-regulate their nervous systems and scaffold their exploration.

Sean was a grade seven student who had struggled behaviorally throughout his grade-school career. He had had a diagnosis of attention deficit hyperactivity disorder at the age of five years, oppositional defiant disorder at the age of 8 years, and recently the school psychologist diagnosed him with a reading disorder. He lived with his grandparents in a small apartment with his nine-year-old half-sister. His parents had separated when he was four years of age. He had inconsistent visits with his mother, but had not seen his father for five years since he had moved to another province.

In the classroom environment, Sean was easily stressed and would respond quickly with verbal aggression, a refusal to comply with requests, and the adoption of an intimidating physical posture. He did best in one-on-one interactions with his teacher or educational assistant, but as soon as they exerted some authority, he became angry with them and would distance physically and emotionally. He would then wander about the classroom disrupting the other children. If his teacher approached him too quickly, his behavior would escalate. His teachers were puzzled about how to help him.

His teachers were experiencing the struggle of not knowing how to create enough safety for Sean to settle into learning. If they left him alone, he could not work independently and would start to be disruptive. If they worked beside him, he managed better until he experienced a challenge. If the work was too difficult for him, he felt inadequate, experienced shame, and did not feel safe. If his teachers exerted some authority, his need for control was challenged, which also left him feeling vulnerable. He could not access his social engagement system to allow for negotiation or collaboration. As soon as he started to feel unsafe, his sympathetic nervous system provided the fight or flight defense strategies required to manage the challenge. The difficulty was that there was no relief. He could not manage independent exploration nor could he manage the intimacy and uncertainty associated with being close to his teachers. For his teachers, they struggled to know how to reach him because they felt that whatever they tried wasn't helpful for him.

Again, the horizontal and vertical bridges were very poorly built. Since he constantly felt anxious, his limbic system bridges developed to allow for hypervigilance. His thinking was concrete, he could not think what might happen if he behaved aggressively or with defiance, and he was at the mercy of his amygdala that couldn't turn off the signals of danger. He could not access what he knew or new learning to help him experience himself and others differently

Luckily his teachers had some knowledge of trauma and were able to recognize that his difficulty settling was a function of his lack of safety. They focused on relating with him with soothing voices and clear facial expressions that communicated their interest and delight in him and their belief that he could learn. They did not experience shame or anxiety in response to his difficulties, and they had each other to consult and debrief the particularly challenging days. They continued to spend one-on-one time with him in small chunks of time. By the end of the school year, Sean could allow himself to take the risk to read with them. He still was quick to anger and would storm out of the room, but the time he could stay with the challenge increased and the time it took him to return to class decreased.

Disorganized

Main and Soloman (1990) in their research of infant/parent dyads discovered that there was a small group of children who had no consistent pattern of responding and engaging with their parent/s. They considered them to have insecure features, but they could not easily classify them. They eventually described this pattern as being disorganized in contrast to the other two insecure patterns that reflected organized ways of responding. They called this pattern—or effectively a lack of pattern—disorganized attachment. For this group of children, the parents had been so frightening, unpredictable, or so anxious themselves that the infant could not find a way to have their parent attend to them or find a way to avoid harm and to find moments of rest and restoration. The child was faced with an unresolvable dilemma: they must have a parent to survive, but that parent was a constant threat to that survival or was always communicating that danger was imminent in their face and voice. Under stress, the child with the avoidant pattern learned that it was best to rely on himself.

Under stress, the child with the ambivalent pattern learned that it was best to rely on others. The child with the disorganized pattern could do neither. As a result, the child with the disorganized pattern is the one most likely to manifest signs of mental illness as an adult, with both externalized (conduct and oppositional-defiance disorders, ADHD, and explosiveness) and internalized (anxiety, mood, and dissociative disorders) symptoms.

Behaviorally in the classroom, these are the children who bounce between the fight, flight, and freeze strategies. They at times are hyperaroused showing aggression, hyperactivity, pressured speech, and running away and at other times are hypo-aroused. At those times, they appear to be "shut down" and may have slow speech, depressed or flat affect, loss of muscle tone, and a look of despair or fear. They have learned to be rigidly in control of others and their environment as a protection against any potential harm and resist any attempts by adults to direct or comfort them. They may lie and steal frequently as they find ways to stay out of trouble and meet needs without depending on others.

Sometimes their behavior can be quite bizarre. We had one student who would only interact with his teachers as a cat. He would meow and wind his way around their legs and when frightened or angry he would spit and claw and retreat to underneath a desk. Being a cat was protective for him. Perhaps it represented a fantasy where cats are strong and beyond hurt or perhaps it represented magical thinking where at one time he was not hurt by his parent when he was pretending to be a cat. Being a cat was equated with harm avoidance, so it made perfect sense that he would persist in being one.

Children with disorganized attachment tend to have such difficulty in classroom situations. They see danger everywhere, and have been so badly frightened by adults that they can't trust anything about them. They project their fear, loss, and rage onto everyone, and are blind to the safety that is being provided by the school staff. They have no functioning bridges to their cortex, so can't be "taught" that things are or can be different. In fact, any attempts to teach them are experienced as attempts to control them and most often met with strong and aggressive opposition. Their alarm system is so finely tuned that even positive interactions or events can set it off and can result in explosive or withdrawing behavior. Teachers struggle to know how to approach such a frightened yet frightening child. Without cues to guide them, they often fail to offer what is wanted or needed, perpetuating the child's belief that adult relationships are not to be relied upon. It is often these students who are suspended or expelled in response to their aggressive and disruptive behavior, leaving us feeling discouraged and exhausted.

Lucas would have been classified as having a disorganized attachment pattern when he first came to us. Sophie was another student who had experienced an environment that had been so frightening that she could not find a way to be with others that felt safe.

Sophie was 8 years old and had been apprehended two years previously from her aunt and uncle's care. A neighbor had reported that Sophie and her younger brother were being yelled at and dragged by their hair by their uncle when they didn't listen. When workers investigated, they found that the children had been locked in their room for days at a time with limited food and water and a dirty mattress on the floor. A routine medical exam revealed that both had been sexually abused.

Both children were placed together in a foster home. The foster parents reported that they would get up at night and scavenge in the garbage for food and drink from the dog bowl. Sophie could scream for over two hours at a high pitch scream. At these times, she wouldn't let her foster parents anywhere near her. Eventually she would tire herself out and fall asleep curled into a fetal position underneath her bed. When her foster parents tried to wonder with her what had been upsetting, she had no recall of how upset she had been.

Sophie would approach her foster father, or other men who came to visit, provocatively and rub herself against their laps with a glazed look on her face. She would look hurt when she was gently redirected and told that it was an adult's job to keep children safe and no adult should have sex with a child. She would then quite often urinate or defecate in her foster parent's room or on their belongings. Many nights Sophie would have nightmares and scream out in her sleep but would have no recollection of what she had dreamed.

During the day, she was defiant and hyperactive. Occasionally she would allow her foster parent to sit beside her to read or watch TV but would then suddenly attack her physically and shout at her to go away. She would hurt the family pets and show no remorse. She would be covered in bruises as she was continually falling, sometimes it seemed to her foster parents deliberately. She showed no pain if she received a large cut or bruise, but would scream hysterically if she had a tiny cut. She would demand a band-aid, but then reject any attempts to put it on her.

Her foster parents worried because Sophie would approach any stranger and engage them in a conversation. She required such tight supervision to ensure that she didn't leave with someone else claiming that she was lost or that her foster parents were abusing her. Although she needed this supervision, she constantly fought against it, demanding that her parents trust her and yelling that she hated them when they gently insisted that their job was to keep her safe.

At school, the same volatile pattern was evident. Sophie could be calm and engaged in an activity one minute and raging the next, with no apparent reason for her upset. Her upset was so immediate that her teachers would be taken by surprise. Their experience of the interaction was that it was going positively or that they had been having a good morning. This may have in fact been the trigger for Sophie. She had no experience with safety or positive interactions and could not trust them or her own feelings about them. If someone smiled at her or gave her a compliment she would rage or look away and down, appearing to have not heard. Given her past history of sexual abuse, a smile may have been associated with impending harm. Her amygdala would have signaled danger loudly and persistently. She either responded with her sympathetic (aggression and running out of the classroom) or parasympathetic defenses (staring into space) as she attempted to keep herself safe from what she believed was coming.

At home and at school, if Sophie had had a good day, the adults could expect the next day to be difficult. Again, Sophie couldn't allow herself to trust this new experience of herself and others. Her underlying sense of self was that she was an unlovable, rotten kid. She couldn't risk having people come close and see her shame, so she rejected others before she was rejected. Given that she had needed to develop a strong sense of control, venturing into new possibilities or experiences was too risky and it was better to keep her environment similar to the one she had learned to adapt to.

Not surprisingly, Sophie found it very difficult to get along with the other children in her class. If they came too close she typically screamed at them. She wanted to be first in line all the time and couldn't tolerate waiting for a turn or whatever the teacher was distributing to the class. When the other children would signal their anger or frustration with her, Sophie would cry and blame them for upsetting her, wanting the teacher to give them trouble. If her teachers didn't comply, she would run from the room screaming she hated everyone.

Children like Sophie really challenge the resources available in a school setting. Unfortunately, there may be more than one Sophie requiring an intense level of supervision and support from the school team, further stretching the resources available. These are the children that can't yet respond to our traditional cognitive behavioral supports or interventions. They do not have any clue why they are behaving the way they are and have absolutely no choice in altering their perceptions or regulatory abilities. They are in a constant state of neurocepting danger or life threat. Helping students like Sophie is a long game and it requires a team of dedicated professionals who understand how developmental trauma has impacted her psychological, emotional, cognitive, social, and neurological development, and who can provide the felt sense of safety she will need to settle and learn.

Before introducing you to the Dyadic Developmental Practice framework that helps us play that long game, we need to touch on one more area of research. Intersubjectivity is the third area of research that informs DDP.

4

Lessons from Intersubjectivity

Attachment theory underscores the importance of a safe relationship for our brains to develop properly. The concept of intersubjectivity helps us understand how through those relationships we develop our understanding of ourselves and our world. Intersubjectivity in psychology is defined as the sharing of subjective states by two or more individuals, and it refers to shared emotion (attunement), shared attention, and shared intention (Scheff, 2006). Trevarthen and Stern are two researchers who have studied the shared, reciprocal experience of the parent and child, where the experience of one of the partners has an impact on the experience of the other. This is an important concept for Dyadic Developmental Practice. How we experience our students can have a profound impact on how our students experience themselves.

One of Sian's adult clients once stated that it was his grade three teacher who had saved his life. This man had experienced terrible violence at the hands of his parents, and at school he was an angry, aggressive, and frightening young boy. He fought any child that he perceived was making fun of him. Given his safety blindness, this was really anybody who came near him. Now, as an adult healing from his past, he could recognize that his teacher saw something in him that he at the time could not. He was intellectually gifted. Although his teacher never knew the impact she had, this terrified boy found a part of himself that year that allowed him to finish school, go to college, and hold down interesting and demanding jobs. That didn't mean that his life was easy or that he stopped being aggressive, but this part of himself was only seen because his teacher had seen it first.

Trevarthen and Stern call this process *primary intersubjectivity*. It essentially means that an infant or child will experience themselves as lovable, valuable, and delightful whenever their parents experience them that way. The opening scenes of the movie *Inside Out* by Pixar illustrate this concept beautifully. As Riley opens her eyes to experience the joy and delight in her parents' eyes, the first emotion formed is that of Joy. She experiences herself as joyful because when she looked into her parent's eyes she sees that they are filled with joy.

When children are abused and neglected, they learn to experience themselves as unimportant, defective, unlovable, unlikeable, and disgusting because that is how their parents experience them in those moments where abuse and neglect is perpetrated. A pervasive sense of shame develops where the child experiences themselves in the presence of their parent as unworthy. As they get older, this experiential sense of self is reinforced by their cognitive understanding that these bad things that happen to them must be because there is something wrong with them. Young children who are developmentally egocentric can only think in this way.

Children then learn to avoid intersubjective experiences for fear that they will be painful. They fear that if they look into our eyes, they will see the same things that were in their parent's eyes. This is so challenging for educators and professionals who know that the way to help children with developmental trauma is to be in relationship with them. Shared attention and intention is difficult to establish when the child's motivation is to avoid and protect, and the educator's intention is to approach and connect in order to understand and teach. This difficulty being "with" one another can easily perpetuate misattunements, reinforce the child's blocked trust—being with someone is not comfortable—and make us increasingly vulnerable to blocked care.

As professionals and teachers, we like to argue with children who have learned to see themselves as defective or bad. We try to give them examples of good things they do as an antidote to their shame. Unfortunately, such cognitive arguments cannot change the underlying experience of shame. This can only be changed through repeated intersubjective experiences where they feel liked, loved, valued, enjoyed, or delighted in.

When we outline Dyadic Developmental Practice in the following chapter, we provide examples and language of how to invite students into intersubjective experiences. As we facilitate moments of shared attention and intention, we can start to influence our students and help them recognize that they can influence us in positive ways.

Intersubjective experiences require three different mutual or shared states. The first ingredient for intersubjectivity is to have shared emotions. If one member of the dyad is angry and the other scared, they will be having different experiences and not a shared one. To invite a child into an intersubjective space, the adult needs to be attuned to the emotions the child is experiencing. It doesn't require the adult to be scared, angry or confused, but they must be able to recognize it and have empathy for the child's emotional experience no matter how different to their own. This attunement is the first step in helping a child "share" an experience rather than be left alone in it. For teachers, this means that they need to take the time to notice and accurately read the child's emotions. This is why taking care of teacher brains is so crucial important. If we are in blocked care, we will fail to notice or we misread the child's emotional experience, thus perpetuating their loneliness rather than offering them a more positive experience of being in relationships.

Once we have attunement, we must both agree to attend to the emotional state. Shared attention is evident when teachers and students work together to understand something or when students work together in a group to solve a problem. It is also evident when a school staff member and student work together to understand why a child is feeling a particular way. Shared attention is particularly difficult with a child who wants to avoid intersubjective experiences. Typically, the adult is curious and excited and the child is wary and avoidant. The adult's attention is on knowing and the child's attention is on threat of being known. The teacher's attention is on teaching and the child's attention is on the sounds in the hallway, the clouds he can see out the window, or the discomfort of his socks. Attaining shared attention is such a challenge for us with children who have blocked trust as being with us in any way sets off the alarm bells. Not paying attention to what we want them to do is probably the number one frustration for parents and teachers. Many a report card or referral to support services includes symptoms of lack of focus, distractibility, and impulsivity. For our hurt students, regulating their attention is impaired both by the lag in the development of islands and bridges that allows for good attention regulation and the psychological vulnerability associated with being "with" us.

How do we invite students to share emotional space? Sometimes the key is to attend to the difficulty connecting rather than the thing you wish to discuss. *"Boy! I really want to talk to you about this math problem but you want to do anything but talk to me about math!"* Such a statement lets the student know you have noticed their internal state and are not upset about it—just interested in why it might be difficult. For a brief moment, there is shared attention on the common experience—the difficulty connecting. The compliance has to be less important than the understanding. If the adult can stay regulated and interested in the underlying reasons for lack of shared attention, the student can experience briefly the interest and feel interesting or discover his own curiosity. If we are irritated or frustrated by the lack of compliance or the attempts to connect, then we will continue to reinforce the student's experience of relationships being something that causes harm and strengthens his intention to avoid them.

Shared intention is the third essential ingredient of intersubjective experiences and is also hard for our students with developmental trauma. Teachers' intentions are typically to teach the curriculum, instill order in their classroom, have fun with a student, and get to know a student. A child who has been hurt may have the intention to avoid the challenge of learning, create chaos that mirrors his own internal state or family dynamics, cause the teacher to be angry as that is familiar, and to avoid any attempts to get to know them. Without complementary intentions, we will be frustrated and outside of a comfortable connection. If both partners can stay in their social engagement system, then they will be able to negotiate and collaborate, finding their way to stay in connection and to manage these differing intentions. However, if one or other of the partners is being driven by their sympathetic or parasympathetic systems, the competing intentions quickly result in an argument, aggression, or withdrawal as each insists on control. Since our students with developmental trauma do not yet have the circuitry that allows them to be in their social engagement system, they most often respond to our attempts to teach, direct, influence, and understand with the tools available to them: fight, flight, or freeze.

The lack of shared intention can also be a frustration for educators within their system. Often, teachers recognize that a child is not yet ready for learning, but they run into criticism from administrators that insist on curriculum delivery. When we lose the collaborative stance, we are at risk of becoming reactive and defensive because our fundamental sense of emotional safety is challenged. What each party wants or believes is pitted against the other in the attempt to control.

If someone doesn't want to do what we want them to do, rarely, if ever, does insisting on it work. Control typically reflects underlying fear. For the child, the fear is of more harm. Perhaps for the teacher the fear is loss of efficacy and impending sense of inadequacy if we cannot make the child comply. If we can understand the other is fearful, name it so we can organize the experience for them, and have empathy for their fear, we will more likely create the safety needed for the other person to move away from defense into a social engagement system. The creation of safety again is crucial for us to move toward joint intention.

Secondary intersubjectivity refers to the way we come to understand our world. If our parents view the world from a particular belief system, we too will come to learn about it that way. Securely attached children learn from their parents that people are there to support and be helpful, that obstacles can be overcome, that others have value and must be treated as such. Children with insecure attachments learn from their parents that connection is tenuous and that the world must be tightly controlled to ensure that things turn out as expected and relationships sustained. Babies and young children with disorganized attachments learn that others can never be trusted, aggression is powerful, and weakness is to be avoided at all costs. They learn to view the world through stereotypes and to be highly suspicious of others' motives.

One of the goals when we work with children who have experienced developmental trauma is to help them learn about themselves and the world in a different way—ways that open up different possibilities for behaving. If we have deep shame, we will try our hardest to hide our true selves from others for fear that they will see us as disgusting and reject us or hurt us further because we have no value. Our fear won't allow us to lean into relationships. If we believe that others are hurtful, maintaining a hypervigilant and reactive stance makes all the sense in the world. As we work with children with developmental trauma, we offer them a different viewpoint. Not by insisting on it, but by communicating a different possibility. Because our view of the world is integrated into who we are, being present and authentic, accepting, and curious will allow our students to "feel" and to come to "know" a different possibility because we feel and know it.

Just as our students experience themselves in our experiences of them, we experience ourselves in their reflection of us. It is easy to be with students who are securely attached because they give us cues that we are on the right track and doing well in our teaching or caregiving. It is easy to keep going. A mutually positive, reciprocal interaction communicates to both parties that the other is liked, respected, and valued. Students who have less trust or no trust at all give messages that we are not liked, not helpful, stupid, or even hated. We become vulnerable to believing their reflections and moving into blocked care, believing that we don't have value. This is especially true if our own attachment histories or experiences make us vulnerable to having feelings of inadequacy or shame.

Understanding the concepts of primary and secondary intersubjectivity again reminds us of the importance of supporting the adults who work with children with developmental trauma.

Scott was a grade three teacher who was an experienced teacher and a strong advocate for his students. As part of the process of becoming a trauma-informed school, he and his two educational assistants were receiving regular supervision from a consultant trained in Dyadic Developmental Practice. The team had a number of highly dysregulated students with histories of developmental trauma, and their consultant met with them regularly to help them understand these student's behavior and what fears the students were bringing into the classroom.

It became apparent that Scott really struggled with one child in particular. In contrast to his easygoing demeanor with other children, he seemed to find it hard to like this child. The student found it hard to sit still at his desk, often chewed his pencils and his shirt, and there were signs of other sensory integration difficulties. He would sometimes be disruptive to others as he wandered around the classroom, but was not aggressive or destructive. Scott would be quick to set limits with this student, insisting that he went back to his desk, and if the child did not comply promptly, he would be sent to the Principal. Scott would be sharp, have irritation in his voice, and signal to the student that he was a nuisance. The student would then signal to his teacher that he was irritating, not liked, and not-worthy of compliance.

When asked to reflect upon what might be causing the student to have difficulty sitting still, Scott believed that he was deliberately defiant and should be able to choose an alternative behavior. He would become defensive when the support person gently asked him to wonder about the difference in the way he understood this child than the other children he had in his class.

As Scott felt safer with his consultant, he began to talk about how he felt anxious when this student would get out of his seat and wander the classroom. When the student ignored directives, he admitted to feeling angry. As Scott and his consultant began to explore what might be behind his anxiety and anger, Scott talked of his own history of abuse and neglect. When his student needed to move his body given sensory difficulties, Scott felt a challenge to his need for control. If he let one student walk around the classroom, all the other students would want to do the same and he would lose control of his class. This loss of control felt dangerous, and he would find it difficult to stay in his social engagement system. The brakes would come off, and he would become organized by his sympathetic nervous system. He was more reactive and forceful than he would normally be and would engage quickly into a power struggle with this student. He then admitted that when the student ignored him, he felt rejected. It felt to him just like times that he had been ignored by his father. He believed that the student's ignoring was a confirmation of his lack of worth and it caused him pain. Again, his sympathetic nervous system activated defenses to avoid that painful early rejection.

Once Scott and his consultant had discussed his experiences, Scott could be more aware of why he felt the way he did and could find ways to keep the brakes on his sympathetic nervous system. He started to be more gentle with the student as he gave directives, and the student began to respond differently to Scott's different voice tone and facial expressions. By the end of the school year, there was no question that teacher and student liked each other. They had been able to engage in repeated intersubjective interactions where Scott could communicate understanding and value. As the student began to trust his teacher, he returned the favor. They became much more practiced in sharing positive emotional experiences. They could share attention both on their experience of the other as well as academic tasks. The student, because he felt safer in Scott's presence, could now trust that being taught wasn't going to lead to humiliation, harm, or rejection. He was beginning to learn that Scott's decisions and actions were about helping him learn. Both shared the intention to keep working together. When ruptures occurred, as they invariably did, they were able to return more and more quickly to intersubjective interactions.

As this example shows, being reactive and defensive will prevent both primary and secondary intersubjective experiences. We will not want to approach someone who is displaying these signs of danger. Any attempt to control rather than understand and mutually influence will prevent us from being together in that intersubjective space. Coercion, withdrawal, lecturing, and monopolizing the discussion are one-sided and will not help us understand what lies behind the child's behavior or what might be behind our own reactions to it.

Given that primary and secondary intersubjective experiences are so crucial to our sense of self, it is easy to understand why the attachment system is a primary instinctive drive. We need to be *with* one another in a comfortable, mutually influencing manner to develop in a healthy way. Chapter 11 covers the use of technology in classrooms and families as a barrier to intersubjective experiences. So often students are receiving their feedback from a device rather than another person and are missing so many intrinsic, reciprocal interactions that are essential for human development.

5

Dyadic Developmental Practice and Its application to Education

Dyadic Developmental Practice integrates what we know from interpersonal neurobiology, intersubjectivity, and attachment theory to inform us how best to provide intervention to mistrusting children. All three underpinnings of the model highlight the crucial importance of a safe relationship for well-being. Dyadic Developmental Practice places the need for a safe relationship front and center, as does behavioral or social learning theory. Where we might differ is our emphasis on the recognition that co-regulation of affect must precede the development of self-regulation and that a child will require repetitive intersubjective experiences before they can be influenced by the incentives that are more standard practice in our classrooms.

We ourselves are our best tool for inviting children into relationships, to help strengthen the bridges toward the prefrontal cortex, and to find a new experience of themselves in our eyes. Once the child experiences through primary intersubjective interactions that they are liked and have value and once they have repeated experiences of their emotions being co-regulated by their teachers, they will be more settled to learn. The resourcing of islands in the cortex that will allow for better learning and problem-solving are secondary. They are not targeted until a safe emotional connection has been made.

When using Dyadic Developmental Practice as our framework, we work to:

- Accept that if a child (or parent) could do better then they would.
- Understand that co-regulation of affect must occur before self-regulation can be learned.
- Recognize that behavior will be changed by changing the felt sense of safety.
- Know that a child must "feel safe" and not be told they are safe to learn.
- Understand that fight-flight and freeze behaviors associated with blocked trust are adaptive.

- Recognize that controlling behavior reflects underlying fear: resisting authority, opposition, avoidance, hypervigilance, inability to recognize or unwillingness to share, thoughts and feelings, lack of reciprocity, and the myriad of other ways our students attempt to control us make sense when children have learned that adults cannot be relied upon.
- Adjust our expectations to meet the emotional age of our students and not the chronological age. Chronic stress delays the growth of our brain in ways that make it difficult to meet developmental expectations.
- Know that in order to survive, our students must suppress curiosity. They, therefore, have little knowledge about why they do what they do or why adults behave in the way they do. We must help our students come to know about themselves and others not expect that they know but are not telling us.
- Understand that in order to survive, our students must suppress empathy. When they feel safe, they will take the risk to feel their own pain and by extension that of others. Empathy will become unblocked.
- Recognize that behavior therapy or cognitive behavior therapy as means of classroom management best suits students with secure attachments. They have little effect on students who cannot identify their internal states or keep the bridge to their cortex in place to access the strategies to change their thinking or calm their feelings.
- Look after our own brains. Our students' relentless attempts to control us and the lack of reciprocity make us vulnerable to slipping into blocked care. As our caregiving systems break down, we become less hopeful for change. In blocked care, we might keep trying, but it is much harder for us to stay in our social engagement system that is so crucial for signaling safety signs to our students.

As we have learned, the forming of relationships with mistrusting children is not easy. We need knowledge of how to use what we know about interpersonal neurobiology and intersubjectivity to by-pass our students' adaptive defense systems.

Often teachers have anxiety that their role is not to be the student's therapist, and are fearful of delving into the emotional realm out of concern that they will make things worse for the child. The purpose of this book is not to turn teachers into therapists, but to provide a framework that allows teachers to create that felt sense of safety that is the crucial first ingredient for learning.

PLAYFULNESS, ACCEPTANCE, CURIOSITY, AND EMPATHY (PACE)

In order to learn anything, we have to feel safe. As we have mentioned previously, telling someone that they are safe rarely translates into feeling safe. Playfulness, Acceptance, Curiosity, and Empathy provide the foundation for that felt sense of safety as they are experiences that our brains instinctively respond to with pleasure and sense of calm. They allow for an intersubjective experience of being seen, which as we have learned is essential for the brain's circuitry to develop in the way that optimizes physical and mental health. Our brain is a social organ, and playfulness, acceptance, curiosity, and empathy bring us into connection. They are signals of safety.

Playfulness

Trauma shuts down the capacity for intimacy and play (Porges, 2017). Jaak Panksepp studied the importance of play for our development. He discovered that our instinct to play is an ancient one, independent of the resources in our cortex. In fact, he surgically removed the cortex of rats and they still engaged in the physical play with other rats whose brains were intact (Panksepp, Normansell, Cox, & Siviy, 1994). The play impulse comes from a deep and primitive part of the brain, and we share it with other animals. If it has continued over many thousands of years to remain a vital part of our brain, it must be fundamental to our survival. Panksepp posits that play is vital because it helps us develop the reciprocity and social skills that will allow us to live in social groups. If we can be successful in social groups or communities, we have a much higher chance of surviving than if we are on our own (Panksepp & Biven, 2012).

One of the things that is so noticeable with our students who have been hurt is that they are very clumsy when it comes to social interactions. They typically try to control play, having little sense of the give and take needed to advance the fantasy or creative play. They are impulsive and they can't wait for others to suggest ideas or take the reins for a while. They are often aggressive in their rough and tumble play, resulting in others being hurt and not wanting to play with them. So many times, they have difficulty recognizing when enough is enough, and what started out as positive turns into something negative for all participants. Sometimes we have students who are just so fearful that they stand on the sidelines and can't approach others to be included in playful interactions. Learning how to play is, therefore, a crucial skill to develop to help students who have brains compromised by trauma.

Play in Dyadic Developmental Practice is less about teaching our students to play snakes and ladders or cards but more about the delight that occurs when we are engaged with someone in a light, spontaneous, and positive manner. We find it difficult to play with people we don't like. When we are truly playful, we engage with others in a way that communicates unconditional acceptance and delight, enjoyment, excitement, creativity, and joy. As we know from intersubjectivity theory, our experience of those emotions will be experienced by the child in similar ways, awakening in them a sense of being delightful, enjoyable, and of having value, emotional states that are so different from the ones that get created through the experiences of abuse and neglect. Play—and the attitude of playfulness that underlies many of our interactions with traumatized children—offers a different possibility of the child's fundamental sense of self, and it gives a welcomed break from the toxic nature of a shame-based narrative.

In a healthy parent-child dyad, the parent is constantly attuned to the child's emotional state and to upregulating positive emotions and down-regulating negative emotions. Playing with infants creates the experiences of mutual delight as parents discover toes, play with disappearing and appearing (Peek-a-Boo or hide and seek), and regulate surprise (tickling or blowing raspberries). Playfulness in Dyadic Developmental Practice mirrors this opportunity to help children learn that they can elicit delight in others. It is about finding every opportunity to communicate to our students that they can make us smile and our eyes sparkle by what they say, what they do and who they are underneath their behavioral symptoms.

Playfulness can also help us approach serious content in a casual and confident way so that the child can feel safer attending to something that is difficult. When we can use playfulness in this way, exploring and learning is an experience of mutual discovery rather than a less reciprocal process that is evaluative or judgmental.

> As Lucas began to feel safer, his capacity for teasing and play started to develop. This allowed us to interact with him differently and to use humour to help him understand himself better. When he was anxious, Lucas would behave in very controlling and rigid ways. He could not tolerate change, and everything had to unfold the way he dictated it otherwise he would become quite dysregulated. Staff had been talking to him about how he got "Rock Brain" (from Michelle Garcia Winner's Superflex poster) when he was uncertain and had helped him see how fear made it difficult for him to be flexible and to be in the thinking part of his brain. Rock Brain was in constant use for the first few months, but as the bridge to his cortex became stronger we saw it less and less. When he had Rock Brain, he couldn't think about anything else but what he wanted.
>
> One day when Lucas was starting to look anxious, a staff member rushed over picked him up and turned him upside down gently shaking him. As he righted him, the staff member reached into his pockets and grabbed a pocket full of stones and shouted with delight, your Rock Brain is now a bunch of pebbles, I think they are small enough to come out your ears when I shake you!" He called over the other staff, "Look! Lucas's rock brain is now Pebble Brain, that means it's not so heavy and difficult for him to manage!"
>
> Lucas and his teacher lined up some pebbles on his desk and talked more about how Rock Brain comes when kids are scared a lot. The more scared the bigger the rock could get. He gave Lucas lots of empathy for how big his Rock Brain had been and shared how delighted he was now that it was just a bunch of pebbles.

Playfulness is not always indicated of course. We must be careful not to use it to "jolly" students out of their difficult emotional experience or to distract them from emotional pain. We must be attuned to what our students can accept in terms of playfulness. Lucas would never have been able to tolerate the aforementioned interaction until he felt safe enough. Playfulness when used within the Dyadic Developmental Practice framework communicates unconditional acceptance, delight, hope, and a way of being with children that develops the child's ability to have fun with others, while sometimes also assisting in processing trauma or behavioral infractions.

In our section about the Belong program, play and a playful attitude are an integral part of everyday activities. Our students come into the program tense and defensive, and finding it very difficult to play. Thankfully, our staff team, particularly our educational assistant, Mr. Hepburn, is skilled at being playful. He playfully greets each student at the door with a constantly evolving handshake. For one of our students who remained in the program for four years, the ritual took over four minutes and involved picking him up and touching his head on the ceiling, then turning him upside down and touching his head on the floor! Each child's ritual is different and is co-created to be a communication of mutual delight. You may be thinking this is impossible with one teacher and 28 students—112 minutes of greeting rituals would likely result in chaos. However, a smile and communication of delight, a teasing comment or sharing of a private joke takes very little time and can be woven into regular interactions with students either individually or as a whole class. Our educational assistant writes a joke every morning on the board with accompanying illustrations for the students to ponder throughout their day. The answer is unveiled with great ceremony before the children leave for their buses.

A playful stance is a nondefensive one. We don't play with people we don't like or are fearful of. As we learned about in polyvagal theory, our job is to remain in our smart vagal system while our students struggle to find it. Children will adopt the same emotional stance as the adults who are important to them (Schore, 2017) If we are too serious, our verbal and nonverbal cues communicate danger to our students who have been hurt, and they remain wary. If we can be more playful in our interactions, we communicate that problems can be overcome. Behavior is just behavior and is not representative of who we are.

In the words of Julie Salverson who is a professor of drama at Queens University and a writer, "play is another way of looking, a quality of attention, an openness to options, a provocation to our imaginations, an attitude to Living, an enrichment of meaning" (Salverson, 2018). Philippe Gaulier, a French master clown, teacher, and founder of a famous French Theatre School who taught people like Emma Thompson, Roberto Benigni, and Helena Bonham Carter, stated that play is "as vital a function as breathing or laughter." When we play, there is a perpetually creative give and take, the story that is, the story that is becoming (Salverson, 2018).

Although play is a big part of kindergarten, it tends to be less and less part of a regular school day as the priorities of resourcing cortical islands takes precedence. Relational opportunities decrease as the opportunity for play decreases. This is even more evident in classrooms now as technology becomes an integral part of teaching, and children spend time on individual devices rather than in shared activities. Research is starting to highlight the negative impact of this lack of shared attention. We are also beginning to see the negative repercussions of technology use by children. Youth between 8 years and 18 years spend on average seven hours and 38 minutes a day on screen media. This is outside of school technology time. Researchers looking at the rise of reported clinical levels of depression and anxiety in our youth point to the amount of time youth are on smartphones or tablets as a significant factor in this rise of mental health problems. It is not the technology per se that is creating the difficulties, rather the amount of time that children are missing shared activities, the face-to-face, intrinsic, reciprocal social interactions (Twenge, Martin, & Campbell, 2018). Increased screen use is also interfering with play and sleep, activities that we know to be essential for growth and restoration of all our vital organs.

You will see as you read about our Belong program how play is present through-out the school program and ongoing interactions with staff. We may have structured play activities. Recently the students designed board games to illustrate the concept of probability and would play in small groups. There may be familiar games such as Jenga, Connect Four, and cards available for play; there is always an elaborate Lego world in construction or puzzles in protected corners of the room. These activities offer the opportunity to practice taking turns and to invite peers to collaborate, problem-solve, and to enter into a shared enjoyable experience.

What is more striking if you walk into our classroom is the playful attitude of the staff. There are frequently inside jokes, teasing, and uproarious laughter at something a child has said or done, along with quiet smiles and glances, a light touch, and a confident, hope-full, attitude. There are many ways of communicating that the student is enjoyable, delightful, and has the capacity to move us emotionally. Play and playfulness are vital if traumatized children are to move from the many negative experiences and expectations of the past to a life that offers hope and joy, laughter, and contentment.

Acceptance

Sometimes when people hear about parenting or teaching from an attachment perspective, they believe it means no limits and consequences. When they hear that acceptance is a crucial part of the framework to bring students from mistrust to trust, they worry that they will be required to ignore big behaviors in the service of making the child feel better. As parents and teachers, we are often heard to describe behaviors or actions as "unacceptable." Acceptance in Dyadic Developmental Practice is about the unconditional acceptance of the emotional experience that lies behind behavior, while communicating that the behavior is indeed unacceptable for the child's life as it gets in the way of healthy relationship development or learning.

The child's experience includes his thoughts and feelings, likes and dislikes, and goals and values. We can accept that a student is angry, but not accept the throw-ing of desks or destruction of property. We can accept that the student thinks that the teacher does not like the student, without accepting the student swearing at the teacher. We can accept that the student likes playing with a screen, without allow-ing the student to play with the screen during classes. The adage of we love you but don't love your behavior is something we all might have said from time to time as a way to communicate unconditional love. However, this is a difficult statement for hurt children to understand as they are not able to separate their behavior from who they are, given the insufficient bridges to their cortex that allow abstract and reflecting functioning. However, to help, we need to find a way to communicate that their behavior makes sense given their underlying experiences and that there is no emotional experience that we can't accept and come to understand. When we feel unconditional acceptance and belonging, Dan Siegel states that our brain produces re-growth of damaged brain tissues, especially in the hippocampus. Acceptance simulates what was missed in those early months and years, what the human brain is designed to receive in order to develop properly.

Acceptance toward the other's experience means that we do not evaluate or judge it. When we judge others, either negatively or positively, it makes us feel less safe. It is easy to understand that if we judge someone critically, the sense of safety is decreased. That person is likely to feel badly about themselves, perhaps experience shame, and definitely will not be in a good place to take the risk to learn something new. So many of our students are always in trouble. The mutual expectation that trouble is coming makes it very difficult for anyone to feel safe or to promote the operation of the smart vagal system.

It may be harder to understand why positive evaluation or judgment can create less safety for our students. In North America, our culture has become increasingly determined that good self-esteem is built by telling children that whatever they do is a "good job" even if it isn't particularly good. Young soccer players are given medals even if they did not play. High school students are rarely failed. We have decided failure is to be avoided. We worry that all this is doing to our young people is making it difficult for them to tolerate making mistakes or failing and that anxiety and depressive systems are increasing as this tolerance decreases. Children are not stupid. They know what a good job is and what is not, and when adults try to reassure them that something bad is good, it is confusing and is communicating that there is something to be feared about failing, that adults need them to be doing well all the time and that acceptance is conditional on doing a good job. Evaluations of the child's specific behavior or academic progress is necessary in the classroom. But such evaluations need to be a small aspect of our relationship with the child. Unconditional acceptance of the child is more crucial if the child is to experience safety within the relationship.

Compliments and positive evaluations are really tricky for hurt children as they do not experience themselves as having any worth. They are notoriously rejecting of positive evaluations, and it often sets up a continuation of the need to mistrust adults: "You are telling me I am a good kid but you don't really understand that I am a no-good, throw-away kid." They may believe that we need them to behave particular ways for us to be OK and the relationship is then conditional. We must accept first the child's experience if they are to learn to accept that we really do see them as a good kid. This is not easy to do, for most of us find hurt children's underlying experiences very painful and find it hard to sit alongside them in their pain. We want to reassure or jolly them into an alternative emotional state. Acceptance, however, is the first step toward a different possibility.

In addition to accepting the child's underlying experiences, we must also accept that if a child could do better, the child would. We have to accept that they do not yet have the neural circuitry that will allow them to behave in ways that promote relationships and learning.

With Dyadic Developmental Practice, we will work to change the behavior by first working to change the child's experience of safety. As a child begins to feel safe, there will be no need for the reactive-defensive behaviors. Typically, the education system has operated by trying to change the behaviors through behavioral methods—reward good behaviors, and punish negative ones. If we understand and accept that the behavior we find challenging is actually an adaptive response to feeling unsafe, then trying to change behaviors through reward and punishment is akin to playing whack-a-mole. We may be able to stop a child stealing others' lunches, but then lying increases. We may succeed in decreasing hands-on behaviors at recess, but then discover that the student is soiling and rubbing feces over his peers' backpacks. We have to change his experienced sense of safety and to accept the underlying emotional experiences of shame, fear, and rage that drives challenging behavior if we are to change problematic behaviors.

Staying aware of the child's fearful or shame-based experience helps us remain more compassionate and empathic toward a child and reduce the likelihood that we became harshly corrective in response to big behaviors. As soon as we become harsh, angry, or fearful ourselves, we have lost the opportunity to invite the student into a different possibility for relationships. We have no safety. We may get compliance, but only because the child is frightened of us or the trouble they will be in if they don't comply. Acceptance allows for psychological safety. With repetition, the child begins to learn that although there might be some limits and consequences, the relationship never wavers, and they can begin to experience the difference between who they are and what their behavior is. This is the beginning of integrating and reducing their sense of shame and the development of the sense that mistakes don't rupture the relationship and that repair is possible.

So what do we do with big behaviors that are unacceptable because they interfere with their own or others' learning? We must first know what these behaviors mean—what are their roots in the child's past and present experiences.

Tristan was a grade seven student who really struggled to manage a regular classroom environment. His tolerance for frustration was poor. When he didn't know how to complete academic work or when his peers would say something mean to him he quickly became verbally and physically aggressive. He would yell obscenities at the teacher or peers and quite frequently flip his desk and throw objects. Others were either frightened of him or irritated by him and would behave towards him in ways that confirmed to Tristan that he needed to stay ready to defend himself against harm.

Tristan was frequently the topic of staff meetings. He had already had several suspensions given the zero tolerance for violence and staff were really struggling to know how to engage him in learning. The principal was aware that the staff were losing patience with this young boy and had called a staff meeting to discuss what they might be able to do differently. The staff had all received training in PACE and were learning how to become a trauma-informed school using the Dyadic Developmental Practice framework.

The principal accepted his staff's frustration and provided them with empathy. He did not judge their attempts at connecting or correcting this student just wondered with them what Tristan's aggression might be communicating. He reminded them that Tristan was doing the best he could and that his behaviour was not likely to reflect a motivation to be in trouble. The staff brainstormed together what might be fueling his aggression. The list included, the need for control, shame, fear, learning disabilities, language delays, sensory integration difficulties, hunger, lack of sleep, substance abuse, worry about what was happening at home. It was then clear that some of these possibilities had to be addressed if he was to find a way to be in class safely. An alternative plan was needed.

The plan required the development of relationships as the first step towards providing a felt sense of safety. It was decided that when Tristan first came to school he would go to the Principal's office where he would be greeted and where there would be breakfast for him. One of the administration team was committed to spending 30 minutes with Tristan sharing breakfast and talking about things that felt comfortable to him, getting to know him. From there, Tristan would be met by an educational assistant and taken to the library where she would read stories to him. There was no expectation for him to produce academic work, just to choose a story and listen. Sometimes they listened to music and discussed lyrics to songs or looked at graphic novels, but still there was no expectation to produce any work for evaluation. Tristan liked to lie on the floor with a beanbag chair over the top of him. This was accepted and his educational assistant would often playfully sit on the beanbag before rolling off to one side to read. Some days, Tristan would fall asleep under his bean bag chair. His educational assistant would sit beside him while he slept and smile warmly at him when he woke.

Recess was too difficult for Tristan. The staff needed to accept that he could not be with the other children for fear of aggressive outbursts. He, therefore, remained with the education assistant who would play cards with him in the library or often suggest a walk to the nearby park just before the main recess began so that he didn't have to contend with the bells and rush of students that would often overwhelm him. After recess, the education assistant and Tristan headed to the Kindergarten room where Tristan was enlisted to help her work with a young boy with physical disabilities. This student was a very positive young man who loved attention and would greet any adult positively. The hope was that his ready smiles and willingness to engage could give Tristan some safety signals and give him an experience of being valued. Tristan was encouraged to read to him and to push his wheelchair to alternative spaces in the classroom. If he didn't feel like it, that was accepted and he was just asked to stay close to the educational assistant who would then read or re-locate the young student.

Tristan and the educational assistant would help the kindergarten children with their lunch and then Tristan would head home for the afternoon while the assistant was allocated to a different classroom. The modified day was implemented so that Tristan could be successful for a short period of time rather than reach his limit of tolerance and fail to manage. With the removal of academic pressures or the requirement to be in his class, Tristan was rarely aggressive.

The principal removed any expectation of academic performance making the priority the establishing of relationships with Tristan. All staff were encouraged to smile at Tristan and to say hello warmly when they met him in the hallway so as to give him an intersubjective experience of being liked. As these connections strengthened, the educational assistant began to wonder with him about his behaviour. Occasionally, he would come to school high on marijuana. On those days, he was not allowed to work with the kindergarten students and he would be required to hang out with the administration team until lunch time. His EA made sure to pop her head in to say that she missed him and hoped that he would help her tomorrow. The next day she would wonder about his need to be high and guess that it probably made him feel less anxious or gave him a break from feeling stressed. She reiterated how he would not be allowed to work with the young students if high but understood given how much stress he had in his life, why he would need a break. Lecturing him would not have worked and would have likely resulted in him getting angry and defensive. Accepting the underlying motivation to be high while placing a limit on what he could do while at school allowed for the connection between them to stay strong.

The priority on making connections accepted that Tristan could not be in class safely. Rather than provide consequences for his aggression, the team recognized that he would need them to help him. First, they needed to get to know him. He was not yet settled to learn so there was no point in asking him to do it at the risk of his frequent outbursts. When Tristan asked why he couldn't go to class he was told the truth, "You are not yet able to be in class safely and you have enough trouble in your life without the risk of charges against you because you have hurt someone. Until we can figure out how best to help you manage in class you will learn a different way."

Tristan did not attend his grade seven class for the rest of the year. He gradually was able to extend the time in school and would spend the extended time in one-to-one situations. Toward the end of the year, the team included someone that Tristan thought he might like to have as a friend for short periods of time. The supervision allowed for that interaction to be successful. If Tristan was high or volatile, he was told with empathy that he needed more adult time that day and that he could try again tomorrow to hang out with his friend.

When Tristan returned after the summer for grade eight, the team were prepared to provide the one on one support again. To their surprise, Tristan stated that he was ready to be in class. His team stated their fear that he would return to using aggression if he was scared or overwhelmed and negotiated a slow return to his classroom so he could test out his new skills. Tristan would leave the classroom when he felt he couldn't manage and go to the grade one class where the young boy with physical disabilities was now enrolled. He had an open invitation as long as he felt he could be regulated and was not high. His educational assistant often popped into classroom to check on him as did the administration team.

The team's acceptance that if Tristan could do better he would allowed them to focus on the provision of safety so that his need for defence wouldn't be necessary. Tristan was helped to see that his aggression was a way of communicating underlying emotional experiences such as fear, embarrassment, shame or anger and that those experiences were accepted without judgment. Staff were clear with him that there was nothing acceptable about hurting others or school property, and that they would work with him until he was able to manage school expectations more successfully.

We will discuss in chapter 9 how to use PACE to implement limits and consequences for some of the most troubling of student behaviors while also helping the student get a better understanding of why they do what they do and how they can repair their relationships.

Curiosity

Curiosity immediately follows upon acceptance, and it is another crucial component of helping a child feel safe. Given that behavior is a communication, we need always to be curious about what the child's behavior is telling us about their underlying experience—their thoughts, feelings, wishes, fears, and insights. In our experience, there are some consistent emotional themes that underlie a vast array of challenging behaviors in our children and youth. Shame, fear, and desire for connection while also not trusting connection would be among the top three. However, there are so many possibilities for beliefs, perceptions, thoughts, and emotional experiences that we need to make sure we slow down and never assume that we understand why our students do what they do. There are of course other motivations or underlying issues such as sensory integration difficulties and learning disabilities that may contribute to behavior. Our job is to figure out what might be contributing to our student's challenges and then to help them understand. The number one answer when we ask students what's going on, how they feel, what they think, or why they behaved a particular way is "I don't know!," to which we answer with confidence "Then let's figure it out together!"

In addition to curiosity helping us understand what is behind behavior, it also helps strengthen bridges between the child's left and right hemisphere, cortex and subcortex, and front and back regions, and moves us toward helping the child develop the circuitry to better support reflective functioning. If we assume that the child is operating from the more emotionally reactive right hemisphere that is registering alarm, the more cognitive analytical processes are very weak or off line all together. How can we invite those processes on board so that the child has a better ability to understand and regulate their emotional experiences? In the same way that we don't assume that our toddlers know what they feel or why they did something, we also do not assume that our hurt students know. It is up to us to assist them in organizing their experience and in exploring its possible meanings by wondering out loud with them about what they might be thinking and feeling.

Recently in our Belong program we had a student who came in one morning and was quite agitated. Karlee was really struggling to regulate her emotions and her attention—skills that she was only beginning to master. She was a student who lived with her grandparents as both her parents had issues with substance abuse. Her mother continued to struggle and would be in and out of her life. Typically, there was a lot of animosity between Karlee's mother and grandparents as they vied for control. The previous evening, the grandparents had let us know that Karlee's mother had arrived late at night wanting to visit her daughter. She had assaulted the grandfather and he had had to call the police. Karlee and her grandparents had worked hard with us to communicate and develop appropriate rules and boundaries for visits so that Karlee could know what to expect and have a sense of safety. She had overheard the altercation the night before.

The staff immediately noticed that Karlee was struggling and started wondering out loud:

> Karlee, you are really having a hard time right now with everyone and everything. I kind of remember you like this when you didn't feel safe. I wonder if you are not feeling safe right now? Grandpa let me know that mom made a surprise visit last night and you sure didn't expect that. You helped make the rules for mom and I am wondering if you feel unsafe again because she didn't follow that rule?

Although it took a little bit of time, Karlee was able to communicate with her teachers how she struggled with being both angry and worried about her mom, and was better able to reflect on how that impacted her and how she found it much more difficult to be in charge of her attention and emotions when her mom was unwell.

Another example of using curiosity to help a student become more aware of underlying experiences is illustrated in the following dialogue. This student's early history was marked by many frightening experiences of abandonment as her teenage mother would leave her for hours to go drinking or to meet friends. When she first came to our program, she might be playing with another child. If her friend left the play for a moment, even if it was with the intention to return, Sara would get a look of panic on her face, her body became rigid, and she would say mean things to her friend who would then be quite confused by Sara's reaction.

Staff wondered out loud:

> Sara, I noticed that when Jenna left just then your face and your body changed. You looked really worried. I wonder if you thought she was leaving you? That's a tricky worry because you've said before that your mom left you all the time. I wonder if you think Jenna is leaving you and not coming back. Do you think it would help if we asked her to let you know her plan when she gets up—just so you know?

In both these examples, the student is in no way obliged to agree with the teacher. Wondering out loud is just offered as a possibility and a contrast to what we believe the child's meaning-making system is telling them: "*I am a bad, no-good, unlovable, crazy throw-away kid.*" Initially, our students find it impossible to engage in wondering themselves. Their brain circuitry doesn't allow for it. Why would we then expect that they will ever figure it out themselves without our help? In the same way we help our toddlers associate their behavior with their feelings (*"You are mad because mommy said no!"*), acceptance and curiosity help us provide the same service to our children who have experienced abuse and neglect so they can learn to understand why they do what they do and what, importantly, they can begin to do differently.

Being curious and wondering out loud is also a lovely way to bring in playfulness and to communicate that behavior is just behavior, and that what is important is figuring out together what the underlying experience is. A current favorite is to wonder if the child is growing too much too quickly and that their jeans are too tight, cutting off the circulation to their legs and making them grumpy. Obviously, any use of humor must be attuned and correctly timed as it may not always communicate a sense of safety.

Lastly, when we are curious, we communicate to the other intersubjectively that we really want to know all about them. It is hard to feel unimportant when someone is relentlessly interested in everything you think and feel without judgment. As we share the attention and intention to understand our students, they can begin to feel safe enough to risk seeing themselves the way that we see them: as having value, being interesting, being creative, and being lovable.

Teachers may worry that curiosity brings them too close to being therapists or that if they wonder, they are putting words or ideas in children's mouths or minds. It is important to recognize that it is the process of wondering rather than being correct that helps to co-create meaningful stories from the many stressful events of their lives. Children are always given the option to disagree or agree, and they readily exercise that right. Sometimes we find that children will disagree with our guesses even when we are quite sure that we are right. Again, we accept the disagreement and suggest that we will keep trying to figure out what might be at the root of their behavior or stressful experience. Curiosity and acceptance communicate to the child that what is important is understanding the adaptive nature of their actions rather than being left with their shame-based narrative. Our hurt children repetitively communicate their belief that they are bad and that others are not trustworthy. Curiosity and acceptance lead to new understanding of the intentions and actions of themselves and others.

Empathy

Empathy is the vehicle for communicating that we understand—and to some extent experience—the other's experience. It is not sympathy, nor is it reassurance. It is not fixing, and it is not an attempt to change a child's mind. Empathy is about being with the other in an accepting, nonjudgmental way. When we experience empathy from another person, we feel "felt" and that helps us feel safe in the relationship. If we feel safe, then we are less likely to use our behavior for fight, flight, or freeze.

It is easy for us to imagine how to use empathy for students who are crying, who are sad and withdrawn, but how do we have and communicate empathy for the student who is swearing, yelling, throwing things around? This calls for us to stay in our ventral vagal organization where we can stay open and engaged and can override our amygdala's desire to propel us into fight, flight, or freeze. This is no mean feat! Holding on to the acceptance of "If this child could do better he or she would" helps. Being curious about what might be underneath all this behavior helps. Being well ourselves helps. Often before we are able to experience empathy for the angry and challenging child, we first need to experience compassion for the child. Compassion, which is a more reflective neurological response, emerges when we are able to know the child and the meaning of the anger. Knowing the stressful events of the child's life as well as how the child experienced those events (shame, terror, loneliness, and despair) evokes our compassion for the child and opens us—and the child—to our empathy.

Attunement with the child's affective state is important if our expression of empathy is to be accepted by the child. If we are to express empathy for the highly aroused child, we must match the affective vitality of the emotion the student is expressing for them to feel like we understand them. If the student is yelling and we are whispering, the lack of affective matching will most likely make the student feel annoyed and further escalate in their attempt to get us to understand. Matching the vitality of the affect, the student is expressing does not mean getting angry ourselves. Rather we match the energy through which the child is expressing his emotion. *"You are so big mad today! So mad! You are shouting and yelling and trying to tell me how mad you are! I get it! Thanks for telling me! I'm so sorry you are having such a struggle today!"*

Expressing your empathy with matching energy enables the child to feel that you understand and will enable the child to begin to feel better. We then naturally slow the prosody of our voices and our tone reflects the more familiar empathic stance of lower, softer tone. When we are attuned in this way, matching the child's energy and then moving with them to a slower more regulated place through the use of our voice, it is hard for the child to remain reactive and defensive.

CONSEQUENCES

You may be wondering about consequences. Providing limits and consequences before the child has become calmer and more regulated will likely result in another escalation or emotional shut-down. Consequences may indeed be part of the way forward together, but must wait until a connection is formed. Co-regulation of affect must occur for the bridges to the cortex to be rebuilt so the student can engage in a reciprocal conversation. If and when consequences are necessary, they too can be given with empathy.

> You may be a little cross with me, you ready? I'm sorry but we are going to have to figure out how to fix the damage done to the classroom and to other's people's hurt feelings. You will have to miss gym time to figure that out with me. I'm sorry because I know you look forward to gym, but this is really important to figure out. Besides, my worry is that there is something big on your mind and gym tends to be more difficult for you when you are worried about something. Do you have any guesses why you are so mad today? I may have a few guesses, want to hear some of them now or should we wait until we have time together later?

Giving consequences doesn't have to be done in a way that causes hurt and more dysregulation. In the given example, the adult was regulated and was clear about what needed to happen, while at the same time maintaining an empathic connection. The end result of missing gym is the same whether said with PACE or whether said in anger. However, the intent of the teacher in causing the child to miss gym is very different. In a Dyadic Developmental Practice framework, the consequence was given as a way to ensure the child didn't get into further trouble and as an opportunity to figure out what was going on underneath the behavior. Also, when the consequence is given with PACE, the child is likely to trust the teacher's motives and not believe that the teacher is being mean or getting even with the child for what the child did. In the behavioral method, the consequence would most likely be experienced as a punishment with the child believing that the teacher was paying the child back for making the teacher's life difficult. This method also assumes that the child "chose" to misbehave. As we have learned, however, for the child with developmental trauma, behavior is an adaptive defense and not an active choice.

Curiosity communicates the desire to understand. The curious stance both helps the adult stay focused on what is underneath the behavior and starts to offer the student some possibility of understanding the emotional experience. Curiosity is also essential if we are to know what consequences would be appropriate. If we do not know what is causing the behavior, how are we able to make an educated guess as to how best to influence the child's behavior? Behavioral methods stress that consequences to be effective must be given immediately to maximize influence. This might be true when we are training dogs or other animals, but human brains are more relationally oriented and are not so much motivated by immediate reward and punishment. Rarely does a consequence need to be given immediately to be effective. It's ok to take our time to understand. The aggression that is instrumental and the aggression that is born from fear may require a very different sort of consequence.

Given the relational focus of DDP, as a model of psychotherapy and practice, consequences or incentives should also be relational. If a child has been aggressive with his peers because he or she wanted to play with the basketball first, the consequence may be that he can't play until he is more able to trust his temper, but he also needs to be helped to repair the relationship with his friends. The removal from play is an immediate consequence, but the intention of the consequence is not to punish, but to ensure safety for all parties involved. We then can use our curiosity to understand what is happening. Once cortisol levels have receded enough, we then help the student repair his relationships.

The following conversation occurred with one of our students.

Deni: "Ben you are so mad right now! You are having a hard time" (Matching the vitality of affect and expressing empathy). "It's not ok to hurt your friends. Come let's go for a walk together so we can figure out how you can play."

Ben: "No! They are not letting me play. It's not fair! It's my turn!" Ben then swears at his friend.

Deni: "Oh you are so upset that this isn't going the way you want it to! I'm so sorry. It's so frustrating isn't it when things don't go the way you want! So hard!" (Still remaining in empathy).

Ben: angry, but more tearful, "It was my turn and Jack took the ball away!"

Deni: "Ahh! so frustrating when you were looking forward to it being your turn, you were disappointed and mad! You were having fun and then just like that you weren't." (organizing his emotional experience with acceptance and empathy).

Ben: "He shouldn't have taken my turn!"

Deni: "It is really hard for everyone to take turns sometimes isn't it? I'm sorry that this isn't working out the way you want it to."

Ben: now responding to the co-regulation of his anger Ben is becoming more tearful. Once there is enough co-regulation of affect, we can move into curiosity.

Deni: "Let's figure out why this was such a struggle. I know you know it's not ok to hit other kids, so let's figure out how that ended up happening just now. Do you have any guesses about why your temper got so big when Jack took the ball and you thought it was your turn?"

Ben: voice rising again, "But it was my turn!"

Deni: "Oh boy even just thinking about it again makes you mad doesn't it! We've got to figure this out Ben we do! I know you love to play basketball and I know you love to play with Jack. We have to figure out how to make things better for you two! Are you ok to wonder about this with me or should we think about it later when you feel ready?"

Ben: Regulated by the acceptance and empathy for his increase in emotional arousal offered "Now I guess."

Deni: "Excellent! Now, where were we? We were guessing about why your temper gets so big when you are disappointed." The teacher has introduced the concept of disappointment as a possibility of what led to the anger. Her tone is all the time regulated and her physiology is open and engaged. She is communicating that she really wants to understand now and not evaluate him. "Being disappointed I think is something that has happened a lot for you Ben."

Ben: Attentive and listening

Deni: (Being attuned to Ben's nonverbal messages, she continues with being curious about disappointment.) "I think so many people have let you down in your life and I wonder if in that moment where you thought it should be your turn and Jack took the ball that your brain said 'Oh No! Here is someone else that is going to let me down! If he is my friend, he should let me have my turn!' Then your brain got scared that he wasn't really your friend. When you get scared Ben, I think you have learned to hide it by being mad. Do you think I might be right?"

Ben: nods

Deni: (Back to empathy.) "So hard when you have had so many disappointments. I'm glad we are figuring this out. We have got some other things to figure out too Ben. Hurting other people is not ok in our class and you really hurt Jack when you punched him. He is going to be really angry at you for hurting him. Do you have any ideas what you are going to do to make things better between you?"

Ben: "No"

Deni: "That's ok, we will help you with that when you are both ready. I think also you need to stick really close to me today. No more basketball until we can be really sure that you can manage being around Jack. I know that must be another disappointment for you as you love basketball, but I don't want you to get into any more trouble today and I don't want for any other kids to get hurt or be mad at you. We good to go?"

This interchange used PACE in an integrated way (in this example, playfulness was not evident, though the light and confident tone is one feature of it). The focus was first on co-regulation through empathy and then on understanding and co-creating a story through curiosity. Limit setting was introduced only when the teacher felt the connection was truly established. The concept for the need to repair was introduced so Ben knew that he would be expected to apologize. Again, waiting for Ben to feel regulated enough to apologize is crucial. Once the anger is regulated, we are often left with shame, which also needs to be co-regulated. Asking a child to apologize before they feel ready is typically met with opposition (blaming, resisting, and minimizing) or rarely feels genuine.

Dan Hughes talks about discipline requiring two hands: one for attunement, nurturing, and acceptance, and the other for limit setting. The child is much more likely to accept the limit when the teacher has shown an interest in the child's inner life that enables both teacher and student to make sense of the behavior. We need to use both to help students learn to self-regulate. Teaching with PACE does not mean that you should never provide a consequence. Consequences, when given with PACE, allow for the co-regulation of the shame, anger, and fear that the student might feel and makes it much more likely that the circuitry that develops self-regulation gets a chance to grow.

It is important to recognize that the use of PACE is not linear. They are ingredients of safety, but are not ingredients that are measured in an exact fashion. Acceptance must always be part of the mix, for without acceptance we are likely to be in an evaluative, reactive-defensive state ourselves. Helpful interactions may just involve acceptance and empathy— *"I'm so sorry you are having a rough day today"*—or acceptance and playfulness— *"Oh my goodness did you eat five boxes of sugar cereal this morning for breakfast? You are a jumping bean and can't listen to a word I say! Maybe five Mars Bars? Maybe a box of worms that are wiggling inside you? I will have to talk quickly today to make sure I can keep up with you!"*

Sometimes acceptance and curiosity might be called for: "Hey! There is definitely something on your mind today, you are having such a hard time paying attention to me. What could it be? What could it be? We have to figure this out! Do you have any guesses?" We might combine playfulness, acceptance, empathy, and curiosity as in the following example:

> Imani was angry. She had ripped up her work and disappeared under the table, scowling and refusing to come out, swearing at anyone who tried to become engaged with her. One staff member had tried playfulness, but it was too early and misattuned, and it resulted in increased anger. Another staff member tried starting with empathy "Oh Imani, I'm sorry you are so upset, I can see you are really bothered." She matched the vitality of Imani's affect when offering her empathy. She then started to be curious, not talking directly to Imani, but to herself "I wonder what is going on for Imani today? I think she came to school feeling ok . . . she came in put her backpack away and had a big smile, and she talked with the other kids and had a good recess time then all of a sudden there was big upset! What could it be about I wonder" This curious stance involves using a storytelling prosody that is co-regulating the emotional arousal being activated in Imani's brain and communicates only a desire to understand, not to fix or to give a consequence for her behavior.
>
> The wondering continued; "I wonder if it was something to do with the math I asked you to do? Or I wonder if there was something on your mind that was upsetting, and it was too hard not to think about that hard thing?" Wait a minute! This is really important to figure out, I need some help. Imani, would you be ok if I lay on the table and hung my head off it? I won't bother you but I think if I do that I might have a better idea what is upsetting you because all the oxygen in my blood will go to my brain and give it a boost!" By this time, although still a bit grumpy, Imani couldn't resist the thought of her teacher hanging off the table. Imani started to talk, and her teacher quickly said, "Shhhh! Don't talk. I'm letting the oxygen go to my brain and I can't be distracted!" again the playful nature of the interaction made it safe enough for Imani to start to engage again. With a few more guesses from the teacher, Imani was able to say that she thought the teacher had given her math that was way too hard. Her teacher could then go back to an empathic response "Oh, that would be so hard if you thought you couldn't do something I had asked you to do! That helps me understand now why you were upset! I'm sorry! You might have been worried that I would be mad at you for not knowing how to do something." The last part of this interaction was again a

curious statement that was starting to organize for Imani what was behind her distress. The teacher, because she knew Imani well, could make the link for her "I know when you were a little girl, people got really mad at you when you made mistakes or didn't know what to do. You were worried about that here too. What a big worry you had. I'm glad we figured it out!"

As we become more practiced at using PACE, we can start to use the Affective-Reflective (A/R) Dialogue, which is a way to have safe and transforming conversations and relationships with students in the classroom. Chapters 6 and 7 illustrate the use of the A/R dialogue to deepen our connections with our students.

6

Co-regulation of Affect

The Affective/Reflective (A/R) Dialogue

PACE allows us to use safety signals to increase the felt sense of safety. Often just the use of playfulness, acceptance, curiosity, and empathy is enough to co-regulate a student's arousal and allow us to get on with our day. The use of the Affective/Reflective (A/R) dialogue provides us with some additional ways of helping our students stay connected with us.

The A/R dialogue is an integrative safe-conversation that weaves together the emotional meaning of an event or experience, the affective expression of that event or experience, and the cognitive understanding of it. The affective component refers to the creation of emotional safety in which the adult and child can reflect together upon what the child has experienced or what has happened. If thinking or talking causes emotional upset, any exploration of meaning stops, and the adult co-regulates the child's emotions until the child feels safe to go on. The child then experiences over and over again the experience of being protected from experiences that overwhelm them but with the concomitant expectation that the child and adult need to understand. It is not an avoidance of stress, but a managing of the stress that can interfere with the cognitive and emotional integration of stressful or traumatic experiences.

The ability to manage distress through the A/R dialogue is in essence a replication of the co-created coordinated regulation that Stern (1985) and Trevarthen (2013) outline as a crucial building block of a secure attachment. A child who has the luxury of engaging with their parent in a continuous and reciprocally coordinated dance learns to expect that their distress will be noticed and will not overwhelm the parent. The expectation is also that the parent knows just the right way to make them feel better—not too intrusive and not too withdrawn. The parent "knows" them and helps the child know himself.

A child who has not had a parent who could engage with them in a coordinated and interactive way have the opposite expectations—that their distress will not be noticed, understood, tolerated, or soothed. Through the A/R dialogue we try to change these expectancies. When we are attuned to the child's emotional experiences again and again and hold them in those experiences in ways that feel safe, the child can begin to experience being known by another. As we describe what we believe a child might be feeling, help the child's arousal to decrease with PACE and patience, and communicate (consciously and nonconsciously) that the relationship will survive this rupture and repair that rupture, the child will become much better at knowing why he does what he does and why adults do what they do. This is the beginning of a more coherent narrative.

STORYTELLING PROSODY

Engagement in A/R dialogue is tolerated better when the adult is using a storytelling voice. Our brains like the storytelling prosody. It is hard to resist when a storyteller uses enthusiasm, pauses to create suspense or punctuate the importance of the something, and uses higher or lower frequencies to engender different emotional experiences and different speaking voices. Our inner ear actually has small muscles that respond to frequency. Higher frequency voices are experienced as safer than lower frequency voices, which are experienced with more anxiety. Moviemakers know this when they pair romantic positive scenes with higher frequency music to make us feel good and manipulate us with lower frequency music to make us feel scared.

As parents or teachers, we often switch to a serious tone of voice to discuss infractions. Lectures sound very different from stories, and as most children can attest, their parents' lectures were met with rolling eyes and escape to fantasy until it was over. With children who have experienced trauma and are hypervigilant, any shift downward in tone signals impending danger and results in anxiety. If we can maintain a storytelling voice to discuss things that are more stressful or serious, there is a better chance that they will stay present for the discussion than use dissociation or other forms of disconnection to manage their anxiety. It is something that is so difficult for us when our arousal systems are fired up to remember that children do not need to be told for the fiftieth time that what they did was wrong. They know right from wrong. What they do need is to understand where that behavior is coming from.

Humans have learned from stories for centuries. We can use the same tool to help students learn to be more reflective. A story may sound like this:

Teacher: "Hassan, I've been thinking about something. Do you have any guesses about what I am thinking about?"
Student: "No" (looking a little anxious)
Teacher: with energy and enthusiasm "You don't! Let me tell you, I have really been spending a lot of time thinking about this and I want to tell you all my thoughts! You ready? Ok here goes. . . . So, I was driving to school this morning and the lights, they were all red, all of them! I was sitting at the lights waiting for them to turn green,

drinking my coffee and thinking about what we were going to do today. I was excited about our art project today because I know you and the other kids like art and we've been working hard lately so I figured we needed to do something fun. But then instead of feeling excited I started to feel a bit sad. Do you know what I felt sad about?"

Hassan: That your coffee was finished?"

Teacher: laughing "No silly! That's a good guess because there were a lot of red lights and I did get through a lot of coffee but it wasn't that! Any more guesses?"

Hassan: looking anxious again. . . . "No more guesses"

Teacher: "Ok let me tell you! I was feeling sad because yesterday you were having a hard time with your friends and I could see what a struggle you were having but I didn't understand why. So, I was thinking and thinking about that, and wondered if you might have been having a hard time because you are worried about your dad getting out of jail soon. That I thought would certainly make a boy feel worried and make it hard to get along with friends if something that big was on his mind. I was thinking that you and your mum have had times when you have been frightened by your dad and you might be getting scared again."

Hassan: looking down, nods

Teacher: slowing her voice and using lots of empathy "Ahh! that is hard Hassan, I am sorry."

Hassan: "I want him to come home and I don't want him to come home."

Teacher: "Yes I can understand that. You miss him, but you are scared that he will get angry and scare you again. So tricky when you have opposite feeling like that."

Hassan: "Yeah"

Teacher: "That is a lot on your mind. No wonder yesterday was tough for you. I tell you what, I don't know that we can fix those opposite feelings, I think they both make sense, but what about if it gets too hard, I will come close to you so I can share them and they won't be quite so heavy for you?"

Hassan: nods.

Teacher: "Deal!"

This interchange involves PACE and the introduction of something serious in the context of a story so Hassan could more easily *hear* it and have his experiences organized. His teacher traveled the horizontal bridge and the vertical one, made the implicit into explicit, and maintained the interpersonal bridge. There was no need for problem-solving because there was no real fix for his ambivalence, but the interchange allowed Hassan to feel understood and not alone.

FOLLOW-LEAD-FOLLOW

Follow-lead-follow is a term that reflects the back and forth of reciprocal conversations. Sometimes we follow and sometimes we lead. Students who have learned to be in control are not practiced at being led, and they resist our attempts to direct them. Everything is fine as long as things are going their way, but as soon as a teacher tries to talk about something stressful, the child uses all of their avoidance strategies to move away from the attempt to direct them. Students with developmental trauma are experts in avoidance, which makes it difficult to talk about what assignments need to be handed in, what went wrong in a test and why, a fight on the playground, and other behavioral transgressions. If we are always following a child or waiting until they feel ready to talk, we might never get to discuss any problems. Allowing them to avoid will not help our students learn, but we can never make someone talk when they don't want to. Avoidance is a reflection of the blocked trust. A child who has been hurt by adults assumes that all adults will not hold their best interests in mind. They can't expect it. As their felt sense of safety increases, we should expect to see more readiness to engage in difficult conversations.

If we insist on compliance, we will immediately get into a power struggle. Generally, the rule is to follow first, to allow the child to talk about what he wants to just because they are the child. Being engaged with them about a topic of conversation that feels safe to them allows for a rhythm to be established and for the child to feel less defensive. Using the same storytelling voice, we then shift to leading the child toward the more stressful things he doesn't wish to speak about. Typically, when we want to talk about a problem with someone, we shift our tone of voice into a lower register. That shift is immediately neurocepted as an impending lecture or other aversive experience. A healthy child can tolerate the aversive nature of a lecture or difficult conversation that might induce shame. A child with developmental trauma adaptively gets rid of the conversation in any way possible.

If we can maintain the storytelling prosody, we can move toward the serious topic in a way that communicates that we wish to understand not give trouble. Even with that storytelling voice, our students may give us a clue that they are anxious. They may stop talking and look down or get more agitated and may try to change the topic of conversation. In order to co-regulate their affective experience, we must then go back to following the child, notice the anxiety, and wonder about it before we lead again toward what must be talked about.

Ashley's teacher had asked her to put her coloring away and join the others on the carpet. Ashley kept coloring and ignored her teacher. The teacher signaled nonverbally to the educational assistant that Ashley needed some help to transition from one activity to the other. She was needed on the carpet to organize the other children and couldn't take the time at that moment. She was accepting of Ashley's noncompliance, understanding that it may reflect an underlying fear or difficulty making a transition. Insisting on her compliance at that moment would have caused an escalation in behavior as well as disrupt the rhythm for the other students. Luckily, she had an educational assistant Ms. T. who could help.

Ms. T: calmly approaching Ashley's desk. "Wow, I really like the colors you chose in your picture! I like how the orange goes really well with the purple in the dress. You love colors! How do you decide what colors to use?"

Ashley: shrugs her shoulders (probably expecting that she is going to be given trouble for noncompliance).

Ms. T: "Maybe you will be a fashion designer when you grow up! Sometimes it's hard to know why you choose something, it just feels right doesn't it?"

Ashley: keeps coloring, head down but nods. She then starts to talk about a TV program she likes, Say Yes to the Dress, and asks Ms. T. if she has seen it.

Ms. T: "Yes I have seen it! Some of the dresses are gorgeous but some of them I really don't like. It's a good thing everyone has different tastes." See here, you have another color combination that looks just right." Ms. T. just waits for a while watching Ashley color. "I can see that it's hard to give up something you love to do. You didn't want to go to the carpet when Mrs. F. asked you to, did you? I'm not surprised when you are practicing your art."

Ashley: stiffens and leans her body further over her art work.

Ms. T: noticing Ashley's discomfort "Oh, did you think I was going to give you trouble for not listening to Mrs. F.?"

Ashley: nods

Mrs. T: "I'm sorry Ashley that you thought you were in trouble. I was worried that you might miss the activity Mrs. F. is talking to the other kids about, and I know it's really difficult for you when you don't understand something. I was wondering if there was anything I could do to help you find your way to the carpet." Still using a storytelling prosody "I couldn't tell if you just wanted to finish your picture or whether there was something on your mind or whether you were scared that you wouldn't understand the project Mrs. F. is introducing. I just couldn't tell! Do you have any ideas why it was hard to listen right then?"

Ashley: identifies the choice that might be the easiest for her "I just wanted to finish my picture."

Mrs. T: accepting her answer, even though she guesses that there is something more on Ashley's mind. "Ok! Thanks for letting me know!" Do you think if we move ourselves closer to the carpet you could draw and listen at the same time and I can help you remember any bits that you might miss?"

Ashley: nods

Ms. T: "Ok then! You chose the right spot that will work best for listening and drawing!" Ashley gathered her pencils and paper and moved closer to the group.

This example illustrates how the educational assistant first joined Ashley in discussing her picture and the TV show *Say Yes to the Dress* rather than address the issue of noncompliance. She then led her to why she hadn't listened to the teacher. As soon as she mentioned the problem Ashley became anxious, which was noticed and organized for her in the question "*Oh did you think I was going to give you trouble?*" Mrs. T. further organized Ashley's emotional experience by guessing at some possibilities for the noncompliance, communicating that understanding was more important than the compliance at that point. The possibility of a solution was only offered after this attempt at understanding and once Ashley felt ready to hear a solution.

One of the aims of Dyadic Developmental Practice is to help a child learn how to be reciprocal so that they can have those difficult conversations. Being able to engage in conversations allows for negotiation and learning as well as the development of a more coherent narrative. But what if we attempt to lead and the child is just not interested?

Talking about or for the child are two possibilities when we meet our student's fear of engaging with us.

Chapter 6

TALKING ABOUT

Talking about a child in front of them is such a helpful way to co-regulate their emotions. By talking about them rather than directly to them we can relieve the pressure, reducing the intensity of their emotional experience as well as organizing for them what they might be thinking and feeling. Again, the use of storytelling prosody and the intent to understand rather than control is important. Talking about can be done between staff members or by wondering out loud if you are by yourself.

Ms. T. and Mrs. F. had noticed Michael was having more than the usual difficulty getting along with the other students. Mrs. F. approached him and tried to engage him in conversation.

Mrs. F: "Michael, you are having a really rough day today! I wonder what is going on that is making it so difficult for you today?"

Michael: ran to the activity center at the back of the classroom and started pulling out games from the shelf

Ms. T: joining Mrs. F., "Hey Mrs. F. I notice that Michael is having a really tough day today. Do you think something might have happened and he has something big on his mind?"

Mrs. F: "Yes, I think you might be right, Ms. T. We know that when big things are on Michael's mind, his body has such a hard time settling down. I wonder what it might be that is on his mind?"

Mrs. T: "We need to figure that out don't we! So hard for Michael when he doesn't understand!"

Mrs. F: "I know that Michael and his brother are staying with his grandmother right now because his mom is in the hospital. I wonder if Michael is worried that his mom is so sick that she may not come back to him? It's also so different at his grandmother's house. The bed is different and the rules are different. Michael doesn't like change like that. He likes things to be the same"

Mrs. T: "That's so true. We have learned that about Michael, haven't we? That would be a big worry if he's worrying about his mom in hospital."

Mrs. F: "I wonder if anyone has spoken to Michael about what kind of illness his mom has and whether he needs to be worried?"

Michael's now playing with one of the games he pulled out, trying to set out the pieces and he looks up.

Mrs. F: "Michael do you know why your mom's in hospital? Has anyone told you why?"

Michael: "No, but she had to go in an ambulance because she couldn't breathe very well." (loudly) She shouldn't smoke! I've told her she shouldn't smoke!" more quietly "Why doesn't she listen?"

Mrs. F: "Oh Michael how hard for you to feel like your mom doesn't keep herself healthy."

Mrs. T: "Mrs. F. Do you think that Michael worries that he is not important enough for his mom to keep herself healthy? That if he mattered she would stop smoking so she can be as healthy as she needs to be to look after him and his little brother?"

Mrs. F: "Mrs. T. that would be a huge worry for a kid wouldn't it!" (turning to Michael) "Michael would you like for you and me to give Grandma a call to ask her what's wrong with mommy? I think she told me that she has what's called bronchitis, which is something that gets better with rest and the right medication. Let's go call her to make sure I got that right."

Michael was not yet ready for a conversation, even something that was light. By talking about him in this way, his teachers could communicate that his upset was noticed and that they really wished to understand and help him. Mrs. T. led deeper into his experience by wondering whether he might not feel important enough for his mother to stop smoking. This kind of guess about his inner experience is informed by our understanding of how children think. It wouldn't have been something that Michael would have been able to articulate. By Mrs. T. wondering about whether he did feel that way offered Michael some insight into his inner world. He was free to acknowledge or deny that he felt that way. We certainly might guess that a young child might feel unlovable or unimportant if a parent continues to engage in harmful behaviors, but we can't assume that it was Michael's experience. The intent to understand is what is healing. Often when we have a relationship with a child, we can make accurate guesses, but we don't have to worry about making inaccurate guesses as they are just offered as a possibility.

If you don't have an educational assistant or another adult with you, talking about can still be a way to co-regulate a child's emotional experience. It might require a bit more confidence to construct the story but is equally as powerful. If Mrs. F. did not have Ms. T. to help her, the narrative may have sounded like this:

Mrs. F: "Michael, you are having a really rough day today! I wonder what is going on that is making it so difficult for you today?"

Michael: ran to the activity center at the back of the classroom and started pulling out games from the shelf

Mrs. F: "I wonder! I wonder what it could be that is upsetting Michael today? I need to get my thinking cap on, I just know something must be on his mind because his body is like a jumping bean today! Usually when his body is a jumping bean it means that something is on his mind! What could it be?" Mrs. F. paces back and forth scratching her head, "Oh I have an idea!," paces some more and says, "No, I don't think that could be right, let me think some more. . . . Wait! I have it! Michael's grandma called me and let me know that his mom is sick right now, in the hospital kind of sick and he and his brother have to stay with grandma. I wonder if that is what is on his mind? Michael must be worried about his mom and he probably doesn't like staying at grandma's and probably wants his own bed and his own toys!" Mrs. F. notices that Michael's frantic behavior has slowed down and so she slows down the rhythm of her voice and gets softer in her tone to match this change and begins to talk directly to him. "I wonder though whether the worry about your mom is the biggest thing on your mind. Has anyone spoken to you about why your mom is in the hospital?"

Michael: "No, but she had to go in an ambulance because she couldn't breathe very well." (loudly) She shouldn't smoke! I've told her she shouldn't smoke!" more quietly "Why doesn't she listen?"

Mrs. F: "Oh Michael how hard for you to feel like your mom doesn't keep herself healthy."

Mrs. F: turns away from Michael slightly and her nonverbal messages communicate that she has another idea. She uses talking about a little bit more: "Oh I have another idea about something that might be upsetting for Michael. I wonder if Michael worries that he is not important enough for his mom to keep herself healthy? That if he mattered she would stop smoking so she can be as healthy as she needs to be to look after him and his little brother?"

Mrs. F: turns back to Michael "Is that a worry for you too?"

Michael: "No! I just want her to come home!"

Mrs. F: "Phew I am glad that that isn't a worry for you Michael!" (acceptance, even though she is pretty sure that it is a worry for him) "Michael would you like for you and me to give Grandma a call to ask her what's wrong with mommy? I think she told me that she has what's called bronchitis, which is something that gets better with rest and the right medication. Let's go call her to make sure I got that right."

Talking about can sustain a conversation so we are not limited in our engagement by our student's lack of desire or ability to have a conversation. We might wonder out loud about their emotional experience, what they might be thinking, or what the motivation might have been behind the behavior as well as talking about what we as adults think about the child and the situation.

Another example of talking about occurred after one student in our Belong classroom barricaded herself under her desk with chairs. She was not interested in a conversation, and her head was down and her arms hugged her knees. The teacher and our child and youth worker were trying to understand what had happened to upset her:

Deni: "Mr. Fowler, it seems like Cassie has been really upset by something. Do you have any guesses what upset her?"

Mr. Fowler: "No, Mrs. Melim. Cassie was playing with the other kids outside when all of a sudden she was angry and ran inside the classroom."

Deni: "She did? Wow! I know she loves to play outside so there must be something big on her mind. She is saying to us that she doesn't want to talk to us about it right now. I wonder if you and I might be able to help her if we figured it out?"

Mr. Fowler: "I think we could"

Deni: "Ok! Let's figure it out. I know Cassie has been really brave lately and playing with the other kids at recess even though she worries that they don't like her. She has been out every recess this week!"

Mr. Fowler: "I have noticed that courage too! She is trying so hard to be in charge of those nasty worries!"

Deni: "So today it sounded like the worries might have won?"

Mr. Fowler: "Possibly. . . . Cassie started off playing tag with the other kids. They were all having a good time and I could see how much Cassie was enjoying the game. She was smiling and laughing, and it looked like her worries were nowhere to be seen!"

Deni: "Mmm I wonder then what could have upset her?"

Mr. Fowler: I know Cassie has been brave with playing outside. I think she will be brave enough to tell us when she is ready. I think I will just sit here a bit and keep her company."

The two staff were talking about Cassie and highlighting their experience of her courage rather than the shame that she herself was probably experiencing. Talking about her took the pressure off having to respond, but allowed her to listen about what the staff thought about her and her emotional experiences. The storytelling prosody, acceptance, and empathy were able to co-regulate her distress and help her reconnect the bridge to her cortex.

TALKING FOR

Talking for is another way to help students understand their inner experiences or to articulate something that they are afraid to say or are not yet clear about. Talking for helps the child stay in the conversation with us. Teachers and therapists sometimes get anxious that talking for is putting words in the child's mouth. When we talk for our student, we guess about what the child might want to say if they could, or what they might be experiencing or thinking but can't articulate. Talking for is not about putting words in our children's mouth, but is a way of offering possibilities and maintaining the conversation when we hit the child's limit for reciprocity. Once we have guessed about what the child might want to say, the child is invited to say whether we were right or wrong in our guesses. Again, it is the process of guessing that is important, not whether we get it right in the end. What we are communicating through guessing is that we really want to understand. Intersubjectively then the child can feel they are worth knowing. We are also communicating by talking for that there is nothing a child can say or do that will threaten our relationship. Talking for a child in the classroom setting might sound something like:

Teacher: "Imani, you are having such a hard time getting your work done today! What's going on?"
Imani: Ignores the teacher and keeps playing a game on her phone.
Teacher: "I wonder if you might want to say something like, "Mr. P., I don't want to do any work today! Work is stupid! In fact, you are stupid Mr. P. for making me do work. Don't you know I just want to play on my phone!" Smiling "Is that something you might want to say to me right now?"
Imani: smiles but doesn't look up from her phone.
Teacher: playfully "I'm right aren't I? You are just being too polite to tell me I am stupid for making you do work when you don't want to!" thoughtfully "I wonder why work is hard for you today?"
Imani: shrugs but still doesn't look up.
Teacher: Talking for Imani, "Well Mr. P., work is hard for me every day not just today! I don't think I'm very good at learning so it's easier to play on my phone." He turns to her and says, "Did I get that right Imani?"
Imani: nods and looks sad.
Teacher: "Thanks for letting me know that, Imani" Since Imani nonverbally acknowledged that Mr. P's guess was right, he could respond to her as if she told him verbally. "It must be hard to feel like you don't understand the work. I can understand why it would make you think you were not a good student and why it's easier to play on your phone. Thanks for helping me understand. I clearly am not doing a good enough job helping you understand the work. Would you please give me an opportunity to do a better job after school today? I think I might have some ideas about how to explain it better."
Imani: nods and says "sure"
Teacher: "Awesome, I am looking forward to spending some time with you and we will see if we can make learning this stuff a little less tricky.

Talking for often increases the emotional arousal because it makes explicit what the child might be experiencing. It is really important to stay attuned to the child's emotional state and stay only with what the child can tolerate.

USE OF TOUCH

Safe touch is a powerful way to co-regulate someone's affect. When our own children are hurt, we might kiss where it hurts, scoop them up, and give them a big hug. Or if they are sad, we may stroke their hair, rock them slowly, and dry their tears. Given the potential for misinterpretation and the safety of both teacher and child, the use of touch in the classroom is generally not permitted. You will see in our description of the Belong program that touch is a regular and integral part of our interactions with the students. However, we have three or four staff that are always present to ensure that safety for everyone is maintained.

The use of touch must be comfortable for both the giver and receiver. Adults vary in their comfort giving touch given their own backgrounds, personality, or sensory needs. Children too vary in their need for or comfort being touched. Developmental stage may also determine the use of touch. It is easier to imagine enveloping a junior kindergarten student in an embrace when they are hurt than a grade eight student, no matter how much we feel they may need such an embrace.

The experience of being hurt physically or sexually or the absence of touch in the case of neglect makes it hard for children with developmental trauma to receive physical affection or be soothed by touch. They have no experience with how being held can make them feel better. The loneliness of never being touched intimately or being punched, kicked, or slapped is so incredibly painful that their brain adapts to avoid touch. Somehow, we have to make it safe enough to allow them to take a risk to receive safe touch and learn to discriminate between touch that hurts and touch that soothes. This may not be possible in all classrooms or school situations, but given its importance, we need to be thoughtful about how we provide the opportunity to receive safe touch during a school day. Occupational therapy, recreational activities, gym activities, or deliberate use of gestures like rubbing a child's head on the way by or high fives can be some ways to weave in opportunities for touch in a safe way.

Trauma also may have created difficulties with sensory integration as the bridges in the brain stem and limbic system are altered by stress. We often have students in a classroom who wrestle or bump into others as they try to get their proprioceptive needs met. Often their attempts to satisfy their sensory needs are misunderstood as aggression and result in consequences and frustration. Other children might try to avoid touch and might react negatively when others brush by them in the hallway or bump into them in gym. We know that touch will be difficult for children with developmental trauma, so it is important to provide opportunities to address this difficulty as we plan our curriculum, design our school spaces, and interact with students each day.

CONNECT-BREAK-REPAIR

Given the complexities of social interaction, there are multiple times where we fall out of connection. Infant research indicates that mismatched states between mother and infant are very common, occurring once every three to five seconds (Tronick, 2007). It is the maternal facilitation of repair that is crucial. The rapid rematch between mother and child within two seconds of falling out of synch predicts secure attachment at one year (Cohn, Campbell, & Ross, 1991). When a parent fails to notice the rupture or responds to the rupture with poor sensitivity, the baby is likely to develop an insecure attachment—a lack of trust in the parent to make things better.

Disconnections are inevitable. We may deliberately or nondeliberately fail to notice someone's needs, misinterpret or misperceive needs or actions, and be thoughtless, careless or engage in other behaviors that result in disconnection. In any interaction, there are multiple episodes of disconnection that are unconsciously repaired. We neurocept the other's distress and modulate our behavior to communicate that we are sorry. Sometimes our mistakes are within the conscious realm. We may know immediately when we have made a mistake and can address it.

Zak was a grade three student who had recently changed foster placements. He struggled to regulate his attention and emotions at the best of times, but since his move, he was more noncompliant, easily brought to tears, and seemed to be instigating conflict during any unstructured time. His teacher who was normally quite attuned to his needs this morning said with a great deal of frustration in her voice *"Zak, sit down and do your work as you were asked! Your behavior is disrupting everyone around you and it needs to stop!"* She knew immediately by Zak's face that she had caused him distress. This was not what he was expecting from her. He had a momentary freeze response, the muscles around his eyes drew down, and his open mouth half closed. Within two seconds, he was angry and yelling that he hated everyone in this class and he didn't want to be in this school (with the requisite swear words) and ran out of the classroom. The teacher was immediately aware of her mistake. She called for someone to come and watch her class and then went to find Zak. Her repair sounds like this:

> Zak, I am so sorry that I got frustrated with you just then. I made a mistake. I used a voice that made you think that I didn't like you or I was mad at you and that made you feel horrible. No wonder you thought you didn't want to be in this school! I know your brain and your body aren't under your control as much as we would both like, are they? Moving foster homes has been really difficult and you are telling us clearly that you don't like it one bit! And then I added to your difficulties when I used a sharp voice. I think I too had other things on my mind this morning and didn't take the care I needed to help you settle down to learn. You think we could go back to class and start this again?

Sometimes the other person fails to give us a clear signal that they have been hurt by our actions, or perhaps it was given, but we failed to notice it. The break in connection becomes apparent later. There is nothing wrong with apologizing once we recognize the break, even if that is a week or month later. Recently a grade eight teacher decided not to put a student's name forward for a leadership camp. His fear was that the student would be overwhelmed and away from her usual supports. When he told her that he hadn't put her name forward, she shrugged and said that she hadn't really wanted to go anyway. The teacher was relieved that he hadn't disappointed her. Over the next two weeks, he began to notice that his student was more withdrawn. She didn't ask questions in class anymore, and interactions between them felt superficial and flat. She skipped a few classes and didn't put as much care into her assignments. In his puzzlement about what might have changed for her, he began to wonder if she was upset about not going to leadership camp. Here is how his conversation went with her.

> "Miriam, I have noticed that you are not as happy in class this past two weeks and perhaps not as happy with me. I have been wondering about that and wonder if you are upset that I didn't put your name forward to the leadership camp like I said I would?" Miriam's breathing rhythm changed and she looked down, suggesting that this was what was upsetting her. "I think I made a mistake and didn't tell you why and now maybe you are thinking that I didn't think you were a good enough student or didn't deserve it or something?" Miriam was quiet and still looking down "I'm sorry. I worried that you might find it too hard to be there without your usual supports and that if you had a hard time you would be mad at yourself. I think I was trying to protect you, but I didn't do it in a good way. I should have asked you what you thought first before making the decision. You didn't know my reasoning and worried it was because you weren't good enough." Miriam looked up then and the teacher continued, "Do you think if it's not too late we can see if there is still time to put your name forward and we can make the decision together if it's the right time for you to go this year?" Miriam nods and the relationship is starting to repair.

When we go back to address a rupture, we provide an important message: you are important enough to me that I will think about you. We also communicate that our relationship will survive ruptures and disagreements.

ELEPHANT IN THE ROOM

Ruptures that are not repaired often become elephants in the room. If someone is mad at us or a family member, it is very difficult to find shared attention or intention unless it is all of us paying attention to the elephant. We generally start to get a sense that something isn't quite right. Perhaps someone is more distracted, preoccupied, angry, or withdrawn. When connecting feels difficult, the best plan is to name it and use curiosity to discover what the obstacles might be. Even if we all end up paying attention and being curious about obstacles to connection, we are paradoxically in connection! Better to ask and wonder than keep our suspicions to ourselves.

7

Using A/R Dialogue to Explore and Discover the Meanings of the Child's Behavior

Once we have helped to regulate a student's upset, we want to help them discover the meaning of their behavior. As we have mentioned previously, we all tell ourselves a story to make sense of our own or other's behavior. The typical stories of children with developmental trauma are shame or fear base: "I am a bad kid" and "Others are sources of potential harm." If we allow the child to stay with these stories, it will be impossible to move them from mistrust to trust or to help them find their social engagement system. In this chapter, we offer some examples of how to use PACE and A/R dialogue to co-construct different narratives. Together we discover narratives that help children integrate their implicit memories so that they no longer hijack their nervous system. We want also to help them see the adaptive quality of their fight, flight, or freeze responses and to find different meanings for adult inter-actions. Because the integrative function of their brain has been impaired by their early—and sometimes ongoing—trauma, our students need us to weave together their thoughts, perceptions, body sensations, and feelings into a coherent whole (Siegel, 2012).

The co-construction of such narratives may create anxiety for teachers who think that this crosses into the role of a therapist. We believe that teachers and educational staff are uniquely positioned to have such conversations with students, and we hope to offer you some ways to have conversations with your students that create under-standing and safety for you both.

Let's start with a conversation about a child's insistence that they are "a bad kid." Veronica was a grade three student who had already had three changes of school. Her father was in jail for assaulting her mother, and they had moved to Kingston to be close to him while he was incarcerated. She was impulsive, distractible, and desperately wanted to fit in with her classmates. Unfortunately, she tended to be intrusive, controlling, and reactive, which made her peers wary of her at best and actively rejecting at worst. Veronica would frequently be in tears. She had so much frustration and sadness about not being able to make friends, but had no insight into her role in the difficulties. She would wail *"Nobody likes me! I'm such a bad kid!"* Her teacher was also sad as Veronica's pain was clear, and was frustrated that whatever strategies she offered were not making a difference. Mrs. O. had received some training in Dyadic Developmental Practice through the school board, and she gave herself permission not to fix Veronica's difficulties but to use PACE to co-regulate her affect and the A/R dialogue to help her be more aware of why she had so much shame. She arranged with her educational assistant that following the next upset she would take some time with Veronica while the educational assistant worked with the class.

Veronica: "Nobody will play with me. They all hate me! I don't want to go to this school anymore!"

Mrs. O: using acceptance and empathy, "Oh Veronica, how hard it is to feel that other people hate you. Such a hard thing to think!"

Veronica: "Why won't anybody play with me?" She became quiet and looked down "It must be because I am a bad kid."

Mrs. O: "Oh boy, you have so many hard things on your mind, that people hate you and that you are a bad kid! So much for a kid who is only in grade three."

Mrs. O and Veronica sit quietly for a moment.

Mrs. O: "I am guessing that these hard worries have been with you a while. I think you have been worried that you are a bad kid for a long time. You are not sure why other kids don't play with you and what has made the most sense to you is that they must hate you and – and if they hate you it's because you're a bad kid! I see how that might make sense to you."

Veronica: "I am a bad kid. My mother always says I'm bad and my dad is in jail so he's bad too!"

Mrs. O: "Then I can really understand why you think you are a bad kid."

Veronica: hangs her head further and pulls her hair over her face

Mrs. O: "Veronica do you worry that I think you are a bad kid?"

Veronica: is quiet

Mrs. O: In a relaxed story-telling voice "It's hard for you to imagine that anyone sees you as a good kid, isn't it? I've been wondering if there is a different reason why you have difficulty making friends. Want to hear some of my ideas? (playfully). Tough luck! I'm going to tell you anyway! I think you have had LOTS of hard in your life. You have moved a lot and had lots of different schools and houses to get used to. You don't see your dad now, and before he went to jail, I wonder if he was a bit scary sometimes. Then that was hard because you probably had mixed up feelings about your dad: you love and miss him but you are also angry and scared of him? The hard keeps piling up! It sounds like mom sometimes gets angry at you too. More hard! Then kids won't play with you. More hard! – just too much HARD Veronica!"

Veronica is listening, but her head is still down.

Mrs. O: "You know I have been doing a lot of reading and learning about what happens to kids' brains when they have too many big, hard things in their lives. Their brains can't work like they are supposed to. When there is too much stress, kids find it hard to concentrate, are jumpy a lot of the time, can't control their emotions easily. They often get into trouble with other kids and adults. Because they are just kids, they think that all the hard things in their life must be their fault. They don't know how to think any other way! I wonder if you've made a mistake Veronica! I wonder if you thought you were a bad kid, but really you are a STRESSED kid!"

Veronica looks up at Mrs. O. who notices and nods her head excitedly. "I think we have just figured it out, haven't we? You are a stressed kid not a bad kid! Now, the other thing I know about kids who have too much hard in their lives is that they are not going to give up the idea that they are a bad kid very easily. So you probably want to argue with me? "Mrs. O., I am a bad kid what are you talking about!" It's ok if you want to argue and don't believe me yet, I'll remind you lots while you are learning. Phew! I am glad that we are figuring this out together. Is it ok if I give you a hug right now, it's hard work figuring out new things, isn't it?"

This conversation took approximately seven minutes. You will notice the use of acceptance and empathy throughout, and the introduction of curiosity when Veronica was regulated. Mrs. O. didn't reassure or try to fix Veronica's belief that she was a bad kid. Her attunement, all of her nonverbal signals and use of touch communicated that she didn't *experience* her as a bad kid. She could then challenge Veronica's belief further by creating a story about how stressed brains cause the difficulties that Veronica was having. The story was offered as a different way of understanding her friendship troubles. It weaved together her thinking, feelings, behavior, and body sensations, and linked them to the experience of stress. Her teacher wisely offered the story as a possibility rather than as a definitive explanation, and she communicated the expectation that Veronica wouldn't be able to believe this new story without time and practice. Her own enthusiasm and confidence, however, communicated to Veronica that she was sure this story was the correct one.

Veronica's impulsivity and reactivity wouldn't improve until she could begin to experience that she was liked and enjoyed in the nonverbal attunement of her teacher. The story gave Mrs. O and Veronica another way to understand her difficulties and led to conversations about what they could do to manage stress. Shame makes us want to hide and avoid, which makes it hard to have conversations and explore different possibilities. With a less shame-based narrative, Veronica could start to be more reflective about her behavior, which led to some collaborative problem-solving.

The following conversation took place between a principal and a grade 12 student who was in danger of failing two of his classes, thus risking his graduation.

Mrs. A: "Hey Jeremy, come walk with me, I need some help."

Jeremy: defensively "What! What did I do?"

Mrs. A: (playfully) "You know, I have never quite got used to how kids automatically think they are in trouble when the principal talks to them. I should get a t-shirt that says Here Comes Trouble! Did you do something I should give you trouble for? I just need some help bringing some things in from the car. If you are quick about it you might even have time for a cigarette before you go into English and torment your teacher!"

Jeremy: "Fine!"

Mrs. A and Jeremy headed to the parking lot to pick up some donated groceries from the car. Mrs. A. grabbed a granola bar from one of the bags and tossed it to Jeremy saying, "Think fast!" then hands him some bags to carry. As they head back into the school, Mrs. A. starts a conversation;

Mrs. A: "Your teachers are telling me that you have not been handing in your work this semester. I wondered if you had any ideas about why?"

Jeremy: "Who cares about school! If the teachers were better at their jobs, I'd do the work. They don't teach. They are just getting fat paychecks to do nothing!"

Mrs. A: matching the vitality of Jeremy's affect "Oh dear! You are not happy with your teachers!"

Jeremy: "They don't teach us nothing!"

Mrs. A: "Then I can understand if they are not teaching you anything why you don't have anything to hand in. I am sad that at the very end of your time with us that you have teachers that you don't feel are good teachers for you. This is your last semester with us and I wanted it to be a great one for you."

Jeremy: "Whatever!"

Mrs. A: gently "Jeremy I wonder if I have got it wrong. I am excited about you leaving high school and going to college, but I wonder if you are not excited. Maybe you are worried about what it is going to be like for you? It's hard to meet new people and maybe you are worried that you aren't going to do well at college?"

Jeremy: "Whatever!"

Mrs. A: "I wonder if not handing in your work is a way that you get to stay here another year. How smart of you to figure that out! You could do a gap year and not have to leave us. Is that it?"

Jeremy: "I'm not staying in this stupid school! I can't wait to get out!"

Mrs. A: "Then I am a bit puzzled. Why would a boy who is on track to get out of here start to not hand in assignments. I wonder what I'm missing? Is there something going on at home that's making it hard for you?"

Jeremy: looked down but didn't say anything. Mrs. A felt she had guessed correctly.

Mrs. A: with empathy "Is mom sick again?"

Jeremy: nods

Mrs. A: "I'm sorry Jeremy. You work so hard to look after your mom and your sisters. I wonder if part of you is saying I can't wait to get out of here and another part saying who is going to look after everyone if I go away to college? Failing your semester would delay that decision for you wouldn't it?"

Jeremy: nods

Mrs. A: "This sounds like something that you need some help with. I don't know what the right answer is for you. If you go to college, you will worry about your family. If you stay, you may be angry that you can't get on with your life. Would you be willing to talk to the counsellor about your dilemma? I could set up an appointment for you?"

In this example, Mrs. A sought to understand Jeremy's behavior and with him find the meaning of not handing in assignments. The conversation helped Jeremy move from blaming teachers to understanding the difficult position he was in. Once that meaning was discovered, they could make a plan to seek counseling. Giving him trouble for not handing in assignments would have likely caused an escalation is his defensiveness and left him without the discovery of the difficult position he was in. Once he could identify the dilemma, he would be in a position to find strategies to manage it.

The co-construction of narratives integrates elements of PACE and A/R dialogues. They are conversations that look for the adaptive meaning of behavior and make the bridge between past, present and future, thoughts, feelings, beliefs, and experiences so that we can arrive at a different understanding and, subsequently, a different approach. The following example illustrates how a change in understanding can lead to changes in behavior for both the adult and child.

Samuel and his grade five teacher, Mr. D, were frequently locked into power struggles. Mr. D would give directions, but Samuel would not listen. Mr. D would then threaten him with consequences, which he couldn't enforce because Samuel wouldn't follow them. Mr. D would then insist that he spend the day in the office given his lack of cooperation. Mr. D felt frustrated and inadequate. The more he tried to get Samuel to do work, the more resistant Samuel became. Mr. D was ready to give up. The principal first met with Mr. D to explore his own emotional experiences;

Principal: "Mike, I see that you are working so hard to get Samuel engaged in class and it's been a frustrating process for you. He really doesn't seem to want to engage, does he?"

Mr. D: "He is so disrespectful! He thinks he can do whatever he wants whenever he wants! He has to learn that is not the way the world works!"

Principal: "I think you are right he really does struggle with letting other people be in charge. That makes it very hard for you to influence him or teach him. I can see why you would worry that he will have a more difficult life if he doesn't learn to listen to others."

Mr. D: "He is so unbelievably frustrating. I don't think I am the right teacher for him."

Principal: "What makes you think you are not the right teacher?"

Mr. D: "He has absolutely no interest in listening to me?"

Principal: "Why do you think that is?"

Mr. D: "He just thinks he knows everything?"

Principal: "You have so much to teach him and he just won't let you! Do you have any idea about why getting through to him matters so much to you? Maybe some other people would have given up by now, but you haven't; you keep going back at it day after day? You keep going back into battle with him. How come?"

Mr. D: "I don't know."

Principal: "Lets figure it out. There is something about this kid that makes you crazy, but you won't give up!"

Mr. D: "He is wasting his potential. I think he is a smart kid and I think he would have a good life if he just tried."

Principal: "Ahh! You feel responsible for him having a good life."

Mr. D: "I think he reminds me of my brother. He was a difficult kid growing up. He was probably smarter than me, but he didn't do well at school and got into drugs as a teenager and doesn't have a relationship with any of us now."

Principal: "I'm sorry. That would have been hard on you growing up. Maybe one of the reasons you became a teacher?"

Mr. D: "Probably. I didn't think of it like that before."

Principal: "I'm glad you became a teacher Mike. You really care about kids and are good at what you do. We have to figure out how you are going to get through to Samuel though. I think it's important to you and I think you could be a really positive influence for him. Let's meet tomorrow and see if we can come up with some ideas together."

This conversation helped the teacher become more aware of how his own background with his brother was influencing his interactions with Samuel. He saw Samuel's potential and wanted to change the course of his life in ways that he had not been able to do with his brother. Samuel's resistance caused him to feel powerless, much like he had felt growing up with his brother. His vulnerability became masked by anger and impatience. Once he became aware of his motivation, he was able to recognize that his anxiety was causing him to approach Samuel in ways that led to conflict rather than safety. He and the principal were then able to puzzle together about why Samuel was so disengaged in class. Once they had some ideas, they made a plan for the three of them to meet.

Principal: "Hey Samuel, thanks for joining us! I have some cookies there. Would you like a juice to go with them?"

Samuel: looking suspicious, shrugged.

Principal: "I'll get you a glass just in case you get thirsty. Don't feel pressured to drink it. I love lemonade so I'll finish it off if you don't! You are probably feeling a bit worried that you are here to get trouble. I asked you because Mr. D. and I have been talking together and we need your help to figure something out. Want to tell him what we have been wondering about Mr. D.?"

Mr. D: "Yes! First Samuel, I have to apologize."

Samuel: looked surprised

Mr. D: "Yes, I have not been able to be the teacher I have wanted to be for you. I think you are a smart kid and wanted you to see that too. I am always pressuring you to do work rather than asking you what makes it hard for you to do it. I think I have communicated to you that I think you are not a good kid because I am often frustrated or mad at you. I'm sorry. I think I have been achieving the opposite to what I wanted! It would be hard for you to trust me when I am always mad at you. The principal and I have been wondering why it's so important for you to be in charge. It must be pretty tiring."

Samuel: shrugged.

Mr. D: "I wonder if it's hard to trust all adults not just me? We know that your parents have not always been able to look after you and you have spent some time in foster care and with your grandmother. I think maybe you have had lots of practice figuring things out on your own and not a lot of practice having adults help you with things. Or maybe it feels like it's the wrong kind of help – like me getting mad at you to get your work done! Either way. I think you decided somewhere along the line not to bother too much with what other people want you to do. That's a problem for school because there is always an adult who wants you to do something!"

Principal: "Mr. D and I have been puzzling about how to get you to see that you are a smart kid that could do well at school without arguing with you. We have decided that you are the better arguer. but wonder whether you aren't arguing with accurate information. I think maybe you want to argue that all adults are useless and unhelpful and rude and let you down so why bother with them. Some adults definitely are but not all adults are useless. Would you be willing to work with us to teach you which adults might be useless, and which might be useful—and not just to buy you stuff!"

Samuel: "I guess"

Mr. D: "It might take us a while to help your brain recognize helpful adults. I promise not to get so frustrated at you; that will probably help! I will find other ways to let you know you are a smart kid and could do well at school and go to college or university if you want to."

Samuel: "Yeah, right!"

Mr. D: laughing "OK, I'm getting carried away with enthusiasm. Thanks for letting me know! One small step at a time."

Mr. D was able to release the pressure on himself and on Samuel to get work done. He prioritized getting to know Samuel, and he communicated that he liked Samuel and believed in his abilities, which allowed Samuel to experience being liked and valued. Samuel didn't immediately start to comply. He needed to test whether Mr. D would return to anger and frustration. Mr. D teased him about how smart he was to test him this way, and that he would be patient while Samuel learned what a great teacher he was missing out on. Gradually, Samuel started to complete his work, and by the end of the school year was learning at grade level.

The co-construction of narratives takes us back to what we learned in our chapter on interpersonal neurobiology. The integration of our experiences in the context of a relationship is the foundation of resilience. Many children with developmental trauma have a disorganized attachment. They have been terrified by their caretaker, and the stress, or their ability to dissociate and not pay attention to the traumatic event, has meant that the memory stays at the implicit level. When we can notice and link for the child their perceptions, emotions, bodily sensations, and behavior, we can help strengthen the bridge between the amygdala and hippocampus and can allow implicit memories to become integrated. As they become integrated, the individual has more control over them and is ready for being taught strategies for better self-regulation.

We know that adults who have made sense of their lives, even when they had experienced trauma, are much more likely to be well than individuals who remain at the mercy of their implicit memory system. Using stories in this way with our students helps them make sense of why they do what they do, or why adults do what they do, and help move them toward resilience.

In the next part of our book, you will find many other examples of PACE and A/R dialogue with the staff and students enrolled in the Belong program. Not everyone will have the luxury of working in such a small classroom, but we hope that the examples of conversations help you in whatever role you play in children's lives.

II

"We can't always ask our students to take off the armor at home, or even on their way to school, because their emotional and physical safety may require self-protection. But what we can do . . . is create a space in our schools and classrooms where all students can walk in and, for that day or hour, take off the crushing weight of their armor, hang it on a rack, and open their heart to truly being seen . . . They deserve one place where they can rumble with vulnerability and their hearts can exhale . . . we should never underestimate the benefit to a child of having a place to belong—even one." Brené Brown (Dare to Lead, 2018, p. 13)

8

Belong

A Classroom for Children with Attachment and Trauma Difficulties

The need to belong is a powerful motivator of our behavior. Maslow in his hierarchy of needs placed belongingness right after the physiological need for regulated and integrated biological systems and the need for safety from our environment. As we have seen, many children with developmental trauma are stuck in trying to get those basic needs met and can't yet develop their social needs of affiliation, love, and acceptance. Their family, school, community groups, and peer groups don't offer them a place to form those relationships from which they can develop self-esteem and wellness or, if they can, the student is not able to access the opportunities to belong.

In 2013, we proposed an educational program that could also meet both the basic and social needs of elementary school children who have experienced early relational trauma. We were lucky enough to secure ministry funding for our program that we called "Belong." The name of the program was conceived so that the very children who didn't feel that they fit in anywhere could say that they now had a classroom where they did belong. The program is informed by Dyadic Developmental Practice, and the staff are trained to use PACE and A/R dialogue to create a learning environment that stems from an underlying sense of relational safety.

THE BELONG PROGRAM

Our program is a clinical and financial partnership between Algonquin and Lakeshore Catholic District School Board, Limestone District School Board and Family and Children's Services of Frontenac Lennox and Addington, and it is funded by the Ministry of Education. At the time of writing, our community partnership changed to our local Children's Mental Health Organization, The Maltby Center. Belong is part of a larger school and is supported by the principal of that school. The staff are required to follow Ministry of Education expectations regarding math and language curriculum and to complete provincial report cards, but have flexibility about how curriculum is delivered and assessed. An alternative report card assesses executive function, affect regulation (identification, modulation, and expression), and social competence rather than the assessment of academic achievement. An example of this alternative reporting can be seen in Appendix A.

Staff

We have three full-time staffs: a teacher, Deni Melim; an educational assistant, Doug Hepburn; and a child and youth worker, Gerry Fowler. The child and youth worker is provided by our community partner. Lisa Fitch has recently joined our team. We also look for support from postsecondary students enrolled in programs such as social work, occupational therapy, child and youth worker, or psychology. Students work with the team for eight months to ensure our children have the experience of stability. Unfortunately, we are not able to offer placements to education students because their practicum placements are only three or four weeks. That is not enough time to build trust, and would cause too much disruption for the children. We offer students regular supervision so that they can learn the principles of Dyadic Developmental Practice and complete their course work. Whenever possible, we include them in local training opportunities. Supply teachers are sometimes needed. Every effort is made to keep supply teachers consistent. Our teacher ensures that they understand the different approach in the classroom before they come, and have them come in to meet the students prior to the day they will be teaching.

Since the whole program is predicated on the building of relationships, the quality of the relationships between staff members must be high and be supported on an ongoing basis. It is essential for the staff to work as a team and to have a high degree of trust and enjoyment of one another to be able to support the students. As such, the composition of the team must be a thoughtful and essential process. The team receives regular supervision from Sian as a trained therapist, consultant, and trainer in DDP, and at the end of each day, the team members have time to check-in with one another about the students and about each other so nobody every feels that they must handle things on their own.

The staff spend from 9:00 a.m. to 2:30 p.m. with the students, eat lunch with them, and supervise recess times. Unlike regular classrooms where teachers are released for recess times and planning times, the staff and students spend the whole day together. Planning time occurs at the end of the day and is part of the team check in.

One of the exciting things about our team is that if you walk into the classroom, it is not immediately apparent who is the teacher, who is the educational assistant, and who is the child and youth worker. Although the teacher is responsible for the teaching of new concepts and curriculum planning, the co-regulation of students is seamlessly passed from one adult to another. This may be very different from a regular teacher–support staff relationship where roles are more clearly delineated. However, in the Belong program, it is expected that all staff are equally as responsible for being attuned and offering co-regulation of students' affect to prepare them for learning.

Children

A Section 23 Classroom allows for eight students. Students are selected for the program when it is clear that their schooling is compromised by behavior indicative of attachment and trauma issues. Students are not taken on a first come first served basis, but are carefully selected to ensure that they will manage as a group within the classroom. For example, we would not place two or three students who have a history of acting out sexually in the same school year. We would not have siblings on the same school year, or even two students from the same school, to maximize their sense of psychological safety. Occasionally we have struggled with two students coming from the same neighborhood where complex family feuds and parent relationships have made them wary of talking openly. When this happens, we address the student's wariness openly and with empathy. We are certainly not going to be able to change long-standing family feuds, but we can talk openly about the challenge of being in such a position so the students are aware.

Referrals are accepted from any of the three partners and are reviewed as a clinical team. The staff will then observe the students in their home school to have an idea of how the child manages relationships and learning. All three staff will have an opportunity to observe the prospective student. Their observations are then related to the larger team, and decisions about placements are made. To this point in our development, we have deliberately not accepted students who have an autism spectrum disorder, intellectual disabilities, or fetal alcohol spectrum disorder given the additional challenges these diagnoses have for education.

When grouping students, we recognize that emotional age may be very different from chronological age, but we try to ensure that there is not too big a range of ages and stages in the group. Currently we are trying to focus on our grade one, two, and three students, with the hope that if we can help them settle to learn earlier that success will breed success throughout their elementary school time. Belong is an open-group concept so new students will join students who have already been in the program for a year. The students who already have experience with the program then provide a core stability for those new students who are anxious because they don't know what to expect.

Program

When Sian was thinking about how to develop the program, she wanted to ensure that interactions and conversations were being informed by Dyadic Developmental Practice, but also the program structure and curriculum.

Attachment theory highlights the importance of stable primary relationships. For most children, they have a teacher from September to June and then will have a new teacher. For some, that is ten crucial adult relationships in their elementary school experience. In Waldorf-inspired schools, the mandate is for the teachers to be an attachment figure for the student and travel with them throughout the grades. Although this might backfire if a teacher is ineffective or a student and teacher really didn't get along, the attention to the importance of teachers to a child's life is exciting, and we wanted to ensure the same concept for our Belong students. We ensured from all of our partners that the team would not be changed based on issues related to seniority. All staff members have a long-term contract.

One of the anxieties we hear from teachers is what happens if children get too attached. It is often the same question that foster parents worry about: "Perhaps it is better to keep a child at arm's length so that they won't attach and experience the trauma of losing another important relationship?" Earlier we outlined the crucial implications of the lack of connection. Our argument is that children can't afford to wait for the "right" person. We all have the potential to be the "right" person. Our students need the repetitive experience of co-regulation of affect, intersubjectivity where there is shared attention and intention, and ongoing bombardment of safety signals if they are to have a hope of learning how to trust relationships. It is true that separation from an important adult is difficult for both parties, but avoiding the pain of separation means avoiding the very opportunities that will allow a child to find different possibilities.

We also understand that relationships take time to develop. Many Section 23 classrooms in Ontario offer programs for only one year. For children who don't trust adults, one year would certainly not be enough time to bring them from mistrust to trust. Students, therefore, come into the program with the expectation that they will be there for two years, and if more time is needed, we will advocate for the students to remain for another term or full school year. We had one student who was getting ready to transition to his home school after his second year with us. Unfortunately, his fifth foster placement broke down toward the end of the school year. The school team were the people who knew him the longest in his 10 years, and a transition was just not clinically indicated at that time. He stayed with us for another two years to support him through the ongoing instability of his foster placements. For grade six, we moved him into a learning center at the main school so he could be close to us but could start to integrate into the regular classroom. At the time of writing this book, he attended his grade eight graduation, wearing a suit and a fedora, proud of his accomplishments and ready for high school.

Over the six years we have run the program, we consistently see that the first year is needed for students to learn to trust adults and the second year is about them learning to trust peers. During that second year, we often hear students talking to each other using PACE, being attuned to a peers' emotional experience, and wondering out loud about their own or their friend's behavior. Recently, one child was overheard saying to another while they were both playing a card game *"I think Cassie must have something on her mind, she's not usually that mean. I'm sorry she is having a rough day."* Neither student was fearful or annoyed, just accepting that their friend was having a rough moment and trusting that the adults would do their job and help her out.

In normal child development, when young children feel safe, they learn to explore their world. They use their parent as a "secure base" coming or looking back if they feel anxious about something or have a need for comfort. Our program initially keeps our students very close. We are housed in a portable classroom on the school property, which helps us create our own small world. Our schedule is designed to have break times at different times than the whole school to ensure that our students are not overwhelmed by recess. Recess is so notoriously difficult for our hurt students, given overloaded sensory systems and immature regulation. Staff are continuously with our students during outside time or break time, and they become the secure base when students are ready to develop the capacity to develop friendships with students outside of Belong. When they are ready, our students join the larger school population, always with a staff casually watching in case of need. In fact, given the fun and level of attention our students receive from staff, we frequently have students who wish to refer themselves to Belong!

As students feel safer, we also offer the opportunity for integration into the larger school community. This may first occur as a group in the form of joining an assembly or large-school activity. Our group recently felt secure enough to be part of the audience for a rock band contest. The students steadfastly supported the other students, and they tolerated the noise, sudden shifts in lighting, and the proximity of 250 unfamiliar students and adults. The activity was one for shared attention and shared delight. As it feels safe to be in the larger world as a class, some students start to feel safe enough to venture out on their own. Sometimes this means integration into a regular classroom. Sometimes it is trying out and making a school sports team. A staff member always accompanies them into these new environments, gradually increasing the distance between them.

Students immediately respond to the ongoing implicit safety in the Belong program, and when it is time to transition to their home schools, anxiety levels can be high for them and their parents. We start talking about the transition in early February. Graduates are invited to visit to talk about their new school, and students are encouraged to ask questions about what to expect. The staff prepare the groundwork with the new administration and teacher if known. Written reports as well as face-to-face consults outline what we know about our student, and examples of the PACE language are offered for situations that might make the student's defense system operational. As indicated, students may join their previous school for a morning prior to the end of year. One of the big anxieties for our students is whether their teachers will see them differently now. Going to their homeschool allows for a re-introduction and re-appraisal for both the student and homeschool staff.

One of the big anxieties for homeschool teachers is often related to the stress associated with the challenging behaviors that precipitated the referral to Belong. They anticipate the same struggles, which means that their nonverbal messages may communicate their wariness and may be neurocepted by our students as a reason for caution and defense. If teachers have this worry, we invite them into our classroom to observe the student who is managing learning and social interactions in a very different way than when he left his home school.

To support the transition, the Belong program does not open until the second week of the school term. During that first week, the staff visit the graduating students in their new schools, providing consultation to teachers as needed and a safe familiar face that can help calm the student's amygdala and can communicate our sense of optimism and certainty that they are indeed ready for this new challenge. One of our recent graduates articulated that his biggest worry was whether our team would forget him. Being there during those first few days and the occasional drop in during the first term helps our students know that they always belong with us.

The primacy of the relationship in our program is crucial also because it is the only way that students will develop the circuitry in their brains that will allow them to succeed as students. As we have learned, children only learn to self-regulate when they have had the experience of having their emotions be co-regulated by a caring adult. Because children with complex developmental trauma don't trust adults, they are not in the position to be comforted and regulated by them, and so self-regulation problems continue to interfere with the child's development. At Belong, staff use PACE to create emotional safety as well as affective-reflective dialogues to help them make sense of what they are thinking and feeling.

Academics, therefore, are not the priority initially, and are not introduced explicitly until there is evidence of the child beginning to trust one or more of the staff team. Initially, emphasis is placed on storytelling, sensory motor activities, and play-based activities. Learning is introduced in a way that allows children to start with success and in partnership with a staff member. As we mentioned in part one, Coen (2016) from the University of Virginia discovered that children can learn better for longer when in the presence of their attachment figures. Consequently, staff stay close to the students until they feel more confident of their abilities and can move to being more independent in their work. Staff are often heard to ask students whether they would like to borrow their brain.

Given that all students have experienced attachment difficulties or disruptions, and/or neglect and abuse, staff members help the students become more aware of how these experiences impact the way they think and feel so that the students learn to have a more coherent narrative and to move away from shame-based beliefs that the difficult things in their life are their fault or related to them being bad or unlovable. These conversations happen naturally rather than in "lesson format." Examples of these safe conversations facilitated by the use of PACE can be found throughout part I of this book as well as in the following chapters.

Learning consequently focuses first on emotion and attention regulation. It is subcortically driven and focuses on right brain functions prior to strengthening left brain functions. Once there is evidence that the vertical bridge is being built, we can add in more structured teaching. In addition to regular curriculum, our curriculum includes the following:

- **Teaching the parts and functions of the brain:** Children are helped to understand how their brain functions and how that leads to behavioral responses. Students may learn how they might become rigid in their thinking, "flip their lid," or lose the bridge to their cortex, which results in big emotions or behaviors.
- **Stress and shame:** Students learn about where stress comes from, how it impacts their brain and their behavior, and become more aware of their core beliefs. This allows for more open curiosity and awareness, which is the beginning of a new narrative.
- **Coping:** As the bridge the cortex strengthens, students are introduced to different coping strategies such as breathing, distraction, meditation, and visualization and are encouraged to use them first with an adult helping and later more independently.

To support this additional focus in our curriculum we ensure that we emphasis the following:

- **Relationships:** Students first learn to trust the adults in the room and are then helped to build peer relationships. Connection is always primary, and proceeds any limits or consequences.
- **Safety:** Teachers go beyond fire drills and lock downs, and talk frequently about emotional safety, but more importantly, through primary intersubjectivity and PACE, provide repetitive signals of safety in every interaction.
- **Dependence versus independence:** We believe that children can't be independent until they first learn to be dependent. We allow students to depend physically, emotionally, and cognitively on the staff even though they may be capable of doing things themselves. We see that our students who have experienced trauma are experts at controlling things and doing things themselves and have very little practice doing things with someone or allowing someone to help them. Relinquishing control has placed them in far too vulnerable a position. Over and over again, the staff model asking each other for help and offer to do things for the student. Once we see that our student is able to let us to take control and make decisions for them, we have the beginning of trust.
- **Reparation:** Fixing ruptures in relationships is crucial for helping students trust them. Adults always assume responsibility for repairing relationships when there is a disruption. We assume that if a child is becoming dysregulated, it is because we were not attuned quickly enough or failed to step-in at the right moment. Adults also are the partner that have more flexibility and capacity for self-regulation, and so are in the better position to bring the relationship back to a comfortable connection. Our apology may be immediate. A student may easily get dejected when they don't get the attention they need right away. We

notice and may say something like "I'm so sorry! You wanted an answer to your question right away and I was so busy trying to get the buses sorted out that I wasn't listening properly." If we have time we may stop and pay attention right then. If we do not we may ask for more time, "Give me five minutes to get this off my brain and then I will be able to listen properly." The key objective is to help the child understand that the relationship is not lost because needs were not met immediately, and that the staff's intention was not a rejecting one.

- **Play is crucial:** Panksepp (2012) identifies that play requires completely different neural pathways than does a stress based response. Children who have been hurt rarely know how to play, and this prevents them from building neural networks that allow them to relax, have fun, learn to take manageable risks, and be open and engaged in relationships. It is as crucial to teach the students how to up-regulate positive emotions as it is to down-regulate more negative emotions. Our day has many opportunities for play and for playful interchanges with staff.

In being together every day, there are countless intersubjective opportunities. The staff genuinely like the students, and there are many shared experiences of delight, but also of sadness or maybe even of anger. A team member may accept the student's anger at moving foster homes again and may share the anger that the system has not done a good job of taking care of him. Being with someone in that experience helps the student organize it and keep the bridge to the cortex working so that they can regulate and integrate their anger. Through these many repetitive, intrinsic reciprocal interactions, the students start to experience themselves as having worth, start to be more reflective about their inner world and the environment around them.

The following chapter outlines what a typical day might look like with examples of how we use PACE and A/R dialogue to create emotional safety and strengthen bridges that will allow for better reflection and self-regulation.

9

Our Day

Structured Flexibility

What does a typical day in Belong look and sound like? The best way to describe it is "structured flexibility"—necessary flexibility within a planned structure. There are established routines and daily, weekly, and monthly schedules with organized lesson plans to meet curriculum goals and individual education plan goals, just like any other class. There is also a necessity to take an alternative route at any given moment.

In our class, all staff are constantly attuned to students and they recognize the moments that we must deviate from the schedule. Structured flexibility allows us to find that balance between follow and lead, direct and indirect that we discussed earlier. The need for control is such a behavioral reflection of the fear our students experience that if we prioritized the lesson plan at times where they require emotional co-regulation we would end up quickly in a power struggle and learning would not occur anyway. Having no structure or lesson plan is also not indicated. Lack of predictability or structure makes our student's anxious. Uncertainty or ambiguity is not yet tolerated by their alarm system, and we need structure and routines to provide a sense of safety. Having a plan for learning also ensures that we can help our students who fear failure learn that they can tolerate frustrations and conquer their fears and can experience the pride of learning. If we just followed their lead without having expectations, we may strengthen their avoidance and inadvertently communicate that they were not capable of learning.

In this chapter, we hope to illustrate how a day may unfold with this flow between lead and follow, and the use of PACE and A/R dialogue, recognizing that this luxury is not as available to all educators.

SAMPLE DAY SCHEDULE

- Welcome activity
- Group Language (focus on story and complementary activity)
- Break
- Language Just For Me
- Break
- Math (group followed by a small group, partner, or individual)
- Lunch
- OTTER (Our Time to Enjoy Reading) teacher reads a chapter book to the class
- Science/Social Studies/Art
- Prepare for home
- Break (time to establish transition bridges for kids who need it)

*Note: students in Belong are exempted from French as a Second Language (FSL) instruction.

**Times are not listed, but rather the sequence of events so that we can adjust as needed throughout the day.

Welcome Activity

In a typical classroom, there always seems to be an urgency to the start of each school day that can quickly turn into a frenzy of voices, backpacks, movement of feet and hands, and what looks to the outsider like pure chaos. There is an organizational goal for most teachers each morning—agendas need to be submitted, backpacks hung, notes or money for field trips submitted, and so on. Support staff (if available) also get pulled into this hustle and bustle, and often start collecting envelopes and checking off names, finishing quick photocopying tasks so that the classroom day can begin. This busy establishing of order is really tough for students who have experienced trauma. There is often a sensory overload on top of long bus rides that set up students to have challenging behavior even before they are asked to learn. Other classrooms may be organized to have "bell work" (completing a worksheet independently or reading quietly) until all students have arrived and the day can begin. Our students with developmental trauma do not yet have the self-regulation skills to quieten their arousal systems to be successful in such quiet, independent tasks.

What if the day started a different way, with the opportunity for connection and co-regulation of affect? Our day at Belong begins with staff welcoming students by name and greeting them at their buses rain or shine. This is an opportunity to communicate our intersubjective experience that we are delighted that the child is there today, a repetition of that safety signal that contradicts their assumed narrative that there is nothing special about them and that they are not wanted. It also allows us to be highly attuned to what the child is bringing emotionally to school that morning and have an indication of how much affect co-regulation they may need to settle to learn. We provide structure for this connection time by offering activities. Some activities are deliberately chosen given what has been happening for specific individuals or for the group; for example, if the group has been struggling to get along, we might offer an activity or two that requires collaboration. Students are also free to pick their own activity if appropriate. Staff stay both physically and emotionally close to the students during this time, listening and offering intersubjective experiences of enjoyment, co-regulation of heightened arousal levels, and opportunities to practice reciprocal conversations and storytelling. We have discovered over time that we need approximately an hour of this connection time. If we miss it or transition prematurely we find that our day does not go as smoothly, and we are forced to abandon planned lessons or activities and return to settling arousal levels and again working our way from the bottom of the brain up to prepare for learning. If we address these needs early in our day, then our student is better able to manage when expectations for learning result in fears and frustrations.

This hour is certainly not possible in a regular classroom but could be in specialized smaller classrooms. For us it has been learning to give ourselves permission to play the "long game." We have learned to trust that a deviation into playtime inside or outside the classroom, the spontaneous offering of a story, or on the spot science activity does not prohibit learning, but actually accelerates it. Why is this? When we can whisper to the amygdala, as Jon Baylin encourages us to do, then the circuitry between the amygdala and the hippocampus is facilitated, allowing for new learning. Calming that amygdala also allows for the hippocampus to more effectively manage the production of cortisol, which in turn allows for the bridges between the amygdala, ACC, PAG, and VMPFC to operate. These are the bridges that, when strong, allow for emotion regulation. The main bridge from the limbic system to the cortex is able to remain functional so that the student can hold on to what they know and not be hijacked by their emotional arousal. As this internal neurological structure strengthens, there is less need for an external structure to establish a sense of safety and regulated functioning. This is the circuitry that is strengthened by good care. When babies and toddlers have enough external support early on, they enter school with the circuitry that allows them to manage independently. Children who have experienced developmental trauma just don't have the circuitry that allows for that independence. We must offer dependence and co-regulation of their affect before expecting independence and self-regulation.

If teachers don't have the luxury of an hour for connection time or the permission for structured flexibility to the degree that smaller classrooms may have, initial connection time is still possible. Greeting students at the door or within the first few steps into the classroom is very effective. Make sure as a teacher that you look each child in the eyes (if they allow it) and share something unique with them. Notice who might need a bit more proximity or attention later in the morning. For some of our highly aroused students, this may not be enough, and they may need to find a relationship outside of the classroom each morning that can co-regulate their overwhelmed sensory systems and offer them interactions that are full of signs of safety so that they can be prepared for a later entry into the classroom. Another possibility is to offer 20 minutes of enjoyable or low-stress activities with carefully chosen tasks that can be completed as individuals or in small groups before starting lessons. Again, although not all students need this transition time, those who struggle will appreciate a chance to transition to learning more slowly and to have the opportunity for positive, fun interactions rather than jump into activities that feel too challenging and that set off the alarm system.

Whatever the classroom situation, the important part is that adults are available—eyes, body, voice, and attention—to communicate signs of safety. There are always last-minute things to do that can pull teachers back to their desks or send them on a quick hike to the photocopier, but being present and available upon student arrival can make a huge difference to the trajectory of the day for many students.

> A student entered the classroom with his hood up, seemingly unaware of who he was bumping into on his way to hang his backpack. Mr. Hepburn noticed this and quickly moved toward him, said good morning and then offered to hang his bag for him. This simple act put us into a nurturing position and allowed us to see if the student was open to being cared for (it only took about 5 seconds on this particular day). Offering to hang his backpack when he was obviously capable of doing it communicated that we are very willing to do something for him that he didn't want to do, and we likely avoided a power struggle of asking him to hang his bag when he was obviously emotionally aroused. While taking his bag from him, we could also quickly see whether or not his shoulders were rigid or relaxed, which would give us further information about his current state. At that point we could do some wondering in a playful way to see if he could tolerate a verbal interaction. "Hmmm, your hood is up this morning. Are you our class ninja?" Silence. "Or maybe you are sleepy and not quite ready to wake up." Silence. "I have it, you got a really cool haircut and you're waiting for the big reveal when we gather as a group." By this time, the student peeked out from his hood and said "I'm really tired. I didn't sleep last night because we didn't sleep at home. We slept at my aunt's again." This instantly gave us insight into his physiological state (he was tired and probably worried), which also meant he probably didn't eat breakfast and he would need some time to adjust. Had we made him rush into a cognitive task at that moment or not noticed him, his morning would have likely been pretty tough. Instead, acceptance, curiosity, empathy, and a little playfulness allowed him to feel noticed and to feel safe enough to say what he was really experiencing. During our morning welcome activity time, he was able to have a snack and gradually wake up at his pace.

Once we see that everyone (or almost everyone) is settling, we can then use this time to ask groups of students, rather than everyone at once, to bring forward their agendas, notes, and the like before transitioning to our first lesson. The children have already had the opportunity to talk with one another, get out all those "I have to tell you something!" moments, so they are usually ready to settle in for a more structured task.

One of the big questions teachers often have is why would they want to stop playing to come to lesson time—work must come before play? How do we manage noncompliance?

Not being ready to transition can also be met with PACE. We must accept that if the child could do better, they would, and that there is an obstacle to the natural desire to learn and do well. To pressure a child to join, counting down from three or explaining that there will be a consequence for not transitioning will just ensure a power struggle and reinforce the need for control. Acceptance might involve naming what we see; "I really see that you are struggling to join the group this morning." We might first use empathy "I'm sorry you are having a tough morning, is there anything I can do to help?" or move from acceptance right to curiosity and ask ourselves what might be happening that makes it difficult for the child to do as requested? What is that child's experience in that moment? We wonder out loud so that the student can experience our interest and receive help to organize what he is thinking and feeling: "I wonder what is making it tough today? I wonder if you might be worried that what we are doing might be too difficult for you?" Or "I wonder if you would rather play all day today and would like to tell me that you are on strike today!" Thanks for your honesty!." The use of playfulness can also communicate that you are not interested in a match for control: "If you are not ready yet to listen could you make sure you stretch your ears so you can hear me, I'll be testing your super-duper listening ability because I think I'm going to teach in a whisper today. You are really going to have to stretch your ears!"

Group Language

We join together and review the day's schedule, including any information on our "What's different today?" board. This is extremely helpful for our kids that need predictability throughout the day. We include visitors, changes to the schedule, or anything that can be perceived as a disruption. In this way we are offering the children's amygdalas a "heads up" as surprises and changes are typically so anxiety provoking.

We then read a story followed by a structured language lesson. All of the texts we read are chosen to highlight something within the curriculum (i.e., text form and features), but additionally may target themes that are occurring within their lives (it may even be only one child). Part of almost every text gives the opportunity to explore students' experiences and help make implicit memories explicit so that they can be integrated into their narrative that is being constantly co-created while with us. For example, if a child is being disappointed repeatedly by his or her parents, the teacher may choose a book with a character experiencing that emotion so that the experience of disappointment can be explored indirectly first, and then with reference to the student's experiences of disappointment. There may be just one sentence in a book that is a golden opportunity to talk or wonder aloud about. In Belong, all of our students have experienced relational trauma. Through storytelling, they will often make comparisons to their own experiences. We have been repeatedly impressed by the insights our students have and the compassion they show to one another when one reveals that they too struggle with what the character in the story has tussled with. Our favorite stories are offered in textbox 9.1.

TEXTBOX 9.1

Beautiful Oops by Barney Saltzberg
The Invisible Boy by Trudy Ludwig (she has a number of wonderful books)
Ferdinand the Bull by Munro Leaf
The Boy Who Built a Wall Around Himself by Ali Redford
Enemy Pie by Derek Munson
Julia Cooke has a number of stories (e.g., "Thanks for the Feedback, I think")
The Dark by Lemony Snicket
Margot Sunderland Series
The One and Only Ivan by Katherine Applegate

In response to a story, about loss, our students had the following conversation;

D: "My dad went to jail when I was just very young. I don't see him anymore."
S: "I don't see my dad either, my mom says it's because he doesn't make good choices."
K: "What does that mean?"
S: "I'm not really sure, I think it because he takes a lot of drugs."
M: "My birth mom took a lot of drugs and she would leave me alone when she wasn't supposed to."
     The students were quite matter of fact in their conversation, and the teacher led them deeper into their emotional experience of these losses.
Deni: "Oh my goodness, you have all had to manage such big losses when you were so little. So hard when you are so little! I wonder if any of you felt that your parents went away or didn't look after you properly because there was something wrong with you? Little kids sometimes worry about that."
     The students were quiet and thoughtful but quite regulated. The staff remained quiet to let them think, and eventually, S expressed;
S: "I get mad sometimes that my dad doesn't work harder to stop taking drugs because then I would get to see him."
Deni: "I can see how much you wish to see your dad. I'm sorry he can't beat his addiction. He sure is missing out on a terrific kid."
D: "I don't know if my dad would even recognize me; it's been so long since I've seen him."
Deni: "He may not; you have grown so big and strong. I'm sorry he can't see what an amazing young man you are. I think all of you have been faced with big adult problems that have just been too difficult to understand. I think sometimes you worry that it's somehow your fault that your parents have problems."

In this example, the teacher gave the students a sense of safety to explore their emotions associated with their statements. The teacher led the students to the experience that the abuse or neglect is somehow their fault, a belief that is ingrained for so many children with developmental trauma, but with no expectation that they talk about it. She just named the possibility. The staff stayed emotionally present with the students and did not give them false reassurance. With acceptance and empathy, the shame associated with the losses could begin to be integrated rather than remain an emotion that led to avoidance and dysregulation.

Storytelling is a very powerful medium for learning about ourselves and others. It is very hard to resist a good story. However, when children have experienced too much stress, their capacity to tell a story is very limited because the neurological bridges that help integrate the complex set of skills required to tell a good story do not work well or were never built. Before we learn to read, we hear others reading to us. Before we learn to tell a story, we need to hear many stories. Discussion following the story helps students practice reciprocal conversations, and how to organize what they have heard and how it impacts them. These are the beginning skills of learning to tell their own story.

In our Belong program, the students are invited to come to the carpet where the staff will be sitting. Some students may find this too threatening initially, and they will often lie beneath a desk, or be in an egg chair or play tent. We allow the students to approach at their own pace and trust that the rhythm and content of the storytelling will capture their attention. At the beginning of our first year, storytime consisted of the four adults on the carpet and four boys all in separate tents in the classroom. As trust develops, students find their way to laps where they are welcomed and held for as long as they are comfortable. Again, if we think of how young children learn to read, it is often in the laps of their parents or grandparents. Such physical proximity allows for affect co-regulation when the story gets scary, too exciting, or too sad as well as providing a powerful association between comfort and storytelling.

Touch in this way will not be possible in a regular classroom as the teacher's own safety must be considered. It would not be safe for a teacher to hold or rock a child without the witness of other adults in case the child misperceives the intent of that touch or the student themselves become sexually provocative or behaviorally reactive in response to the intimacy. Touch as we have mentioned is a very powerful aspect of affect co-regulation and the provision of comfort. We often see in classrooms dysregulated students who so desperately need a hug or to be rocked to help them regain equilibrium, but who cannot receive this given the policies and regulations that are understandably set up to keep everyone safe. Having additional support staff in classrooms where there are vulnerable students can make the use of safe touch for comfort possible.

Storytelling at Belong is not always tied to a text. We use storytelling to organize a child's experience in the moment, as the prosody and rhythm of good storytelling are safety signals and they are inherently experienced by the limbic system as soothing. The following example illustrates how storytelling was used to help a student make sense of her upset.

Cassie completed her language work beautifully. Mr. Hepburn, sitting near her, asked if she was finished. She said yes and slid it over to him. He noticed her name wasn't on it and he quickly printed it for her, thinking nothing of it. The student immediately began to cry. In that moment, he could have peppered her with questions, minimized her distress, tried to distract her or cajole her into a better mood, or reassured her. None of those responses would have helped Cassie or staff understand what lay beneath her response. She was likely, given previous experiences, expecting the staff to be cross, impatient, or dismissive. This is one of those moments where staff needed to move off of the planned schedule and take time to be curious and support this student.

Here is what staff did. Since Cassie was holding a small animal in her hand (she had been working with it as part of her task), Mr. Hepburn and Deni also got small animals and started to talk as animals in order to wonder aloud about what might be happening. We knew she struggled with making mistakes, but she hadn't made any throughout this task. We also knew that she was nervous when working with male staff. These were the two wonderings we started with. Deni sat close to her as Cassie was usually comforted by her proximity and Mr. Hepburn sat two chairs away so that she felt physically safe.

Deni (bear): "Cassie is really upset. Do you have any guesses about what is bothering her?"

Mr. Hepburn (giraffe): "Not really, Bear. I know Cassie hates to make mistakes and I wonder if she thinks she made a mistake just now?"

Deni (bear): Mmmm! She does really struggle when she thinks she made a mistake. I also know she struggles when Mrs. Melim is not nearby, and she has to work with Mr. Hepburn and Mr. Fowler. Men are a bit scary to her."

Mr. Hepburn (giraffe): Oh boy, Bear! What if she was worried about making a mistake AND worried whether Mr. Hepburn would be mad at her. Two big worries!"

Cassie was quiet while Mr. Hepburn and Deni spoke but she did not move away from the discussion and eventually brought her animal out to join the staff's duo. There was no definitive resolution to her upset, just a conversation that communicated that staff were interested about what was behind her behavior and the shared intention to figure it out together. When the staff noticed her affect, they co-regulated it through physical proximity and storytelling (with attention to prosody and tone) so she too could notice and organize her emotional experience. The staff's acceptance allowed her to maintain connection rather than the loss of connection she expected in response to her behavior or emotional vulnerability. The entire event lasted approximately four minutes, and those four minutes influenced her experience of safety and created a building block for trust. She was able to return to classroom activities.

Staff, however, remained curious about what had caused such upset in that moment and discussed it together at the end of the day. Cassie was not yet able to offer those insights, so after school, the teacher connected with Cassie's caregiver. She gave her an account of what had occurred and wondered if she would be able to wonder with Cassie about what had happened that evening. The next morning, her caregiver let us know that the act of printing her name was the triggering event. By printing her name on her page (something teachers do all the time), she believed that her parents would find her. Cassie had been removed from the care of parents who had been very frightening to her, and we had not realized how fragile her sense of safety was. We were then able to connect with her the next morning and apologize for not understanding how frightening it was for her to have Mr. Hepburn print her name. We told her how her caregiver had let us know how brave she had been to let her know what it was all about. We used acceptance and empathy liberally, and then were curious about how this must have been an experience for her at her previous school where neither she nor her teachers understood her fear. Her teachers had thought she was deliberately controlling or defiant, and Cassie had thought she was bad or crazy.

So often we make the assumption that a student is angry, defiant, or noncompliant when the underlying motivation for the outburst is fear. When we can maintain our curiosity combined with knowledge of how trauma impacts our brains, we will minimize the chance of misperception and avoid slipping into providing danger signals rather than signs of safety.

Break

We take breaks between lessons requiring sustained attention. Being attuned to the students' needs determines the type and length of break we take. The break activities may include finishing something (i.e., a Lego structure) from our morning welcoming activity, talking with one another, a quick game of cards, or having a snack. It's not the time to get out the paint and items with multiple pieces. All students need brain and body breaks, not just those who have experienced trauma. Yes, there is curriculum to cover, but our team has learned that if our kids are not settled enough to learn, then the same curriculum will need to be taught two or even three times and will actually take longer. Giving them the chance to move throughout the day and recognizing when movement is needed is important. It may be a five-minute break or a 15-minute one, but it's necessary, and it makes a huge difference to the rhythm of the day. During our breaks, we continue to be attuned and ready to support where needed.

> Two girls were playing Lego together on the mat during a break. Sarah upset, claimed "I can't find my Bat Girl. I don't know where she went." Lucy quickly said, "I'll help you find her." Staff was thrilled that Lucy was jumping in to help and by doing so actually co-regulated Sarah's affective state. Staff watched the interaction to see how they would work together and what would happen if Bat Girl wasn't found. What they saw was Lucy putting her hand in the Lego bin, taking the figure out and then hiding it under the mat. She continued to 'look' for the figure with Sarah. After a couple of minutes, Sarah stopped looking and said she would look later. Sarah and a couple of the other students headed outside and Lucy (unaware that staff were watching), reached under the carpet for the figure and then went to her backpack and put it inside. She said she was going outside too and off she went. It looked like Lucy deliberately hid the figure and then stole it from Sarah. Did she just want it? Was there another motive for taking it? That was the mystery staff needed to solve. What the team had learned earlier in the school year was that Lucy tended to steal when there was instability or uncertainty at home. Staff brought Lucy back inside and spoke with her. They were direct and concerned about what they had witnessed, but were careful to highlight that their

current concern was figuring out what taking the figure, hiding it, and then stealing it was about (curiosity). Deni started the conversation naming with acceptance what the team had seen "Lucy, I noticed that you wanted to help Sarah find Bat Girl. You helped her to look for it. I saw you find it, hide it and then put it in your backpack. Help me understand what happened. I know it all went really fast." Lucy said "I don't know" put her head down experiencing shame. To help her regulate her shame, Deni started to tell the story of what happened using a rhythmic storytelling prosody outlining the sequence of events without expecting a response from Lucy. Then she introduced what the motives might have been, again without judgment and to stay with the intent of trying to understand: "I was surprised, and I wondered 'what is happening here?' I know Sarah and Lucy are pretty good friends and they love to play Lego together. Maybe Lucy was hiding it so she could be the one to find it for Sarah, but if that were the case Lucy would have just pulled it out of the bin and said 'I found it!' Sarah would have been so happy. But then Lucy put it under the carpet and I thought maybe she's going to pull it out and say, 'Sarah I found it!' but that didn't happen either! Then it went into Lucy's back pack and I got super confused. I started to wonder if maybe Lucy just wanted that figure, but then I remembered that she already has that exact same one. Maybe Lucy wanted something of Sarah's so it's kind of like having Sarah with her at home." Lucy peeked up suggesting that this last guess might be close to the mark. The teacher then invited her into the conversation. "Do you have any ideas?" Lucy said "I think I'm moving again and I don't have mine (the figure) with me. If I move, then I'll still have one." Deni then could thank her for letting her know and give her empathy for how hard moving again was for her.

The staff's guessing had been wrong, but the mere fact of noticing and guessing was enough to help Lucy feel safe enough to share very vulnerable information. After giving her lots of empathy, the staff wondered with her how she was going to let Sarah know what had happened and would she like some help with that. No heavy consequence was needed to "teach" Lucy that stealing was wrong. This she knew, and it was clear that she experienced shame. Lucy needed to approach her friend, return Bat Girl to her, and repair the relationship, which she was able to do.

The acceptance, curiosity, and empathy embedded into a storytelling prosody helped Lucy regulate her shame and keep her level of arousal within her window of tolerance. If staff had moved too quickly into lecturing they would have risked increasing her shame and if they had moved too quickly into problem-solving, that is, how was she going to fix the behavior, they would have missed understanding what lay beneath the behavior, and Lucy would have been left confused about why she took it and alone with her anxieties about moving again.

Structured Language Tasks

Following our break, we move onto a structured language task with modifications and accommodations when needed. All students work on targeted areas individually, in partners, or in guided groups. It's a busy time, with students needing different levels of support. For some, sitting beside or near them is enough to maintain a balanced state and keep them working. Following Coan's (2016) work that illustrates how our cortices can work better for longer when we are in the presence of a safe attachment figure, we often refer to lending our brains. Such an offer again communicates that help is unconditional, and students are aware that their brains will work better with this kind of help and why.

Other students may need more direct support with the task, staying on task or with managing complex feelings such as making mistakes, being "stupid" for not being able to do something they think should come naturally, needing to control the task, making mistakes on purpose to sustain adult attention and proximity, and managing corrective feedback or praise. Students with trauma may experience one or all of these during a task, and determining which one is at play at any given moment can be challenging. If we have the luxury of knowing what a student is most likely to feel based on previous events and experiences, then we have a chance to talk about it, but otherwise our PACEful stance allows us to co-regulate the affective state and to organize what is happening so that it doesn't overwhelm anybody.

> Kristin sat at the table and looked eager to get to work on her individual language. She loved this time of day. She had all her materials—her pencil, eraser, notebook with questions and her latest book, The Perfect Pony. Knowing that she sometimes got distracted, all of her materials were ready, she was seated at a table with her back to most of the other students, and staff had already given her instructions and a checklist to follow (i.e., read chapter 1 and answer questions 1–5). Deni looked over to see Kristin had started her work. She was often inconsistent in her performance, so the teacher would check in at frequent intervals. Within a few minutes, the teacher did a closer check-in to see if she had understood what she had read and was following task instructions. Deni noticed that she made errors on the first two questions and would need to make corrections before continuing. Deni asked Kristen if she could read her first two answers to her and asked her to listen carefully to see if it is what she meant to say. When she finished reading Kristen didn't say anything. Deni asked "Can we talk about this answer? I want to make sure I understand what you're saying." She suspected that Kristin actually understood the question and was able to give an accurate answer, so she playfully said, "Hey wait a minute, you know this stuff. You were just trying to confuse me and make me think I was reading answers about a different book! I wonder what that's about? You know I'll come and help you if you're stuck, but you weren't really stuck. I think you like me to check in so I'll sit with you. How smart you are! Guess what? I'll come and check on you whether you make mistakes or not."

As Kristin returned to working on her questions, across the room Seth threw his book across the room and yelled, *"I'm so stupid!"* This is a terribly sad statement to hear from a seven-year-old, and the almost unanimous adult response is *"No, you're not!"* However, in that moment, the child does feel stupid, and by contradicting or minimizing his experience, he or she will not feel understood by you. This will increase the likelihood that the student will not learn to trust you. Moving over to Seth was crucial because he was in an emotional state that definitely needed co-regulation, and it is easier if he allows proximity rather than for us to try to help him from the other side of the room. The quick offering of empathy *("How hard it must be to feel that you are stupid when you are not able to do something!")* communicates that his frustration is understood, and that understanding trumps consequences at that moment. If he can experience that acceptance and empathy over many repetitions, his arousal system will become better managed, and he will learn how to self-regulate in the face of learning challenges. If we had asked him to leave the room until he could be calmer or were irritated at the outburst, he would have responded defensively and a power struggle would occur.

Acceptance of our student's emotional state is so crucial to build trust. When we argue with, dismiss the child's experience, or reassure them, we perpetuate their feelings of not being understood and we reinforce their sense of being alone with their thoughts and feelings. Empathy is required alongside acceptance in order to communicate that you understand how hard it is for that child if they feel stupid, bad, crazy, alone, or rotten. Once the child feels that you understand, they are more likely to take the risk to enter into intersubjective experiences. If we move too quickly to problem-solving or to giving consequences, we lose the opportunity for understanding.

Recess/Break

Language is wrapped up and it's time for another much-needed break. Recess has arrived, and our kids are generally anxious to get outside. Recess and lunchtime are two of the trickiest times of the school day for students who cannot yet be in the dorsal vagal system that allows for positive social engagement. Typically, we send students into a field of unknown and unpredictable social situations that require independence and an established capacity for self-regulation. Just as we identify students with physical exceptionalities that need close supervision outside, our students who have experienced trauma also require such supervision. It is important to see the need for this supervision as a way to help the student be successful rather than as a punishment or a constriction of freedom for the behavioral transgressions that are a function of being in the sympathetic nervous system or dorsal vagal organization. Given that their brains have developed to see signs of danger and not of safety, the fast-paced, often ambiguous, or capricious interactions are too much to process, and they create great alarm, which typically ends in fight or flight behavior. Providing them with a regulated adult brain to decipher and organize what is happening socially and what they themselves might be experiencing can keep the student regulated and help these times be less overwhelming.

> Sam and Andy entered the classroom arguing. It was hard to decipher what each were saying, and they were clearly invested in their argument, indifferent to the growing audience as others entered. Rather than limit them, staff adopted a playful attitude which served to interrupt their argument with an unexpected response. Staff said in an elevated storytelling type of voice and pretending to hold a microphone: "And in this corner dressed in black and grey and standing at 4 feet 3 inches tall is Super Star Sam! Hold the applause! And in this corner, ready to jump right in wearing a blue shirt with the golden hammer is the Always Aerodynamic Andy! Before we start round two, boxers,

can you go to your corners, get a drink and be ready for action." At this point, the boys (and those entering) are more interested in what the teacher was saying and less in what the boys were arguing about. The arguing boys are surprised by the playfulness and find it hard to resist. Their escalating aggression was curtailed as they were invited into the unfolding story.

Another staff quickly volunteered to be Andy's coach and another Sam's coach. Both coaches used empathy and acceptance to hear each boy's story and co-regulated as needed so that we could talk about the boys without them becoming embroiled in the argument again. The conversation between staff went like this:

Mr. Fowler: in a storytelling voice: "Super Star Sam was super excited to play the Manhunt game with the grade 4 class at recess and thought that Aerodynamic Andy was going to play too."

Mr. Hepburn: "Sounds like a good plan so far."

Mr. Fowler: "Yes, Sam was excited to play especially when Andy agreed, but then something happened a few minutes into the game. Sam thinks Andy gave away his hiding spot and told the person who was 'it' where to find him."

Mr. Hepburn: "Ah that would be so frustrating! Sam was happy to be playing Manhunt and excited to be playing with Andy because they're such good buddies and then Sam saw Andy point to him and give his spot away! Wow—that must have been a bag of mixed feelings for Sam."

Mr. Fowler: "I think so too. He was excited at first and then all of sudden confused and maybe even felt betrayed because Andy gave him away."

Mr. Hepburn: "I talked with Aerodynamic Andy and he said that he didn't really want to play the game, but he played because Sam kept asking him to and he just wanted him to stop asking. Then when they were playing, Andy got caught by 'it' and he thought if he pointed out Sam, then Sam would get caught too and he and Sam could just go and play something else together on their own."

Mr. Fowler: "Oh, so maybe Andy was playing something Sam wanted and hoped they could play something different after. So, they both just wanted to play together but they got some messages mixed up."

Mr. Hepburn: (in the announcer voice but much quieter) "Both boxers to the center of the ring." Both boys had heard the conversation between staff and re-joined. They were not asked to apologize to the other because their intentions were actually to play with one another. The way it unraveled was a deficit in social competency skills and making their wishes known. It's hard to consequence that! The last thing Andy said was "What does aerodynamic mean?"

It's important for staff to be attuned to each other, and not just to students. When one of us needs the other to be part of the response, it's important that he or she can insert effectively into the scenario. Staff may talk about the child, using wondering-out-loud and storytelling prosody, signs of safety that will support the bridges between the amygdala and hippocampus and from the limbic system to the prefrontal cortex to help that frustration level stay within the window of tolerance. Two staff can also enter into wondering, where one speaks for the child *"If I were Sam right now I might want to say something like, 'I'm really mad at Andy because I thought he was my friend and when he gave my hiding spot away I thought that's not what friends do! Then I thought he might not want to be my friend anymore.'"* Constant attunement and co-regulation is hard on adult brains, and we too benefit from working with another brain in our attempts to co-regulate a student's affect. Talking about and talking for can certainly be used when you are only one person, but perhaps it requires more confidence with dramatic performance as you shift between voices or characters.

This high level of supervision is very difficult to find in a regular school system. Recesses and lunchtimes are typically supervised by teachers or volunteers who may have no relationship with the children or who lack the knowledge and skills to be able to notice and soothe a child who is in self-defense mode. It will require flexibility and creativity to offer vulnerable students more structured recess opportunities with a caring adult who is knowledgeable about trauma and versed with some skills for affect co-regulation. Our trauma-informed schools that we introduce later offer clubs at lunch with a particular student in mind. They make sure that there is a teacher who is assigned to a small group of children to ensure that recess time is more structured and successful. Tasks are generated to offer particular students helping opportunities that offer them the success of a one-on-one adult relationship. Although we can all agree that students need social time, if they are not yet equipped to be successful, we do not insist in our trauma-informed schools that a student go out for recess as we might for our securely attached students. The lack of success and subsequent dysregulation can end the day. Whether offering quieter interactions or more supervision, we need to make sure that our modifications in expectations or structure is seen as a "gift" rather than as a burden to the teacher or child. Because the modifications just described are relationship rich, administrators have had to be creative about freeing up staff to provide this supervision. Although difficult, it is not impossible.

At the Belong program, we initially structure recess times so that they lie outside of the regular recess time for the rest of the school. This way, the students remain together as a small group with students they are familiar with and are not overwhelmed by 350 unfamiliar faces. At least two staff stay with the group so as to provide opportunities for mutual delight while playing as well as to offer support should it be needed.

Because a high level of supervision is hard to find in regular school systems, behavioral correction is focused on time-outs versus time-ins. Time-out is predicated on the idea that withdrawal of the student from the reinforcing social activity is averse and will cause them to alter their behavior if they wish to remain with their friends. Such a consequence may work for children who have the self-regulation capacity to modulate their behavior, but it does not work for children whose brains have adapted to danger and where that bridge does not allow access to cognitive resources under times of stress. For our hurt students, sending them away when they most need to borrow our brains will result in further shame, which is likely to increase the impulsivity or defensive response that got them into trouble in the first place. Because we have the luxury of extra brains, we offer time-ins, an opportunity for co-regulation, since self-regulation is not yet a developed skill. If a student is having a difficult time at recess or with a social interaction, they are invited to do something with a staff member. This allows them to stay outside, take a break from what is challenging, and have some pleasure and success that will eventually build the circuitry needed for self-regulation.

We have one staff who is so sensitive to the isolation of time-outs that he can often be found chatting to the students who have been asked to stand on the wall during the whole-school recess. Often the conversation starts with him asking how come they are standing on the wall. The typical response is "I don't know." This may reflect their shame about being singled out in this way or may also reflect their genuine confusion about what they had done or not done that upset the yard teacher.

Math

Math is scheduled for after recess, which means that students have to practice another transition and practice bringing down their arousal levels from play to learn. This is not an easy task for a child who has difficulty with emotion regulation, so it is another opportunity for them to receive co-regulation of their affective state from staff, reinforcing the association between being helped with safe adult relationships. Math is chosen for after recess because it is often a hands-on activity with opportunities for movement. Everyone plans differently, but we have found that after a recess that is too short for some, sitting still is not yet an option. Math centers, small group, or partner math can fill that need. As we work through the morning, it's important to notice that some of the students may be reaching their capacity for learning.

One of the confusing things for adults who work with children who have been hurt is the variability in their capacity to focus or to complete academic tasks. Some days, long division is easy. Other days, it is as if the concept has never been taught. As adults, we run the risk of ascribing intent to this variability and pushing the child to do something he "knows" how to do because he did it yesterday. This variability is certainly not under the student's control. Some days, the bridge to the cortex is under repair or has completely disappeared. It can be as confusing to the child as it is to us, and tends to reinforce feelings of inadequacy and beliefs that they are stupid and will never learn. The bridge to the cortex disappears when there are increases in stress. This might take the form of something happening at home that is consciously or unconsciously on a child's mind, hunger, excitement, fatigue (cognitive or physical), sensory integration difficulties, or even something about the content of the task assigned. If a student knew it yesterday but not today, acceptance, curiosity, and empathy for the frustration and confusion the child feels will regulate the stress rather than adding to it. That task may have to be modified or shelved for that day. We try to make this process explicit for the student so that they are learning when they don't know, and that taking a break or modifying expectations becomes a good coping response. It is a good opportunity to talk about the brain and about how the bridges may need a bit more time for repair before tackling the task.

Often the provision of hands-on activities helps the transition, but sometimes, the frustration of learning leads to avoidance through shutting down or behavioral outbursts. We expect that learning is difficult for a child who has rickety bridges, and the goal is to meet these outbursts with PACE so that signs of safety help the bridge stay functional.

Math for our grade 2–4 class seemed to have a nice rhythm that day. The kids were working well and there was a lovely hum in the air. Staff moved between the students to help where needed, question strategies, and offer alternate ways of thinking about problems. All of a sudden, a container of geometric shapes flew into the air and Stevie yelled "this is stupid." Staff moved to Stevie, unsure of what had led to this response. He had the same partner the day before and didn't have any difficulties with him. He understood the concept well and often took a leadership role within math centers. His partner had no explanation and sat quietly while staff wondered aloud. "Stevie, you seem really upset right now. I'm sorry, I'm not sure what happened. Can you help me understand?" Stevie immediately became agitated and again said "This is stupid!" Staff responded "I heard that part, but I'm not sure what you mean. Maybe I didn't explain it properly or maybe you're missing an important piece or maybe it's something different?" (introducing the possibility of it being something more personal for him). Stevie responded "I want to do the grade 4 work, not the grade 2 work. This is for babies and it's stupid." Staff response "Ah, I get it. You want to do harder work and I gave you work that's just too easy!" Stevie responds "Yes!" Deni replied "Oh my gosh! This is all my fault." At this point Steven looks a bit confused but is curious about why his teacher thought it was her fault. Deni continued in an excited voice "I have been saying how amazing you are in math because I see how you look at questions and challenging problems and you figure them out in all kinds of fantastic ways that I don't think of. I keep telling you how great you are and of course you would want harder work" (acknowledging his experience). She continued in a softer and quieter voice (bringing her own affect down) "What a lot of pressure I've put on you. I'm so sorry!" With acceptance and empathy, Stevie was now able to tolerate a more cognitive or rational discussion. "My worry is that if I don't give you the grade 2 work and I take you right to grade 4 work, then I might miss teaching you something you're really going to need. At your old school, you missed so many days. I know how frustrated you'll be when you feel like you don't know something you think you should. How about this, when I know it's safe and you have all the tools you need, I'll give you harder work and when I know it's something brand new, we'll start with grade 2 work and then move ahead when you feel ready? Deal?" Stevie agreed to this and then rejoined his partner.

Lunch

Lunch, too, is a whole-class activity so staff can offer structure and support as needed as well as provide opportunities to practice conversations and social interactions. It is often in these times that important information is shared ("I was always hungry when I lived with my birth mom") or table manners can be coached or conversations about food developed ("Why is it important to eat vegetables anyway!"). Occasionally lunch consists of a shared feast where all have participated in the preparation and cooking. These are occasions to introduce new foods, teach new skills, offer opportunities to collaborate, and to share attention and intention. Many of our students have not participated in a Thanksgiving, Easter, or Christmas feast, and sometimes the conversation is more difficult as students talk about poverty, parents' mental health difficulties, and limitations. Students are helped to move through these more serious conversations to lighter ones and back again with acceptance, curiosity and empathy, and playfulness as tolerated.

Birthday lunches are a ritual in the classroom. The student is asked what they would like for their birthday lunch, and all efforts are made to provide it exactly as requested. Birthdays can be very anxiety provoking for many of our students. Positive emotions (excitement and joy) can be just as hard to regulate as more negative emotions (fear that parents will not buy them a present, ambivalence about receiving gifts from a family member that has been frightening, or anger at being forgotten). Staff are attuned and help the birthday child organize their experiences with A/R dialogue. These lunches are a wonderful way to experience shared enjoyment and delight, and to communicate genuine celebration of that child. However, we are always careful to be attuned to the child's comfort level. Our students who are still developing trust will typically sabotage positive interactions because they can't yet manage that positive attention.

OTTER (Our Time To Enjoy Reading)

We start our afternoon with another connection time to aid in the transition from active play to learning time. Once the students are settled, we move into a story. We typically have a chapter book that we're reading, and its purpose is to bring the kids back together and offer a shared experience. The way in which the story is read depends on the arousal level of the children. If they need more co-regulation as a group, the story may be read in a whisper so that they start to naturally quiet down to hear. Staff almost always sit on the floor with them rather than above them on a chair. If they are leaning more toward a hypo-aroused state, a different type of voice may be used with hand gestures or body movements that pique their curiosity. We try to up-regulate positive emotions and down-regulate negative emotions to mirror the process in secure primary relationships; our goal always being the practice of co-regulation to build self-regulation capacity.

After any transition, there may be a student or two who just have difficulty getting their arousal level to the right place for learning. It is important not to fall into typical classroom management practices where students are directed to comply before they are able, offered consequences for noncompliance, or singled out where they are vulnerable to feeling shame. Acceptance, curiosity, empathy, and playfulness, when appropriate, will communicate that you understand how difficult it is and help is readily available.

The class was called to the gathering area to listen to a chapter from the book Jacob Two-Two Meets the Hooded Fang. Karlee was staying at the opposite end of the classroom. Staff had observed that transitions to group activities were hard for her. Instead of insisting that she sit with everyone, she was given permission to stay at a comfortable distance. Deni communicated; "Karlee, I notice that it's really hard for you to come to the carpet with everyone at once. I wonder if it feels like you're all squished up with all those kids. Arms and legs everywhere! How about if you listen from wherever you can hear me best and I'll send out a signal and you can let me know if you're okay. Can we figure out some signals together?" The signal was that Deni would tilt her head, which would look natural to everyone else as she read while simultaneously making eye contact with Karlee. Karlee's signal back would be a thumbs up if she could hear and everything was okay. Part way through the year, she started coming closer to the group and finally to the edge of the group.

This example emphasizes understanding the reason for Karlee's difficulty with coming to a common gathering place before jumping to a consequence. Although small, the number of kids felt overwhelming for her. Finding a solution together allowed her the safety and space from which she could observe others, become comfortable with the routine, and decide when she was ready to come closer, all without disrupting the lesson or her classmates. Sometimes the worry for teachers is that if one student is allowed to do something different, then all the others will want to as well. We find this rarely happens—maybe once or twice to test it out—but for the child who really doesn't struggle with transitions or with groups of kids sitting too close, he or she will quickly tire of being at the back of the classroom when he or she really wants to be in the middle of the group. When students become aware that their need for control is named, accepted, and not met with matching force, they gradually have less need for the opposition.

The class has been called to the gathering area again to listen to a chapter from the book Jacob Two-Two Meets the Hooded Fang. Dan often found a toy to play with along the way and ignored all verbal and visual transition requests. This quickly became part of his transition routine and could be disruptive to others if he started adding dialogue to his play. Taking the toy away, allowing him to bring the toy to the carpet or hiding the toy didn't help. As a way of interrupting this routine and trying to figure out what his behaviour was really all about, staff moved to playfulness. When Dan entered the classroom, he expected the same routine. While the kids gathered on the carpet, he would go to the toy, be asked to come to the carpet, he'd refuse, he'd be asked again, and maybe even a couple of the kids would ask him to come too. So much control. . . .

That day, however, staff waited at the table playing with the toy. Dan saw this and immediately came to the table. Deni said to him, "Hi Dan. I totally understand why you love this toy. I've been playing it with during lunch recess and it is pretty cool. I thought maybe today I could stay back here and play with you and Mr. Hepburn is going to read the chapter to the class." Dan was unnerved by this response and immediately said "It's not that fun of a toy." Deni said "But I thought you really must love it if you play with it every single day." Dan said a bit defiantly "No!" This was Deni's opening to explore what was really behind him staying behind. She pretended to talk to the toy rather than directly to Dan since she had already disrupted his expectations and didn't want to add additional pressure. "Sorry toy, Dan just isn't that crazy about you today. I know it's probably confusing because he visits you every single day." At this point, Mr. Hepburn called both teacher and student over for the story. Deni yelled "No thanks!" just as Dan usually did. She noticed that Dan had smiled when she had declined the offer to join. She guessed that he didn't care about the toy and he wasn't overwhelmed by joining the group as Karlee had been. He was seeking an invitation. He wanted staff and kids to want him to be with them. He was used to being overlooked in his home of seven kids. Toys had little meaning to him, they were all shared, but being wanted, being invited was powerful and elusive for him at home. The teacher addressed the toy, "Toy, I wonder if Dan really likes it when I ask him to come over with us and if he likes it even more when the kids invite him. I wonder if sometimes he feels a bit invisible at home with all his brothers and sisters and he doesn't want it to be the same here at school."

Dan was open and engaged, allowing the teacher to make sense of his behavior in a non-shamed based manner. Dan's hippocampus was open to new learning and understanding as the amygdala's alarm system was turned down by acceptance, empathy, and curiosity. He had a new narrative, involving being wanted as opposed to the old narrative of having to listen to adults who were not interested in him. We were able to offer him opportunities for inclusion by asking him to do jobs around the classroom and be conscious about "inviting" him. As the year progressed, he became more cooperative, in part because he trusted the safety of the classroom, but also because his fear of rejection was now explicit and being integrated into his awareness. He was also having multiple repetitions of being included and valued where he could begin to experience staff's delight and enjoyment of him as well as be open to his peers' positive regard.

The more opportunities for storytelling the better, as it provides us with a powerful way of helping our students discover their world and pay attention to their own experiences in response to the story, strengthening the bridge between the right and left hemisphere as well as the vertical bridge that offers organization of the limbic arousal. The choice of a chapter book for OTTER allows us to practice the opportunity of tolerating excitement, surprise and waiting for the next installment, or delaying gratification. It is a shared experience, crucial for intersubjectivity—a building block for healthy brain development.

In our society's increasing use of technology, we have limited or removed altogether the opportunities for shared enjoyment. Often in many schools, each student learns individually from a tablet rather than from each other, and sometimes even instruction is given "online" rather than from the teacher. Earlier we explored the implications of technology for our relationships. At Belong, there is no use of technology as we believe strongly that both relationships and learning are improved through co-regulation and co-construction of meaning. We find that not one of our students complains about the lack of iPads or computers.

Science

Once we finish our story, we transition to science. This is a favorite subject since it's full of "oohs and ahhs" and moments of discovery, again offering students the opportunity to be curious and expand their capacity for exploration. Being curious is not possible when lack of safety is the familiar emotional state. Our students are usually eager to jump into whatever interesting experiment that is prepared, especially when they are starting to trust the safety in the room. In addition to curiosity, engaging with science experiments helps our students experience failure as opportunities to learn. They are encouraged to make a hypothesis, test it in different ways, and then interpret the results. No result is without value. We are offering opportunities to be more flexible in their thinking and more comfortable with the experience of taking risks, to try multiple options rather than apply one thought or strategy, and to prime the skills of observation over time to promote sustained attention and curiosity and delight in discovery.

As with any subject, we often see kids who are excited to try something but simultaneously worry about making mistakes. Usually the salience of making a mistake will trump taking a risk for a student who has experienced abuse and neglect. Remember that their narrative is that they are at fault for the abuse. Making a mistake is associated with danger and with the sense that they will cause others to be angry with (and, therefore, abuse) them. Science experiments allow for much trial and error and a way to bridge the academic learning with the emotional learning of what happens in their brains and hearts when they make a mistake (creating a more explicit narrative), and how that experience is similar to what they might have felt when they were little and were so scared of their abusive parent (creating a more explicit narrative, traveling the horizontal and vertical bridges as well as the bridge between the amygdala and hippocampus that allows the student to be open to new learning.)

Tom was working with a partner on his science experiment. When the teacher checked in he seemed to be on task, working well with his partner and sharing the work load. The next moment, he was crying, ripping up his observation sheet and sitting under the table. The teacher sat down on the floor beside Tom (not directly in front in order to reduce the intensity of the interaction). The conversation sounded like this: "Tom, I notice you're having a really hard time right now. I'm so sorry. I'm not sure what happened. Can you help me understand?" Tom spoke loudly "It's stupid. It didn't work. It was supposed to work and it didn't!" The teacher responded "Ah! I get it, you were expecting the experiment to go one way and it went the other way. That's a surprise and I know you are a kid that doesn't always like surprises, even science experiment surprises." Tom yelled "I do like surprises!" Matching his affect the teacher used an excited but controlled voice with no anger accepting his response, "You like surprises? I like them most of the time too. What was your favorite surprise?" He replied "I got a bird once." The teacher replied still using an excited voice, "A bird? Wow. I don't know if I'd like that surprise. Is your bird noisy?" Tom responded, "Kind of." Tom was starting to manage his upset so the teacher steered the conversation back to what might have created his outburst; "I'm wondering if this particular science surprise felt more like a mistake and I know making mistakes is really hard for you. Maybe you're thinking you did the whole thing wrong and you have to start over. Or maybe you think your partner did something wrong or he thinks you're dumb. What a lot to worry about! Here's the thing . . . science experiments are meant to go all sorts of ways that you don't expect. You were being a great scientist—I was watching you. You were smiling and focusing and following all the steps with your partner. You found out something new and so did your partner. I'm looking at him right now and he seems curious about the results you both got." Tom started to get distressed again saying, "But I ripped my paper. I can't write anything down." Tom's partner had been listening the whole time and made a suggestion to write both their observations on his page. Tom was able to agree and they both went back to work.

In this example, two underlying reasons may have caused Tom to cry and tear up his paper. One, he was uncomfortable with surprises, and two, he was fearful of making mistakes. Knowing that was a starting point for a conversation. You will notice that when Tom contradicted the teacher, his contradiction was accepted, otherwise a power struggle would have occurred with both the teacher and Tom arguing their position. There was also no reassurance (e.g., "Don't worry, you'll get it next time." or "It looks good.") or problem-solving ("Let me rewrite it for you.") or insistence on compliance. Instead, the underlying motivation for the behavior was guessed at, named, and organized. There will be many more opportunities to revisit that theme with Tom and help him be aware of how hard it was to feel like his behavior caused his parents to give up on him and how hard he had to work now to make sure that other people didn't leave him in the same way. Teachers often worry about how much time such a conversation and support would take. This particular conversation took approximately five minutes.

Social Studies or Art

These are also afternoon activities, and again are subjects where we balance academic learning and emotional experience. Often learning for our children has been associated with danger and failure, and as we provide safety and lead them from mistrust to trust, we continually offer opportunities to take safe risks, practice curiosity, and tolerate frustrations, with the opportunity for support from helpful adults. The emotional learning is intertwined with academic learning like a double helix. We do not switch from cognitive learning to emotional and back again or "teach" social skills. The constant attunement, A/R dialogue, and experience of co-regulation allow for our students to travel on highways that head toward the front of their brains rather than the tried and true reactive-defensive ones to the back of the brain. Multiple repetition of these reciprocal interactions and safety messages allow for what Jon Baylin calls interstate highway travel that will allow for new learning in all areas of development.

Transition Toward End of Day

As we near 2:30, the children are often quite tired. They are new to regulating attention and emotions, and it takes a great deal of energy. As they get tired, they are more prone to dysregulation, and we often see more arguments with peers, frustration with themselves, increased anxiety, and decreased attention. To ask for more cognitive learning at this point would be setting the students up for further frustration. We use this time to remove academic demands and to focus more intently on relationships and connection. We start the transition to home, often an hour ahead of bus time so that we minimize the last-minute rush out the door. Transitions are hard, but the transition home at the end of the day can be twice as hard. First, because the student is tired, and second, because often what is at home continues to be frightening or unpredictable, and attention to home becomes more immediate. We have the luxury of having three to four staff for six or seven students, so this is a time where we can offer individual time, small group activities that are pleasurable, outside play where gross motor activities can help regulate, or quiet time for reading with a staff member.

> Laney struggled at the end of each day. It was really hard for her to leave staff. She felt safe in the classroom and felt valued. As the end of the day crept closer, she needed recognition of her struggle. Mr. Fowler said "Laney, it seems so tough for you to leave here. What do you think that is about?" Laney shrugged her shoulders. He asked her if it would be ok for him to guess. He then said, "I think it's tough to go home, because you worry a lot about whether your mum and dad are in a good mood or bad mood. It is hard to worry and you never really know what it going to happen at home. Here at school you get a break from that worry. What do you think about coming up with a handshake that we can do before you leave? That way when you are at home you can remember the handshake and feel me with you to help you with your worry." The hand-shake started simply, but over the year grew into a multi-step shake that was co-created into a 5 minute affair! The student was walked directly to her bus after the handshake and staff stayed to wave to her until the bus was out of sight. We couldn't fix her worry, but we could be with her as she worried.
>
> When things were particularly difficult at home, Laney sometimes needed an additional transitional bridge. Staff might ask her to hold onto something from class (i.e., a stuffed animal, a special bookmark, a small picture) for the night and to bring it back the next day. Sometimes she was given a beaded bracelet to wear home, and staff wore the same bracelet until the next morning. All of these things helped to keep her connected to the classroom and to the people in it when she was at home and felt lonely and scared.

This example illustrates how the attunement allowed staff to notice her shift in mood, and wondering out loud helped her know that she was not alone with her experience. We don't have to have the correct guess. It is the intersubjectivity—the communication of I want to understand—that maintains that interpersonal bridge and allows for co-regulation to occur. The offering of a solution must come after the co-regulation, otherwise it is too much of a cognitive communication before the bridge to the cortex is steady enough to integrate it. If we had rushed too quickly to the solution, we may risk communicating that we can't handle her emotional experience and she might feel that she needed to be "fixed" rather than heard.

While Laney responded well to these transitional bridges, another student did not, and he needed something different.

> Lee typically let staff know a couple times a day that he couldn't wait to go home. On the surface this looked like rejection of us or the program, but we knew it was the exact opposite—he wanted to stay at school but was not going to risk wanting something or feeling vulnerable. We had a lot of work to do to help him understand why he didn't

want to go home. We knew that he wanted his mom to give him more attention, that he was always unsure of where he would be sleeping or who would be visiting at home. He left his house each morning not knowing what or who he would find when he returned. Staff noticed that the last twenty minutes of each day, Lee started to dysregulate physically and emotionally. His social interactions became strained and he became less aware of his body in space increasing the risk of potential injury to himself or others. Lee didn't seem to realize that this was occurring each day or see the impact it had on his peer relationships the following morning. Staff noticed this aloud "Lee, we see that the end of the day is really hard for you. You have trouble with your friends and your whole body changes. I worry that you're going to get hurt or that your friends aren't going to understand what's going on for you." Lee seemed surprised that we noticed this. "We've talked about how hard it is at home before and I wonder if that is part of what's happening. You're worried about what will happen when you get home." At first Lee denied this and staff followed up with acceptance "Oh good, because IF that was something you were worrying about, I can see why it would be so hard for you." By using the word IF, staff were not telling him that's what he was experiencing, but rather offering a possibility and communicating acceptance and empathy. Lee then said "I just want to go home and play on my tablet" to which we follow "Ah, that's a solo game. It's probably nice and quiet for you. What's your favorite game to play?" We talk for a moment about his game and then the staff took the lead again. "I wonder if you like to play your game because you can block everything out. Perhaps at the end of each school day you are pretending to be one of the action figures in your game but you forgot your friends are real people." At this comment, Lee smiled, suggesting that the teacher's guess had resonated with him. No consequence was needed, just understanding—help to make the implicit fears explicit so that over time they could be talked about and a plan developed for how to manage them. The home time conversations took place over a number of days for very brief periods of time so as not to overwhelm him. The team could not change the unpredictability of what he would find at home each day but we could bring awareness to his experience and the impact it was having on his thoughts and on his body and like Laney offer to walk beside him.

Each staff member is careful to say goodbye to all students and to communicate that they will see them the next day. Again, this is a repetition of intersubjective experience of enjoyment and delight so that the student experiences as many times as possible this new self-experience. Until he was asked to stop, given safety concerns, Mr. Hepburn would race each bus down the road, waving as the bus overtook him.

After Children Leave

After taking care of our students' brains all day, the end of the day is reserved for adult connection and brain care. We take at least 30 minutes to debrief and discuss individual students or group dynamics to inform the structure for the next day or days. We also reflect upon our own experiences throughout the day. Holding our student's fears and vulnerabilities can be very hard on us as their home lives remain unpredictable or their past experiences are so hard. Supporting each other is crucial to our own capacity for self-regulation. As adults, we may have had big emotions about what was happening in our interactions with students. When we are so invested, our feelings may be hurt by rejection or angry words directed at us, and we need our colleagues' PACEful support to de-personalize the experience. As a team, we are very playful, and laughter is a big part of every day. We practice PACE with each other so that we can keep our vagal systems in that open and engaged place, keep our important bridges maintained so that we can access resources optimally, and can return the next day ready to help our students organize their less mature brains. We stress that our own oxygen masks must be put on first, and the connection time at the end of the day is an essential part of being able to do that.

This connection time is not easily found in a regular school system, as teachers are busy with their individual workloads and run from school to their equally busy family lives without much time for reflection. Our hope is that once we realize the importance of maintaining our own brains, this opportunity for collaboration and connection can be built into all school systems and seen as an essential ingredient of effective teaching.

10
Meeting Challenging Behavior with PACE

This chapter explores some of the common behaviors and emotional themes that children who have experienced abuse and neglect bring into the classroom. We provide some examples of how we have used the Dyadic Developmental Practice framework to understand what might motivate these behaviors and how then to manage them. We encourage readers to read Sarah Naish's (2018) book *The A–Z of Therapeutic Parenting, Strategies and Solutions* for further resources on understanding what motivates children to behave a particular way and how to respond in ways that maintain our connection to the child.

STEALING

This is a challenging situation. It is one that can have real-world ramifications as our students age and is a behavior that typically gets adults activated and children's freedom restricted. Consequences are laid in an attempt to "teach" kids that stealing is wrong and needs to stop. We don't think we have met a child who doesn't know stealing is wrong, at least cognitively. So why does it happen? Sometimes it is an impulsive desire to have something. Sometimes it is a longing to have something that other children have and they do not, perhaps a way to fit in. Sometimes it is a strategy to create distance in the relationship because the growing attachment or sense of dependence is too frightening. Children know it's a sure-fired way to make others angry at them. Other times it is for need: food, drinks, and money are taken because the child doesn't have enough. Sometimes the reasons are hard to understand as the child seems to have all that they need but still steals.

As with other behaviors, we have to be curious about the underlying intents and motivations. Applying a consequence for stealing without understanding the underlying reason can lead us into a game of Whack-a-Mole, where we may curb the stealing, but another challenging behavior takes its place because we have not paid attention to the underlying emotional experience.

When children have lost the ability to trust the adults in their lives to provide physical and emotional comfort, they become self-provisioners (Baylin & Hughes, 2016). They may not trust that the enough in their environment is truly enough or they think that it may disappear at any given moment. That hippocampus just makes it so difficult to see that the new reality is a safe one. Adults also struggle with a child who steals because it is so hard not to personalize it. It may feel like a betrayal following all that the adult is doing to try to care for the child, an "all I do for you and you repay me by stealing from me?" moment. As soon as we personalize the child's behavior, our amygdala will kick our circuitry into self-protection, and the result will be disconnection rather than a maintenance of connection that the child so desperately needs.

Maintaining PACE when we feel under attack is so very difficult, and we may need others to co-regulate our own affect so that we manage to do so. Curiosity is perhaps the best place to start as empathy for the child who took $50 or their classmate's snack may not be easy. Recently at Belong, one of the students took small toys from the classroom. When we noticed, we approached him and told him we had noticed that he had been taking toys and we wondered "How come?" We did not ask him whether he had been taking toys as his automatic response would have been to say No! Never ask a question to which you already know the answer, best to state what you know so you minimize the likelihood of a power struggle. Our student was able to say eventually that he was taking the toys for his brother to play with. When we were curious about why his brother needed these toys from our class what came out was that he wanted his brother to have a small thing to hold when his parents were arguing. Perhaps for him, the toys represented the safety he felt at school and he wanted his brother to have the same relief. We were then able to have empathy and wonder how he might solve this problem without stealing from the classroom. Understanding in this situation was enough, and no consequences were required.

Other times consequences may be necessary, especially if the stealing has harmed a relationship. Increased supervision is typically the first place we start so that the child is not given the opportunity to steal and get into trouble. The supervision again is offered as a way to help a child rather than "punish" so that we can work together to understand the stealing. We then try to make consequences reparative. If one student has harmed another, we wonder how they are going to make it up to him. We might say something like this:

I think your friend is now going to find it hard to trust you and we are going to need to help him understand why you stole from him. It is going to take a lot of courage to apologize so you let me know when you are ready and if you need any help figuring out what to say. I am

*going to stay very close to you in the next few days to make sure that you keep working on
your friendship and that you are not tempted to take his toys again.*

This, however, is the last stage of the process. If we skip to consequences or reparation too soon, arousal levels are too high, and the child cannot yet access circuitry
that will allow for reflection, empathy, and problem-solving.

What happens if the student does not reach empathy or understanding? There are
still consequences that occur. Again, it is really important to not to rush to consequences too soon as they will elicit an escalation in an already aroused nervous system.
It is hard to wait, as we have the sense that if we miss the window for consequences,
we miss the power of them. This belief is based in the behavioral model that sees
immediate consequence or reward as necessary to ensure the association between the
behavior and motivator. If not immediate, the salience is lost and power to change
diminished. However, for most of us and certainly for our students who have developmental trauma, no consequence needs to be immediate unless it is a life or death issue.
We must build the bridge back to the cortex through co-regulation of their affect if we
are to have any chance that a consequence is understood and implemented. Discipline
means learning and learning can only occur if we first calm the arousal system.

So, what might consequences look like for a student who may still be in defense
mode and not yet in the place where he or she is collaborating in the process of
repair? Putting our own oxygen mask on first is the first step, as when we consequence in anger we rarely get it right. Not insisting on compliance when cortisol
levels are still high is the second step. Then we set a limit or consequence with PACE.
It might sound something like this:

> Ben, I think you will be upset with me because I am going to give you a consequence
> for stealing money from me yesterday. I think I might understand why you took it, but
> stealing is never ok. You will need to work in the classroom to re-pay me the money
> you took. I will check in with you later to see what jobs you can think of that would be
> appropriate. Don't worry if you can't think of any as I have some ideas. I will check in
> with you after lunch.

This allows the student some time to think rather than being put on the spot and risk
shame or anger in response to an exertion of authority, but makes it clear that there
will be a consequence. Increased supervision is also a consequence but phrased in a
way that communicates that we don't want the child to experience failure rather than
as a way to ensure the child feels punished. It may sound something like,

> Ben, I think you are really struggling right now with not taking things from your
> friends. We have to figure that out because I know you know stealing is not ok! In the
> mean time, I want you to stay really close to me so I can help you with that temptation
> and make sure your friends don't get mad at you. You have had enough trouble in your
> life, you don't need any more. Maybe as we are hanging out today we can think about
> why you find it so hard not to take your friends' stuff.

COLLECTING

We have noted over the years that our students are big collectors, and that the need for collections can occasionally extend to stealing. Rocks, eraser tips, Lego heads, sticks, crayon shavings, and acorns are just some of the items our students have collected while in Belong. The focus can change from week to week, sometimes it depends on what we are interested in as a full class and other times it's completely child dependent. When our kids have been able to explain their thinking about collecting, we usually have one of two reasons. First, collecting is a way of owning something. A way of having something of their very own that can be kept with them at all times—during school, on the ride home, and safely stored at home. The items might not make sense to others, but for the student, items are specifically chosen and cherished, and they bring a sense of order when there may be little stability in their lives. For many who have been through the foster care system, clothing, toys, stuffed animals, and pictures have been lost in transitions. Collecting things gives a sense of control and comfort.

The second reason is that students want to keep things that are given to them, particularly by staff. It is a way for them to hold the relationship and the experience that went along with the item. For example, one of our students collected multiple items over his time in Belong. His collecting would escalate when he was experiencing stress. At one time, his caregiver informed our staff that she had found several half-eaten McDonald's cheeseburgers under his bed and was curious about why they would be there. Our student wasn't going to eat them but he wouldn't throw them away. His foster mother also found wads of gum stuck in different places throughout his room. His collecting to that point had been odds and ends, but this was entering into an area that had hygienic implications for his home. Rather than remove the items immediately and lecture him on the perils of rotting food in his room, his caregiver let us try to figure out what was behind this particular collection. We began by letting him know we knew about the half-eaten cheeseburgers and the gum and were curious about it. At this point, we had a strong trusting relationship with the student, and although it took us a couple of days, he did let us know that he didn't want to throw them away because they were given to him by staff. The cheeseburgers were part of a birthday celebration for a student and the gum was given to him to help with his very long ride home each day and, more importantly, was given by his favorite staff member. He explained that he had mixed feelings about throwing them away. First, he did not want to waste it, and second, he felt like he was betraying staff by throwing out a "gift."

We met him with acceptance and empathy, and then curiosity about where those feelings might have come from and how they related to his many transitions in foster care. After we had wondered together over the course of a few days, we started to address the need for a limit on the amount and type of items he was collecting given hygiene issues. We allowed some time to think of a solution. His new foster parent understood the need for security behind his collections and offered him a possibility.

Every couple of weeks they have a bonfire where he is given the opportunity to add things to the fire or keep them. He started to let go of crumpled pieces of paper, sticks, and wrappers and to keep things that he was not yet ready to let go.

SWEARING

Swearing is another problem in the classroom. Adults tend to find being sworn at insulting, disrespectful, or a challenge to our authority. Many a power struggle has occurred when we instruct a child to stop swearing or when we provide a conse-quence for every swear word. Swearing is actually a regulating right-brain activity along with storytelling. A good swear word (or few) tends to make us feel better, at least in the moment!

Putting our own oxygen mask on first is again the first step. As we have already mentioned, we are not a fan of time-outs for our hurt students, but are big fans of time outs for adults in order to get themselves regulated. We have all given consequences in anger, and they are typically overly punitive and most often non-enforceable. Being regulated ourselves is the best chance to regulate our student. Children are likely to reflect the arousal level of the adult in the room. Once we are regulated, we go back to our PACE framework. Acceptance reminds us to see that the child is doing the best they can and to accept the emotional experience that led to the behavior. The swearing is a communication about something that we need to understand. Curiosity reminds us to ask, *"What is this all about?"* Empathy for the struggle that child is having in this moment reminds us that it's not fun to be upset and not something our student would willingly choose for himself. We may start first by matching the vitality of their affect matching their energy with our voices, facial expressions, and gestures, and then gradually slow our prosody and calm our nonverbal messages. Children remarkably follow us from the high energy to low. If we interact with the child at the level of behavior (swearing) then we will most likely enter into a power struggle and miss the opportunity to organize their emotional experiences. When we respond only to the behavior, we risk communicating that the relationship is conditional.

Swearing is a big part of many children's lives. Some use it to test the strength of a relationship or to shock. Children who have expressive language difficulties often fill in with a swear word and don't think anything of it. Other students may start to swear when their arousal levels rise as a signal that all is not right. With these stu-dents, their swearing flows freely and we may often be surprised at some of the words and terms that they know at such a young age. They may be imitating what they hear from their parents or in their community, or for many, through the movies, video games, and music videos they are watching without supervision. Sometimes swearing follows feeling shame. Better to be angry and have people focus on your words than on your mistake. Perhaps it is a habitual shield to keep people away from their painful vulnerability. What we do know for sure is that once a child is aroused, telling them to stop swearing and use their words is an impossibility. The bridge to their cortex is completely washed out. They can't access any other words. Their defense system is fully on and we need to decrease the arousal if we are to get any cleaner vocabulary.

Like other big behaviors, we meet swearing with acceptance, curiosity, and empathy. We also make it as boring as possible. Students have learned that adults get upset with them for swearing, and for our hurt students, anger in others is expected. Anger signals are clear and unambiguous, and therefore are preferred over neutral, novel, or ambiguous signals. We like to give them a response that is not expected. When we can surprise them, there is the possibility of something new. We then get curious: "I notice that you like to swear a lot. What's that about?" One of our students would almost compulsively swear under his breath, every time his mother was unwell. We would then be able to provide him with empathy for how hard it was for him to worry about his mom when he was away from her at school. As we were able to name and organize his worry, he had less need for swearing. If we had given him a consequence for his swearing, he would have been left alone with a very big worry and continued to believe that he should tackle the world by himself.

Sometimes swearing is directed at peers or staff. Again, the swearing itself is not given a consequence, and the focus is on helping the student regain a more appropriate level of arousal. Later, the harm to the relationship is discussed and reparation expected. For example, we may say to a student after his arousal level has decreased:

> Hey! You were really big mad earlier! Any ideas what that was about? You said some pretty mean things to your friends and my worry is that they are probably not going to want to play with you this afternoon and I think that will be hard for you. Would you like some help thinking about how you are going to say sorry and help them trust you again?

Typically, students find their own strategies for reparation, but if they can't, we might suggest a few. If we think that the child's arousal system is still activated, we increase supervision, again to avoid situations that will upset them. Swearing is a symptom of upset. Later, the student will learn strategies to manage their emotions with more school-acceptable strategies, but until that bridge to the cortex is stronger, they will need to rely on adults to help them stay calm enough and swearing won't be needed.

For swearing that feels like a learned pattern of language, we try to discuss being aware of who is around. Many students swear with their friends and stop when the teacher approaches or know not to swear when there are younger children around. If we can teach our students to have the same awareness, we are helping construct that interpersonal bridge, to mentalize about another's experience, and to modulate their behavior (teachers don't like swearing and would rather not hear it), again building blocks of self-regulation.

AGGRESSION

The kids who need the most love will ask for it in the most unloving ways.

—Unknown

Most classrooms and schools have zero tolerance for aggression. It results in suspensions and eventually expulsions. It leaves teachers and peers fearful. Unfortunately, suspensions and expulsions do not work, and students become more marginalized and at risk for further aggression. According to statistics provided by the Ministry of Education, in Ontario, approximately, 2.67 percent of students (over 50,000) were suspended in 2016/17 and 0.02 percent (362 students) were expelled. Almost half of the expulsions were students with special education needs. In Kingston during that time, 882 students were suspended and less than 10 expelled. Ontario's push to develop a positive school climate has resulted in policies for progressive discipline and in attempts to establish safe and respectful interactions in schools. Suspensions and expulsions have halved over the past 10 years, but the issue of violence in schools is currently a priority for discussion both in terms of its impact for other students and for staff.

Because we have the luxury of a high teacher-to-student ratio, we have been able to mitigate most aggressive outbursts by being attuned to any rising upset and a quick offer of proximity and co-regulatory strategies. Acceptance and empathy are our first responses, and when the arousal level has receded enough, we add curiosity. As we have learned, our hurt children move quickly to anger and to physical or verbal aggression because their circuitry has primed them to do so. We can't punish or reward them into having better circuitry, so we have to understand that to build that circuitry requires many repetitions of affect co-regulation. It really helps again to remember that if they could do better they would. It is no fun for a student to be in trouble all the time. They don't "choose" this, even though it may look on the surface as if they enjoy that role or are deliberate in their aggression. The vast majority of students, once the arousal level has decreased, have a lot of shame about the hurt they have caused and fear about what trouble they will be in.

Safety for everyone is of course a priority. We have had on occasion to remove all the other students to the gym or the playground to give the upset student space. Because we have three or four staff, this is a strategy that is easily accessible to us. Two staff stay with the child who is being aggressive to ensure safety. Matching the vitality of the child's affect can be helpful with children who are very upset. Often, we think it is about staying calm and using a calm voice. We do need to stay regulated, but matching the rhythm and energy of the child's upset communicates that we are with them in their upset. They will feel more "felt" by someone who matches in this way, and then the adult can gradually change the prosody, speed, and frequency of their voice, leading the child back to a more regulated state.

Once the student is regulated again, we wonder what must have led to such a big upset and again offer acceptance and empathy. If they are ready, we may use a playful response at this time to further communicate our conditional acceptance and to highlight there is no loss of relationship.

Consequences are again the last part of the process and are stated or negotiated when both teacher and student are calm. They will include cleaning up any mess, fixing any damage, and, importantly, repairing relationships. If we have come to understand what might have led to the upset, we make environmental modifications such as more notice for transition, connections with social workers or parents regarding the stresses at home, or modification of social or academic expectations until the student feels ready for them again.

In our six years, we have twice sent students home for aggression. These send-homes are not seen as suspensions, but are framed to the student as a need to reset and as a worry that if they stay longer in school that their temper will get them into more trouble and that we don't want them to experience any more trouble today. We communicate that we will look forward to seeing them tomorrow. During our connection time the next morning, the events of the upset are discussed and repair is done with teachers and peers. We may continue to offer increased supervision if we suspect that the student's shame is still dysregulating them.

As the student develops trust and starts to allow staff to help them emotionally, we start to offer some possible strategies that they might try. Remember our students have great difficulty recognizing any internal cues that alert them to rising frustration so they go from 0 to 100 in milliseconds, and strategies that are known cognitively are quickly out of access as that bridge washes away. Until the bridge gets stronger, they will need to rely on an adult for help as they learn new strategies. We may offer deep rhythmic breathing as a strategy for calming. Initially we stay and breathe with the student to set the rhythm and to provide the extra support and reminding. Similarly, if we offer the technique of distraction, we first offer it, go with the student to the distraction, and stay with them until they are calm. With many repetitions, we find that students begin to do it themselves. Lending our brains in this way is resource-rich and it will not be accessible to all classrooms and schools. However, understanding that co-regulation of affect must precede self-regulation and connection must precede compliance will avoid setting yourself and your students up for failure.

BRAGGING, EXAGGERATING, AND LYING

These behaviors get students into so much social difficulty. It's not much fun playing with someone who constantly brags or exaggerates. It doesn't foster reciprocity, and leaves peers feeling that they are always put down or that their ideas are minimized or dismissed. Without reciprocity, friendships are not sustained.

Understanding what drives the behavior is essential to reducing or eliminating it. Although it may not look like the child is interested in a friendship, we have found that the very opposite is true, but their deep sense of being unlikeable makes them believe that they need some kind of status or story to make others find them attractive. For others, an alternative reality is preferable to the one that they are in, and they present what they *wish* rather than what they have. We find that correcting exaggerations or tall tales does little to stop them. Naming what we think their intent is and having empathy for the underlying insecurities works better. "Andy, I really see that you always want to one-up your friends. I wonder if you worry that they won't like you just the way you are? That has to be a hard worry."

Often, naming what we see goes a long way to 'tame' the behavior (Siegel & Payne Bryson, 2011). With one student, this wasn't enough, and the Wow game was created. It is essential that the Wow is not sarcastic or condescending but is playful and accepting.

Here's how the game works. To start, our student had said something that we were suspicious about and felt was untrue. For the first example, we knew that he had never broken his leg.

Tyler: "I broke the bone in my leg when I was 4."
Mr. Hepburn: "That must have really hurt."
Tyler: "It did. It broke in four places."
Mr. Hepburn: "Really? How did you do it? (we ask this because it seems plausible so far).
Tyler: "I was doing parkour and I fell off something high."
Mr. Hepburn: "That must have been scary, especially if you were only 4! Imagine a four-year-old doing parkour! What talent!"
Tyler: "I was up on the top of a building as high as the portable."
Mr. Hepburn: (we know this didn't happen so we start in on the Wow game). "I broke my leg too and had to have a cast."
Tyler: (He noticed the staff member jumping in with his own story and immediately reacted). "I had to have a cast too. It went from my ankle to my knee."
Mr. Hepburn: "Mine went from my ankle to my hip."
Tyler: "I had to get mine changed so it went past my hip."
Mr. Hepburn: laughing "That's a lot of cast for both of us. But guess what! I had one cast on and then I broke my other leg and had to get a cast on that one too!
Tyler: (now he's stumped). "No, you didn't!"
Mr. Hepburn: "I sure did! In fact, I was so wobbly with two casts that I ended up breaking an arm too so I had three casts at once.
Tyler: "Wow! You are making this up!"
Mr. Hepburn: smiling, "I was hoping that if I made up a crazy story you would think I was super cool! I was trying to do what you do sometimes . . . tell big stories because I think you think that's the only reason someone will want to hang out with you."

Tyler saying "Wow" told the staff that there he had insight. He recognized that exaggerating wasn't working. By turning it into a game, it allowed the student to safely hear what lying or exaggerating might sound like to a peer. It also allowed peers to listen to the conversation, and since the staff member was talking and being playful, it sounded like a regular conversation rather than a reprimand. The staff member then helped Tyler make sense of what had happened by naming for him what might be behind his behavior.

Often children who have been hurt by others expect ongoing hurt, and lying becomes a very solid strategy for avoiding trouble: "I didn't do it, my brother did it," "I did my homework but I left it at home," or "Yes I brushed my teeth" (despite the toothbrush being dry). When caught in a transgression, the immediate verbal response is "I didn't do it!" The underlying emotional response is likely shame. Shame is so uncomfortable that we find quick strategies to rid ourselves of it. Lying is one of those strategies, as are blame, minimization, and rage. Dan conceptualized these behaviors as shields to protect us from shame. Figure 10.1 helps us understand these very challenging behaviors as adaptive responses to shame.

Lying is hard on adult brains because it erodes a sense of trust. If we can keep in mind that lying is an adaptive strategy for ensuring safety, then we can hopefully be patient. From our chapter on interpersonal neurobiology, we also know that lying is a predictable response to suppression of pain. When we have a strategy that blocks us from feeling pain, we are also prevented from feeling those social emotions like guilt or empathy that would perhaps otherwise guide us to behave in ways that don't upset others.

Once safety is increased and trust is built, the fear of trouble diminishes and lying will no longer be necessary. Also, try to never ask a question to which you already know the answer. It is so common when we find our child or student has lied to us to ask them whether they lied or whether they stole that cookie when we saw them

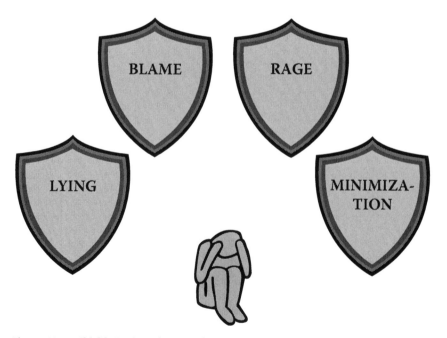

Figure 10.1   Shields Against Shame. Kelcy Timmons.

eating it. Rather than setting them up for another lie, which is adaptive in the face of the adult's nonverbal messages that the child is now "in trouble," be clear about what you know. "Hey! I saw that you took a snack from the basket when I had asked you not to. I wonder what made it hard to wait until snack time?"

Then we can communicate to the child that we intend to understand rather than give trouble and keep the arousal level where a conversation is possible. Understanding may not be enough and a natural consequence may also be needed, but again given with PACE. "I can understand that it was just too hard to wait. You really, really wanted that snack and your brain said take it now! That snack was for snack-time and I am sorry that you will not be able to join us eating cookies together this morning."

Sometimes, our students are so practiced at lying that they are not aware that they are lying and get very upset at our insistence that they are. A power struggle can ensue. It helps to understand that for that student, their lie is their truth, and we may have to communicate that we must agree to disagree. Playing that long game is so important here to recognize that increasing safety will decrease the need to hide behind lying, minimization, blame, or bragging.

> *Tyler:* "I didn't take the toy from John's backpack!"
> *Mr. Fowler:* "I am afraid Tyler that I saw you take the toy. I think maybe your brain now wishes you didn't and expects trouble. Perhaps you think if you can persuade me you didn't do it, I'll stop bugging you and it won't feel like you are in trouble?"
> *Tyler:* "I didn't do it—I told you I didn't! You never believe me!"
> *Mr. Fowler:* "Oh, Tyler it must feel awful if you feel that I never believe you. I think we may need to agree to disagree on this one. I'd like you to replace the toy in the backpack by lunch. If you need help I will help you, but I think you are a courageous boy and will find a way to return it."

Mr. Fowler avoided an argument or power struggle and accepted the child's protest, provided empathy, but firmly set a limit. It is easy to see why we stress putting your own oxygen mask on first as it can be so easy to get drawn into power struggles with children who lie.

RUNNING AWAY

This flight response is something that increases anxiety for all staff members as we take seriously the responsibility to keep our students safe. If they are running away, especially if in a state of heightened arousal, we worry for their safety and our arousal system is preparing us for action. The adage never pursue a distancer is not of great comfort when you have a student who is rapidly increasing the distance and you have visions of them running into traffic. How do we use PACE to manage this behavior? First, we have to accept that their sympathetic arousal system is telling them they need the distance for safety and so pursuit and closing the distance will feel threatening. We must first calm our own nervous system. If you have missed the warning signs or, as often happens, the emotional state shifted in a matter of milliseconds, we are now faced with how to keep someone safe who is scared of us and is too far away for our usual co-regulation strategies to be heard or felt.

In and just outside our classroom, we have tried to create a few spaces to run to that allows the child to hide. However, that plan is not always accessible when arousal levels spike. As we get to know our students, we have found that they don't run far. A staff member will calmly follow them to the yard and sit down somewhere in their proximity and wait, often without saying anything until they feel the child is ready to hear. Once the child shows signs of calming, we start with empathy for the hard time they are having and wondering out loud what might have happened to upset them so. This may not always be so pleasant in the rain and the snow, but we have found that being regulated and understanding the fear behind the anger helps our students become regulated faster.

Sometimes students run so that we will come after them. It is a sign of claiming or caring. If we feel this is the underlying motive, we may have empathy for how hard it is to worry about not being special and how smart they are to test whether we will come for them no matter what. We may then be playful and say something like, "I *think I would come find you if you hid in a basement, a tree, a manure pile*"— basically that the student is stuck with us, but he is welcome to keep testing it out until he is sure.

Obviously, the time it takes to help a student in this way may not be possible in a classroom with only one teacher. This is where it is crucial to be able to call on a team of staff who are knowledgeable about trauma. There are times where we may need to call the police to help us, but in elementary school, these times are rare. If we have enough adult brains to notice, co-regulate the child's affect, and organize the shift in mood, we can often head off big behaviors before they happen. If that is not possible and there is imminent harm, then we might need to close the distance, even if the child is afraid of us and escalates their behavior. In these situations, the repair with the student is essential. We may have to wait until the arousal level comes down and to use ACE to have the difficult conversation.

Hey, you were really mad with me yesterday when I wouldn't let you run off school property. I think you might have wanted to knock my head off at one point! I'm sorry that we struggled. Have you had any ideas about why you were so upset yesterday? No? I was thinking about it last night and had some ideas. Let me tell you what I was thinking. . . . I think sometimes your brain thinks one thing and your body another and its confusing for you. I think you would have liked to stay in class and sort things out, but your body takes over and makes you run away! I think your body learned to protect you like that when you were just a little kid. Of course, when you were tiny you couldn't run, but once you could you would run away from trouble. Smart thing to do. Trouble is now your brain can't tell the difference between trouble like you had when you were little and trouble that isn't really going to hurt you. You just use the same strategy. An excellent one if you were going to get your head knocked off, but not such a good one if someone just wants to help you with your math.

Here, the teacher apologizes for the struggle but doesn't apologize for stopping him as she isn't sorry about that. She then wonders with him about what was beneath the behavior, offers a story that is accepting, and provides a non-shamed based narrative.

Again, giving a consequence with the hope that it will stop the child running away will be futile. His body takes over and he has no control over the flight response. If he could, he would. Our job is to find a way to increase the felt sense of safety so that the running away is no longer necessary. We might, once the child feels safe enough to talk about the problem, start to offer some cognitive behavioral strategies to deal with increased arousal (breathing, counting to 10, or engaging in a relaxing activity), never expecting that a child will know how to self-regulate without lots of supported practice.

NEED FOR CONTROL

Being controlling takes the form of many behaviors, but the underlying emotional experience is fear and the underlying belief is that things will work out better or more predictably if I take charge. There is not yet the trust in adults that the decisions they make are good ones that are helpful. Our students enter Belong with a strong need for control. They attempt to control their environment (I want that desk over there!), their interactions (insisting that play follows their rules or ideas) and others' emotions (physically, verbally, or emotionally hurt us). Power struggles and patterns of mutual escalation are common for our hurt students, and the relentless lack of reciprocity can lead us to blocked care.

Whatever the behavioral ramifications of this need for control, understanding that it is an adaptive strategy for regulating fear can help us stay in our ventral vagal system and avoid power struggles. Curiosity further helps us stay beneath the level of behavior. One of our students insisted that she use a particular pencil for every language task. When she misplaced it, everything stopped until it was found. For adults, a pencil is just a pencil, and there were many others she could have used. What we discovered for her was that it was the first thing she was given when she entered Belong and it was hugely important to her. Just insisting that she use another before understanding and co-regulating her upset was not going to work. Another student insisted that he sit in the same place all the time and he would rearrange furniture and activities to ensure that he could sit where he wanted. When we wondered with him what that was about, he was able to say that he needed to see the door, otherwise he couldn't listen to what the teacher was saying. Once we understood and had empathy for how scared he was, we could offer different possibilities including letting us share the job of surveillance and be in charge of who came in and out of the classroom.

Letting us be in charge is understandably very frightening. We try in many ways to encourage dependence on us so that the students experience that we can do things for them without anger, rejection, or hurt. That may sound counterintuitive to some educators, as the priority is typically to increase independence. However, for children with developmental trauma, independence has developed before dependence, making the balance between the two—interdependence—a real challenge. So we start in small ways to encourage them to allow us to do things for them. We offer to hang up their backpacks, put their outdoor shoes in the right place, help them get dressed, and support them on the playground equipment—even though we know that they can do this or developmentally "should" be able to do this. When they resist our attempts to care for them, we gently label it. *"Hey, I really notice it's hard for you to let me take care of you. How exhausting that must be to always be in charge."* Or we might playfully tease that they need to be the boss and how did they learn those skills by eight years of age when we had to go to school for ages to learn how to be a good boss! We might fuss *"Hey! This is our classroom. You can't be the boss at 8 years old! It's not fair that adults don't get to make the rules in their own classroom. Not fair!"* Fairness is a concept that most latency aged students are all too familiar with, and it can then lead into a discussion about negotiation: when can the child make decisions and when can the adult. This conversation might be a group discussion or facilitated by a book theme.

Staff may also lead students to reflect about their early experiences when adults took too much control and were punitive and harsh, or did not have enough control and were absent or preoccupied. We hope in these conversations to help the child recognize that taking control has been a smart move, but now that strategy is no longer necessary. With repetitive signals of safety, we can travel that bridge between the amygdala and hippocampus to encourage the hippocampus to integrate new learning. If the student can realize that their behavior is adaptive rather than "wrong," we start to reconstruct the shame narrative. Once the behavior is understood and become conscious, there is possibility for change. You can't change what you don't know about.

Accepting that control is a survival strategy and that increasing the sense of trust will lessen the need for it is much easier said than done. The bridge to our own cortices can be easily stressed by the 101 ways that our students resist our caring, our authority, and our opinions and draw us into battles or distract us from what we had initially set out to do or say. Often, as staff, we allow ourselves to be controlled briefly and then playfully notice how skillfully the child has set the agenda. "Oh my! You are so tricky! Did you see how distracted I was? You got me thinking about what you wanted not what I wanted, just like that! So smooth! I'm going to have to work harder on not being tricked by you!" Naming it with acceptance and communicating delight at the child's skill offers a response that is different than the child is expecting, and offers clear safety signals that will hopefully, with repetition, build the sense of trust.

RECEIVING FEEDBACK (CORRECTIVE OR PRAISE)

Receiving feedback whether for correction or praise can be very hard for students with developmental trauma. Given that that is an integral part of an educator's job, how do we understand this reticence and prepare students for receiving the feedback that is crucial for learning.

Correction

It is easier to understand how corrective feedback could make a student defensive. They have not yet learned to regulate their shame around making mistakes. Being told to do something differently or a receiving a correction is equated with being a stupid or bad kid. For a healthy child, struggling with math is simply struggling with math, and they hold onto all of their strengths in other areas. That bridge between emotional states is robust, and they have the regulation skills to know that their global worth is not predicated on whether or not they are good at math. Our hurt students, however, cannot do this, and feedback or correction often tips them into shame where their self-worth is very much tied to the present problem. For some children with quick fight responses, being taught represents vulnerability, a one-down position from which the only way out is attack or defense. Their windows of tolerance are so narrow that any frustration associated with learning dysregulates them. These kids are so challenging for teachers whose job is to impart knowledge as they are thwarted no matter how creative and gentle they are trying to be. The only "safe" interactions seem to be the ones where the child is doing what they want to do and avoiding any challenge. The teacher may feel manipulated into setting lower standards or avoiding constructive feedback, and feel stuck about how to move forward.

We may choose to avoid a conversation until greater safety has been established. We may decide that academic challenge is not yet appropriate, and we allow the child to work at a level below their potential. We will work hard at establishing a relationship with that student through play. One of our students was an excellent athlete, and a staff member made sure to engage him at recess times as well as other times of the day in throwing a football or practicing shooting hoops. As the relationship built, that staff member started to work beside him and occasionally offering some help *"Would you like me to show you a trick about how to do subtraction?"* If our student said, "No!," that was accepted, and there was no further attempt to influence his work at that time. The staff member might add *"No problem, I know when you are ready for more work you will let me help you! I think you think you aren't a smart kid, but I'm smart and I know another smart person when I see one!"* There was no change in the willingness to play with him at recess time, communicating that enjoying him was not contingent on compliance or completion of academic work. Given his strong need for control, if he thought for a moment that completing an academic task was our immediate agenda he would resist.

Educators may at this point be anxious and wonder, "When do you start to insist that a child learns the curriculum?" Remembering that working with children who don't trust is a long game. We also believe that the resistance to learning is a protective strategy, and that the child underneath really wants to learn and be a good student. We might have to wait until he feels safer, all the time accepting and empathizing.

For this student, it took about 2.5 months before he started to show interest in learning. By the end of his first year with us, he started to show pride in his work, asking for worksheets and keeping them in a binder to show his parents when they came to visit the classroom. When he returned to his homeschool, his reading had improved to grade level, as had his math skills.

Naming the struggle is also helpful. A staff member may warn the student that he or she is going to say something that he will find difficult:

> "Hey, I am going to tell you something now that your brain may hear differently than I mean. I think your brain is going to think that I am telling you that you are a dumb kid, but really what I want to say is how hard you are working at understanding something and how happy I am to be teaching you new tricks for understanding. OK, you ready? Let's see if we can trick that pesky side of your brain that tells you things that aren't true. You ready? OK, here is the trick for learning . . . ." We may then check in with the student to see how they are managing their familiar shame-based narrative "How are we doing? is that part of your brain being quieter?"

Positive Evaluation

We often assume that everyone loves praise, and that praise is motivating. When we feel stuck, we may resort to a lot of positive feedback in an attempt to get the student to take the risk and just try something new. For our hurt students, however, it can be scary and uncomfortable. Being told that they have done a good job or an exclamation of praise is so far removed from their sense of themselves that it feels like a lie or a ploy to manipulate them. It might also be communicating to them that the relationship is conditional on doing a good job.

We have in the Western world equated the building of self-esteem with telling students that they do a good job at everything. While we don't advocate never giving feedback or praise, we must be careful to not label something as a good job when it really isn't. Children see when the adults in their lives are just trying to make them feel better about a mediocre or inadequate job. For a non-trusting child, this makes it harder to trust. This tendency to be effusive about jobs well done reflects our increasing tendency to be intolerant of emotional discomfort. As adults, we don't want to make kids feel bad, especially if they have a lot on their plate. We argue, however, that all we are doing is creating increasing anxiety about emotional discomfort, fear of failure, and narcissistic needs for affirmation.

Never giving corrective feedback or praise is not the answer either. We have to be able to tolerate both to be in reciprocal relationships. As with other fears, we start by naming and organizing for the students what we feel might be their thinking or emotional experience.

Lucas, whom you met earlier, could be very rigid in his thinking. He was very clever and often wanted to be right. It was really hard for him to be wrong because it meant he wasn't good enough. Not being good enough was why he thought his parents didn't care for him, why his adoption didn't work out, and why his foster homes just never went quite right. He sought perfection, and this tiring pursuit made it very difficult for him to accept corrective feedback as it automatically meant he hadn't produced something that was good enough. Working with a partner whose answers or responses he felt were not adequate or larger groups that had even more variability in response was so anxiety provoking. This was an area of control that we had to challenge if Lucas was to find any relief from the constant self-deprecating comments or if he was to find a way to have relationships. When he returned to his homeschool, he would have to work with others and he would have to manage feedback.

Because his response to any perceived mistake was immediate and involved a strong temper outburst, we needed to start with acceptance and empathy to help him regulate his arousal. There were no words that would have been helpful for him to hear or that would have convinced him to behave otherwise. Matching the vitality of his affect and the giving of other regulated nonverbal signals gave him the message that his frustrations were accepted and understood.

This is SO difficult for you, so hard! I'm so sorry this is so hard . . . so very hard. . . ." Our voices trail off to invite him to follow us down the gradient of emotional arousal. As his arousal level came down, we then used curiosity to help him be aware of where his frustrations were coming from, as Siegel and Payne say, naming them to tame them. 'I wonder where this needing to get it right all the time comes from? I wonder if it came from when you were a little baby boy who wanted to get it right so people didn't give up on you all the time?

Lucas initially responded with denial and tears, but with gentle persistence, we started reframing his attempts to get things right all the time as strengths, for example, resilience and pursuit of knowledge. We linked his belief that the rejections he had experienced were because he was not being good enough with his drive for perfectionism. We gave him lots of empathy for how tiring it was and how worrisome it was that his performance might never be enough. He started to understand that he wanted to be perfect so that adults would want to keep him and give him a forever home. Who could reject a perfect kid?

Understanding was not enough; we needed to give him practice. We started more explicitly with positive feedback. For him, we needed to remove the words "smart" and "perfect" from our interactions and to replace them with skill-specific feedback. We started with playfulness. Staff would slide sticky notes with a smiley face or a compliment on his work before frustrations were apparent. Sometimes we hid them in his backpack so 3he would find it later or in his lunch box or his shoes. This eventually led to verbal praise being more playful *"Are you ready Lucas? This is going to be really tough. Are you ready? I'm going to tell you something you did well. Here it goes . . . you put such detail in your science report. I learned at least three new things!"*

Corrective feedback was more difficult for Lucas to tolerate. Like with positive feedback, we would warn him that it was coming, and if he became dysregulated, we would sit close to him and offer empathy if he could manage it. We didn't want to get rid of his upset as we wanted to create a new association: upset does not equal rejection or harm and he was not alone. Once he was calm, we offered him our perspective, that he was brave to let himself have these big feelings and to let us help him. Mr. Fowler repeatedly told him that he had never seen a perfect person but that he was always looking, as he'd never seen one and wondered what such a person might look like. Lucas slowly began to tolerate feedback and eventually began to regulate his frustrations himself, stating, *"I'm going to try this again!"* He needed multiple experiences of failing and experiencing that nothing bad happened. Once he got better at tolerating his mistakes academically, he started to explore the possibility that he had made a mistake about thinking his apprehension and adoption breakdown were his fault. When Lucas comes back to visit us from his homeschool, he still playfully asks Mr. Fowler *"Have you met the perfect person yet?"* a sign that this particular trauma is integrated into his narrative in a non-shame-based way.

MAKING MISTAKES

Most of our students struggle with making mistakes as it is tightly tied to feelings of impending danger. For some, making a mistake at home could have resulted in a pinch, a punch, name-calling, or isolation. For most, they have no idea what the mistake was that led to the abuse or neglect just that they must have done something wrong. When they then do something wrong in the classroom, their amygdala expects the same original abuse or neglect, and their sympathetic or parasympathetic systems drive a flight, fight, or freeze response.

One of the first concepts we highlight at the beginning of the school year is that making mistakes is expected and safe. The teacher and staff deliberately and routinely spill things, spell something incorrectly, bring the wrong book to the carpet, or put on two different shoes. We read the *The Beautiful Oops* by Saltzberg, and model noticing mistakes ourselves or having another staff point it out and laughing about it before correcting it. We are very attuned to the students' responses to these mistakes and help organize their experience *"I notice you got really quiet when I spilt the paint. Did you think I was going to get really big mad and yell or blame you for my mistake?"* We want to really highlight that mistakes don't end in adult dysregulation that is frightening to children, and we do this over and over again until the fear decreases.

We then encourage students to make mistakes to see if we can notice them. We playfully guess at what the mistakes might be, before landing on the correct one. Our message is that no behavior will result in harm or loss of the relationship.

This doesn't mean we're always playful about mistakes. It is important for the children to understand that some mistakes can be serious or cause others harm. We focus on what the child's experience was before they made a mistake to explore whether there was any intent, whether it was due to emotional arousal that made it hard to engage in thinking, or whether it reflects a skill deficit. Students are then given practice making amends and repairing the relationship, an essential part of moving them from shame to guilt.

SAFETY

As we established in Chapter 1, physical and emotional safety must be purposefully planned before any academic or relational work can be done. We go beyond school-wide fire drills and lockdowns. We talk about safety in our homes, in our community, and with our caregivers. How confusing for our kids that the people that are supposed to keep them safe are often the ones making them feel most unsafe. Our students need to know that when they arrive on school property that it is the staff's job to keep them safe no matter what. This is no easy feat with children who have spent years not relying on others. We wish it could be as easy as just telling them that their amygdala can now rest because we are on watch for danger or harm. Reassurance or cognitive statements do not translate into feelings of safety. Students have to *feel* safe not be told that they are safe. We start by staying physically close to them and attuned to their affect as much as possible. We note what and who makes them nervous, and when and how they respond, and we do our best to modify expectations and environment to minimize stressors and to co-regulate their upset when they are experiencing lack of emotional safety.

We are careful to remember that our perception of safety can be a student's perception of danger. One of our students hid any time an unfamiliar visitor arrived. It was very important for her to know ahead of time if someone was visiting and why, but that wasn't always possible. If she hid within the class, another staff sat beside her and told her she was safe and who the visitor was. Eventually, her classmates told the visitor that she was nervous and would come out when she felt safe. They started using our language! Each experience of an unfamiliar visitor ended with her seeing that nothing bad had happened. One day while we were gathered on the carpet reading a story, our director of education entered the classroom. He was not expected so there hadn't been a chance to prepare the children. He was wearing a suit and tie and looked very serious. All of our kids visibly shrunk in their seats and looked directly at the teacher, much like babies orient to their attachment figure to decide whether they should be fearful. One student sitting closest to the teacher whispered, *"Is he a lawyer? Who is he coming to take?"* Staff responded to his shift in affect and moved closer to establish immediate physical safety. Deni welcomed the director and introduced him to the kids by his name and position along with a quick description of what his job was in a playful way. He asked to speak with the teacher privately on the porch. Our educational assistant resumed reading the story while she left the classroom. Our director said that he did not need such an introduction, he had just wanted to observe the class quietly. He had not understood the immediate unease with a stranger or the negative association for most of them between his clothing and negative outcomes (being taken away).

Helping the amygdala discriminate between who/what is safe and who/what is unsafe is one of our main tasks during the two years the children are with us. In addition to helping them feel safe with our staff in the classroom and in the wider school community, we discuss who might be safe in their own communities. How to tell who they could approach and who they should avoid?

Some of our students are really frightened of police. Many have had to call 911 to save their mother from abuse or because a parent is unconscious due to substance abuse. Many have witnessed loud and aggressive interactions between adults and police in their communities and have grown up with a visceral mistrust of police: "Police are bad and are not helpful." To reconstruct this belief, we have regular visits from our community police officer. Cassie was visibly anxious given past experiences with police being called to domestic violence incidents. While some of the other students had many questions about her gun, Taser, vest, and baton, Cassie hung back, reading a book in the corner of the room. Questions about weaponry changed to questions about why police had to arrest and hurt people, and over time changed to questions about what classes she had to take to be a police officer and what did she like about the job. Her acceptance of their fears, empathy for how hard it would be for them to feel police were safe people if they only arrested and hurt people, and her curiosity about the work they were doing allowed them to feel safer. As they felt safer, their questions reflected very different curiosities and allowed for respectful and reciprocal conversations that challenged their earlier beliefs. Repeated exposure in this way allowed them to build a different perception and add this particular officer to their safe adult list and consider that other police officers could also be helpful.

A consistent feedback we get when our students graduate is that they know how to ask adults for help. Although our students may struggle with the concept of mistrust for years to come, that ability to ask for help indicates that trust is now developing and they have a different possibility for relationships.

SABOTAGING

As safety develops and children are allowing themselves to be closer in relationships and more vulnerable with us or one another, there is often a sudden behavioral regression or increase in dysregulation. A student who has been doing so well may start to get argumentative, aggressive, belligerent, or distant. For many, this new experience of safety becomes frightening, and there is a sudden and fierce impetus to return to what is familiar and a concomitant desire to push people away in any way that is successful. This can be so disappointing to teachers or parents who have worked so hard and have enjoyed the progress that they have been making. Understanding that this is a normal and expected reaction to building trust can help us manage that disappointment and not personalize it. Change is not usually linear, and there are many stops, starts, and regressions on the journey from mistrust to trust. Our lessons from interpersonal neurobiology also remind us that being close without fear requires a nervous system that is flexible and adaptive. Trauma impairs the child's ability to adapt and change. Although the child may consciously be aware that they want to have relationships and do well in school, their nervous system, which is involuntary, doesn't allow it.

One student, as he began to enjoy and trust the staff, started to complete work (he had never been able to do this in his homeschool) and showed real pride in what he was beginning to accomplish. He also was a gifted athlete and was starting to gain confidence in his abilities with the delight and the positive feedback he was receiving from staff as well as other children. We observed him playing with peers in successful and reciprocal ways. Then one day, he started being really mean to the other students, making hurtful comments, and taunting or rejecting their ideas. His peers at first ignored him, but that strategy seemed to escalate his attempts to annoy them. Eventually, there were tears or verbal fights as his peers voiced their confusion and displeasure at his treatment of them. He also started instigating arguments with staff members, losing the flexibility and more easygoing nature that he had been showing us previously. The climate of the classroom was changing rapidly, and we were worried that the student would damage relationships past the point of repair with his peers. Although he appeared to be mean and uncaring, we knew that what he wanted more than anything was friends.

This student's home life was quite chaotic. He was one of five children, with another baby on the way, and from our family meetings we were aware that his parents' initial enthusiasm for our classroom was waning. We wondered if he was now in a bind. Succeeding at school and positivity for his relationships with staff and peers might have become threatening to his parents at home and perhaps he was now in a loyalty bind? Perhaps this new feeling of accomplishment and pride was so novel and frightening his amygdala and hippocampus refused to let him learn the new state and were pulling him back in to the familiar fight state that precipitated his referral? Adults can become so confused when children avoid or mess up what is clearly good for them. For children who don't trust, they can also not trust that this new feeling will stay. Better to reject before being rejected. Better not to have than have and lose it. The alarm system orchestrates distance between relationships so that the danger associated with need and intimacy is decreased. It is so difficult for us when we experience this sudden and explosive rejection and so adaptive for children who have to manage this fear.

We brought our wonderings to our student. We would like to say that this naming and attempt to organize his experience was enough, but the bind he was in was significant, and although the intensity of his attempts to reject others decreased, he could not find that easy, settled pride that he had found earlier in the school year. We hoped that making his bind explicit might help him organize it. Of course, he needed to choose his parents over us at nine years of age, but maybe now that he had experienced a different possibility he could find it again when he was older and more independent.

LOYALTY BINDS

Helping students deal with such loyalty binds is a frequent occurrence. As children begin to feel safer and experience new relationships, they also become more aware of what *lack* of safety feels like. They begin to ask questions about why their parents haven't kept them safe or continue to interact with them in ways that make them feel uncomfortable. How do we as staff support these questions? First with empathy. These are incredibly difficult questions and bring up many mixed feelings. We then through curiosity and A/R dialogue start to organize explicitly what the student is thinking and feeling, and what the parent might be thinking and feeling. In this way, we are able to co-create a different narrative than the one where the student believes it's their responsibility to take care of their parent or where parent limitations are seen as their fault.

One of our students was struggling with his increasing awareness of how he needed to take care of his mother. His mother viewed him more as a friend and expected him to collaborate in making decisions for the family. He was often the one to protect her from aggressive partners—as best as he could at nine years of age. Prior to joining us, he would often run away from school so that he could make sure she was ok and his help was not needed. When he came to Belong, the distance from his house made it difficult to run away, and we saw a very anxious boy who couldn't settle to learn with the fear that his mother was being hurt. We started to name the struggle he was having and give him much empathy for how hard it was to have this big worry and responsibility. Gradually, we started to introduce the possibility that his mom was an adult who had additional resources than relying on her son for help. We gave him a lot of positive feedback about his courage and strength to take on such a huge responsibility at his age, and began to wonder what his life might be like if he could share this responsibility or get rid of it. As we came to know more of his story and talked about it with him, he started to see that he was just a little kid and wanted to start to act like one. He expressed that he did not want to have to take care of his mother, but was worried about who would look after her if he didn't. Although he was learning to trust the Belong staff and beginning to entertain a different possibility for his role, he remained very careful not to divulge all that was happening at home. His need to protect her physically may have lessened, but his fear that someone would take him away from his mother if he spoke about what was happening at home stayed.

Our program also works with parents so we have the ability to help parents think about how their behavior, past or present, impacts their children. In the same way that we accept that our students would do better if they could, we apply the same respect to our parents. We have not met a parent who has had a child so that they can deliberately abuse and neglect them. Over time, lack of skills, mental health issues, and projection of their own survival strategies have led to difficult parent-child interactions. Although it can be difficult for us as adults to understand why parents harm their children, it is important to be curious about their underlying motives and intents. Often the intent is different than the outcome. For our student who needed to protect his mom, we worked hard to gain her trust and to understand her fears and worries. We connected her with community resources that could be supports for her and could support her to meet her son's needs. We were aware that PACE with her was essential as, like our students, she was being driven by her sympathetic nervous system and was so often ready to respond defensively. We had to make sure our nonverbal signals were clear and unambiguous, otherwise they would be misinterpretated. We needed to send as many safety messages as possible in all kinds of creative ways to help her learn to trust that we had her child's—and her own—best interest in mind.

Some of our students live in foster care and they struggle with their increasing attachment to their foster parent and with what that means for their relationship with their biological parent. Whatever the loyalty bind, we attempt through PACE and A/R dialogue to organize and walk beside them through their struggle. We may not be able to fix it, but by using PACE, we communicate that the child is not alone with their experiences.

SEPARATING ENVIRONMENTS

We recognize that although we work intensively and purposefully with caregivers while students are with us and even after they've graduated, some home environments will not change substantially. This is especially difficult when we see such beautiful potential within the student. We know that when he steps onto the bus and waves goodbye to staff, he prepares himself for another environment that lacks the safety and structure he has come to love and trust at school. One of our students expressed this distinction in environments. He noted that his neighborhood was one that he hoped to "escape" someday, but that while he lived there, he knew he had to take care of himself. We have learned that as much as we'd like to make significant changes within families, it is not always possible.

The focus for us then becomes acceptance and working to make the difference in environments very explicit so that our student can be more aware of what behavior is needed in different environments. Greater awareness has the capacity for better control over our physiological state. If the student can now "choose" adaptive strategies to match different environments, he is at less risk of being hijacked by his nervous system. Having more conscious awareness will allow for better problem-solving and a different narrative than "I am a bad kid." Recently, a clinician shared an anecdote about an adolescent with whom she had built a positive relationship. They had worked together for two years, and the youth had learned that it was safe to share her vulnerabilities and discover more about herself with her therapist. The child unfortunately was charged with assault of a peer and transferred to a youth custody facility. The therapist went to visit and was shocked to experience the change in their relationship. Her client was rude, belligerent, and dismissing of her during the visit—a stark contrast to their previous warm and easygoing interactions. The therapist left very upset and wondering if she had done something to contribute to her client's anger. She decided to return but to ask for a private place to talk. What then became clear was that for her client to survive in this new culture she had to mask any sense of caring or vulnerability. The therapist's acceptance of such an adaptive strategy allowed her client to maintain a sense of safety in their relationship. They talked openly about the benefit of having different ways of responding for different environments, and they both could be grateful that their relationship was an opportunity to take a break from that defensiveness.

Even if change in family or community circumstances is not likely, the conversations about it can help the child be more reflective and aware of why he or others do what they do, and, importantly, is not left alone in the experience.

FOOD

All schools include scheduled times for eating, including breakfast programs where snacks and lunch are available. These are regulated times so that all kids are doing the same thing at the same time. In Belong, the student's relationship to food tells us a great deal about their ability to be aware of and regulate their physiological needs and what their past experiences with this aspect of security have been. We have students who have been denied food, others who have chronic food insecurity, others who were punished with food, and others who hoard food. In our classroom, we allow students to eat when they are hungry. This may mean that a student eats everything on arrival while another waits until the last fifteen minutes of the day to eat. Power struggles around food are avoided wherever possible, but we also plan to help students become more aware of what their bodies need and when. They will also be returning to their homeschool where constant snacking will not be tolerated.

In the classroom, we make fresh fruit, water, juice, and snacks available. We do have a scheduled, although flexibly scheduled, snack- and lunchtime where staff sit at the dining table and eat their food. We invite all students to come to the table for conversation and food if they choose it. We share our food and talk about favorite things to eat and growing food what is on the grocery list later that day. It becomes a time to share experiences about food, and this is often where we might have students open up about being hungry at home or discussions about what being a vegetarian means and extensions to animal welfare. We try to make our mealtimes about connecting rather than eating. With this routine, our students gradually adapt so that by the time they leave us, they are in the regular school routine.

We also celebrate with food and have feasts on occasion. Students are asked what they would like for their birthday lunch and to choose a cake. The staff make sure to prepare it and the student is celebrated by the whole class. At Thanksgiving and Christmas, the class shares a turkey and the students are invited to help with preparing the vegetables and setting a festive table. We always make extra so that food can go home to parents. Field trips may also be arranged to go for a meal at a restaurant. Many of our students have never had this experience, so we try to offer this opportunity to learn about how to order from a menu, and what table manners and social skills are expected.

A caution about making assumptions about celebrations. During our first year, we had asked a student to plan her lunch and cake. She was not able to choose a cake and had asked Deni to choose for her. Following what seemed like a very pleasant lunch of pizza, we brought out the cake with candles and our birthday student became angry and burst into tears. Surprised, the team did everything we could do to regulate her and understand her experience with little success, her mood stayed low. We wrapped up her cake to take home and the next morning learned that she had thrown it across the kitchen. For her, birthdays were associated with a birth mother who had repeatedly said to her that she wished that she had never been born. We had done too much too quickly for this student and made the mistake of assuming that all children enjoy being celebrated on birthdays.

THE BUS

Transportation is a very difficult time of the day for some students. Many have to travel over an hour in a bus and arrive at school quite dysregulated. School bus rides are unstructured and noisy, overload sensory systems, leave the student without the support of an adult to co-regulate their increasing arousal, and are unpredictable, given the many moods and personalities of students. Often, the morning starts with an altercation and being in "trouble."

When we started our program, we originally wanted to limit the drive to school to 30 minutes. Unfortunately, it was difficult to sustain, given moves in foster homes or family mobility. Our recourse was then to elicit our bus drivers into the team. We work with the bus company to ensure the shortest route or smallest bus. We then work to know the drivers and share information about our students that will increase the chance for successful travel. One of our students could not sit at the window as he couldn't tolerate the feeling of having no ready escape. His anxiety would rise quickly, especially if an adult monitor would sit beside him, and lead to a fight reaction. We try to share some knowledge about trauma and how it impacts on children's behavior, and how the bus driver can communicate safety. We teach them about PACE and communicate that we are open for consultation at any time.

Sometimes our bus drivers become additional safe relationships, but sometimes we meet drivers and bus monitors where that working relationship is not possible. Recently, we had one very significant episode of aggression when a monitor did not remember that a student could not tolerate any physical direction. That student would escalate rapidly if he perceived that authority was exerted and he had no way out. Unfortunately, the monitor was badly injured, and it underscored the need for not just supervision but also the right kind of supervision with adults who understand the need for safety and how to communicate safety signals. For some students, we have needed to advocate for alternative means of transportation to limit the possibility of aggression.

We also try to work with our students to be aware of how difficult bus rides are and what could make them easy. We have no technology in our program, but might offer a tablet or a MP3 player to students for bus rides so that they can limit the sensory overload and have something that commands their attention.

Our connection time at the beginning of each school day is an essential part of helping the arousal system relax before asking anything of the student. We meet the student at the bus in an open and engaged stance, and communicate our delight at seeing them. We then often play outside and encourage running, jumping or swinging to regulate their body before coming into the classroom for social and learning time. This may not be possible in a regular classroom, but the understanding that cortisol levels can be very high following a long bus ride and the student is primed for fight or flight reactions can help us reduce demands until cortisol levels have receded. Perhaps there is another relationship in the school that can co-regulate the student's arousal until ready to learn or a quiet corner of the classroom that the child can use to recover.

FATHERS

There have been very few kids in Belong who have had a positive or consistent relationship with their fathers. Some fathers left long ago, some are in and out of jail, others call infrequently or pop in unexpectedly, and others refuse any type of contact. No matter the level of neglect and abuse, we find our students long for a relationship with their father and blame themselves for their absence. They wonder if they had been better behaved or smarter or faster or taller or thinner, that their father would have stuck around.

Their narrative around fathers is typically fragmented. Their mothers often are fearful of telling their child the truth, sometimes out of fear and sometimes because they are trying to facilitate a positive relationship with the father because they know that to paint him in a negative light would not be good for their child. Some of our students have been told that their father had to go away to work or was on vacation to make sense of long absences. Although well meaning, the child is then left with the puzzle of why work or vacation was more important than them.

When we know our student is struggling with this issue, we accept it and use a lot of empathy.

"I really notice that you are thinking hard about something. Is it ok if I make a guess about what you are thinking about?" If the student says no, we accept the refusal, thank him or her for their honesty, and say that we are open for help if needed. If the student says yes, we may say something like *"I think you are worrying a lot about your dad and a bit confused about why he hasn't been to see you lately. It's so hard isn't it to figure out why he doesn't see you as much as you would like."* We then try to engage the child in that conversation *"Do you have any guesses about why he doesn't visit as much as you would like?"* Typically, the child will respond with *"I don't know."* Again, we accept that and wonder out loud some more, *"I wonder if sometimes you think you are not interesting enough or good enough for him to visit. How hard that would be if you think that—such painful thoughts."*

This is an issue that we would work closely with parents about. It is our belief that children need the truth about their lives. Obviously, they don't need graphic details about abuse and neglect, but they have lived through it and know it implicitly if not explicitly. When we as adults ignore it, sanitize it, or minimize it, we are inadvertently causing more shame as what we are communicating is that your life is so bad that even adults don't want to talk about it. Our brains don't like not knowing, so we make up stories about events that help us make sense of them. Our students' stories are typically shame-based: I did something wrong, I am unlovable, no good, a throw-away kid. We cannot leave them with these narratives if they are to be healthy. They need to know that their parent is in jail, addicted to drugs, struggles with their temper, and has hurt family members. We work with their parents to take responsibility for the hurts caused and to communicate to their child that it is not their fault.

We have also had the luxury in our program of having two male staff who are available to model healthy relationships with men. Often the students project onto them their anticipation of harm. This is accepted, named and organized for the student through curiosity and then through empathy for how hard it would be for them to always be worried about being yelled at or harmed. Having an alternative successful experience helps our students over time become more clear that it is their parent who has the difficulty, and not them.

In a regular classroom, there are often curriculum demands that are opportunities for this type of discussion. Father's Day and Mother's Day, or assignments about family trees are difficult for children with developmental trauma. Some students have more than one father or mother, and possibly several foster parent relationships. The stress of whom the Mother or Father's Day gift and card should go to can lead to some highly dysregulated behavior that communicates the confusion and the loyalty binds that the child is experiencing. Recognizing ahead of time that conversations and assignments that recognize parents can be stressful is helpful because then you can prepare yourself and the student for what might be coming. Empathy for the confusion and struggle can help the child feel understood, and curiosity about their experience can help them organize implicit thoughts and feelings so that they can be more fully integrated.

Given the high frequency of divorce and separation, many children can relate to stress concerning parents. Even if a student has not experienced divorce they are likely to have experienced conflict where a limit was set that the child didn't like or the parent was considered unfair in their interactions with their child. Talking with everyone in the class about what we experience when we don't like what our parents say or do gives permission to have worry or anger and can make explicit the thoughts we have (my mother doesn't love me) when we experience our parents as unkind. Our students with developmental trauma may have experienced unkind on the extreme end of the unkind spectrum but will benefit from frank and open discussion about child/parent conflicts at less extreme ends. Teachers understandably feel anxious about wading into commenting on parents' actions or inactions but keeping the discussion to experiences that we all feel when we struggle with our parents offers our hurt students a different perspective. They will not relinquish their shame-based narrative upon the first exposure to a different possibility, but they will have had an invitation to think differently.

11

Lesson Planning

We often get asked how the teacher plans lessons, given the complex profile of each of the students. Part of the challenge of teaching in a specialized classroom is that there is an expectation that students catch up academically. Before coming to us, most of our students spent the majority of their time in the principal's office, wandering the halls, hiding in the classroom, or running away from school. They are often far behind academically. Despite being behind, curriculum is not what they need when they first come to our program. School to this point has been a source of stress, shame, embarrassment, fear, and failed relationships, and they bring this expectation through the door when they arrive at Belong.

As we have identified previously, our first goal is to provide a felt sense of safety so we can prepare them for learning. We approach getting them ready to learn much like we would approach a toddler who will enter kindergarten. We work relationally and from bottom-up of the brain. Many of the activities in the first days and weeks are ones that are play-based and involve storytelling. Through both these avenues, we introduce children to novelty, exploration, discovery, and making mistakes. These are the prerequisite skills for learning and children, with developmental trauma struggle with all of these concepts.

Our role as staff is to stay attuned to their experiences, upregulating positive emotions and down-regulating negative emotions—much as we would do for infants. We use the metaphor developed by Circle of Security researchers—one hand supporting the innate desire for independent exploration and the other supporting the need comfort or limit setting (Powel, Cooper, Hoffman, & Marvin, 2014). Given that most, if not all, of our students have a disorganized attachment, they struggle with both of these hands and need a great deal of practice with limit setting, receiving comfort, and having the confidence to explore their world and relationships.

Play and storytelling are the two main avenues for practicing being held by these two hands and through which we will eventually begin to teach academic content. Staff find out what the children are interested in and join with them, sharing their interest. If they like a sport, we play the sport. If they like collecting coins or Pokémon cards, we learn about that, and if they can only talk about a favorite video game, then we learn about that too. By joining them in their interests, we can assess so many aspects of their cognitive development. For example, we can assess reflective capacity, problem-solving abilities, ability to take turns, ability to manage winning or losing, the capacity to sustain or divide attention, courage to take risks in learning, their vocabulary, and visual-spatial and visual motor skills, as well as their literacy and numeracy skills. We can start to add our own knowledge to assess how they can integrate new information. We ask questions to see whether they can make inferences or understand abstract concepts, and we can begin to "teach" using their interest.

We often play structured games like board games or cards as ways to practice the skills that precede academic demands (e.g., reading instructions, counting the dots on a dice, and following instructions). Outside play may include playing hide and seek, which helps children practice the tension of will they matter enough to be "found" and experience the staff's playful delight when they discover their hiding place. Grounder is a "tag" game that requires staying on the playground equipment to avoid capture. First it is a staff member who is "it." Another staff member protects the students from being caught, communicating urgency and excitement, and providing breaks as needed. So many things are being developed through games such as these: gross motor abilities, eye-hand coordination, and spatial awareness. The key skills we wish to build however, is the child's ability to self-regulate, first through the experience of having their emotions co-regulated and then with more independence.

The staff's attunement and intent to help the students manage is ever-present. If a child gets upset with their friend, a staff member stays beside them and uses PACE to help the child understand their upset, and to offer ideas about how to repair the relationship. If a child becomes overly competitive and struggles to stay in the game if they are not winning or getting their way, again the child is helped to understand what they might be experiencing and is given empathy for their struggle. As their arousal levels decrease, there may be a conversation about what it means to lose or not have control. Managing their emotions in these play activities are ways to practice managing the frustrations that will come with learning.

Storytelling is the other main strategy we use to prepare our students to learn. Listening to stories is the precursor to learning to read. Staff read to the group and to individuals many times a day, often while a child is cuddled up beside them or on their lap, following the pictures and discussing what they see in the pictures or what they think about the story. There is no expectation initially that the child attempt to read themselves if they don't want to. We trust that when they feel safe, they will start to spontaneously read words or ask to learn.

Jack had missed multiple days of school prior to coming to our program. He had witnessed domestic violence repeatedly between his parents and was very protective of his younger siblings. During his first few weeks with us, his eyes were constantly scanning his environment expecting harm. He often flinched when the door opened or when someone came too close to him. Three months later, he was still quite hypervigilant, but had communicated he liked this school because the adults didn't fight. He was never too far from a staff member, but had not yet showed an independent desire to learn. By Christmas, he was noticeably less hypervigilant and had begun to join in group activities. His need to scan his environment had lessened to such a degree that he could allow himself to be interested or engaged in something other than surveillance. Our class has both group and individual ("language just for me") language times. Jack was encouraged to sit wherever he wished during group language times, but during language just for me times, we would pair him with a staff member with whom he was most connected that day. We initially chose books, and started with a book about snakes since he had one at home and would be able to share some knowledge rather than feel vulnerable reading about something he knew nothing about. He was not expected to read or provide written answers, but would be drawn into learning by the staff member's excitement about what was being read. The staff member might model looking up unknown words in a dictionary or comment about things they were learning. Hands-on learning opportunities were created. For example, Jack and the staff member covered a fake textured-snake with glue and let it dry for a day so that the next day it could shed its skin.

The next book was Jack's to choose—a first step in independent exploration. Three months later, Jack asked staff to teach him to read so he could read to his little sister, but still felt too frightened to try reading. Three months after that, he started to attempt to read words, started to ask clarifying questions, and was curious about texts. He could answer comprehension questions by attempting to print or by allowing a staff to scribe for him. It was sometimes hard to be patient and to trust that Jack would take the risks he needed once he felt safe enough. We had to calm our own anxiety about teaching him such an important skill. Although we may have been able to more formally teach him reading skills earlier in the school year, it might have taken just as long to learn and be without the concomitant relational learning.

As students feel safer, we see less physical tension, less reactive or startle responses, and more engagement in classroom activities. We start to see that students start to ask what is happening that day or when they can expect to play a game. These signs of relaxation give us a clue that more traditional academic tasks could be integrated into the day—for example, expecting some reading time with a teacher, math worksheets, or written work. When work is first introduced, we make sure to have a staff member work with a student. We offer to lend our brains to each other many times a day, reminding students that brains that work together are more effective. Staff may read to a child, lead a discussion based on what is being read, scribe, or offer a trick or strategy for organizing ideas.

One of the hardest things for Deni to adjust to was her anxiety about waiting to teach curriculum. She struggled with knowing that the children would be returning to home schools and needed to learn like their peers. She felt so responsible to the children, families, and home schools, and worried that without learning, these children would have further disadvantage in their lives. What becomes clear, however, is that our students are nowhere near ready to learn and that we have to give again ourselves permission to play the long game. Being settled enough to learn can vary in time for each child, but it is not something that can be rushed or moved along on an adult's wishful timeline. Our first year with students is about establishing trust, safety, and routines, and by the end of the year or sometimes sooner, they begin to show greater curiosity, pride in their work, and a willingness to take risks, knowing that they might get it wrong but nothing bad will happen.

Many of our initial activities are hands-on and based on their interests. This may require spontaneous lesson planning! For example, when a couple of students expressed an interest in King Tut, it led to some quick planning of an Around the World Unit that started with Egypt. We made things together, including masks, pyramids, hieroglyphics, and Egyptian food. We didn't expect a lot of written output, but we did read together, watch travel videos, and have discussions about why people would want to go to Egypt. We discussed how Egyptian culture was different from our way of life, and how there were so many different cultures in the world. This turned into looking at our world map (always a favorite anchor in our classroom) and choosing other countries that piqued their interest. By the time we were done, we had learned about Italy, Mexico, Kenya, Australia, and Portugal. They had passports and suitcases to hold all their treasures, and proudly took them home to share with their families. This unit integrated geography, social studies, art, and language, and, importantly, stretched a growing sense of safety. Students could move from the security of their own backyard or city block to exploration of a wider world.

At other times, we may plan from an off-the-cuff comment. For example, one of our boys lost a button from his shirt and we asked if he wanted us to sew it on for him. He was thrilled that we would do that. We noticed that he looked extremely interested in the process, so we paused and asked if he wanted to take over. After a moment of hesitation and weighing whether or not he could do it, he agreed to try. We showed him how and then let him continue. He did a beautiful job and the button held! Since he enjoyed sewing so much, we wondered whether he would be willing to try other similar activities. We introduced knitting, looming, and weaving. He did a brilliant job at all of the activities and was proud to bring home artifacts—he knit a beautiful scarf, loomed a tiny blanket for his sister, and weaved a decorative coaster. His classmates were observing how this student was excited by what he was making. They were also observing that he got frustrated at times, made mistakes, unraveled his work, and started again—without anything bad happening. They too were able to take the risk to try. The knitting became a great time to have hot chocolate together and talk (they thought it was an "old lady" thing to do while knitting). Everyone weaved coasters, and when the students studied Kenya, they sewed them together to make a quilt. Looming was a little more challenging, but was a great group problem-solving exercise!

Having a smaller class and the permission to play a long game allows for spontaneous and creative ways to introduce curriculum. Many of our academic lessons are tailored to individual and class interests, but they will incorporate the main concepts outlined in ministry curriculum requirements. Curriculum expectations are modified in breadth and depth, depending on the student. We are exempt from teaching French as a second language and do not formally teach drama. Given our small class size, we have the luxury of following interests for longer periods of time or exploring tangents related to a topic of learning. We have additional topics we teach that are not found in a regular classroom-learning about the brain and the impact of stress on brain development, what core beliefs mean and how they might be changed, or the importance of relationships to being well. We also try to incorporate mindfulness and yoga into our routines.

LESSON PLANNING THAT INCORPORATES SOCIAL AND EMOTIONAL LEARNING

In many specialized classrooms, social skills or topics related to mental health are taught as separate subjects. You will have seen in our previous chapter that we are constantly helping our children through PACE to understand their behavior and manage their relationships, and that it is integrated into everything that we do. There are some more explicit exercises that we might use to develop our students' knowing about themselves and others. A few of these are provided later in the chapter.

Our teacher typically engages in cross-curricular planning so that the emotional themes that interfere with learning are purposefully and intentionally considered. Our structured flexibility protocol may mean that the concept of "planning" is dynamic. Although we may plan to address fear of taking risks through a particular activity on Friday, a conversation that happens after a story on Monday or an interaction between students on Tuesday may require us to make use of that opportunity even if we are not fully "prepared." Our in-the-moment learning takes precedence over our planned curriculum.

Deni recalls one of those times:

"It was the Friday before Thanksgiving long weekend. We had prepared a Thanksgiving lunch together and were just waiting for the turkey to cook. We settled in for a story to help pass our time—Bear's Thanksgiving by Karma Wilson. It's one of her many wonderful rhyming books featuring gentle woodland creatures. Everyone seemed content as I read the story, and our affect by all accounts was well regulated! I anticipated that we would read the story and then move right to lunch since everyone was hungry. One word stopped my plan. Grateful. One of the kids asked what the word meant and I asked if anyone else knew. One of the boys said, "It means thankful." I paused and consciously made the decision to delay the turkey and expand this conversation. I asked, "Does anyone have something they are grateful for?" One of our new students said, "I'm grateful I was adopted." It took great bravery and trust to share that with the group. She hadn't shared it to this point, and she probably wasn't expecting the supportive response she received from her classmates. This then led to other things the students were thankful for, and the planned ten-minute story turned into a thirty-minute talk that included some hard memories for several of the students and the recognition that they were now in a different situation. This was a reminder to me that entry points for discussion can occur at any time, a validation that flexibility is always needed, and an understanding that opportunities for reciprocal dialogue that expands a student's understanding of themselves can be more important than an arbitrary deadline or an adult priority. The turkey waited . . . what was important was allowing for time and space to explore their thoughts, the experience of joint attention, and intent to understand. Our food didn't burn and we all enjoyed the afternoon together—with an increased intimacy.

This story beautifully illustrates the concept of structured flexibility. The student's discussion of their experiences in the past and present—that was then and this is now—is a sign that the hippocampus is allowing for new learning.

We still, however, need a structure and activities that allow us to develop both academic and emotional learning. Planning for the first month includes an overarching framework for establishing physical and emotional safety. Our first month prioritizes social interactions so that we can allow the students to experience playfulness, acceptance, curiosity, and empathy many times a day without the additional challenges of academic learning. Staff play with the students at recess, providing structure and reciprocal conversations and mutual delight. While the weather is nice, we spend as much outside time as we can playing different sports and games.

We try to use the "yes . . . and" rule of improv when playing with our students. So many of our students are reactive to the word no, and play can easily be derailed by limits that start with "No!" or "Stop!" The "yes . . . and" principle helps us avoid power struggles. If a child asks to climb a tree, we say *"Yes, and I am coming with you to test whether the tree is safe enough for you to climb."* Or if a student wants to go outside to play ball in the middle of math class, we might say *"Yes, you certainly may after you have finished that page of questions. Would you like help to make sure you don't get distracted and then you can get out faster?"* Our brains respond so much more favorably to the word "Yes," so we try to use it as much as possible!

Of course, sometimes the answer must be No. We deliver "No" with empathy *"I'm so sorry that you are not allowed to do what you want to do right now, it's tough to hear no isn't it?"* or with playfulness *"Oh No! Here comes the word that you really don't like to hear! Are you ready? No, you aren't? Maybe if I say it in German? Japanese? Russian? What if I whisper it in your left ear? Right ear?"*

Providing a response that the child is not expecting can often circumvent those power struggles. Sometimes a No will quickly send a student into an angry or aggressive outburst, despite all efforts to avoid upset. When your survival depends on control, someone thwarting it will be a threat to survival and will require a big response. If we have missed the precipitating cues and we end up with a child who is dysregulated in this way, we have to accept this is the best he can do right now. Our job then is to help him reduce his level of arousal so that we can start to wonder what makes hearing "No" so hard and can begin the process of helping him understand that adaptive nature of his behavior and how it is connected to his early frightening experiences rather than to his belief that he is "a bad kid."

Being with the children, playing, talking, and listening, allows us to teach social skills or emotion regulation skills online in real time. We do not have a set time of day to present children with information regarding social and emotional learning in lecture format. As we mentioned earlier, our students are skilled in telling us what they should do or should have done. They need the most help when their arousal levels are high and the bridge to their cortex is rickety. Lending the child our brain allows them to regulate faster and be open to using strategies such as breathing, visualization, and meditation with our help—co-regulation before self-regulation.

There are ways, however, that we plan to draw the children's attention to their inner world or to help them explore how their thoughts and feelings or past experiences impact on their day-to-day functioning. We have provided some examples of some of the lessons intentionally planned to target either social or emotional themes. These activities are designed to generate discussion among the students and allow staff to engage in A/R dialogues.

Sunglasses Activity

This is a favorite activity. Deni usually starts by reading a text that highlights how kids see themselves versus how others see them. Some good texts to use with this activity are *A Pea Called Mildred* by Margot Sunderland, *Stand Tall Molly Lou Melon*, or *Ferdinand the Bull*. These books highlight both the concept of self-perception as well as how others might perceive us. There are three parts to this activity.

Day 1: Read the text and introduce the chart paper that outline some core beliefs (see table 11.1). We might include "I'm unworthy," "I'm ugly," "I'm no good," "I can't learn," and "People are bad" and ask students to add more if they are able. We then discuss how each one of the core beliefs can color how we see ourselves and situations. Students, when they feel safe, are able to acknowledge which of the beliefs resonate with them and how they see them operating in their lives. This is usually enough for one day. They are being introduced to concepts such as unworthiness and shame-big feelings. It is often an important realization that others have the same beliefs and feelings, and lets each student know that they are not alone.

Table 11.1   Core Beliefs

• I'm unlovable	• I'm stupid	• I'm boring
• I'm not good enough	• I'm ugly	• I'm worthless
• I'm bad	• I'm abnormal	• I'm undeserving

Core Beliefs

Everyone looks at the world differently. Two people can have the same experience, yet have very different interpretations of what happened.

Core beliefs are the deeply held beliefs that influence how we interpret our experiences. Think of core beliefs like a pair of sunglasses—everyone has a different "shade" that causes them to see things differently.

Day 2: We review the chart and the students are asked if anyone has anything else they'd like to add. Each time we do this activity, we are amazed at the thoughtfulness and insight that students have. One student asked to add "silenced" to our chart. He explained that he wants to say how he feels at home, but he always has to be quiet; he can't speak about what he wants or needs. In fact, he went further and said that while speaking to his father on the phone, his dad told him to stop talking about his new class. The student said his father doesn't want him to learn, and that he made him be silent about something he was excited about. We meet this painful insight with empathy. There is nothing we can do to fix his father's belief, but we can make sure that our student feels supported in the painful realization that his father cannot share his excitement. Another student asked that the word "numb" be added because he often didn't know what to feel so he just sat in a numb state. When examples are given or new beliefs added, it highlights that there is a sense of trust developing. We are in awe of how much courage it takes for our students take the risk to let us know more about them.

Once we make additions, we discuss the internal states and feelings that are associated with core beliefs. Perhaps the feelings come first, perhaps the thinking comes first, but we discuss the bi-directional impact of hard feelings and negative core beliefs. We then introduce how they impact our behavior. If we feel that we are not good enough, how does that impact making friends or learning?

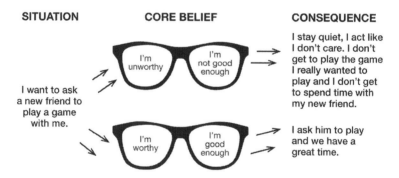

Figure 11.1   Core Beliefs: Sunglasses Activity.

We then ask the students to list on their paper all the things they feel they are good at. Some students have a difficult time with recording anything positive. Some may have a long list but become aware that their attention is on negative core beliefs rather than on positive accomplishments. This is an important building block for later development of cognitive behavioral strategies. We cannot use strategies if we lack the awareness of our inner world.

The students are then given a pair of sunglasses and asked to color in the lenses with colors that represent the feelings they have. They create a legend for their colors and corresponding feeling states. When they are finished, staff meet with each student individually to have them explain their glasses to ensure that they have communicated how they see themselves to their satisfaction and to make sure we are understanding. We have found that students are very honest during this activity and are interested in knowing themselves better. This particular activity is a way to expand their awareness of emotional states, which is typically narrow (happy, mad, and sad), and to build sturdier bridges between emotional states. Often, they add in adjectives rather than beliefs, but every word is accepted and explored to help the child and us understand their inner world more deeply.

Day 3: The child's glasses are attached at the top (or one side) of a blank piece of paper and held by the teacher. Next, a blank pair of glasses is given to each student along with the name of a peer. The goal of this step is to have each student identify how he/she perceives their classmate—does he see him as lonely most of the time or as disappointed? Does he see her as happy half of the time and mistrustful the other half? It is key that no one knows who is completing each pair. It is also important when planning that consideration is taken to ensure that two peers that really dislike or mistrust each other are not paired. This doesn't mean that the glasses are all positive and are laced with nothing but compliments, but we also don't want students to be crushed as they are taking the risk to make themselves vulnerable. We meet quietly with each of the students to again ensure we understand what they are saying so that it is clear for their classmate. If we're unsure, we'll ask for an example. The glasses are handed in and each pair is added to the student's piece of paper and set aside.

The final step is for staff to complete the third set of glasses. This is how we see the students. Sometimes our staff work on it together, and other times we might each complete the activity for two or three individuals. We use the same color scheme the student chose for their glasses and then use new colors to introduce different things that we see. This is another example of "yes . . . and . . ."; we see the loneliness and the sadness and the jealousy that the student sees, but we also see other qualities. The "yes," communicates acceptance of the child's perception and the "and" introduces new possibilities, something we see that the student doesn't see yet. This third set of glasses are attached below the peer perception. When all three glasses are complete, we ask each student to find a quiet place in the room with space to be comfortable and have privacy. Staff move among them as they look at their glasses. It is always amazing to watch their faces as they realize that others see them differently in some ways and the same in others. We have had students cry and ask, "But how can you see bravery and worthiness in me?" This allows us to engage in A/R dialogue to further their understanding of mixed feelings (how can someone be brave and worthless at the same time) and begin a challenge to their core beliefs that continue to compromise their learning and experiences.

As a final step, staff print additional things we notice about feelings, core beliefs, or behavior on small sticky notes and place them on their paper with the three pairs of glasses. For example, sometimes I need to slow down and read all instructions; I'm happy to play on my own; It's important to me that people think I'm smart; I really want to have friends; I love to play video games; I can be a good support to others; I am really curious; I like to learn; I worry other kids won't like me; I have a hard time trusting new people; and I get worried when I don't know something. The student is asked to read them privately and told that if they agree, they can stick them back on their poster. If they don't agree they are encouraged to rip them up and if they are not sure yet, they put them in a corner on the back of the paper to consider at a later date. This part of the exercise encourages the student to be more self-reflective, lets them experience that others can be wrong in their perceptions, without it resulting in the loss of a relationship and expands the intersubjective experience.

This is an activity that can easily take a week to complete and is one that students ask to repeat throughout the year or to return to and make adjustments. The first part (self-perception) is also a great activity to complete just prior to graduation and then compare to the glasses they completed in their first year in the program. There is always a remarkable difference in core beliefs.

You're Such Rubbish!

Many of our students feel that they are no good, throw-away kids, and one of the ways we tackle this feeling is to address it explicitly. The book *Ruby and the Rubbish Bin* by Margot Sunderland is used to introduce the discussion. The story is about a girl named Ruby who feels that she is rubbish and thus belongs in a rubbish bin. Luckily, when we were considering exploring this tough feeling, the Trashies™ characters and, more importantly, the trash cans they came in were readily available to use for this activity. We start by reading the book together and discuss the parts that stand out for the kids. We talk about examples of when they feel like "throw away kids." While the kids are talking, another staff member writes down their statements on a chart. All staff stay attuned to the student's verbal and nonverbal signals to ensure that they don't become overwhelmed emotionally.

Once we finish our discussion, the staff ask students to choose a garbage can and a piece of clay. Their job is to decide if they feel like rubbish sometimes, all of the time or never. We have yet to meet a student who says never. Then they make themselves out of the piece of clay—quite often they make themselves into creatures or blobs rather than a person. They sometimes don't see themselves as kids at all. Next, referring back to the chart if needed, they write on pieces of paper the things that make them feel like rubbish. The staff are readily available to help them write if they need help. Once written, they are encouraged to tear or crumple the statements. Many of the students put their body into the trash can put the paper reasons on top and then close the lid.

We keep our collection of garbage cans for "garbage pick-up" day. At that point we take the garbage out (the paper) and staff says something like "*Hey, there is a kid in here! How did this kid get into the rubbish bin?*" Since we have had a chance to look at what they've written, we see common feelings among them all, and are able to name them and talk openly about their shared experience. The hope is that the students will realize that they are not alone in their feelings. Students may talk more about the events that have made them feel so horrible and experience empathy from the staff as well as their intersubjective experience of their courage to talk about such hard and painful events.

Once we are finished our discussion, a staff member will provide empathy to all the students "I'm so sorry you have all felt like garbage at some point. You certainly have had lots of hard things happen or heard lots of things that would have certainly made you wonder if you were loveable or special. You may not see it now, but we see you a bit differently." Staff then say something positive about each student as we pull him/her out of the garbage can. We leave the cans in an easily accessible place so that if they ever want or need to put themselves or part of themselves back in they can. If that happens, staff will be spend some individual time with that child, using acceptance and empathy, and then curiosity, as they wonder about what might have happened to activate the core-belief that they belong in the garbage.

Timeline

At some point in every student's academic career, he will be asked to complete a timeline. It's not a big deal for most students but is a very big deal for students who have experienced relational trauma. They don't know how to tell their story as their narrative is so fragmented. Times and events are often mixed up. Events that occurred long ago are presented as having happened last month. Other big events (e.g., a change in foster placement) are not depicted on the time line. When attention has had to be on survival, the student cannot yet develop the neural circuitry that allows for reflection on the events that occur in their lives, cannot orient between past, present and future, and do not have the executive functioning skills to sequence and organize life events. Even if they do have some of these executive functioning skills, the shame attached to certain events makes it very difficult to share with a teacher or their classmates. Often a student's arousal levels will flare as they wrestle with wanting to please the teacher or fear that they will get into trouble if they don't comply alongside the fear of communicating events that are so filled with shame and unresolved trauma or loss.

Before we work on personal timelines, students will have already learned about the features of a timeline by reading and listening to books that include them. We look at how they're used in nonfiction texts (i.e., the timeline for the sinking of the *Titanic*) and in biographies or memoirs to see the more personal aspects of a timeline. The teacher then introduces the book *The Day the Sea Went Out* by Margot Sunderland. This is a story about a critter who has a relationship with the sea. The waves come in with the tide and disappear when the tide goes out. One day, the waves don't appear as he expects. He waits and waits, keenly feeling the loss of his beloved sea.

The concept of timelines is reintroduced and connected this time to the waves that have disappeared in the story. We talk about the difference between calm and rough waters, walking in ankle deep water and trying to swim in deep water, and how each might feel. This leads us into looking at how our lives might be represented by rough or calm water, big or little waves. We start to plot our lives as if it were the sea. The higher waves represent hard times or tough interactions with people, while the still water represents times that felt calmer. The students are encouraged to include as much or as little detail as they wish. Staff move among them and support as needed. Some students have far more waves than others. Waves can range in size and shape, and sometimes they are separated by space. The waves help the students visually see events and the progression of those events in their lives, think about how they might have felt differently in rough or calm water, explore what was happening for them or in their lives at the times of significant events, and experience the organization of their narrative through shared experience, curiosity, and empathy. Some examples of timelines are depicted in the figures below.

Figure 11.2 Examples of Timelines to Build Coherent Narratives. Provided by author.

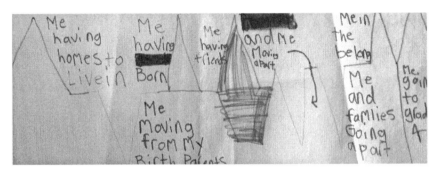

Figure 11.3 Examples of Timelines to Build Coherent Narratives. Provided by author.

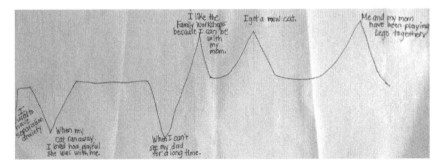

Figure 11.4 Examples of Timelines to Build Coherent Narratives. Provided by author.

Preparing for Transition (graduation)

All of our students are anxious about transitioning from Belong. They have so many worries and are able to identify the biggest ones (usually around friendship), but sometimes are more private about other worries. To help start the dialogue, we get our graduates thinking about the upcoming transition. This allows staff to identify as many worries as we can so that we make them explicit and they are not alone with their worries. By the time they are ready to transition, we are able to problem-solve *with* the student rather than *for* them, and we can generate possible solutions to all of the identified worries.

As a collaborative activity, we begin by drawing a door in the middle of a large piece of paper and on the door, it reads: "How I think I will feel walking out the Belong door on the last day of school." The graduates pick a different section of the paper. They can use pictures and words—whatever they wanted to express their feelings. Here are some of their thoughts. . . .

> "I feel much happier than when I first came here!"
> "I will be heart broken when I leave our class."
> "I will miss the people." When asked about a picture he drew as he articulated this thought, he responded, "Mr. Hepburn has wings because he is a superhero."
> "I will miss all the extra help I get."
> "I want to watch my new class first, so I know what to expect."
> "It's hard for me to tell my new teacher that I have a hard time sitting at the carpet with a group."
> "I will worry about Mrs. Melim, Mr. Hepburn, and Mr. Fowler when I leave. I want to know they are okay and I want them to know I'm okay."
> "I want to make sure that I understand the lessons."

A student who was not graduating also wanted to share in the experience of the graduates. He anticipated what he might feel and said, *"I'm staying next year, but I am already thinking about how it will feel when it's my turn to leave. I think my heart will break and I will cry. But what I like about my first year is new friends. I think I am stronger and can handle things better."*

Follow-up activities focus on specific worries and specific coping strategies. The student develops a list of things he or she might do to tame their worry. This may include the typical cognitive behavioral repertoire of relaxing, breathing, and visualization, but also importantly includes when to ask for help.

Feels Like . . .

This activity is presented as a flip booklet (see figure 11.5). We usually work on this after we've completed the sunglasses activity so they have a good sense of core beliefs and some of the harder emotions attached to the beliefs. The flip book is easy to create ahead of time with "feels like," "sounds like," "looks like," "smells like," and

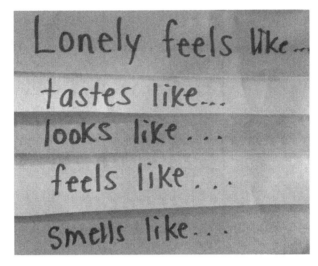

Figure 11.5   Activity to Help Students Develop Reflective Capacity. Provided by author.

"tastes like" already printed. The student chooses the belief or emotion that resonates most with them and then completes the book.

Examples:

LONELY feels like . . . an empty home
Tastes like . . . nothing
Looks like . . . sad love
Feels like . . . empty
Smells like . . . dirt.

AFRAID feels like . . . being trapped in a box
Looks like . . . people fighting
Smells like . . . lots of smoke
Sounds like . . . a loud booming jet engine
Tastes like . . . being thirsty and there's nothing to drink.

EXCITED feels like . . . tense muscles
Sounds like . . . a concert
Looks like . . . jumping up and down
Smells like . . . chocolate
Tastes like . . . strawberries.

This exercise helps students further develop reflective skills. It is similar to Dan Siegel's SIFT game that helps individuals become more in charge of where they allocate their attention and develop the skills to be mindful. To answer the questions, students have to look both inward and outward and have to integrate past with current experience. Many important highways and bridges are being traveled with the outcome of strengthening the self-regulatory set of bridges.

One of our students had such a traumatic history that, despite being a very intellectually bright child, he had no capacity to describe emotions. Listening to his classmates play with this exercise allowed him to listen to emotional language and experience others' curiosity about internal experiences. Over time, he started to participate and be present with his emotions rather than to immediately dissociate.

I am Pharaoh, Ruler of Egypt. These Are My Rules!

We usually use this activity while working on our Egypt unit. The students understand what a pharaoh is and that he gets to make all the rules no matter what. We tie this into their experience with adults by having them pretend they are a young pharaoh and they can make as many rules as they like. The kids are asked to choose an adult that must follow their rules. The following are some examples of answers that our students have given, which gives us an insight into what they are thinking about and wishing to change.

Examples:

Dad has to tell me why he left.
Stop doing drugs.
Eat well.
Sleep well.
Four hour movie night.
One hour dinner time with me.
One hour gaming time with me.

Dad has to see me every other week without cancelling.
He needs to get a job that he can stay at.

For mom to get a house.
Get more money.
Get a car.
Come to my house more to see me more.
Nan to listen to my mom and talk to my mom more.

Stop fighting.

I don't want my step-dad to leave.
If he drives somewhere, he has to come back.

I want my mom and dad to not fight and get together again and live with me and
my brothers and sister.
Have a happy life and be happy.
P.s. I have been in five homes in CAS
P.p.s. My sister is ---. I think that's her name.
P.p.p.s. My brothers are --- and -----.

Making the rules for the adults in their lives helps us understand what our students
wish for. Although we may not be able to grant their wish, we can provide acceptance and empathy for what we too would wish for them for there to be less stress
in their life.

Given that we have regular contact with parents and have monthly parent workshops, we can bring the children's wishes to the adult's attention. Recently in a parent workshop we asked the question, "What do you want from your child?" Answers
included things like respect, truthfulness, happiness, and to have manners. We then
asked, "What does your child want from you?" Answers were initially funny (a new
x-box, money, and to let him do what he wants whenever he wants) perhaps reflecting the discomfort or shame of being needed and failing to give what was needed.
As arousal levels settled, the answers became acceptance, to feel safe, to play, and
time. We then looked at the barriers that were preventing us from giving our children what they needed from us. The two biggest barriers were fatigue and finding
time to give time. Parents then began playing with the idea that their own histories
made it hard for them to believe that they were anybody that people would want to
spend time with, and the barriers were actually adaptive strategies to protect from
their own painful feelings of inadequacy. Although we encouraged parents to look at
something they could do to free up time and discussed self-care strategies that could
decrease fatigue, we knew that change would be less likely if parents did not feel the
acceptance and empathy from us about their own shame, and find the curiosity to
discover why barriers are there for them and the intersubjective experience that communicated value and respect for their courage.

Parents are often surprised by how much their children notice, and are often
motivated to change more for their child than for themselves. We work closely with
parents to connect them with additional adult services that might support them with
addiction, housing, or mental health issues that are getting in the way of what they
want for themselves or their child.

Paper Dream Catcher

Paper dream catchers (figure 11.6) are a fast way to "catch" thoughts and worries.
Sometimes students are asked to put things they worry about or don't like inside
the dream catcher and more positive thoughts, or things they are excited by, on
the outside (see figure 11.6). Other times they might reflect on what they can or
can't control. It depends on the group. Once they've written the harder or more

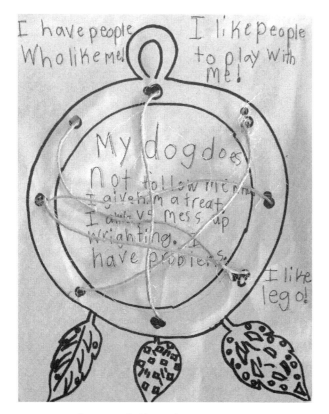

Figure 11.6   Dream Catcher. Provided by author.

worrisome information inside the dream catcher, they color the frame (if they want) and then trap the thoughts and worries with string.

Below are some examples of what students have written.

- Inside: Sometimes I fight when I play with people; I don't like my rules at home; I have trouble learning to read.

    Outside: I love to hang out with my papa; I love school because I have friends here.
- Inside: If I don't get a computer, I'm not happy; I get scared that I'm not going to get computer time (at home); When I'm upset, I feel like I'm going to have a heart attack; I feel sad.

    Outside: I love my cats.
- Inside: My dog does not follow me when I give him a treat; I always mess up writing; I have problems.

    Outside: I have people who like me now; I like people to play with me now; I like Lego.

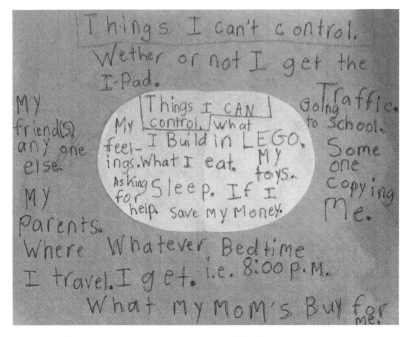

Figure 11.7　What I Can and Can't Control. Provided by author.

This same exercise might be done in a number of different ways. The goals, however, remain the same. The exercise offers the opportunity to develop reflective capacity, to practice mindfulness and discuss worries in a way that integrates them into a more coherent narrative. Figure 11.7 is an example of one student's representation of what he can and can't control.

Upstairs-Downstairs

We use the resource *The Whole Brain Child* by Dan Siegel and Tina Payne Bryson to help students understand what happens in their brains when the amygdala takes over. As a science class, we look at brains, sculpt brains out of paper maché, and learn about how different parts of the brains are responsible for different feelings and behaviors. We teach the students about how fight, flight, or freeze responses are a result of the brain's job to protect us from danger and discuss the brain's tendency to overgeneralize: it will keep you safe even when you don't need it to. We identify how those 3 F's have many different forms but are adaptive and necessary to protect them from harm. Student's name different parts of themselves, for example, Rock brain, Bossy Betty, Jokester Jeff, and Calm Carl (characters from Michelle Garcia, Winner's poster), and talk about how different parts of themselves pop out given different emotional experiences. Knowing the science and reason behind certain behaviors really helps our students develop a less shame-based narrative, and to develop a more realistic perspective of their abilities and limitations.

Each student makes a poster or Lego figure to represent what happens when the upstairs of their brain, which is the planning and doing, gets disconnected from their downstairs brain, which is responsible for their feelings and for keeping them safe (see figures 11.8 and 11.9). They are asked to reflect on what internal or external events precipitate flipping their lid, again encouraging their ability to control their attention and develop their reflective capacity. The acceptance of all internal and external cues communicates that understanding and relationship take precedence over behavior. Curiosity helps us expand a child's understanding and lead us into possible strategies for preventing flipped lids or to repair once the lid is flipped.

Figure 11.8　Lid Flipping. Provided by author.

Figure 11.9   Lid Flipping. Provided by author.

Tell It to Me Straight . . .

Recently, Deni started to introduce group time to develop self and other awareness. She had noticed that the students were not skilled at reciprocal conversation. She wanted a way to help them practice listening to others, add to a conversation rather than control the conversation, and to practice staying on topic. She also wanted to prepare for upcoming writing instruction and hoped to build a bank of topics for the students to write about later that term.

Initially asking direct questions resulted in suspicion and a reticence to answer. To make it less threatening, our teacher came up with "catchy" titles and started with questions that were not personal in nature. *Would You Rather Wednesdays* started with . . . Would you rather chocolate or vanilla milkshakes next week? Some other examples included:

Made it Monday—What's the coolest thing you ever made?
March break Monday—What was one thing you did on the break?
Travel Tuesday—If you could travel to any country in the world, where you go?
Top it off Tuesday—What do you like to top off your icecream-sundae?
Tickle me Tuesday—Where are you ticklish?
Theme Park Thursday—What theme of amusement park would you design?
That Darn Groundhog Thursday—What do you predict the groundhog will tell us this year?

These nonthreatening ways of starting a conversation allowed the students to practice communicating their wishes, thoughts, and opinions and listening to others. The staff would respond with acceptance of their ideas and often delight providing safety for the child. Students will not take the risk to communicate and explore their own ideas and opinions without this sense of safety. As the children started to feel comfortable engaging this way, the staff started to occasionally add questions that were potentially more emotionally challenging, for example, *Weeping Wednesday* . . . When was the last time you cried and why?

Sometimes the staff expected a silly or matter of fact answer to a question, and were surprised by how the group offered more emotionally vulnerable answers. For example, in response to *Fix It Friday*. . . .What do you want to fix that is broken? The staff expected the students to talk about broken toys or games. Instead, a student stated, "*I wish I could fix my mom and dad's relationship.*" Another student added "*I wish my mom and dad would get along, but I don't know how to fix them.*" The other four students declined from answering the question, which was unusual. Up to this point, all the students had answered questions and looked forward to this part of the morning routine. Students are always given the option of adding their answer later in the day if they need time to think. One student later whispered to the teacher her answer and gave her permission to write it down.

Perhaps later that day or week, the teacher would help the students make sense of their experience with this question. The teacher may say "*I really noticed that Fix it Friday was a tough question. It seemed to make some of you very thoughtful and some of you uncomfortable. Do you have any ideas why it was tough?*" Students may or may not have an answer, but the attempt to understand can help the students be aware of their emotional experience and perhaps reflect on it. The staff may help the reflection by offering some of their own ideas. For example, a staff member may say "*I wonder if sometimes it feels like big people problems are just not fixable and it makes you both sad and mad.*" or "*I wonder if you have tried and tried and tried to fix some things in your family and when it doesn't work you worry that you are not smart enough or maybe you even worry that you are the cause of these difficulties your parents have.*" The students may want to take the conversation further or may not be interested. Either decision is accepted.

Some of the questions encourage the student to ask questions about someone else, helping them practice initiating conversation but also the practice of curiosity, which is often a skill not yet developed. *My Teacher Mondays* was a topic that invited students to be curious about the staff.

My Teacher Monday . . . What is one thing you want to know about Mrs. Melim, Mr. Hepburn, or Mr. Fowler?

Why do you take so many pictures of our class?
Where have you traveled?
What hair colors have you had?
Why does Mr. Hepburn support the Habs?

Sometimes questions encourage collaborative problem-solving such as *Find the Pattern Friday* . . . I'm going to the beach and I'm bringing a PIG, GIFT, and TOY, what are you bringing? They worked together to figure out the pattern (last letter of word is the first letter of next word), and then continued to play the game by taking turns to offer an answer.

Samples of Questions and Answers That Elicit More Personal Information:

Magical Monday—if you could have one magical power what it would be and why?
 Teleportation—I could get away when I am scared
 Invisibility—I could hear what other people are saying and I could hide
 World famous magician—I could trick people
 Fastest in the world—I like to run
 Hit a baseball across the world—I would be strong
Merry Monday—where are you merriest (happiest)
 School
 Ice rink (at school)
Tell Us Something Tuesday—What is one thing most people don't know about you?
 I can look like a crazy person sometimes
 I can hack a candy machine
Try It Again Tuesday—What would you like to try again?
 I wish I could try to skate again because I gave up at first
What Age Wednesday—If you could be any age what would it be and why?
 One, so I can grow teeth again
 100, so I can die and meet my Nan in heaven; she died from taking the wrong drugs
 Twenty, so I can buy an M-rated game
 Ten, so I can wear a crop top
 Fourteen, so I can help my brother with his girl problems and he can help me with my boy problems
Weeping Wednesday—When was the last time you cried and why?
 I couldn't fall asleep because all the other kids were so noisy and I was so tired.
 I cried when my fish died.
 I cried when hot gravy from my poutine spilled onto my belly and burned me.

One Word Wednesday—What is one word that describes how you feel right now?
Happy
Tired
Mixed
Mad
Normal

Throw It Out Thursday—if you could throw out one thing of an adult's, what would it be and why?
Dad's money, unless he gives some to my mom (he never gives her any money)
My foster parent's bed (when asked about this further, she said she wanted it for herself)
My mom's phone, so she'd spend more time with me
My dad's work schedule
My papa's CNN; he watches it too much

Take Over Thursday—If you could take over anything, what would it be?
My house!
Our principal's job
I want to be in charge of all dogs
I would like to take over my parents and be their boss

That's It Thursday!—What do you find frustrating?
My mom's boyfriend and all his kids
Being sick
When my iPad dies when I'm playing it

Take That Back Thursday—If you could take back something you said or did, what would it be?
I wish I didn't tell my dad's wife I don't like her because that's how I lost my father
I wish I didn't take my sister's slime away because then she cracked my video game
I wish I could take back what I did to get grounded
I wish I didn't run away from school

That's Love Thursday (it was Valentine's Day)—How do you know when someone loves you?
When they say it
They give you kisses
When they smile
They have kind eyes
When they give you a hug

Friendship Friday—What is one thing you look for in a friend?
Smiles
Likes to play
Kindness
Being nice
Dependable

As the students move from mistrust and suspicion to trust, the answers to these questions reveal more about their emotional experiences. We also see more sophistication in their ability to articulate their experiences, listen empathically to their friends, and sustain their attention while the whole group is offering their answers. We also see increased motivation to take risks and explore their own and others' experiences. One day, Deni didn't write a question on the board. All the children noticed and were concerned that they wouldn't have the opportunity to engage in the activity and demanded that she write a question.

The given examples are more deliberate ways into helping our students become more aware of why they do what they do and why others do what they do. There is no way that our students can utilize cognitive behavioral strategies until they have developed a better connection to their inner world and find a way to know and describe their thoughts and feelings. These activities are ways to do so, traveling and strengthening bridges between the right (emotion) and left hemispheres (language and explicit memory), vertically between the brain stem (awareness of sensations), limbic system (feelings) and cortex (planning, organization, language), and between memory systems—explicit and implicit—expanding awareness of emotional states and past-present-future orientation. As you will have already realized, the introduction of such activities are predicated on first having the experience of safety. Introducing them too soon will result in superficial results or dysregulated students. Online learning precedes more formal cognitively biased exercises.

A word about technology here. Many IEP's will recommend the use of assistive technology. We have stayed away from technology use in the classroom given the priority for the establishment of healthy relationships.

Why is limiting of technology important to us?

TECHNOLOGY AND ATTACHMENT

As we have learned in part one of this book, our brains are social organs and require attuned, repetitive, and reciprocal interactions with our primary caregivers to allow them to develop the neural circuitry that form the basis for attention and emotion regulation. Good attention and emotion regulation are important for mental health, doing well at school, and forming positive relationships. We now live in a digital age where the required attuned, repetitive, and reciprocal interactions are limited or interrupted by technology. Both parents and children are increasing their use of smart phones and tablets. Although technology can be useful and beneficial, the irony is that in a more "connected" age, we are actually not engaging enough in the face-to-face contact that builds the neural circuitry that allows us to be successful in relationships and other cognitive and emotional skills.

More than 50 percent of parents allow their babies and toddlers to use a phone, 1:7 for four or more hours a day. Ninety percent of modern two-year-olds use a tablet (Hourcade, 2015). We have I-potties and I-bouncy chairs, where infants and toddlers are "entertained" by a screen, not by the conversation and companionship of their parent. When traveling, eating dinner at a restaurant, or waiting for a bus, children and parents are engaged with their screens and not with one another. By age eight, 96 percent of children have watched TV, 90 percent have used a computer, 81 percent have played console video games, and 60 percent have played games or used apps on a portable device (cell phone, handheld gaming system, iPod, or tablet). This is not unusual, given the access children now have to technology; however, the amount of time spent on these devices for children 8 years to 18 years is on average seven hours and 38 minutes a day (Rideout, Foehr, & Roberts, 2010). This is on top of the screen time allocated in school. Both American and Canadian Pediatric Societies have come up with guidelines that children under 18 months should have no screen time, 2–5 years should have one hour a day, and for those over 6 years, families should set limits on screen time, prioritizing school, homework, at least one hour of physical activity, social contact, and sleep. Whatever is left over can be screen time, but parents are encouraged to be aware of what effects screen time is having on that child.

As with many of our innovations, the consequences are not always readily apparent. Research is now beginning to ask questions about the impact of our relationship with screens. About 56 percent of parents of young children believe that baby videos are good for child development, and the most common reason parents give for infant and toddler screen time that it is educational and beneficial to children's brain development. There is no research, however, that indicates that programs aimed at young children have any efficacy (Guernsey, 2015; Chiong & Shuler, 2010). There are some studies that show that the opposite is true (Nathanson, Aladé, Sharp, Rasmussen, & Christy, 2014). Young children who interact with e-books actually have more problem with comprehension because they get distracted by the interactive features of the e-book (Bus, Takacs, & Kegel, 2015). Adult interaction with a young child during media use and video chatting is crucial for infants and toddlers to understand what they are seeing (Radesky & Christakis, 2016, Kabali et al., 2015, Strouse, O'Doherty, & Troseth, 2013).

Internet addiction is associated with structural and functional changes in the brain regions involving emotional processing, executive attention, decision-making, and cognitive control. FRMI images show an atrophy of both gray and white matter effecting executive functions and impulse control (e.g., Zhou et al., 2011, Dong et al., 2012, Wang et al., 2015). Volume loss was also seen in the striatum, which is involved in reward pathways and suppression of socially unacceptable impulses (Hou et al., 2012, Kim et al., 2011). Damage was also seen in the insula (Hong et al., 2013), an area crucial to our ability to develop empathy. Compromise in these areas of the brain have negative implications for the making and sustaining of relationships. Other brain changes involve the atrophy of white matter, which translates into loss of communication within the brain, leading to more difficulty making appropriate decisions; reduced cortical thickness, leading to impairment in cognitive processing and overall impaired cognitive functioning; and reduction of dopamine receptors and transporters (Hong et al., 2013). Much of the damage of excessive gaming and internet addiction occurs in the frontal lobe, which has implications for all areas of life.

Not everyone is at the level of addiction, but there is growing awareness that regular exposure (remember that most youth are engaged with their screens more than seven hours a day) is creating damage such as sleep problems, hyperaroused nervous systems, and sensory overload. One study found that infants between 6 and 12 months old had significantly shorter night-time sleeps after exposure to evening screen time (Vijakkhana, 2015). Increased impulsivity, moodiness, and inattention are often seen in children who have regular exposure to screens (Twenge & Campbell, 2019, Hinkley et al., 2014). Physical health problems such as obesity (Cox et al., 2012), posture and respiratory function (Jung, Lee, Kang, Kim, & Lee, 2012), and vision problems are also being associated with increased screen use (American Academy of Ophthalmology, 2018).

Between 2010 and 2015, the number of teenagers in the United States who admitted to feeling useless and joyless, classic symptoms of depression, rose by 33 percent in large national surveys (Tweng & Campbell, 2019). Teen suicide attempts increased by 23 percent, and completed suicides for youth 13–18 years rose by 31 percent. Twenge, Joiner, and Rogers (2016) found that those born after 1995 were much more likely to experience mental health issues than the previous generation. The authors identified the sudden introduction and ubiquitous use of smartphones as the reason, ruling out economic issues, homework pressure, changes in family structure, or substance abuse. They found that teens who used social media for five hours a day were 71 percent more likely than those who spent only one hour a day to have at least one suicide risk factor. Two hours a day seemed to be the point at which risk factors increased significantly. The authors also pointed to the lack of sleep that occurs for teens who are on their phones at night. Not sleeping is certainly a risk factor for depression, and it may be that the lack of sleep is causing the rise in depression and not the smartphone use per se. However, what is clear is that teens spending more time on social media activities are at increased risk of mental health issues (Twenge & Campbell, 2019) and spend less time on activities associated with decreased risk of mental health issues such as face-to-face interactions, sports, and religious activities. It is likely then that teens who are more vulnerable are having mental health difficulties because of the combination of increased smartphone/technology use, not enough actual face-to-face interaction, and inadequate sleep. The rise in depressive symptoms and suicidality was exclusive to females, suggesting that our girls are more vulnerable to the impact of screen use.

Adults are also spending much of their time connected to their smartphone (Felt & Robb, 2016). We only have to look up to see most adults engaged with their phone while walking, traveling, waiting, and eating, even when doing these things with a companion. What is this adult use doing to our children's brains? (See figure 11.10).

In order for children to grow healthy brains, they need those repetitive, attuned, and reciprocal interactions with their primary attachment figure. But what happens when those interactions are repeatedly derailed by notifications from social media, emails from work, and news headlines. What does that infant experience? Dr. Tallie Baram, professor of pediatrics and anatomy-neurobiology at University

Figure 11.10   Lost Opportunity for Communicating Delight and Interest. Mehdi Azizi.

of California, Irvine, and her colleagues used a rat model to study how good but disrupted attention from rat mothers can affect their newborns. Baram placed some mothers and their pups in modified cages that did not have sufficient material for nesting or bedding. This was enough to distract the mothers into running around looking for better surroundings and end up giving their babies interrupted and unreliable attention. Baram then compared the development of newborns raised in this environment to those raised in the normal cages where mothers had enough material to create a comfortable home. When the offspring grew older, the researchers tested them on how much sugar solution they ate, and how they played with their peers, two measures of how much pleasure the animals were feeling and a proxy for their emotional development. The rats raised in the modified environments consistently ate less of the sugar solution and spent less of their time playing and chasing their peers than the rats raised in the normal setting. Their conclusion was that there may be a crucial window in which newborns need to be exposed to certain behaviors from their primary parent in order for their nervous system to develop properly. In this case, the lack of consistent, repetitive, and reliable attention appeared to affect the animals' ability to develop proper emotional connections to help them understand pleasure. Predictable and consistent attention was essential. Given the parallel to human parents and infants in the digital age, researchers are now investigating brain changes in infants in response to maternal attention.

Linda Smith and Chen Yu at the University of Indiana tracked the eye movements of 36 parents and their one-year-old children by using head-mounted cameras. The parents didn't know the purpose of the study. Findings indicated that the longer a parent, and therefore their baby, paid attention to an object while playing, the longer the baby kept paying attention to it, even after a parent stopped. The shortest attention spans in babies were among those whose parents got distracted and looked elsewhere or sat back and did not play along. The ability to pay attention is indicative of success in many areas of life. Smith and Yu, like Baram, are suggesting that the lack of consistent, predictable, and reliable attention from parents is negatively impacting the child's ability to develop good attention skills at a crucial stage of development.

Attachment theory and intersubjectivity theory also underscore the requirement of attuned, reciprocal interactions for the healthy development of an infant's brain. Colwyn Trevarthen, Daniel Stern, Edward Tronick, and Beatrice Beebe have been researching the crucial importance of the interactive regulation and coordination or empathic joining for the development of later self-regulation for years. Infants have the capacity to notice if their partner matches or mismatches their behavior as well as if the mismatch is repaired to a more matched state (Tronick, 2007). Beebe's (2016) work identifies that being seen and "known" is key for the development of a secure attachment. When parents are distracted by their phones, they are not seeing the reactions of their infant and so cannot recognize, match, or repair their dynamic emotional experiences.

Our students who have had developmental trauma have developed circuitry that prepares them for fight or flight, and keeps them in an organization that promotes mistrust and distance from others, which limits the opportunity for mental health. Our students must develop the capacity to be in relationships before they engage in an activity that keeps them out of them. They certainly don't have the self-regulatory capacity to monitor their use and to stop when they feel they have had enough. So many times our students are offered iPads as a way to settle. Given the dopamine surges that occur during screen time, settling comes relatively quickly. When it is time to give it up and go back to class, however, our students protest loudly and the adult and child quickly fall back into a mutually escalating power struggle.

Last year, we arrived back to school in September to see that a *smart board* had been installed. After an initial impulse to send it back, we were able to see its potential use! When we do use it, it is an activity that promotes shared attention. Together, the students interact with videos about science concepts, create power points, or use it as an interactive math center. The children have also watched live feeds of the pandas at the Toronto Zoo before they headed to their new home on the West Coast or reindeer feeding in December or dog teams racing in the Iditarod in Alaska. Sometimes we use it playfully. On cold winter days, we turn it into a fireplace or a beach. Sometimes when we need to move, it becomes a dance center. It has become another way to facilitate our social, emotional, and academic learning.

MINDFULNESS AND YOGA

Mindfulness has become a subject in many mainstream classroom schedules, given its connection with good self-regulation. We again see that students with healthy brains make excellent use of these opportunities, while students who are still operating form lower parts of their brain don't benefit. We have found that trying to introduce mindfulness activities in a subject-like manner creates great anxiety for our students. They don't know how to notice their body sensations or pay attention to thoughts and feelings. Some are truly frightened by silence or a calm environment. They know what to expect from a noisy and chaotic world. Asking them to sit still with their thoughts while breathing in and out feels too frightening. Some are worried that if they close their eyes, something bad will happen to them while others worry that they will look silly. What works for one student is threatening to another making it quite challenging to have a prescribed program for all at one time. We have had to be creative about weaving opportunities for mindfulness into our day-to-day routines.

Stella, a grade three student, was hypervigilant. To ask her to close her eyes or to remain still with her thoughts was too threatening for her. Focusing on her breathing would require that she draw her attention away from her need to be attuned to others. Deni became Stella's safe person initially. She was never very far from her and would for much of the day be physically connected sitting or standing with her back to Deni's front, often bringing Deni's arms around her. She could then watch the classroom from this safe space. It was through this connection that Deni started to find opportunities to engage in mindfulness activities that worked for her. If she changed her breathing patterns, Stella would immediately notice. Deni would then ask Stella if she could match her breathing pattern to hers. Deni would then change her breathing rhythm to see if Stella could follow her rhythm. The next step was to give Stella a turn to lead and notice whether Deni could notice and change her rhythm to match. Playing in this way helped Stella focus her attention on her breath and consciously make changes. While playing, Deni could offer some information about how breath was linked to our feelings, and the two of them could identify different situations where breath might be fast or slow. They then built to the concept that breath could be changed. Deni would ask Stella to think of a time where she was anxious or needed her breath to be activated and then ask her to slow her breathing until she noticed her body could be more relaxed. Initially Stella could do this when she knew it was a game, but not able to use the strategy when engaged in classroom activities that made her fearful. At those times, Deni would go to her, pull her close, and ask Stella to notice and follow her breathing rhythm.

Another opportunity to practice mindfulness arose following the reading of *Wilma Jean, Worry Machine* by Julia Cook. The discussion led to what we do with our worries, and the class very quickly agreed that "It depends." Staff expanded the conversation to worries that were common to many kids (i.e., taking a test or talking to a new classmate for the first time) and worries that were unique to each of them (i.e., worries about dad calling from jail that night or mom living on the streets again). Collectively, the class wondered what could be done with worries that just wouldn't go away. One of the students laughed, *"We can blow them away!"* The staff immediately set about getting water, dish-soap, and pipe-cleaners. The students made different sized wands and were asked to put their small worries into a small bubble and for big worries use a larger wand. They were then asked to use different speeds and types of breathing—slow and long or short, sharp bursts of breath—and also watch what happened to their worry bubbles. Stella piped up *"Hey another reason to have short or long breaths!"* Students were able to notice that when they had slower, longer breaths they could form bigger bubbles, which could float away. This was another game where the students could practice allocating their attention to their breath or to bubbles and could manipulate the outcome.

Reading time is often a time to practice finding relaxation. Each afternoon staff read a chapter book. Staff give the students approximately five minutes to find a place in the classroom where they can stretch out and find a feeling of comfort. Deni waits for everyone to give a thumbs up before she starts the book. Staff may sit beside a child and rub their back or have a quiet conversation if they think they need help to wait until everyone is ready. Deni uses a calm and relaxed voice to read the story. Often the light is turned off. Students now are able to transition quite quickly into a slower regulated breathing pattern. Sometimes one of our boys closes his eyes while listening. A new skill for a boy who tends to be hypervigilant!

Yoga is another activity that is known to help individuals with trauma have more control over their nervous systems. None of our staff are yogis, but luckily there are some great beginner yoga resources. One day, the class were discussing names and who wished they had a different name and why. Deni took out the yoga book and asked students to look through and find a pose that looked like the first initial of their name. They then had to demonstrate it for everyone else to follow. There was some nervous giggling, but soon it turned into concentration. Each student had a turn at being the leader. Then one student asked if they could spell their whole name using his friends. By the end of half an hour, the children had been letters, trees, water, and certain animals. We were able to ask them if they noticed whether they could balance better or worse with different breathing rhythms or on their right or left foot, again a fun way to focus their attention on their bodies and breathing. The team is now working with a yoga master to first experience how changing their own breathing and bodies can change their levels of arousal. They then take this learning to the students. The hope is that our students will develop another coping tool that will extend beyond their time with us at Belong.

Staff spend a lot of time teaching children about their bodies, how different parts function day to day, and how they may be impacted by stress. One unit explored senses. You may have recognized by now that every curriculum lesson is also an opportunity to help make sense of their personal experiences. Smell has a strong tie to memory. When exploring this sense, staff placed a variety of materials in covered jars. Everyone sat in a circle and were directed to take a small sniff at first and when they were comfortable a slower and longer sniff (another chance to be aware of breathing). Once the student felt they knew what the smell was, they passed it to their neighbor without saying anything. When everyone had had a turn, Deni asked the group to shout out their guesses all at once. She then had each student say their guess again and link it to something the smell reminded them of. Some smells reminded them of an activity—sunscreen a day at the beach or a sunburn—and some of more difficult times. Soap reminded some students of times they had had soap put in their mouths for swearing or being rude. Touch was explored in the same way with students being asked to touch things like peeled grapes, noodles, shaving cream, or slime that were in covered containers. Interestingly, this caused much more anxiety. The students were able to explore how faster breathing sometimes communicated excitement and sometimes fear and could link it to what they had learned in science about the nervous system.

Spontaneity and creativity in lesson planning allow us to follow our student's needs and lead them deeper or to new learning opportunities in a lovely rhythm. You can see how playfulness and curiosity is embedded in teaching activities as well as in our interactions and conversations. Deni has become confident that her students will leave us being able to hold their own academically, but more importantly, with skills that reflect more healthy brain functioning.

12

Working with Parents and Community Supports

PARENTS

Working with primary caregivers is a crucial component of our program. When students are accepted into the program, their parents, grandparents, or guardians must agree to being part of the team. We ask them to commit to attending monthly workshops so that they can support what their children are learning in school. We operate from the belief that parents are doing the best they can and want the best for their child. Intentions may not always be reflected in practice, and our aim is to create safety for parents so that they can recognize and lessen the obstacles in the relationship with their child. We offer additional knowledge about child development, some "cool" interpersonal neurobiology facts, how to use PACE to manage behavior, and other topics that are relevant to the children in our class. Our groups also provide a safe place for parents to listen and support each other. In the same way that the students in Belong have experienced a great deal of stress and trauma, so too have some of our parents. Many continue to struggle with mental health and relationship difficulties. Some struggle to hold down a job or to stay in one place for any length of time. Some of our parents may be foster parents or adoptive parents, and have varying degrees of experience with parenting children with developmental trauma. We use PACE with our parents also, and work hard to forge a trusting relationship. In a parallel process, we help them develop their reflective capacity and consider a different possibility for their relationships with their children. There are several elements to our family program.

Everyday

Each day, our teacher communicates with parents or grandparents. This may take the form of sending a photo or text of something positive that their child has said or done. Our parents have communicated how they welcome this type of communication is. For years, the majority of communication with school staff has been negative; a call to come pick up their child or meetings where they have felt overwhelmed, suspensions that require them to be home from work that is not flexible about taking time off, and shame or anger at their child for "messing up *again*." We try as many times as we can to send pictures and positive texts to communicate to parents that their children are succeeding. With repetition, we find that our parent's arousal systems begin to calm, and they don't immediately anticipate threat when a communication comes from school. Quite quickly, the children look forward to school, which also serves to move a negative experience toward a positive one. So many of our parents have come to understand their child's difficulties as a function of something they are doing wrong. They have shame or have come to resent the child's needs for the impact they have on their ability to work or the demand on them psychologically when dealing with persistent behavioral challenges.

Each Week

During the week, our teacher may send a reminder about something coming up at school or a caring inquiry about what might be happening in a child's life if we notice a change in behavior. Our parents are expected to be part of the team, and their knowledge about their own child is respected and valued. Typically, conversations occur by phone or by text but may require a face-to-face conversation. The parent is then invited to pop in after school or our child and youth worker will visit them at home.

Our child and youth worker also may drive a student home once a week and visit with the caregiver(s) to encourage them to respond to behavior using PACE, to ensure that they are connected to services that they need and again to foster a collaborative relationship. Initially, these home visits are more social in nature, a chitchat at the door or a shared cup of tea. Often, they will bring some donuts and cookies, and will focus on telling parents positive and funny anecdotes about their child. As trust increases, the conversations may turn to potentially more stressful topics. For example, the staff member may bring up a fear that the child has expressed during the day or a concern we may have about the parents' stress levels. Parents are helped to see how their own mental health or self-regulation difficulties impact their children's well-being and are offered a safe relationship in which they can begin to address these issues.

Occasionally

Parents are invited in to discuss their child's progress, to discuss stresses and concerns, and to develop a collaborative plan to ensure continued success. If the child is in care, their social worker and the parent's family services worker are also invited to ensure that everyone is aware of areas of growth and areas of continued need. Using PACE, we help parents stay regulated and start with lighter more tolerable topics before moving to more serious issues.

As we get to know the parents, we start to communicate about some of the stresses in their lives that are not directly related to their child's school experience, but nevertheless impact on the child's mood and level of stress. From time to time, the school staff facilitate referrals to physicians or other community services that are necessary for parent success and, as a consequence, student success. Consistent, open communication helps us stay informed of the ups and downs in our families' lives, and as trust develops, parents are able to reach out to us. One parent called us frantic one day because her wallet had been stolen so she had no money for groceries. Our staff drove over after school and provided them with a week of groceries and helped the parent connect with the appropriate resources to re-issue identification. We have parents who will reach out to us even after their child graduates when they need that extra level of support for their child.

Monthly

Parents are invited to have a shared breakfast with staff and students, and then stay for a workshop facilitated by Sian. We just recently moved our shared meal from lunch to breakfast as the students were so anxious on the morning of the family workshop, fearing that their parents would not come and that they would be the only child who didn't have a parent attend. Moving the workshop to the morning meant that parents could come with their child in the morning and anxiety levels could be better managed.

The overall goal of our workshops is to help parents understand the behavior of their child differently and to respond to their children in a way that strengthens rather than weakens their relationship. The focus of the presentation may be an aspect of the PACE model and a discussion of how to apply PACE to stressful behaviors at home, issues that are arising in the classroom, or personal issues that impact on parenting. We may use some of the same exercises that we have used with the children to help parents become more aware of their own beliefs about their child's behavior and where it comes from, and how it may make them feel like an inadequate parent. We might explore their own attachment history and where their beliefs about child rearing emanated from. The ultimate goal, whatever our focus, is to help them develop better empathy for their child's struggles, to de-personalize their behavior, improve their reflective capacity, and find new ways to respond that strengthen their relationship.

In the same way that we don't "teach" social skills to the students, we don't present information to parents in a lecture format. We start with light and playful interactions with parents while we share food, gauging their mood, levels of fatigue, or ability to be present with us. Sian then leads to a topic for discussion, and it is presented in a way that it is something that she has been thinking about that she would like to share, or something the team has noticed about what the children have been experiencing. New information is presented in a storytelling format to maximize the chance that it can be heard effectively and tied to examples of things parents bring up as challenges. Parents are asked to reflect upon how that information resonates with them or how it pertains to their child. We encourage parents to wonder about their own or their child's behavior, with all guesses having equal value. Often the conversation leads us away from the original topic, and we have to be prepared to follow and lead during these times. When trust has been established, we often have parents who take the lead in supporting other parents. The facilitator then sits back and steps in only to guide the participants back to the use of PACE with one another if they stray into problem-solving and provision of solutions before the other parent is ready to hear them.

Follow-up with the teacher and child and the youth worker helps consolidate the skills. A summary of each workshop is written up and sent home with the parents so that they can refer to the information as needed. Appendix B gives an example of information that might be sent home.

Like many programs, engaging parents is not always easy. Often parents' trauma histories make it hard to ask for or receive help. Transportation or procuring childcare is frequently an issue. Sometimes the dynamic of the group works, and sometimes it doesn't. There are often community or family feuds that we are not aware of that find their way into the classroom. During our first year, we struggled with having parents who had such diverse experiences that it made it difficult to find safety together. Given that we were all just getting to know each other, we hadn't had enough time to build the necessary trust. Now that we have been operating for six years, we have parents who graduate with their child, but other parents who are staying for their child's second year. The fact that the parents who are staying have built trust with us and are comfortable with the program goes a long way to help parents who are new to the program.

Over the years, we have become more successful delivering this part of our program. We ensure that at the beginning of the referral process, parents are aware that their involvement is mandatory if their child is accepted into the program. We provide transportation as required to ensure the parent(s) are able to attend. We start the relationship with parents and students well before the start of the new school year, and maintain frequent contact to minimize anxiety and to build trust. Again, the framework of Dyadic Developmental Practice and PACE is crucial to help parents feel accepted and encouraged to be the best parents they can be and to feel that there is no judgment only an intention to support them and their child. Our hope is that by the end of our time together, both parents and children no longer focus on what they can't do but have an idea about what they can do.

During the past academic year, our group of parents developed relationships within the group and then started supporting one another outside of school. Parents became trusting and willing to talk about personal issues with one another in the same way that their children were learning to do during the school day. The network of parent relationships started to allow for playdates and sleepovers, activities that other children had access to, but had not been available to our students.

The success of family workshops is so dependent on the trust that is being built in the everyday interactions that occur between the staff and parents. Safety is established so much faster in the group when each parent is learning that the program is working for their children and that their own struggles are met with acceptance and empathy. Below are some comments from parents over the years:

> Thanks so much for the last two years of hard work you put into my son. I never would have thought we could get over our little struggles until he started your program. He's so much more confident and sure of his decisions.

> In preparing for her son's upcoming transition from the Belong program, one parent wrote, "Realizing it is actually all me that is nervous about next year, which in turn makes me nervous that he'll notice my anxiety. . . . I fully trust you guys."

> Parent—"I am really exhausted . . . can I give you a call sometime today?"

> A parent sent a text after her child opened a small birthday gift from the team when he arrived home "*OMG * loves his gift. He said, 'Best gift ever!' I could cry from happiness!*"

> A grandparent had popped in to drop something off and stood watching her grandchild play with two other students. She stood staring and didn't say anything for a couple of minutes. Staff asked if everything was okay and she said, "I've just never seen him play with any other kids before and I want to watch."

> A parent of a recent graduate wrote to let us know; ". . . had an episode at school today. It was handled really well and, apparently, he used a lot of words he learned through you and your program to express his feelings. I was really proud!"

We often stay in touch with our graduating parents, checking in occasionally with them, or receiving a text or email that communicates both successes and struggles. We have become a secure base for many parents—one hand, to encourage their exploration and independent parenting, and another hand to provide comfort when needed.

Lucas's parents wrote:

> When we first met Lucas, we knew he was an incredible little man who had a really tough start in life. We were committed to help him, but really didn't know how to go about it. We were new to parenting, new to fostering, and new to Lucas. We were fortunate that Lucas was enrolled in his second year of the Belong program. The Belong program and PACE were the foundation upon which we built our new family. Our success as a family, and Lucas's amazing change and development started in that classroom. He came to believe he belonged somewhere and was special and worthy. Once he believed in himself, he started believing in other people and in his future.

We benefited greatly from the structure, regular updates, and constant support. Daily communication between us and the team was encouraged and supported. We were able to share our successes and challenges at home and hear the successes and challenges that had occurred at school. Lucas was then able to learn that he had many adults in his life that were interested and engaged in his life. We think Belong helped Lucas build loving, trusting relationships with adults for the first time in his life.

Monthly meetings allowed us to see Lucas in his school environment. He loved to show us his work and see his classroom. The team supported us through our fears of doing or saying something wrong. They let us know when we were on the right track, and gently redirected us if we were struggling.

Belong helped us better understand Lucas and work with him as he worked through his challenges. We learned so much about him and ourselves. A key learning for us was: "If kids could do better they would."

Lucas graduated from Belong after two years. The team helped him transition to a different school and a regular classroom. They worked with the new school and teachers to help them understand Lucas's strengths and suggested strategies they had found worked—or didn't work—for Lucas. They made regular visits to his new classroom to help him.

Now, even three years later, the folks in Belong continue be interested in Lucas and his successes. Lucas often asks us to share his successes with the team. Mrs. Melim was his anchor, and Mr. Hepburn and Mr. Fowler were and continue to be positive male role models in his life. Dr. Phillips is "a great lady," according to Lucas, and one of the few people he unreservedly trusts. Years later, he still talks about them and things they did together.

WORKING WITH BROADER COMMUNITY SYSTEMS

Many of our students have complex needs and come to us already working with the medical system, mental health professionals, or allied health supports. If not already involved with community supports, we may need to make a referral. Children who are in foster care are supported by social workers who have responsibility for their care. Our team offers to communicate with all supporting professionals if we have parental/guardian consent. Our hope is that that communication is mutually beneficial and that we work together to support the child and family.

Community professionals who work with the child may be invited to attend the classroom for a visit, and are formally invited to any progress meetings or meetings called to discuss concerns. The staff are available to accompany parents to meetings that might be held at the hospital or community agencies. Typically, other professionals do not have the time to come to the classroom, but the offer is always available. Most of the time, we are able to work collaboratively, communicating by email or phone calls when necessary. We often need to access psychiatric services either as a way to get additional information about our students or to ensure that medication is monitored. Some of our students have neurofeedback, occupational therapy, or receive therapy with community professionals.

The biggest challenge we face in our collaboration with community systems is when the family is involved with a professional who works from a fundamentally different theoretical model—most typically a behavioral approach. Our children are not yet ready to work within a behavioral or cognitive behavioral approach. It can be very overwhelming for parents who are hearing contradictory advice and can add stress to an already stressful family experience.

If we find ourselves in situations like these, we use PACE with both the family and professional, naming and having empathy for the frustration that comes when we don't all speak the same language. We all have the same intent—to be helpful. We offer to share our understanding of how developmental trauma impacts our students and what we have learned about meeting their needs relationally. We ask for some more time to get the student ready for their service and suggest that in the meantime the family not receive services that are contradictory in approach. The family is always free to withdraw their child from our program if they feel that another service better meets their needs better. If they wish to have their child in the Belong classroom, we will ask that they withdraw from services that are providing an approach that will not yet be helpful to their child.

One of the ways we try to reduce the possibility of conflict between approaches is to build capacity in our school boards and community resources. Sian and Deni are always available to provide workshops or to attend meetings where we can share what the research is telling us about working with trauma and how we are learning from the successes and challenges of the Belong classroom. We are currently consulting to a number of school boards across the province of Ontario who are experiencing that traditional behavioral classroom management techniques are not influencing their students to settle to learn. There are also community mental health agencies who are adopting Dyadic Developmental Practice as their framework, and their staff provide additional consultations and become advocates for services that best meet the needs of our most complex families. There is no question that behavioral and cognitive behavioral approaches have value. Children who are not yet able to construct that bridge to their cortex are not yet ready for them and will require interventions that will allow for co-regulation of affect before self-regulation.

13

Case Study

There once was a boy named Stevie. He is this kid with blond rock star hair, interesting hats (a purple one in the winter and a baseball cap in the spring), and who reads with amusing accents. Stevie is clever and creative, and has these bright blue eyes that sparkle when he is happy or when he is mischievous. He loves words and seems to have just the right ones at the right time to make people smile. He loves to use words like magnificent and majestic. Stevie is one cool cat (oh by the way . . . he loves his cats . . . and seals).

Stevie seems like he's got it all. He has a mom and grandparents that love him and care for him. He has a home he says he loves and never wants to leave, and he's got some new friends that are true and kind. He has a class where he feels valued and respected and where he's even learned a thing or two. For those who really know him, however, it's easy to see how behind those big blue eyes, there is still some worry and uncertainty.

Stevie still seeks to understand some pretty tough stuff about his birth dad and why he can't see him and he has some worries about his mom's health. He's trying to figure out how to tell people when he is worried. It's tough when you're just a little kid and things are going on around you that don't make sense. Your brain tries its best to figure it out, and many times needs some help to do it. Even adults need help figuring things out sometimes.

This is the beginning of Stevie's coherent narrative given to him upon graduation. It was a two-year process to co-construct a narrative that was less fragmented and shame-based.

Stevie is a boy who struggled with understanding how relationships worked. He had missed at least 70 school days, and had drawn the attention of the school youth worker and the school board attendance counselor. Stevie lived with his mom, Jennifer, and her boyfriend. He did not have contact with his biological father, who had substance abuse issues. His mother didn't feel it was safe for Stevie to have contact with him, but had not explained to him why she did not encourage their relationship. Stevie had made up his own stories, the most predominant one being that his father must not love him.

Stevie's mother was a bright and articulate woman, but she had some significant health and mental health issues. She had had some seizures that had required Stevie to call 911 on more than one occasion. She had significant anxiety that made it difficult for her to go out of her house or to allow her son to attend school or outside activities. Even on the days when she felt better, Stevie would refuse to go to school because of his own anxieties about what would happen to his mother if she were to have another seizure. Jennifer found it too difficult to override his strident protests, so the two would stay home together. Stevie would play video games and his mom would feel shame about her inability to parent her son the way she wanted to. Jennifer had been bullied in school and she was aware that Stevie was being picked on, which was another reason she didn't push him to go to school. Staying home seemed safer for both of them. Stevie quickly assumed control of their relationship, recognizing that his mother was not able to make decisions. On bad days, she struggled to decide what to have for dinner or what to watch on TV. Stevie just started to make the decisions for both of them.

Agreeing to be part of the Belong program took great courage for both Stevie and his mother. Jennifer had to overcome her anxiety to attend meetings. She came initially with her social worker with whom she had a good relationship. She was quiet, tense, and overwhelmed, but she stayed for the two hours of shared lunch and workshop. We met her with acceptance and empathy, and with delight and respect for her courage.

Stevie noticed that his mother came to these meetings. We had recognized quickly that he had anxiety about his mother, but it also became apparent that he had some anger toward her. Initially this anger was outside of his awareness. He was not yet aware of the tremendous responsibility he felt for his mother's safety and how it was the wrong way around. He needed to rely on her and couldn't, and that led to feelings of fear, anger and sadness. His mother's courage to come to meetings at the school and the staff recognizing the bind he was in was the beginning of moving these feelings into his conscious awareness. Once he was aware of them, they could be organized and woven into a more coherent narrative.

As we got to know Stevie and his mother, we identified an ambivalent attachment pattern. He was too anxious to be independent and would coerce his mother into paying attention to him by being whiny, demanding, intimidating or throwing tantrums. She couldn't ignore him if he was coercive in this way. Although Stevie tried desperately to cling or reduce the distance between him and his mother, he failed to find comfort in that. Being too far away from her didn't work and being too close to her didn't work either as nothing she could do assuaged his anxiety. He was expert at poking at her insecurities, and Jennifer would alternate between trying to soothe him, ignoring him, or shouting at him all the time, feeling ashamed that she was not being a good enough parent.

For Stevie, we knew that we would need to first establish a sense of physical and emotional safety for him. This meant first making sure he had connection points with his mother throughout the day. He was worried about her health for good reason, so we needed to make sure he knew that she was healthy if he was to turn his attention to learning. This initially meant hourly phone calls or texts. It wasn't enough to just tell him that she was alright; he had to know for himself. Within about three months, the phone calls and texts lessened until he didn't need them at all. Instead, he would only ask for a text to be sent if he wanted his mom to know about something he was working on. This constant communication with his mom also helped to build trust with our staff. We always kept a close eye on his arousal level, and when he seemed either over or under aroused, wondering aloud with him and asking him if he needed a "Mom Hello" often helped to bring him back to a more balanced state.

When Stevie first joined the class, he was extremely fearful. His sweatshirt hood was constantly up and his long hair covered his face. If staff tried to touch his head whether in play or to communicate empathy, he shrank away. He often put items in his mouth (toys or pencils) and had his hands in his mouth when objects weren't within reach. If he did communicate with peers, he used finger gestures, covered his face, particularly his eyes and hunched his shoulders forward. Stevie also used a number of animal or non-descript noises to communicate when he was feeling unsure. His peers would be puzzled, but would, with staff support, give him the space he needed to feel more secure. He began to tolerate some touch on his shoulder or hand, but remained quite fearful of unexpected contact. When he thought we were not looking, he could be seen to carefully watch the interactions between staff and other students from beneath his hair and hood. Then one day, he sat very close to one staff member while the teacher was reading a book on the carpet. The staff without looking at Stevie put his arm around his shoulders. It was tolerated! About a week later, he plopped himself on the staff's lap during story time and allowed for two arms to hold him. Initially we didn't say anything to Stevie about his seeking out relationships in new ways for fear that he would feel shame and retreat. Through acceptance, gentle rocking, and nonverbal messages, we communicated our enjoyment of this time together and placed no additional expectations on him. It was really important that he didn't feel that he had to please staff and take care of their emotional experience in the same way that he had had to do at home. We accepted and waited for him to make the next move.

We started to witness that he was taking more risks with his peers. The noises disappeared. He had been very frightened of any physical contact with peers for fear of being hurt. At his previous schools, he had been shoved, hit, or physically intimidated. He started to appear more often from his hoodie and began to engage more with staff and peers. He started to learn that adults were in charge of keeping him safe, and that staff would step in consistently if rough and tumble play was getting too rough for him. He was also learning that he didn't need to be in charge of other kids or the staff.

As he started to feel more secure, we started to talk to him about his parents. He had two very different sets of worries and relationships with his parents. With his mother, he had the conflict of both wanting to care for her and not wanting to care for her. He had not been able to learn to trust that he could rely on her, so he did the best thing possible, be in charge himself. This led to many power struggles when his mother did ask for something or set a limit. With his biological father, he needed to know where he was and why he didn't have a relationship with him. He had not seen him in over a year and understood that it was because his father needed to fix some of his problems prior to seeing him. Stevie alternated between feeling that he was the problem that made his dad stay away and feeling anger at his father for not working harder to fix whatever he had to fix so that they could have a relationship.

As we started to build a trusting relationship with Jennifer, we were able to help her see that she needed to tell Stevie the truth about why he could not see his father. With her permission, our staff (along with mom's support at home) began to tell the tale of his father and his limitations. There was no reassurance given, no excuses made for his dad, and no promises that they would be reunited. Once this truth was shared, Stevie was then able to make sense of his parent's relationship, why it couldn't work. He was able to see that his mother had made a very important decision about leaving his father so that they could both be safe. If she could make that decision, perhaps there were other good decisions she could make for them. Perhaps he had made a mistake in thinking she was incapable. It was agreed that whenever Stevie asked a question about his father, his mother and our staff would answer to the best of our knowledge with truth and empathy. Rather than see himself as being the reason for his dad leaving, he had a different narrative. He was able to express sadness and anger and he began to compile a list of questions that he would like to ask if he ever had the chance.

Attunement, acceptance, and communication of interest and delight were key signals of safety for Stevie. As soon as we noticed a shift in his mood we would notice and be curious about what he was experiencing, guessing at first and then later asking him if he had any ideas. If we missed the affective shift, he would retreat, shutting down emotionally and hiding behind his hair sometimes for an hour or more. He would later tell us that he kept his bangs long so he couldn't see anyone and no one could see him, and if his hood was up as well, then he truly felt invisible and invisible meant safe.

Staff worked with this flight response and they were able to use A/R dialogue to explore why he might be hiding. For example, when Stevie withdrew from an academic partner task, staff let him do so for a few moments, and when he started to peek up, we were able to begin a dialogue that would help him to understand both the emotions he was experiencing and how they were connected to an event, thought, belief, or interaction.

To match his affect, we often sat beside him and put our arms on the table and held our chin in our hands. This allowed Stevie to avoid a face-to-face interaction. Starting with empathy was most helpful as was using a quieter voice to keep him in the conversation:

> "Stevie, I'm sorry this is so hard for you. You seem so sad right now. You have huge crocodile tears flowing from your eyes. You're not turning into a real crocodile, are

you?" He would either smile and shake his head no or would remain silent. "I wonder if you're not sure about the activity or if you're not seeing crocodile eye to crocodile eye with your partner. I noticed that you didn't want to use his idea to solve the problem. It sounded to me like a really good idea. Do you think if you use his idea that means that yours isn't a good one?" Silence. "Hmm, if yours isn't a good idea, then I wonder if you think that makes you a dumb kid." We didn't expect him to answer, just to communicate that we wanted to understand.

As he began to feel more confident, Stevie started to try new things. When he started new physical activities (i.e., frisbee, softball, and skating), he needed to learn the most basic skills. He had not learned to catch or throw a ball, and had not had the opportunity to develop gross motor coordination. This made most physical activities challenging for him. Throughout this trial period, he experienced common injuries such as getting hit with the Frisbee or ball or falling when he attempted to skate. This was incredibly frustrating for him, and he quickly withdrew from all activities and said, *"I should go back to my old school. I'm getting hurt too much here."* For staff, this was a sign that he was not seeing all the physical safety supports that had been in place for him, and that he definitely wasn't feeling emotionally safe. He was taking a huge chance trying several new activities and he didn't think it was working out for him and it just might not be worth it. We knew that he could easily revert back to avoiding risk taking in all areas—academic, social, physical—and we wanted to start the discussion about the underlying causes of why it was so hard to take risks.

As we got to know him better, we saw the role of disappointment, the fear of making mistakes, and the overarching fear of being hurt (remember he had watched his mother go in and out of the hospital, and he assumed the same would happen to him) interfering with taking risks. We took on a playful stance when engaging him in physical activities. For example, when learning to catch, Mr. Hepburn or Mr. Fowler took on the character of the greatest pitcher to ever live using the announcer's voice, the gestures, and sometimes even the jersey. The staff would elevate their own affect to match that of our panicked Stevie and would then gradually use their voices to co-regulate his fear and help him make sense of what his real fears were. It sounded something like this:

"And the pitcher takes the mound. He sees the batter has stepped up to the plate and is looking a little nervous. It might be the pitcher's lucky day. But wait, the batter is stepping away from the plate. What is happening? The pitcher is confused. Did he do something wrong? Oh wait, maybe the batter is worried that he isn't going to be able to hit the ball or that the ball will hit him! Ouch—that might hurt!" Staff was quiet for a moment while watching Stevie's reaction. If Stevie moved away and said he wasn't playing, the affect was too much for him to tolerate; Staff said "The batter is taking a break. Maybe next inning."

Stevie typically said, "I can't do it. I'm going to get hurt!" Staff responded with acceptance and empathy, "Wow that must be tough thinking that ball is coming right at you and you're going to get hit. I bet that would be scary!"

Later in the day when we had a moment alone with Stevie, a staff member would offer him some guesses about why he worried about getting hurt so much. They might say something like, "Stevie, I've been thinking about your worries about being hurt when we play ball. It suddenly came to me why you might have these big worries. You've had to deal with your mum's hurt a lot and seen ambulances coming and taking her to the hospital. I think your brain has learned that being hurt is really dangerous and it wants to keep you away from anything that might hurt you. That would make so much sense wouldn't it?"

We didn't expect Stevie to respond to our guesses, just to experience that we wanted to understand and to offer him a different possibility for understanding his behavior. Eventually he would engage with us more actively in trying to understand but first he needed to learn more about how to understand himself so that he could have reciprocal conversations.

Stevie loved video games and spent most of his free time in front of a screen. He often related to the characters within his game more than to real people. Every conversation was about a character or a game. It was very challenging for Stevie to talk about day-to-day events, to share in a reciprocal conversation, or to enjoy activities requiring joint attention. It was too difficult for him to engage in anything that felt unfamiliar because unfamiliar automatically meant unsafe. It was through follow-lead-follow conversations using his computer characters that we were able to safely engage Stevie in conversations, first about safe topics and then about hard topics such as his worries about his mother and his wonderings about his father.

At the same time, we taught his mother how to engage in follow-lead-follow conversations and to explore her own fears about tackling hard topics. She always worried that it would be "too much" or "too stressful" for Stevie to talk about some topics, but she learned that not knowing the truth and avoiding the tough conversations would only lead to Stevie making up his own stories, and they would be far worse than the truth.

Often his mother or staff carried on both sides of the conversation to model for Stevie the reciprocity required to have social interactions.

Mr. Hepburn: "Hey Stevie! I wonder if you have anything on your mind, your face looks serious?"

Stevie: continued to play with his Lego and ignoring the question starts a story about the video game he likes to play.

Mr. Hepburn: following . . . "I really see how interested you are in that game, is it your favorite or do you have others that you prefer?"

Stevie: "My favorite game is this one you get to play on line with people all over the world. You have to shoot people and you can earn different weapons or money to buy weapons."

Mr. Hepburn: leading . . . "That sounds like a complicated game and I can see that you like, it, but I think you are distracting me! Yes, I think you are! I had asked you if there was something on your mind and I don't think you were thinking about your exciting video game right then because your face was sad and not happy like it is when you are talking about your video game!"

Stevie: smiling mischievously tried to re-engage the staff in video game chat but Mr. Hepburn resisted and started to talk for him

Mr. Hepburn as Stevie: "Well, Mr. Hepburn I am not a big fan about talking about my feelings you know."
Mr. Hepburn: "Yes, that is something I had noticed and wondered about."
Mr. Hepburn as Stevie: "Mr. Hepburn I have some big feelings and big worries but I don't know that anything will help."
Mr. Hepburn: "Ahh, Stevie! It sounds like you don't have any trust that things can be different. That is tough and maybe that's what I noticed in your face?"
Stevie: "No, I was thinking about my dad."

One day, Stevie started to cry, and staff could not see an immediate trigger or cause. He was reading his book (he loves to read), he was in a comfortable favorite seat, and he looked very content and relaxed. Staff approached him and sat with him. By this time, Stevie had developed trust in our staff and was able to almost immediately tell us what was on his mind. He said, "*I'm crying because I can't remember the color of my dad's eyes anymore.*" It wasn't enough for us to call his mom and ask the color of his eyes. That would solve the immediate problem, but for Stevie, the scarier prospect was that he was actually forgetting his father. Empathy was needed in that moment—not reassurance, not problem-solving, just empathy. We sat with him in this moment of pain and held him. Later in the day, he remembered that he kept a picture of his father in class for him to look at when he wanted. He carried the picture with him for the remainder of the day, and then safely tucked it back into its special envelope before heading home.

Talking with, for, and about can be done by one person or between two parents or staff members. To help Stevie learn the back and forth of conversations, staff would often talk about him in front of him.

Mr. Fowler: "I'm wondering if it's really hard for Stevie to make a mistake. He might feel like it's the end of the world. I get that. He's kind of learned that some mistakes lead to disaster, especially with his mom's health."
Mr. Hepburn: "Ah, maybe. That makes sense! So, Stevie might think that if he makes a mistake here that something bad will happen. Wow, what a huge worry! I'm glad I understand that a bit better. What do you think we could do to help out with that?"

While Stevie initially could not tolerate participating verbally in such a conversation, he would stay and listen. After about a year in the class, he was often able to fully participate in these conversations and talk with staff, rather than staff talking for or about him.

Talking for Stevie was necessary in all early social interactions. When he came to us, he did not have a friend to speak of, which was expected, given the amount of school he missed. He did not know how to initiate, join, or respond to an invitation from peers. Stevie was lonely while surrounded by kids who wanted to play with him. At first, staff helped peers to understand that it was really tricky for Stevie to jump right into play. Staff would say, "*Thanks for asking Stevie to play. I think sometimes he really wants to join, but it's still a bit scary for him right now. Is it okay if he just watches for a while?*" Since all kids entering our program have social competency limitations, they are typically very understanding of the fear in this domain and are often respectful and patient. As Stevie observed, with constant running social commentaries from staff, he slowly began to engage in repetitive play with toy cars and a track. He began to tolerate another student joining his play and eventually two. He maintained these two friendships even after graduation, despite going to different schools.

Due to his small size, Stevie was often viewed and treated as much younger than he was. We watched Stevie use this to his advantage to get peers to give in to him and to allow him full control of all activities and choices. This is when talking about Stevie in social interactions became important for him and for his peers. He needed to start to make sense of why control was so important for him as well as why he used his size to coerce peers. For his classmates, it was important for them to know what he was doing so that they could make more informed decisions.

Early in the program, Stevie escaped a social situation by taking an item the group needed to continue a game saying, "*Now no one will have fun. I'll ruin it for everyone.*" He used nonverbal gestures (typically the one finger salute) and glared at the perceived offender. Staff initially talked about Stevie during these incidents to draw his attention to what he was doing while helping his peers make sense of it at the same time.

> *Deni:* "I wonder if Stevie is worried that he isn't going to win this game. He seemed so sure that he was ahead and now Jack has caught up."
> *Mr. Hepburn:* "It isn't always fun to lose especially when you think you're going to win. The other boys were having a lot of fun though and so was Stevie. I was watching their faces and they were all lit up."
> *Deni:* "I saw that too! How confusing it must be to be having fun one minute and then feeling pretty lousy the next. I wonder if it's really about losing or if Stevie is still getting used to actually having fun while playing with friends. Sometimes it's scary to have fun when you haven't had much. Do you think he's worried they'll tease him if he loses or think he's dumb?"

Although he tried to give the impression of not listening, Stevie was taking in staff's wondering but also the acceptance, empathy, and desire to understand. His peers didn't always find their empathy for him but were exposed to the desire to understand before the need to problem-solve or consequence. We would then address their need to continue their game and if Stevie wasn't willing to give back the piece or participate we would provide a different option or find a representation of the missing piece, so they could continue. Once Stevie was ready, we would help him repair his relationship with his friends, who were more than willing to forgive and forget.

There were many interactions initially that would require some form of repair. With many repetitions, he began to be more sure that his relationship with staff didn't change. One day, he became anxious about a math activity (definitely not his favorite subject), and he moved away from the task (flight) and then did something we had never seen him do before. He took six or seven chairs and tipped them over. Each time he tipped a chair, he looked at staff to see what we would do or say. We could see that as he tipped them over (it was quite gentle), he seemed to get calmer. When he had them all tipped over, he waited for trouble and we could see that he was getting anxious again. Instead, Mr. Hepburn said *"Stevie that is one amazing chair spider web. However would you crawl out of there if you were the fly?"*

This simple observation and question immediately regulated him and showed him that there was no anger about his chair tipping. What we really needed to look at was what had overwhelmed him to begin with. We took two pictures of Stevie's web (see photos 13.1 and 13.2); the finished product with him standing across the room and one of him as the fly in the middle of the chairs. You'll notice that one of his peers sat just outside the web offering him company. For the next hour, Stevie and his class-mates took turns pretending to be fly in the chair web and moved them around to get the perfect web. Shortly after that, staff was able to then dissect what had happened and work with Stevie to make sense of his response. Stevie had been frightened that he didn't understand the math questions and that others would make fun of him.

With many repetitions of these kinds of PACEful conversations, Stevie and his mother found a more successful relationship. We were able to help him move from mistrust to trust in a way that allowed him to have much more successful relation-ships with his peers and with adults. Academically, he learned how to sustain his attention better and began to manage the frustrations associated with learning.

Our structured flexibility practice allows us to deviate from the planned task to accommodate moments such as these. Some of you may feel that it would have been

Photo 13.1   Chair Spider Web: Before Being Regulated. Provided by author.

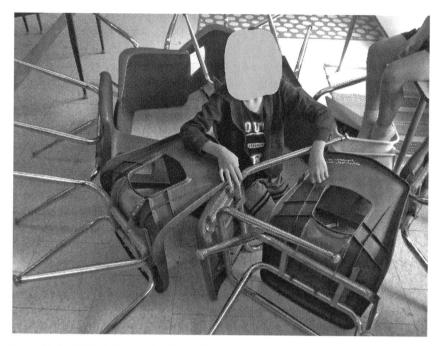

Photo 13.2   Chair Spider Web: After Being Regulated. Provided by author.

better to provide a consequence for the tipping of the chairs and that the priority for Stevie was to attend to the math lesson. A consequence may have indeed got us back to math faster, but it would have left Stevie without the understanding of how his past experiences of humiliation was painful and how he didn't yet trust his classmates to support him. By being playful and then by our use of acceptance, curiosity, and empathy, Stevie was able to make sense of his experience and importantly not feel alone in either past or present painful feelings.

As part of our program evaluation, questionnaires are completed within the first six weeks of entering the program, the end of the first year, and at upon exit from the program. The data from these questionnaires supported what we were observing. Upon entering Belong, Stevie's symptoms of post-traumatic stress disorder (PTSD), anxiety, depression, and anger were all within the clinical range, greater than 98 percent of children his age. After one year, PTSD symptoms had decreased to the normal range, with the exception of intrusive memories, which remained the same. Depression scores decreased from the 99th percentile to just on the cusp of the clinical range, and anxiety and anger were within the normal range. We also saw significant improvements in his executive functioning. He had settled to learn! Importantly, Stevie saw himself differently. When he first came to Belong he rated his Interpersonal Strength at the 1st percentile (on the Behavior & Emotion Rating Scale). Upon exit from the program, he felt he had above average (84th percentile) social skills. Stevie also felt that he had more confidence that he could be successful and was more positive about his accomplishments, rating the intrapersonal strength subscale at the 16th percentile upon entry to the program and at the 75th percentile at the end of the program. His confidence in ability to complete school work went from below average (9th percentile) to above average (91st percentile) and his sense of his ability to give and receive affection from the 37th percentile to 75th percentile. Stevie was feeling different.

UPDATE (ONE-YEAR POSTGRADUATION)

Stevie transitioned to his home school, which was one of the schools we will talk about in part III of this book. The staff understand developmental trauma, and have support in using Dyadic Developmental Practice and PACE in their day-to-day interactions with students. With the staff's help, Stevie found social, emotional, and academic success in his community school. His mother still connects with our staff when she is facing a challenging situation, but she is leading with "*I'm thinking of doing this*" rather than "*Tell me what to do*" or "*I can't handle this.*" She sees possible solutions and is able to maintain the bridge to her cortex so she can engage in problem-solving. She shares successes and proud moments, and asks for help when she needs it. She and Stevie had learned the same lessons from Belong; to recognize what they can do and to ask for help, when they felt they needed it. They had learned that they could trust others to help and not hurt and this had given them both the confidence to manage day-to-day challenges. Both started with their hoods up and eyes down, hoping to be invisible and, therefore, overlooked if others were out to harm. When Stevie graduated, his mother was serving as a mentor to new parents and was offering suggestions for some of their struggles at home. Both she and Stevie carried their new-found confidence with pride.

Stevie still worries about his mom at times. On a visit with him about a month into his new school year, he asked if we could help his mom make friends with the other moms. His mom had simultaneously reached out to us saying that the other moms were being mean to her. We were thrilled that both were feeling safe enough to ask for help. Staff met with Stevie first to help him understand that he was worrying about his mom again and that although his empathy was a strength, it was not his job to find her friends. We then asked his mother to confirm that, although she appreciated his concern, it was not his job to solve this problem for her and she was quite confident that she would find a solution. When we met with Jennifer, we helped her explore whether her anxiety was making her focus on signs of danger rather than signs of safety. She admitted that perhaps she had jumped to the conclusion that they were being mean because they hadn't introduced themselves to her right away. She was able, with our help, to look at different meanings for the slower introductions and to understand how her brain would immediately expect harm given her previous social experiences at school. We had lots of empathy for how she now had to tackle more uncertainty than she had in the two years they were at Belong. She was able to recognize that resorting to her previous strategies of avoidance would no longer work for Stevie or for her. She asked for us to attend a meeting with the principal where they could discuss how to support her in these transition times.

TWO-YEAR POSTGRADUATION

Stevie has grown two feet! He, Jennifer, and her partner have a relaxed easy manner with one another. There were many stories and much laughter around the kitchen table as we asked them if they would be willing to share their story with you. Jennifer is planning to return to school. Jennifer's partner is gentle and loving with Stevie. Stevie can talk about his biological father in a regulated and integrated way. He has friends and feels comfortable in his school community. His confidence seems to have kept pace with his height! He is able to look at the anxious, angry, sacred self that entered Belong with insight and a sense of humor. We are confident that his brain is a healthier one and that he is ready to tackle the world!

Below is the story we gave to Stevie at his graduation so that if he ever feels like he needs a reminder of all he learned he can re-read his story.

STEVIE'S STORY

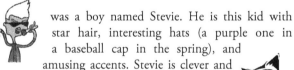

There   once   was a boy named Stevie. He is this kid with blond   rock   star hair, interesting hats (a purple one in the winter and   a baseball cap in the spring), and who reads with   amusing accents. Stevie is clever and creative and has these bright blue eyes that sparkle when he is happy or when he is mischievous. ☺ He has the best vocabulary that makes everyone smile. He loves words like *magnificent* and *majestic*. Stevie is one cool cat (oh, by the way. . . . he loves his cats . . . and seals).

Stevie seems like he's got it all going on. He has a mom and grandparents that love him and care for him. He has a home he says he loves and never wants to leave, and he's got some new friends that are true and kind. He has a class where he feels valued and respected and where he's even learned a thing or two. ☺ But, for those who really know him, it's easy to see how behind those big blue eyes, there is still some worry and uncertainty. Stevie still seeks to understand some pretty tough stuff and to figure out why hard things happen and how to make some changes. It's tough when you're just a little kid and things are going on around you that don't make sense. Your brain tries its best to figure it out and many times needs some help to do it. Even adults need help sometimes.

The teachers at Stevie's school and his mom and grandma knew that Stevie was having some struggles. He really didn't like to be away from his mom during the day. He worried about her and wanted to be with her all the time. It made it tough to get up in the morning and get to school every day. It made it hard to eat, or sleep, or do things that most kids were doing. Stevie worried when his mom was sick that something terrible would happen to her, and when he got sick, he thought something terrible would happen to him too! Well, that makes sense since it had been him and his mom (the dynamic duo) for so long that he thought he needed to take care of her. It made sense that he didn't want to leave her to go to school because if he did, something might happen and who would help her? Those are some pretty big worries for a kid, and when worries get too big, all sorts of things happen.

So, Stevie and his mom went through the struggles together and leaned on each other, but this meant that Stevie missed a lot of school. On the one hand, he loved hanging out with his mom, but on the other hand, he really wanted to go to school and have some friends. It was super tough when he would go to school because he never knew what he missed or what they were learning. It was also hard to make friends. This made him even more anxious, and so it got harder and harder to go to school and easier and easier to stay home. While he was having all these mixed-up feelings, his mom was having some too! He didn't realize that his mom was feeling badly that he missed so much school, and the that more he missed, the harder it was for her to go to the school too. She was ashamed she couldn't be a mom that could help her son with worries. They were just plain old stuck.

Stevie had some other wonders and worries. He wondered about his dad. He knew that his dad had some troubles but he wasn't quite sure what those were. His mom always said kind things about his dad, so Stevie wondered why he wasn't around or why he didn't see him. It seemed to make his mom sad to talk about him so he didn't ask too many questions. That's something you should know about Stevie. He doesn't ever want to make anyone he cares about sad or uncomfortable, so even if he has worries, he sometimes doesn't share them. More about his dad later.

So Stevie's principal, his mom, and his grandma decided that it was time for a school change, and they all hoped it would be a good change. The class was called Belong, and it was further from Stevie's house than his old school. He would have to take a bus every day and he was a bit nervous about the whole thing. He was going to a new school with new adults and new kids. He didn't know anyone and he didn't know what to expect. Stevie liked things to be predictable, so this was super hard for him. His mom knew he could do it, and even though she was anxious *for* him, she got him onto the bus with a smile. Stevie's mom always wants the best for him and she knew this must be really scary for him, but she also knew he could be brave and take that first leap. They were both being so brave!

When Stevie first arrived at Belong, he just watched everyone. He watched the adults, he watched the kids, and he watched the adults with the kids. He wasn't sure how all this was going to play out. He kept his hair long and in his eyes, with his hoodie up all the time. This way people really couldn't see him well and he could peek out only if he wanted to. Great strategy, but the problem was that he missed so much good stuff. He was always on the lookout for possible scary things or people that he missed out on so many things that were safe and even fun. But, the adults in Belong knew this about Stevie, and so they waited. They waited until he felt safe enough to put his hood down. Stevie began to notice that the adults didn't yell and didn't get upset when someone made a mistake or made a mess. In fact, they laughed, they played, they talked gently, and they even made the biggest messes of all! It didn't seem like such a scary place after all.

Once Stevie started to realize that the kids were all in the class for similar reasons, he was able to relax, but only a tiny bit. He was still used to getting his own way . . . he likes to think that because he's small and adorable (yes, he is adorable) that people will just look at him, think he's much younger than he is, and basically give him his way. This had always worked in his other school with adults *and* with kids. The kids thought of him as younger and treated him like a little brother. And . . . here's the secret weapon . . . if he brought on the water works, the really big crocodile tears . . . well, let's just say, he pretty much got whatever he wanted. Who could resist? No one wanted him to be upset so people gave in pretty fast. The problem with this was that Stevie didn't learn how to do some of the things kids his age should be able to do on his own; he found it really hard to make mistakes or not know something right away. You see, when you have a lot of worries, it is easier to avoid the things that make you worry. Stevie found a way to get other people to do things for him. Did we tell you he was a smart kid? Trouble was when he got his own way by making people feel sorry for him or took advantage of people who didn't want to hurt his feelings, he became even less confident and even more worried that he couldn't do things. His brain kept saying "Hey, you don't need to learn this because someone else will do it for you." Eventually he was certain that he couldn't do things and eventually people started to say "Whoa, you should be able to do this for yourself" and they weren't as quick to help. Stevie didn't like that because it made him feel mad (although really his mad hid his worry).

So, Stevie had to think about that one really hard. His old strategies weren't going to work and he would have to make the decision . . . does he keep using his old stuff or does he maybe try something new? Well, we were really happy to see him give some new things a try. Yes, it was painful for him at times, yes, it was confusing and a bit scary to take some risks, but as soon as he started doing that, his smile grew and so did his confidence. He went from playing only one activity with only adults to playing with the kids and trying new activities. It took a long time, but he started to see that maybe starting up the tears wasn't the only way to get some attention.

Stevie has made some pretty cool friends while he's been in Belong, and he's going to keep those connections. His friends are important to him. He has gone from wanting to control his friends and what they play together to being a bit more open to compromising. Control is a funny thing—it's the brain's way of making sure everything is predictable and calm. At first, that's what Stevie needed, but as the two years moved along, he realized that the only predictable thing about trying to control your friends all the time is that you might actually lose them. No one likes to be told all the time what they have to play and when. So sometimes Stevie's control pops up and sometimes, like every other kid in the world, Stevie just wants his way. The difference is that now he can usually tell which it is for him.

So . . . back to his dad . . . this year Stevie has had more questions about his dad. Maybe that's because he's heard the other kids talk about their dads. Some see theirs once in a while, some have never seen them, and some wish they could see them. It's a mix, and Stevie realized that he was part of that mix. He was feeling like maybe he did something wrong to make his dad stay away. His mom felt that it was time to share more of the truth with Stevie—she was confident that he could hear it and maybe better understand why it's so hard for his dad to be around right now. She had tried to protect Stevie for so long and didn't want to bring any pain to Stevie, so she had kept some things from him until she knew he could handle it. It's hard to share that a parent has some limits and that those limits have nothing to do with kids at all. Stevie's dad had and still has his own struggles with drugs. This makes it unsafe for Stevie to be with him, and his dad probably feels ashamed that he can't be a better dad. This is his dad's struggle, not Stevie's, but it sure feels like Stevie's. There's no easy fix to this challenge. I'm sure that there will be a day that Stevie can ask the questions he wants to ask and can hear the answers without feeling that he did something wrong.

Now Stevie is getting ready to graduate. He's heading to a new school and will take the brave step again to get to know new adults and new kids. He's learning to be more independent—getting up and ready for school, getting his work done in class, trying new things, and figuring out what he needs to do to be more successful with friends. He's worked hard on using his voice and his words to tell others what he wants or needs. Sometimes he still needs some help to do that, but he's trying! Stevie has finally looked up from the iPad (and has had his hair cut short) and connected with real people in real time. Yes, he loves his computer games and would gladly play on them at night and on weekends, but at school, he is with his friends. He talks with them, laughs with them, plays outside with them, creates with them, and enjoys their company. No iPad can ever do all that. He has connected with people, and this connection has made those big blue eyes sparkle even more.

It is so important that Stevie see how far he has come. He's not the same guy that walked through the door of Belong on that first day. He has his hood down, his bangs away from his eyes, his shoulders back, and is standing a little taller (well he has grown 2½ inches since he started!). Yes, he's still a bit picky about food and a bit picky about activities, but hey, isn't everyone at some time or another? In the last few months, Stevie has really started to show pride in his work and in himself. He remembers the feeling of missing so much school and of being so unsure of everyone and everything. He knows how hard it made everything for him. Stevie has made the decision to get going in the morning and get to school. He may even sleep on the bus, but he gets through the door and smiles walking through the classroom door because he got to school.

Our hope is that Stevie sees the love and support around him at home and that people are generally good and kind. People will help him, not because he's "adorable," as he likes to call himself, but because he's a *loveable* kid who is *worthy* of attention and understanding. They will want to help him because he wants to help himself, not because he seems helpless. Yes, there will be some struggles and worries that pop up—that happens to everyone—but our hope is that Stevie will carry what he learned in Belong and that his mom will carry what she learned in Belong too, and they will do what they do best and work *together*.

14
What Have We Learned in Six Years?

DDP is a relatively new therapy, and one of the criticisms is that it does not yet have an evidence base. We know that the key theories and principles upon which DDP is built have long research histories. Attachment Theory has numerous research articles proving that an infant's development is dependent on the stable, predictable, and attuned presence of its caregiver. Colwyn Trevarthen's theory of Intersubjectivity has over 40 years of research showing how the reciprocal nature of communication and the emotional experience of the parent effects the neurobiology of the infant's brain (e.g., Jones, Field, & Davalos, 2000, Dawson et al., 1999). Research on intersubjectivity contributed to the development of prevention and intervention programs for infants of young children. The Triple P (Positive Parenting Program) developed by Sanders (2001) is a popular program run by children's mental health organizations all over the world. The Triple P Program is built upon the research showing that attuned, sensitive interactions are necessary for well-being, and it has been widely and positively evaluated (e.g., Thomas & Zimmer-Gembeck, 2007, Sanders, Kirby, Tellegen, & Day, 2014, Totsika, Mandair, & Lindsay, 2017, Lyndsay & Strand, 2013).

Video Interaction Guidance (VIG) is another intervention that has world-wide use and has shown positive outcomes for increasing sensitive and attuned communications between a parent and child (Kennedy, Landor, & Todd, 2011, Vik & Hafting, 2006, Fukkink & Tavecchio, 2010). In 2012, the British National Institute of Health and Clinical Excellence recommended VIG as an effective evidence-based intervention. Parents are filmed in interactions with their child. The clinician selects and shows the parent moments of positive communication to help the parent recognize the power of their influence on their child's experience. Through discussion, parents are helped to recognize and engage in "attuned interactions"—accurately perceiving and responding to the child's nonverbal messages, and co-creation of reciprocal conversations based on both the infant and parent's reading of one another in ways that communicate interest and emotional safety (Hatzinikolaou, 2015). Hatzinikolaou (2015, p. 275) writes, "An attuned interaction creates the appropriate intersubjective space for the "deepening of the conversation, the exploration of new meanings, the collaborative problem-solving, the naming of disagreements and the managing of conflicts."

The reader can see how Dyadic Developmental Practice has incorporated these principles through the use of PACE as ways to communicate safety, the use of the affective-reflective dialogue to encourage reciprocity, shared attention, and mutual enjoyment. DDP and Dyadic Developmental Practice has also incorporated the explosion of interpersonal neurobiology research over the past fifteen years. That research also helps us understand how the quality of parent–child interaction impacts a child's development in very specific ways—neurologically, cognitively, behaviorally, socially, and emotionally.

Although every day we see positive implications of the Dyadic Developmental Practice framework in the classroom, we wanted to see if we could measure it in a manner that might contribute in an evidence-based way.

The teacher and parents are asked to complete a number of standardized measures that reflect aspects of the child's functioning. These measures are completed within the first two months of the school year, at the end of the child's first year, at the exit of the program (typically two years) and within six months of the child being back at their home school.

The following measures have been used consistently since the beginning of our program.

Behavior Rating Inventory of Executive Function (BRIEF)—Gioia, Isquith, Guy & Kenworthy): There is a form for both parent and teacher to complete for children 5–18 years. Eight clinical scales (Inhibit, Shift, Emotional Control, Initiate, Working Memory, Plan/Organize, Organization of Materials, and Monitor) and two validity scales (Inconsistency and Negativity) are generated from parent or teacher reports. The clinical scales form two broader indices— Behavioral Regulation and Metacognition—as well as an index representing an overall score for executive function.

Behavioral and Emotional Rating Scale, second edition **(BERS-2)**—Epstein 2004: This is a 52-item scale for children 5–18 years. We ask the parent, teacher and child to complete this form. It provides five subscales; Interpersonal Strengths (controlling emotions and behavior in social situation) Family Involvement, Intrapersonal Strengths, (child's outlook on his or her competence and accomplishments), School Functioning (competence in classroom tasks), and Affective Strengths (ability to express feelings toward others and to accept affection from others.

Trauma Symptom Checklist for Young Children TSCYC—(Briere): Both teachers and parents are asked to complete this questionnaire designed to measure symptoms associated with trauma for children 3 to 12 years. There are eight clinical scales that are generated (Anxiety, Depression, Anger/Aggression, Posttraumatic Stress-Arousal, Dissociation, and Sexual Concerns).

Delis Kaplan Executive Function System (Delis, Kaplan and Kramer); This measure for individuals 8–89 years assesses the key components of executive function believed to be mediated primarily by the frontal lobe. Students, as long as they are eight years of age or older are administered select subtests to assess executive functioning capacity.

In addition to the responses to questionnaires, we keep a record of the child's attendance, major incidences, and academic levels such as PM benchmarks in reading and grade-level math abilities. We have recently added the Thinking About Your Child Questionnaire by Granger (2009).

Our hope in collecting this data is to show that our program is successful in helping children settle to learn. As our students experience a sense of safety, we expect to see a decrease in major trauma symptoms on the TSCYC and an improvement in the scales measured by the BERS. We also expect an improvement in executive functioning. We would assume that as students are feeling safer emotionally and are not being driven by their sympathetic nervous system or the dorsal vagal branch of their parasympathetic nervous system, they will have better access to their cortically driven functions. Consequently, we expect to see improvements in all three indices of the BRIEF.

BELONG PROGRAM EVALUATION: INITIAL DATA SUMMARY

To date, we have had twenty students complete at least one year at Belong. It is not always easy to get parent questionnaires that are fully completed, so we don't yet have enough parent-completed forms to run a statistical analysis. We also do not have a sufficient number of DKEF protocols to run an analysis. We do, however, have enough teacher-completed forms. Although there were some significant differences in certain children's TSCYC protocols indicating a reduction of PTSD symptoms, we saw no difference on the TSCYC when we analyzed group results. We do see significant change, with large effect size, on teacher-completed BRIEF and BERS questionnaires.

BRIEF

We were able to compare the mean scores of the three indices—Behavioral Regulation, Metacognitive Index and General Executive Index when the students first entered the program and again at the end of the first year. Questionnaires were completed each time by the classroom teacher. Mean scores were within the clinical range upon entrance to Belong and, although still above average, were below the clinical threshold at the end of the first year of the program (see table 14.1).

Table 14.1   Mean BRIEF Scores at Entry and End of First Year

	Mean—Entry to Program	SD	Mean—End of First Year	SD
BRI	73.91	14.649	61.08	11.063
MI	66.64	11.759	61.36	11.896
GEC	70.70	12.673	62.15	10.300

The difference between mean scores was significant, with large effect sizes. This means that the change is unlikely to be by chance. The probability that this change was due to chance was $P = .010$ for the overall Executive functioning index, $P = .012$ for Metacognitive regulation and $P = .005$ for Behavioral regulation. After one year, students appear to be better able to regulate their thinking and behavior. We recognize that it is not possible to say definitively whether the change we are seeing is a result of Dyadic Developmental Practice without the comparison to a control group. Our next goal is to see whether more traditionally focused section classrooms show change in the same way.

BERS

Analysis of teacher-completed BERS showed significant differences, with large effect sizes for four scales: Interpersonal Strength (controlling emotions and behavior in social situation; $P = .002$), Intrapersonal Strength (child's outlook on his or her competence and accomplishments; $P = .003$), Affective Strength (ability to express feelings toward others and to accept affection from others; $P = .063$), and Total Strength Index score ($P = .005$).

Mean scores at the beginning and end of the first school year are shown in the table 14.2.

Although statistical analysis indicate that the differences are significant for interpersonal, intrapersonal, and affective strength scales with large effect sizes, no difference was found for Family Involvement or School Functioning scales. We were surprised that we didn't see a change in the School Functioning scale since we were

Table 14.2   BERS Mean Scale Scores at Entry to the Program and After One Year

	Time 1		Time 2	
	Mean	SD	Mean	SD
Interpersonal	6.80	2.044	9.70	1.494
Family Inv	6.63	2.264	8.90	1.197
Intrapersonal	6.80	1.476	9.50	1.900
School Function	8.00	2.784	9.10	1.729
Affective Strength	7.60	2.011	9.40	2.547
Strength Index	81.29	11.191	95.30	8.314

Note: Statistical analysis indicate that the differences are significant for interpersonal, intrapersonal and affective strength scales with large effect sizes. No difference was found for Family Involvement or School Functioning Scales.

seeing children being able to manage academic tasks better. The measured improvement in executive functioning would suggest that students will do better with classroom tasks. We think the lack of change reflects the fact that the questions that comprise this scale do not reflect the kind of tasks that are typical of Belong (e.g., completes homework), so the scale is not as valid a measure of change than it might be in a regular classroom.

Anecdotally, we do see a shift in the student's attitudes to school. They very quickly come to enjoy being at school and can be heard to say that they are not looking forward to weekends or holidays. Some of our students entered Belong with an exceptionally high number of absences from school, with some students having missed between 50 and 70 days of school. The number of late arrivals was also high for many students (between 30 and 50). Our attendance rates for our students are nearly perfect, with days being missed only due to illness or appointments. It is rare for a student to miss a day because he or she doesn't want to be at school. We have had a number of students attempt to come to school even when they are sick. Their regular attendance continues when they return to their home schools, according to their new teachers.

Deni records literacy levels regularly. When they first come to Belong, most students are behind academically. Many factors have made it difficult to access learning. When they return to their home school, we find that most children's reading and math skills are at grade level, with the exception of a few students who had diagnoses that made learning more challenging despite their emotional growth.

We can conclude that after one year in our program, the students are observed by their school staff to have better behavioral and cognitive regulation when measured by the BRIEF. This is corroborated by a significant change in the interpersonal strength scale on the BERS, which measures the ability to control emotions and behavior in social situations. Students are also seen to have more confidence about their abilities after a year in the program, and are better able to express feelings and accept affection. We are able to say that our program seems to be helping in important ways, but without a control group, we are not able to say definitively that Dyadic Developmental Practice is responsible for the change. It may be that students are responding positively to the small number of children in a class and the high student-to-teacher ratio that would also be available in other section 23 classrooms.

ANECDOTAL EVIDENCE OR "STORIES"

Anecdotes provide powerful evidence for the efficacy of what is being experienced. Still, one of our favorite stories took place four months after starting the program. The students who were in our first cohort had been accepted because of multiple suspensions for aggression, poor attendance, and difficulties learning. Much of the first three months of school as we have outlined focused on sensory play and learning the strengths of their bodies, building trust in the adult relationships, and in their ability to take risks. Our custodian noticed that all the students looked at the ice rink he had built with a mixture of trepidation and desire. None of the students knew how to skate, but they seemed intrigued by the ice rink. Having noticed, he brought in five pairs of skates, helmets, and hockey sticks for the students to use for the winter. They all struggled initially, but with staff support, very quickly learned to skate in a matter of a few days. One recess, the students were all in a "huddle" in the middle of the ice rink. When asked what they were doing, the spokesperson shouted, *"We are just hanging out."* Such a long way from the isolation and aggression these students faced the past academic years and the beginning of being in their social engagement system.

In the same vein, what other children take for granted, our students do not. None of them had had or been invited to a birthday party. Each of our students has now thrown a successful birthday party and had been invited to each of their classmates' parties. Staff work to regulate all the anxieties that come with not knowing what to expect and the nervous excitement of having friends for the first time. Recent parties have included invitations to students who have graduated, highlighting the bonds that these children are making with each other. For the first time, they have real friends. We had one parent call us wondering how to manage the fact that her son now wanted to spend hours on the phone to his classmates. Our students are learning to tolerate increased positive and negative arousal and are finding longer periods of time in their social engagement system.

The structure of this program allows for focus on small things that might get missed in larger more traditional classrooms. One child mentioned casually *"If I grow up . . ."* staff noticed and with empathy communicated how hard it must be for him to not feel like he has a future. That student now says, *"When I grow up."* He has an extended sense of self that communicates movement away from the sympathetic nervous system and integration of brain regions.

Lucas, our student who featured prominently in the first part of this book, was asked what he felt Belong had taught him. Without any hesitation he said, *"Self-control."* He was eight when he came to us, and now four years later, he was able to look back on his younger self and reflect about how difficult it had been for him to control his thoughts, feelings, and behavior. He could laugh at the many meltdowns he had had during his first year with us and was clear how what he had learned at Belong had helped him transition to a new school. When asked what he thought had been most helpful in teaching him self-control, he again without hesitation declared *"The support!"* Lucas had now been able to make sense of aspects of his life in a way that he had not been able to prior to coming to us. We know from the attachment literature that it is the *making sense* of our lives not the incidents themselves that predicts well-being.

Another story that illustrates the making sense or integration of difficult experiences was illustrated when one of our graduates came back to the school for a visit. Staff asked him how things were going. He replied, *"Oh you know! The same . . . mom's having her same difficulties. When she is good, she is good and when she isn't, she is over having fights with my grandparents."* He calmly relayed that his mom still had troubles, but she was getting help and that he just hoped she got better. His tone and demeanor were relaxed and matter of fact. He had integrated his understanding and experience of his mother, and although he still worried about her health, he no longer blamed himself.

When visiting Pete at his home school (about three months into his transition) it was amazing to hear from his teacher that he was one of her "super-stars." When Deni peeked in the classroom, she saw him working quietly nestled between two other students. It was pajama day, and he was sporting his fleece snowman set along with slippers. When Deni approached him, he flashed her a bright smile and said *"Hello!"*, and then introduced her to his desk mates. He got a chair for Deni and invited her to sit with him while he finished his math. After about five minutes, a number of students became very agitated and were swearing and throwing things. Pete looked at Deni and calmly said, *"It's okay Mrs. Melim, they sometimes have hard days and today is one of them. They won't hurt you, they're just loud."* Deni thought two things in that moment. First, she noticed the understanding and empathy he had for these boys which was illustrated in his PACEful language. She noticed his classmates were calmed by Pete's statement. Second, Deni was moved that Pete was worried about her. When Pete had first come to us, his empathy was blocked by his fear and vigilance. We couldn't even greet him in the morning without him getting upset. His entry and willingness to connect had to be controlled by him. Now over two years later, his empathy was immediately accessible, and he could tolerate so much more distress and uncertainty.

One of the signs of success we see with our graduates is their increased tolerance of more traditional classroom management. One of our students transitioned from Belong to the main school for grade seven and eight. That first year he had an excellent relationship with his teacher who had been working from a PACEful approach. She accepted another position at the end of that grade seven year, and our student was then faced with a teacher who worked from a reward and consequence-based framework. This teacher unfortunately didn't communicate that he enjoyed the students and there were many power struggles. Our team was worried and checked in more regularly. Their worry was unnecessary, however. He was able to articulate that he didn't like his teacher and could give specific reasons about how his teacher didn't understand him or had behaved in a way that he didn't think was fair. He was also able to articulate that he would be faced with that problem in high school—with teachers he got along with and those he didn't. He was resigned to doing what he needed to do to graduate and start the next part of his educational journey without regression in his behavior. Even though this year caused some distress, he kept his bridge to his cortex and could now self-regulate.

We also see positive comments from staff involved with our graduates. Teachers are noting the changes they see in the students when they return to their home school. One teacher wrote, *"Hats off to your team . . . he is definitely a much calmer, more secure young man than he was when he left. We are so thankful for your work with him."* Another wrote *"We can't believe the change. He's able to handle things that used to make him go wild.*" We are told that all graduates are maintaining the academic gains they made in the Belong program.

A large component of our program is the support of families. Parents have communicated their satisfaction with the program with comments such as:

- "I'm so happy he's there now. He's been so much more confident and he handles things at home issues a lot better. I'm trying to keep up with the program. I started being more physically active myself and it's been really helping my moods I find which helps me stay calm when he isn't."
- "We had a hard weekend. Trying to comfort was hard. He continuously tried to anger us. If he couldn't let us help, I'm glad he let you do it."
- "Could you help me piece together something? I know it's the weekend. . . . You are just one of the few people who know him and care about him and actually understand how challenging he can be."
- "He's been so happy since he started your program. I love it! Thank you."
- "I know in my heart he's in the right place at the right time. Also, I feel comfort knowing he's in such a caring and safe environment. Thank you for your consistency in keeping me up to date."
- "I love how they comfort each other. You guys have done a great job bringing community, love, and safety to your space."
- "Thank you all for the amazing work you guys did with her. It really shows in her daily life!"

With parents being less stressed by the behavior of their child or with practical issues surrounding suspensions and negative school meetings, interactions at home are likely to be more positive. We have been able to develop enough of a trusting relationship that all parents attend family workshops. Parents who have been fearful are sharing their concerns and experiences and finding acceptance from others. This allows them to be less reactive and defensive and be more open to supports to maintain family relationships.

Often the best results are the children's insights. In preparation for a visit by a team who were set to replicate the Belong program, the children were asked: What do you think they need to know about our school? The students were quite excited. They quite often express their hope that other classrooms like theirs will open so that "more kids can get help." Probably each of our students at some point has been described as lacking empathy. Deni has said on many occasions that she is impressed by their empathy and compassion. They wanted people to know the good, the bad, and the in-between. The group unanimously expressed that their classroom was their "safe place" where they can learn "cool things." When asked what cool things they had learned they talked first about favorite lessons (e.g., learning about Egypt, a science experiment, or a good book). The group reminisced and the staff relished their love of learning. The conversation then turned to relational experiences. We have a digital photo frame that runs continuously through the day and captures day-to-day moments, funny interactions and specific activities or field trips. Students started to express memories of walking down the sidewalk together eating ice-cream, sharing stories with our principal, crying and receiving affection from a classmate, playing sports with Mr. Hepburn and Mr. Fowler, and having the team understand them.

Some of what they wanted you to know is,

- "If you want to be alone, you can be alone."
- "If you have something going on, you can talk about it."
- "I have less worries in this classroom."
- "I feel safe here."
- "We all have something going on in our lives. In a different class, I might be the only one."
- "I don't feel like I'm in trouble every day."
- "We get to play."
- "You care about us."

When Lucas was asked what he wanted other teachers to know, he responded:

- "Let kids do things at their own pace."
- "Trust me."
- "Being strict doesn't help."

SUMMARY

The Belong program is a very successful and innovative program that is improving the learning and emotional experience of a very complex and hard-to-serve group of youngsters. Preliminary data supports the anecdotal evidence that we are making a big difference in the lives of these students and their families. Significant improvements in emotion regulation, metacognitive functioning, intrapersonal strength, and affective strength were evident in only one year. We expect large effect sizes when we add exit data for all students and as we increase our numbers in our sample size. Attendance data highlights a shift in attitude for children and parents. For the first time, students like school, and are missing school only when sick or for appointments. Academic successes are evident in that all children are improving their reading ability.

The success of the program is reflective of the high caliber of the Belong staff, Deni Melim, Doug Hepburn, and Jerry Fowler, as well as the effective partnership between the school boards and Family and Children's Services—and now Maltby Center. These partnerships are crucial to the "behind the scenes" success of the program. Our superintendents, principals, managers, all work to ensure that the program is protected. They support further training to build the capacity within the board and organization to work more effectively with our most complex students. Together we ensure that we continue to be thoughtful about the program and remain open to new learning.

The family component of this program is also a crucial part of the success. With our partner and community involvement, we are able to support families, reduce the stress involved in learning, and reduce the number of suspensions and critical incidences. Parents, therefore, are no longer having to deal with negative interactions with the school or with their child being suspended with the ensuing stress of having to miss work when their child can't go to school. Parents feel supported and feel safe to ask for help and guidance around challenging behaviors, and have ongoing opportunities to learn how to manage their relationship with their child more positively. Our hope is that we can prevent children from coming into care because the child's behaviors become less challenging and because parents have a safe and encouraging partnership with school staff.

Our superintendent, Karen Shannon writes:

The Belong classroom holds a special place in the Algonquin and Lakeshore Catholic District School Board. The theoretical underpinnings, beliefs, and values that form the core of Dyadic Developmental Practice and PACE align seamlessly with the vision and mission of our Catholic school system. All children should experience a deep sense of belonging, the caring relationships of adults and peers, and joy in learning. Seven years ago, when conversations began about establishing this special program to meet the needs of children who were not achieving these fundamental experiences in our region, the decision to enter the partnership was easy. Selection of team members was carefully considered, and the ongoing training, support, and clinical oversight of Dr. Sian Phillips was recognized as pivotal to the success of effectively implementing this new model. This meant that traditional structures and procedures associated with daily classroom operation in a typical school would take a back seat in the Belong classroom to creating the conditions of safety needed most by students. A high level of trust and autonomy has been afforded to the team at the school and system levels, and it has yielded fruit beyond measure.

The learning and expertise developed, over the past six years, within the program have had a direct influence on how many school communities within the district are understanding and supporting students and families, due to the commitment of the Belong team to share their professional insights. Sian and Deni support teachers in numerous school communities, offering workshops, after school meetings, and ongoing communication to extend support as colleagues implement their new learning.

The school community that is home to the Belong classroom has thoroughly embraced PACE as a way of relating to all children. Within ALCDSB, it is understood that trauma-informed practice can and should be utilized at the universal level in all school communities to shift how we see and understand student behavior and to enhance the development of caring and safe schools. The Belong classroom provides a highly specialized program with intensive support for children who are at the top of the intervention pyramid; however, many children can benefit from informed use of this evidence-based and practice-informed model.

The continuous and dynamic learning from inside the Belong classroom is rippling out across the entire school system, and our principals, teachers, and support staff are asking for more—a sure sign of the fruitfulness of this approach.

Karen Shannon
Superintendent of School Effectiveness and Special Education, ALCDSB

15

Bloopers

Where We Got It Wrong

Although Dyadic Developmental Practice gives us a framework and a place to come back to when we struggle, it is not always easy to trust that we are on the right path. Most of the time we can repair our mistakes and come out the other side with greater understanding. However, sometimes we fall off the path and don't get to where we had hoped to go. Perhaps the hardest times for us has involved two students who we asked to leave the program early. There is no question that they needed the kind of support that we offered, but in both cases, their use of intimidation or aggression was creating an environment where the other children were afraid and where we could not establish a consistent sense of safety.

One of these children came to our class at the beginning of our second year. She had a high level of aggression that could not be settled by our routines and our attempts to co-regulate her high levels of arousal through PACE. Although there were short periods of calm, she could become highly explosive with no warning. The staff expected that the transition into a new program would be stressful for her and they initially gave her a great deal of one-to-one support. She was not able to tolerate any social interaction with the other children and would typically say mean things as they came near her or would threaten to wreck their things.

For the staff, having to maintain a high level of hypervigilance and have one staff member allocated to her at all times was exhausting. They began to be more short with her and in supervision admit to feeling less empathy and ascribe more deliberate intent to her behavior. This child's mistreatment of the other children was particularly difficult. Relationships had been established with the children from the previous year and they could see the erosion of trust in the face of such frequent and unpredictable aggression. We were not able to establish the routines and level of safety required for them or for the other new student who had joined the classroom.

Everyone's anxiety levels began to rise, and interactions were starting to become less PACEful and more reactive and consequence based.

We called a meeting of caregivers, social workers. and staff to discuss how to better understand what was making it so hard to settle. In her world outside the classroom. our new student was facing threats to her living situation. Extended family members wanted her to come and live with them, and there were arguments between the adults in her life about what was best for her. She had no idea how to make sense of some traumatic events in her history nor currently what the adults were arguing about so vociferously. She had no safety, and the added stress of a transition to a new school was just too much for her. Not only was it too much for her but her distress was also too much for the other students and we were not able to establish safety in our classroom. We made the decision for her to return to her home school and for issues related to permanency planning to be made a priority. Although perhaps we could not have known just how difficult it would be for her, we all felt badly that we had added another layer of stress to her life as well as to that of our other students.

We had one other student who started to consistently undermine the safety in the classroom. In his previous school, he had often been aggressive and would run away quite frequently. He exhibited explosive aggression only twice in our classroom, but would use subtle intimidation in many of his interactions. He was a bright student and, like the others, needed a strong sense of control. His way of controlling was to draw the other students into a game or seemingly friendly interaction and then say something cutting. He would walk away from them with disdain, blaming them for saying something stupid or for making him angry. His friends were often bewildered and hurt, and given their histories, quick to believe that the rupture in the relation-ship was their fault. Staff would help them understand that they had done nothing wrong and then wonder with our student what would cause him to hurt his friends in this way. During class discussions, this student would begin to "one-up" the other students or mock them for their vulnerability. Staff would quickly intervene, but the damage was done, and our students began to be very wary of this student and they would not open up in a group format about their thoughts and feelings. When he was away, they were so obviously more relaxed and willing to take risks and they began even to articulate that they liked school better when this student was away.

We increased our supervision, but the level of coercion and intimidation increased and our sense of safety in the classroom decreased. Our student's parents also strug-gled with his need for control and his aggressive responses, especially when they set a limit. During our first year, we had been able to have conversations with our student about the need for control, how it made sense given his history, and felt that he was willing to look at alternative possibilities. Shortly after he started his second year, he stopped being part of these conversations. Perhaps he became too comfortable and became scared of the relationships he was forming. Perhaps he really did want to interact in different ways, but his neural circuitry that was primed for survival could not let him learn a different way of being.

As we were losing our ability to influence our student, his parents started to lose trust with us. They became angry with us, believing that something we were doing was causing his escalation at home and his difficulties at school. We ultimately made the decision to transition him to his home school earlier in the school year to preserve and celebrate the gains he had made. Although we would have liked him to stay, we felt we would not be able to influence him enough in the time we had left and that the regressions for the other student would outweigh any gains we would achieve with him.

Unfortunately, we were not able to plan a graduation and celebrate his time with us as his parents refused to let us tell him that he would be returning to his home school and refused to allow us to talk about emotions with him for fear of causing an escalation in behavior. Given that our program is designed to help students with building awareness of emotions, we were not able to comply with their request. The rupture in our relationship with both parents was large, and unfortunately, the child was moved suddenly without any chance to help him process what was happening and why. We all felt sad and worried for our student who now had one more significant loss and burned bridge to bolster his defensive armor.

Where could we have recognized the escalation and provided more support? It is hard to know without exploring the experiences of this particular family or having a chance to repair relationships. It always feels so hard to make a choice between one student and the others. We so want to be helpful to all our students, and often struggle with feelings of inadequacy and fear that we are at fault for the rupture. In those moments, we try hard to have PACE for ourselves, being curious about what might have been different or at the root of the problem, but having acceptance that we do the best we can do and empathy for when it feels so hard.

We often make mistakes in our day-to-day interactions. One of our college students, Cole, recounted the time he got into a power struggle with Alex. He was trying to make Alex complete the work and the child refused. The more Cole insisted that he complete the work sheet, the more and more dysregulated Alex became until he tipped over a desk and called Cole several nasty names. Quickly, Mr. Hepburn came to Cole's side as much to co-regulate Cole's anxiety as to co-regulate Alex's anger. Mr. Hepburn modeled the use of acceptance and empathy for Alex's upset, helping him make sense of why he had become angry. The next day, Cole approached Alex and apologized for pushing him to complete work that he wasn't ready to complete. Alex immediately asked Cole to play baseball with him outside and later worked alongside him with no compliance issues at all. For Cole, he could articulate his learning to be about the skill required to avoid power struggles. Later in his placement, he could reflect how the building of relationships resulted in so many fewer issues of noncompliance.

A common challenge is wanting to fix something too quickly. It is difficult to sit with a student who is experiencing emotional pain and just provide acceptance and empathy. One of our students early in our program would frequently move into a hypo-aroused state. He would withdraw himself from the group and sit unhappily in a corner of the classroom. Staff would find his pain very difficult to tolerate, and they would quickly go to him and try to make him feel better and urge him to come back to the group. They would offer a number of solutions, none of which would be taken. Staff would feel stuck and worried about this student's unhappiness and worried that they were being drawn away from the group for much of the day. There is a lovely sequence in Pixar's movie *Inside Out*, in which Bing Bong is feeling despair at the disappearance of the rocket that represented his relationship with young Riley. Joy is desperately trying to jolly him out of his despair as they must find their way to the train before it leaves. Her attempts are misattuned and do nothing to shift his emotional state. Sadness then sits down beside him and gives him empathy "*I'm sorry they took your rocket, they took something you loved, its gone for ever.*" Joy reprimands her for making him feel worse, but Sadness continues to invite Bing Bong into talking about his memories and gives empathy for his sadness. Bing Bong breaks into tears, receives more empathy and then shifts his emotional state and can lead them to the train. Our staff were falling into the same trap of not accepting our student's sadness. Our student was getting the message that others couldn't tolerate his emotional experience, which would have left him feeling lonely. Our staff were getting anxious about how to meet his needs and those of the group. Once they realized that it was not their job to fix this student's pain, but to notice, accept, and provide empathy, both student and staff were able to find different solutions. Our student began to shift his emotional state more quickly, and our staff could feel more confident that both he and they could tolerate the deep feelings.

The mistiming of playfulness is also another common misattunement. Our staff is a playful group, and they love to tease and play with the students. There have been a few occasions where a staff member has used a playful response and has not received the anticipated response. One morning a staff member teased a student for being slower than a tortoise and that he was going to need to find his inner cheetah if he was going to play tag with them. The student yelled and cursed loudly at this staff member and ran to another part of the playground. The staff member immediately felt terrible and was puzzled as usually this kind of banter was tolerated. He left the game and approached the student who ran further from him, yelling that he hated his teacher, that he was never going to talk to him again and that he should get away from him. Our staff member immediately apologized and tried to understand what had happened to cause such upset, but our student wanted nothing to do with him. It took another staff member to approach our student, first to just sit with him and provide empathy, and as his arousal levels came down to be curious about his experience. Eventually we learned that he thought that our staff member was making fun of him. He had been feeling sad prior to going out for recess because he had been struggling with his project. The staff member had already been outside and so not aware of what had happened in the classroom. Our student was in an emotional state where he was primed to hear danger signals and had heard the words of our staff's comment, but not the playful tone in which it was issued. He believed it was another thing he was failing at and his shame quickly translated to anger. Our staff member had responded based on what he expected their relationship to be rather than paying close attention to our student's nonverbal messages.

Luckily, as we build relationships, most of our mistakes are quite repairable. When our students learn to trust that our intent is to be helpful, they forgive us quite readily when we are misattuned, say something not helpful, or don't meet needs as quickly as they would like. We have frequent opportunities to say to our students "*I'm sorry!*" We also try hard to model making mistakes with one another and repairing them. Over time, our students learn that making mistakes is common place, but they don't result in the loss of a relationship. Our hope is that we can move our students from shame (I am a bad kid) to guilt (I did something to hurt someone). If they can feel safe enough to stay in their social engagement system, they will be able to use what they know to repair their relationships.

III

"I've learned that people will forget what you said, people will forget what you did, but people will never forget how you made them feel."—Maya Angelou

16

The Journey of Three
DDP-Informed Elementary Schools
and One Alternative High School

The Limestone District School Board is situated on the traditional territories of the Anishinaabe and Haudenosaunee. We acknowledge their enduring presence on this land as well as the presence of Metis, Inuit and other First Nations from across Turtle Island. We honour their cultures and elaborate their commitment to this land.

We would like to tell you that in the next four chapters you will find all the answers about how to use Dyadic Developmental Practice as a framework for trauma-informed practice in your classroom or school. However, what we have discovered in our four-year journey with our three elementary schools is that applying a specific template or program would not have worked. Using the framework, taking our time, being open to discovery, and staying connected to each other has been the foundation of our trauma-informed practice. Consistent with Dyadic Developmental Practice principles, the learning and ability to provide trauma-informed education has been co-constructed from repetitive, attuned interactions with staff and students. The teams have noticed, wondered about, and offered a PACEful response that was contingent upon what was noticed, then wondered about and responded again—repeatedly. Although leaders of this initiative were armed with science, information, and data, it has been the voices of the staff and students who have dictated how that has become integrated into practice.

In the next section of this book, we will describe for you the journeys of three elementary schools. The three schools were part of an initiative in the Limestone District School Board to develop trauma-informed practice. In order to be respectful of confidentiality, we do not name these schools or their principals. Names of students have been changed, or examples are composites of students that are typical of all three schools. We will offer you some examples of how we learned to manage some very real tensions between traditional and trauma-informed education, and

then offer you some resources. We hope that this will be a guide for you in your journey toward integrating Dyadic Developmental Practice into your trauma-informed
practice. We also hope that you can learn from our successes and mistakes.

OUR CHILDREN AND FAMILIES

Katie would only communicate as a cat. "Meow" could be said in different tones,
with emphasis on different syllables accompanied by hisses, spitting, and clawing, or
whispered from underneath a desk or while wrapping herself around the teacher's
legs. It might mean, "I think I like you!" or "I'm not sure if you are going to hurt
me" or "Come any closer and I will take your eyes out!" She might stay in one
emotional state for the whole day, but typically moved quite rapidly between shy
feline approach behavior and rapid withdrawal. Katie had recently enrolled in grade
three. She had moved to Ontario from the East Coast to live with her aunt and
uncle. Her biological mother had long-standing mental health issues. Katie had been
exposed to very frightening and confusing behavior as her mother struggled with
violent psychotic episodes and long periods of depressed and paranoid behavior.
Katie had been removed from her mother's care several times and placed in foster
care—a different placement each time. When her mother's behavior stabilized,
she would return home. Following an episode where Katie called 911 because she
couldn't wake her mother, the authorities decided to seek a kinship placement.
Her maternal aunt agreed that Katie could come to live with her and her partner.
Although her aunt had empathy for her niece, she was exhausted by her bizarre and
impulsive behavior. She worried that Katie had the same mental health issues as her
mother and had no tools in her toolbox to address her behavior. Her teacher likewise
expressed frustration and concern, as she had not yet found a way to approach Katie
to assess what learning she knew or to offer her new opportunities for learning.

Trevon, a grade seven student, alternated between sullen withdrawn behavior, refusing to take out his headphones, and reactive explosive behavior, where he would
storm out of the classroom yelling a long list of profanities. Any attempts by the
teacher to direct him were met with resistance. Sometimes he would quietly ignore
them and sometimes he would respond with verbal and physical aggression. This
was a pattern for him since he joined the school in grade one. He had had multiple
suspensions and referrals to specialized programs. He had attended an out-of-school
program for his grade three year, but continued to struggle to access learning when
he returned. He didn't have peer relationships, and the school struggled to provide
him with an adult relationship in which he could feel safe. His teachers were aware
that Trevon had grown up in a family with significant domestic violence. Trevon
and his mother had periodically left and lived in shelters, but always returned. His
father had recently been incarcerated for an assault that had caused serious harm to
his mother. Despite having compassion for Trevon's situation, empathy was harder

to find in the face of his use of aggression, intimidation, and rejection. His mother was overwhelmed, and Trevan often intimidated her in the same way his father had. He refused to listen to her, yet would fight anyone who had a bad word to say about his mother. Teachers struggled with his impact on them and on other class members, and found it difficult to like him. His classroom teacher struggled with blocked care for this student and often wondered whether she could continue to teach this class.

In junior kindergarten, Carson was apprehensive and rarely communicating with classmates or adults. If anyone came near, he would scream and push them away physically and would sometimes throw objects around the room. He lived with his maternal grandmother. His birth mother had been 15 years old when she had given birth to him, and was currently involved with hard drugs and prostitution. She had no fixed place to live. Carson's birth father was in and out of jail, occasionally coming to Kingston for a visit with his son. Visits were short and unsatisfying for Carson, and his behavior would escalate in the days following a visit. When his mother was sober, she would occasionally drop by the house for dinner, but tended to be indifferent toward her son. Carson's grandmother still had two of her own children at home and made frequent comments to school staff that she "had not signed up to parent another kid." She was often short or gruff with Carson, and constantly looked tired and frustrated.

Didi was 13 and had recently moved to Kingston to live with her grandparents. Both grandparents were survivors of the residential school system in Canada and had a deep mistrust of the school and government systems. Didi's father had left when she was an infant and she lived with her mother for the first five years of her life. Her mother struggled with drug addictions, and Didi spent long periods of time with different family members. She had attended ten different schools since junior kindergarten. Didi was disinterested in school, producing the bare minimum of work when asked. She would doodle beautiful pictures in her notebooks. She kept to herself, didn't participate in class discussions, and didn't engage socially with any of her classmates. When teachers tried to talk with her, she looked down, letting her hair hide her face and resisted any invitation for connection.

Katie, Trevon, Carson, and Didi are typical of many of the children who are enrolled in our three public schools. These three schools committed in 2015 to becoming trauma-informed schools using Dyadic Developmental Practice as the framework for achieving this goal. Their communities have more than twice the national average of families living in poverty, and their teachers believe that more than two-thirds of their students have had more than five adverse childhood events (ACEs).

Carol is just about to have her seventh baby. Her three oldest children attend one our trauma-informed schools, Carol has been badly hurt by partners in the past. She is deeply suspicious of the school's intentions to work with her children, and will sometimes appear at school in a rage, shouting obscenities at the principal or teachers, demanding that her children be treated fairly and believing that school staff are intentionally discriminating against them. On other days, Carol can be calm and can engage in social chitchat with teachers or engage in discussions about her children's educational needs. School staff were never really sure which Carol would show up at school and were tentative to call home when one of the children was having difficulty that required that parents be informed.

Many of the parents in these communities are like Carol, with histories of trauma that have made them vulnerable to substance abuse, ongoing mental health struggles, and involvement in unsafe relationships. Despite deep mistrust, they are also the parents who demonstrate fierce determination, loyalty to friends and neighbors, and desire for better things for their children.

In these school communities, there are some families that have been in the neighborhood for many years and the school staff may have taught two generations of the family. We also have four federal penitentiaries in our area, so we also have a more transient population of families who may only be in our communities for 18–24 months. The administration teams in these three schools have worked tirelessly to form relationships with the parents, grandparents, or guardians of their students. Even before adopting Dyadic Developmental Practice as their guiding framework, the staff in these schools understood the need for these relationships. It is even harder for students to feel safe at school when their parents mistrust their teachers and school community. Without a relationship, it is harder to ask for parents to be part of their child's support circle or to provide information about how to support their child's learning.

The administration teams would be the first to say that forming relationships with parents is essential, but requires time. In the same way that children with developmental trauma are mistrusting of others motives and intents, so too are their parents. Shame is readily activated when school staff call regarding a child's misbehavior or request a conference to talk about learning problems. Many a teacher and administrator have been yelled at, blamed for causing the child's misbehavior, or met with a rejecting or minimizing stance when attempting to talk to parents about their child. Shame, as we know, often translates to blaming, minimizing, and angry responses in an attempt to distance from that toxic emotional experience.

These three school communities have persisted in the face of these responses and, prior to knowing about Dyadic Developmental Practice, were intuitively nonjudgmental and empathic. As staff became familiar with the framework, they could bring the research on interpersonal neurobiology and intersubjectivity to mind to help them stay in their social engagement system. By understanding *"why"* relationships were essential for the development of healthier brains, they could persist when their own brains may be telling them to respond in defense or withdraw. By recognizing that the parent's response was likely masking shame, deep sense of inadequacy and fear of judgment, they were less likely to personalize a parent's angry or rude discourse.

WHY DYADIC DEVELOPMENTAL PRACTICE?

The three administration teams had been developing trauma-informed practices by necessity prior to adopting a Dyadic Developmental Practice as a specific framework. They had long recognized that the students brought their experience of domestic violence, loss of relationships, hunger, and fear into the school day. They had established breakfast and lunch programs, safe places in the school where students could go to sleep, staff who were kind and empathic, softer entries into the school day or early dismissals to ensure success for students, and the availability of sensory toys or rituals that communicated that staff liked their students. Staff who worked in these three schools were people who wanted to work with children with complex needs and who had large capacity for compassion and patience. They were skilled at meeting the students at a level where they could be successful, and they knew their student's stories.

So why wasn't this enough? The administration teams all recognized that despite some sensitive and powerful work, there was a large group of children who were not benefiting. Staff were making some short-term gains with these students, but those gains were not sustained. It was clear that staff could manage some of the challenging behavior and could raise the level of compliance by providing incentives and consequences—traditional behavior modification approaches. Like all schools, teachers were getting to know their students better by the end of the school year, but they were not managing to influence the development of a healthier brain. As students started a new school year in the fall, gains were lost, and everyone started the long, slow climb toward managing behavior and settling the students to learn.

The administration teams from these three schools had many discussions about how to better influence their student's trajectory. Behaviors were being managed but not changed. So many of the students remained in biological states that made learning too difficult. The administration team were convinced that they were missing something in the work they were doing. The staff in one of our schools estimated that only 5 percent of their students could be considered to have mental "health" and were settled to learn. If 95 percent of the students were still not reading, despite attending school each day, a great deal of energy and money would be spent to ensure that children learned to read. Why not apply the same logic to over half the students whose brain did not allow them to learn at all.

The administration teams first wanted to understand these children better. They knew that many of their difficult students had, or were continuing to experience, various forms of trauma in their lives. They started to collect data informally. For each student, they discussed how many ACEs were known to them. That exercise brought into focus how many students faced relentless external stressors. They then partnered with Sian to further understand the impact of trauma on learning and how they might use Dyadic Developmental Practice as a framework to meet these children's needs and go beyond managing behavior. Administrators grappled with big questions about how PACE would help children who were aggressive every day and who caused harm to peers and staff. How to balance the needs of one or two children with the rest of a class who are ready to learn? How to get students to stay in the building rather than run off property at the first sign of frustration? How to meet the needs of staff as well as students? The team needed to grapple with these questions and come to know how Dyadic Developmental Practice was a way to address them before they shared the initiative with their staff. As leaders, they would need to be steadfast in their commitment to the initiative. With the financial backing of the Limestone District School Board, we began the journey of learning how to embed Dyadic Developmental Practice within larger classrooms and within the whole school culture.

First, administrators shared with their staff their estimate of how many students in their school communities were living with ACEs, and told stories about what these students were experiencing in their day-to-day lives. The effect was more compassion for students, the beginning of understanding that these children were perhaps not choosing their behavior, and increased desire to do something to help these students manage. Administrators then began to ask whether staff would be willing to embark on a journey to better meet the needs of this particular group of students. The education system frequently has learning initiatives and new programs and the administrators wanted to ensure that their teachers were willing to take a risk to learn something new, not because it was a ministry or board expectation but because they themselves were understanding the moral imperative of working differently with this group of students.

Armed with the knowledge that approximately two-thirds of their students had experienced four or more ACE's, the research that recognizes the power of relationships to develop healthier brains and confidence from the administration team in their staff's ability to take on this challenge—the majority of the staff immediately were open to learn more about their difficult students and to maintain an open stance toward learning.

TRAINING AND CONSULTATION: THREE AREAS OF FOCUS

Information

Given the expense of releasing teachers for training, a summer institute was offered in late August, 2015, 2016, and 2019. Attendance was completely voluntary as union regulations prevent mandatory training outside of school hours. Teachers begin to think about setting up their classrooms during that last week of August, so we wanted to capitalize on teachers who were rested and starting to think about their new students. Educational assistants, student support workers, and support or administrative staff were also invited to attend so that everyone in these three communities could share the same experience.

Our hope from this first day of training was to introduce educators to the following core concepts.

The influencing of student's behavior and learning can occur only through the provision of physical and emotional safety.

If a student could do better, the student would: Staff were introduced to the research on interpersonal neurobiology. They learned how trauma significantly impairs brain function and how such impairment leads to pervasive difficulties in self-regulation. Challenging behavior exhibited by students with developmental trauma is not a "choice," but represents adaptive and complex survival strategies operating outside of the student's awareness. If teachers could understand the developmental lags caused by trauma, they might find it easier to be compassionate and be less likely to personalize student's struggles or to try to influence them only with incentives and punishment.

Connection before correction or compliance. Teachers were introduced to the research that identifies that self-regulation strategies can only develop from having emotional experiences first co-regulated by safe adults. We want to avoid compliance that is driven by fear and increase compliance that comes from our social engagement system.

PACE. A way of engaging and being with children to provide safety in the relationship.

This first day of training was then followed up at our first Professional Development Day at the end of September, with a discussion of how staff were using what they had learned. We also used role-play to develop confidence in using PACE for both co-regulation of affect and making sense of the meaning of the child's behaviors. There were some common questions, experiences, and tensions.

Some staff worried,

- That acceptance and empathy was letting the child "get away with" misbehavior, and that there was a loss of authority both with that child and with other students who were observing.
- That acceptance and empathy were antithetical to having high expectations for students.
- The additional time and resources directed at a child who presented with challenging behavior was taking time away from children who wanted to learn.
- Aggressive or intimidating behavior was making other students frightened, and what was their responsibility to the other children in the class.
- The struggle to balance the child's need for safety with the need to teach curriculum.
- That they were being asked to be therapists, and that wasn't their role.

In addition to worries, staff shared positive outcomes when using PACE.

- Some staff had experienced that empathy in particular calmed a child more quickly than reassurance or the giving of consequences.
- The giving of empathy allowed teachers time to figure out where to go next with the student.
- Several teachers reported how helpful it was to remind themselves to be curious about what the child may have experienced before coming to school or earlier in their school day, rather than be reactive to the behavior.

- Some teachers expressed how liberating it was to be playful and to openly engaged with a student to influence behavior rather than be authoritarian.
- Some staff talked about how easy it was to get stuck in power struggles when they were set on control, and how playfulness and empathy would allow them to step around those struggles.
- Many teachers would say this "feels" right even if it is hard to do.

Safety

Once the information was given, the priority was on creating safety for teachers to talk about their experiences of using PACE and to tell stories—the good, the bad, and the ugly. Administrators met teachers with acceptance and empathy, and they would be curious with them about what made the particular incident positive or a struggle. Together, staff would wonder about their own responses as well as what the child might have been experiencing to cause an upset. Principals in all three schools stressed the importance of accepting their staff's struggles even when it became uncomfortable. Sometimes staff were angry at the leadership for not suspending a child for aggression. Sometimes the whole staff team felt overwhelmed and mistrusting of Dyadic Developmental Practice as an initiative. Sometimes the conversations among the team became quite negative. All three principals felt strongly that if the team was to adopt and embed this framework, all aspects of the journey must be fully accepted. Their role was to accept, have empathy, encourage curiosity, and inject humor when appropriate and to hold the belief that this initiative was in everyone's best interest.

The administration teams recognized that they had a greater luxury in practicing the use of PACE, since typically they were dealing with students individually rather than the teacher who was managing a whole class. They made themselves vulnerable by experimenting with PACE and talking openly about their successes and struggles. As they wandered through their schools each day, they would make it a priority to notice each time someone used PACE, name it for them, and celebrate the commitment to new learning. One of the administrators reported that he would then immediately find someone else to share the story with. It is easy to feel lonely in a classroom, and the administration team became the link to ensure that joint attention and intention remained front and center. Staff were asked to linger when they saw their colleagues use PACE to co-regulate a student's affect in the hallways. This allowed the staff member to know there was support if needed, but there was also a way to have staff witness each other's experiences. Post-it Notes with examples of success were stuck to cupboards in the staff room, as were inspirational quotes for staff to notice as they made their tea and coffee. Noticing also allowed teachers to practice being attuned with their children rather than respond reactively. We start to heal when our needs are noticed and responded to in a contingent way. Noticing, therefore, is such a crucial first step.

Stories about interactions were then shared at each staff meeting. PACE became a verb as teachers shared stories about how a child was PACEd or a noun "I was so

PACEful today!," and staff began to use common language in their thinking and responses to students. Staff meetings became a way to share stories about children and families, deepening the whole staff's understanding of a particular student and helping them stay in their social engagement system. They were also conversations where tears at the struggle to meet a student's needs were as acceptable as uproarious laughter about a student's comments or a staff's response. The freedom to tell stories and struggles contributed greatly to the staff's sense of safety as they tried to embed this new learning.

Just as there are times where limits are necessary for students, the administrators recognized that there were times where they needed to have difficult conversations with staff about how they had responded to a child. This again was done with PACE. Administrators knew that the staff chose to be in these particular schools because they wanted to make a difference in children's lives. Acceptance and empathy were always the place to start, and then curiosity about the teacher's experience. Administrators understood that when their staff was overwhelmed or stressed, they would return to behavioral principles that were focused on control rather than on understanding in the effort to manage their classroom.

Teachers were first given support and then, within the safety of the relationship, encouraged to think about what the student might be experiencing and what they themselves were experiencing. Often teachers came to recognize that they were not in a position to put their own oxygen mask on first, given issues related to their own traumatic experiences as children. Past hurts were being activated and making it difficult to be optimally responsive. Sometimes the hurts were more situational, with worries about family members intruding into the workday, or personal physical and mental health issues that were difficult to ignore. Whatever the issues, staff were encouraged to be aware of them and to use the supports available to allow them to use PACE in their interactions with students. Administrators worked hard to be attuned to their staff, provide an encouraging word or a break when needed, and serve as a constant reminder to practice connection before compliance. Teachers were given permission to be creative in how they looked for that connection and to set aside academics until students were settling to learn. Just as the students were not rushed into learning, the leaders did not rush or pressure their staff to accept Dyadic Developmental Practice. They held the belief that with steady acceptance and relevant information, teachers would become open to new learning when they were ready.

As a general rule, educators tend to be very willing to try new things, but only persist if they see positive results. The difficulty with changing brains from the bottom up is that it takes a great deal of time, and results are not immediately apparent. How to keep staff committed to the long game? Administrators helped by setting goals that were attainable—we want him to be able to enter the classroom by Christmas and have one positive social interaction; we want him to kick you less by the end of the month rather than not at all; if he enters the class, we want him to see your delight that he made it that day. Administrators also were in a good position to see improvements. They were able to communicate to staff the small steps that could lead to bigger ones. Sharing of stories was crucial, and the openness to disagree or challenge the direction for the school culture was accepted and encouraged.

The following story illustrates the importance of playing the long game. One young teacher came to one of our schools three weeks into the new school year. She had missed all the information about developmental trauma and PACE and had only limited experience in the classroom. Jacob was one of the most complex students in the school and he was in her kindergarten class. This young boy at age 5 could not tolerate anything about being in school. He would hide in the cubbies at the end of the classroom, withdrawn and unhappy. If people came near, he would shout obscenities and start throwing things. His preference was to play underneath a table outside the classroom, resisting attempts to play with him or to get him to come back into the classroom. Occasionally, he found his way into the classroom, but quickly became angry and would pull pictures off the walls, tip over desks, or throw things on the floor. The teacher had understood that the school was using PACE as a framework to help students find safety, but because she had missed the training, she was not confident that she could work in this way. She often felt that she was not cut out for this job, and expressed frustration at her inability to connect with this child in particular. Despite her lack of confidence and days where she wanted to find another profession, she persistently communicated to Jacob that she wanted to help him. Each time he would yell an answer to a question from his cubby or from underneath the desk, she would acknowledge his good idea. Each time he tore apart the room, she would fix it, expressing empathy for his struggle.

Jacob transitioned to grade one and continued to struggle. He was physically aggressive with the other students and was disruptive in many other ways. The school team provided an alternative space for him to be, providing for him play opportunities rather than academic learning. He and his educational assistant had a small space in the school that was just for them. Jacob again started the school year underneath the table. He had large cushions and would build elaborate forts with them. Then he started building with LEGOs and Play-Doh, still refusing to let anyone join him in the worlds he was creating. His educational assistant would show delight in his creations and would patiently accept that this was the best he could do at this time. After Christmas, Jacob began to communicate to her while he played and started to let her play with him as long as she did as she was ordered to do. She would sometimes playfully tease him that she wanted a turn to be the boss and asked when would he be ready to let her make up some rules. By the end of grade one, his play was more reciprocal. While playing, he would sometimes talk about some of the things he worried about at home and provide information about his family life.

Grade two started in the same way, with Jacob spending time one-on-one with his educational assistants. He now had one for the morning and one for the afternoon. He started to tolerate being read to and would play many games of cards, practicing the ability to be more reciprocal in his interactions. The team asked him if he would like to choose a friend to spend some time with him in his space. On the days where he could, Jacob would then choose someone from the regular class to join him to play, listen to stories, or play cards. His teachers began to incorporate some learning into his play, for example, a simple math card game or a game where he had to develop memory skills.

Toward the end of grade two, his school team began to wonder if Jacob would be better served in a smaller, specialized class in a different school. His grandmother was adamant that he stay where he was and quite rightly challenged the team that being removed from a community that he knew would not be better for him in any way. Relationships were so frightening to him, so why would we challenge him further with new adults and new school environment? The team recognized her wisdom, and re-committed to providing Jacob with safety and consistency.

For grade three, he was allocated to the teacher who had had him in kindergarten three years previously. By this time, he was showing the desire to learn and participate with his class, but still had such a struggle to stay in class. In the morning, he would attend his regular classroom with his educational assistant as he felt able. He would still move quickly to aggression when he was frustrated, and at other times was most comfortable hiding in a small space in the classroom. He was met with empathy and a great deal of curiosity about what was making him so upset at that moment. When he became aggressive, either he or the other children were removed from class to ensure everyone's safety. He was able to tolerate some playfulness with adults he knew well, and toward the end of his grade three year, he could even start laughing with peers. With his educational assistant in the afternoon, Jacob was becoming more and more open about the things that were bothering him. He was learning to trust that his teachers were unwavering in their acceptance of him and starting to move toward relationships rather than fight or run from them.

By grade four, Jacob was able to be in his regular classroom for the whole day. He still required his own space for those days that were hard, but trusted that adults could help him with his big emotions. He started to read books independently, and played soccer with his classmates at recess. His grandmother went for coffee each month with school staff and talked about parenting strategies, school, and community supports, and celebrated how far Jacob had come.

Over the five years, there were many times that staff wished they could speed up his progress or fix what was wrong at home, but the reality was that Jacob needed time to connect and heal. His first teacher who had been so new to the school reflected on his progress:

This is a child that we could have easily written off predicting that he would be permanently excluded from school and on the road towards juvenile detention. Instead we offered him a safe environment where he could learn that when it goes bad we are still going to be there. We were always able to say "I am glad that you are with us and whatever you bring today we will figure it out together." It wasn't always pretty but we all learned the power of persistence.

This story, along with others, is shared regularly in staff meetings and professional development days to remind teachers about the crucial role they play in a child's life. Playing the long game requires a huge commitment, both emotionally and financially. Jacob's success in school required the school board to provide full-time educational assistance for three years, ongoing attention to Jacob's needs, and regular meetings to ensure those needs were being met in optimal ways. Is this worth it for one student? Some may question such a rich allocation of resources for one child.

Our argument, and observation over the last four years, is that how staff worked with Jacob impacted the whole school community. Children are astute observers. They watch how adults deal with challenges, and experience safety when they can see that adults don't give up no matter how hard something is and don't respond to challenge with their own fight, flight, or freeze responses. When Jacob destroyed the classroom in anger, students were helped to understand why he was having such a hard day, for example, "*Jacob's brain is having a hard time feeling safe in the classroom today. I think his brain is yelling at him get out get out and causing a fuss is one way to get out,*" Staff helped them organize their own emotional experiences:

> *My guess is that you are feeling angry that Jacob had a hard morning and we were not able to get our work done. You might have wanted to yell and scream too! "Let me get my work done!" I'm sorry your morning was not as you had hoped. Do you have any guesses why Jacob has such a hard time in class sometimes?*

> *I see sometimes you look scared when Jacob has a hard day, I think his yelling and throwing things makes you worry that you might get hurt when he has a hard morning. Maybe you have been hurt like this before and you don't want to be hurt again. It is hard and I'm sorry. Being scared is no fun. Do you have any guesses why Jacob has such a hard time sometimes? Shall I tell you what is happening in his brain at those times?*

There is no immediate solution or fixing offered, although the teacher may finish by offering her help when they are angry or scared. When the students were helped to understand why Jacob behaved the way he did, had their own emotional experiences noticed and organized, and observed that their teachers could cope without becoming frightening, their tolerance for Jacob grew, and by grade four students could be heard saying to supply teachers, "*Jacob needs to be hiding in the cubby right now. He will come out when he is ready.*" Safety for Jacob translated to safety for his class, and it contributed to a school culture where everyone could feel safer emotionally.

Having acceptance and empathy did not mean that there were no consequences for Jacob's aggression. Limits and consequences are also a component of feeling safe as long as they are provided with empathy and repair occurs following implementation. There were times when Jacob was sent home and on occasion formally suspended. The motivation for these decisions was sometimes different. Sending Jacob home at times was a break for staff who had become worn down and were no longer in the position to offer him safety signals. Having him at school at those times was counterproductive because his safe adults were now providing danger signals, for example, irritation in their face and voice, avoidance rather than approach, or flat affect rather than delight. Teachers needed that break to be able to receive him better in the future. This was always explained to Jacob and his grandmother: "*Right now your teachers have to figure out how they can best support you when you come back to school in a few days. Something they are doing isn't quite right for you and they need some time to figure that out. They will let you know what they have thought about when you come back next week.*"

Suspension as a punishment to correct behavior will work best for students whose brains are already healthy. Phrasing the suspension as an opportunity to better understand communicates our intention to be helpful and lets us continue to "*be with*" the student as we try to figure out how to help him or her feel safe. When Jacob returned to school, he was met with delight and excitement that he was at school. He was not required to attend a "re-entry" meeting and discuss his behavior, which would have increased his shame and made it difficult for him to come back to class. At some point in the day his teacher, educational assistant, or principal would initiate a repair in their relationship. A repair may sound something like "*Jacob it's so nice to have you back in school. Last week was so tough wasn't it—tough for everyone! Did you have any thoughts about what made it such a tough day?*" Jacob, like many students who do not yet have good reflective capacity, did not usually have any ideas. The staff then could offer some guesses:

> *How difficult for you to not know! I think these big feelings just hijack your brain so quickly don't they? Your brain was certainly telling us that you didn't feel safe in that moment. I wondered if it had something to do with not understanding something I had asked you to do. I think you worry so much that you will get big trouble when you don't know how to do something.*

The staff member is carefully attuned to Jacob's responses to see whether her guess resonates. She might then give empathy if she is close to the mark or let him know that she will keep trying to figure it out.

Sometimes suspensions, formal or informal, are offered because someone got hurt and there needed to be a clear communication that hurting people is a significant infraction. Again, how the suspension is communicated is important. Jacob knew that hitting people was not ok, so lecturing him or shaming him wouldn't be helpful. We do like to tell kids what they already know! The principal may say something like:

> *Jacob you had such a difficult day today and I think if you stay in school any longer you might have more difficulties and we don't want to pile more hard on top of hard. I know you know that hitting people is never ok, and you are probably feeling badly and don't really understand how that happened. You are going to go home with grandma and your teachers will try to figure out how to help you when you come back tomorrow.*

The intention with such consequences is to be helpful rather than to provide an aversive experience, with the hope that the punishment will influence different choices. Jacob did not yet have the self-regulation skills to calm himself down. He was very dependent on the adults at school to notice when he was starting to get agitated and to co-regulate that affect so he could keep his horizontal and vertical bridges operational.

Consequences of course do not always involve sending students home. It is often a difficult choice to send students home to situations that are chaotic, neglectful, or abusive. From what we understand about our brain's survival functions, a child who is immersed in a dangerous home environment will come back to school with high arousal levels that will translate into the fight or flight behaviors that precipitated being sent home in the first place. Staff at our three schools tried as often as possible to use time-in school consequences. Time-in requires the availability of a regulated adult, and its purpose is again to provide co-regulation of the student's arousal levels so that they don't get into trouble. As we were learning together, some staff articulated their discomfort that time-in reinforced a child's misbehavior because why wouldn't they want to spend time with an adult photocopying or helping in the classroom or hanging out with the principal rather than do their work? They struggled with the notion that misbehavior was about needing attention so why provide it in this way. This struggle again reflects the difference for students who can self-regulate and those who can't. Those who have had the benefit of secure attachments or who have bridges in their brains that are less rickety can manage consequences that are more behaviorally informed. Children who do not yet have the brain regions and neuronal connectivity that allow for self-regulation require adults to help them. They *are* in need of attention. That attention is not in the service of helping a child avoid expectations in the classroom, but in the service of helping children to learn to rely on trustworthy adults, be regulated, and figure out what the obstacles are and what to do to overcome them. We come back to our mantra that if a child could do better, he or she would. Safety—for the child and the school staff—will allow for different learning.

You will have noticed our bias toward the use of technology in the earlier parts of this book. A huge frustration for some teachers is that they ask a child to leave their classroom and go to the principal's office, where they are given an iPad and allowed to play games. The frustration is twofold: one that the child seems to be "rewarded" by playing games, and two, that when it's time to come back to class, the child is unable to transition from technology and their behavior escalates again. As we outlined in part two, we advocate for limited use of technology. Although sometimes its use is inevitable, a child is not going to learn about why he is having a hard time or what to do about it from an iPad. When our children leave the classroom, the hope is that they will find a different opportunity to relate, one that might bring more safety and success.

Support and Mentoring

DDP is a relational model, so we needed to ensure that to support new learning, everyone had access to relationships that were knowledgeable about trauma and Dyadic Developmental Practice. In addition to delivery of information and provision of safety for staff, we needed to ensure ongoing consultation. Initially this occurred by regular visits to schools by Sian. Sometimes she would visit certain classes to observe and provide feedback to teachers. Sometimes she would attend staff meetings to bring additional information about what might be contributing to challenges. Occasionally, the schools would offer additional staff meetings or professional development days that were open to staff from all three schools. These meetings typically included the delivery of some information, the opportunity to discuss students, and role-play of how to respond using PACE.

Although helpful, the visits to schools were insufficient. Sian was not able to spend enough time with each school or with individual teachers. Support needed to be more consistent and required deeper relationships. The administration teams needed to be that everyday support. The principals and vice-principals were working with teachers every day, and they could witness those everyday challenges and successes. Sian met with the administration teams every six weeks for a period of three years. We didn't have an established program to implement and follow. The work was innovative, difficult, dynamic, and co-constructed from everyone's experiences with applying PACE and A/R dialogue in the school environment. These regular meetings allowed for the sharing of stories. What was working and why? What was not working and why? We would then inject ideas into practice in the weeks between meetings. The constant sharing of experiences allowed us to co-construct what Dyadic Developmental Practice could look like as a foundation for trauma-informed education. We knew that working from this framework was essential for some students but good for all students. Collaboration at all levels was a crucial component of sustaining the work. Having three schools involved helped us all feel that we were in this together rather than isolated. Each school has a different school climate, but the shared experience kept us all feeling excited, fueled our creativity, and bolstered us when we were not sure of next steps.

The school board's commitment to the project allowed us to expand the circle of support by providing more intensive training to student support workers and counselors. These individuals were already in the role of consulting with teachers about challenging students, developing student support plans, and providing additional resources to students. With additional training, they would be able to support teachers in the use of PACE and provide the emotional support required for this difficult work. Sian then consulted regularly with that group of individuals.

Not everyone believes that Dyadic Developmental Practice is a useful framework. Some teachers have been intuitively PACEful before they heard of DDP and now have a language to organize their practice. Others are open to learning, but easily revert to traditional models of classroom management when they are stressed or are not mindful of how students with developmental trauma can't yet self-regulate or learn. There are individuals who actively resist incorporating DDP principles into their work. This may be because they are in blocked care. Working with children who are volatile, reactive, aggressive, and unpredictable is incredibly difficult for our brains. Teachers bring to school with them their own histories and personalities, and there may be many reasons why they are not able to embrace this way of working. In our three school communities, this group of teachers is small, but that does create some tension for their peers. Often these are the teachers who use loud angry voices in response to student noncompliance, insist that students be excluded from their class until they can behave more appropriately, and hold more rigid and negative beliefs about a child's intentions and motivations. Some staff have articulated that it is painful when they believe that some empathy would help a student find their equilibrium and they are torn between supporting their colleague and supporting the student.

Looking after teachers' brains quickly became a key factor in our work. The use of PACE requires us to put our own oxygen mask on first. To be optimally responsive, we have to feel safe and feel well. The complexity of needs in any one classroom can feel impossible to manage at the best of times, and in these three school communities who had such a high number of children with challenging behavior and learning needs, it often felt like staff were moving from crisis to crisis with no opportunity to relax. This was especially true for one of our schools. It was a brand new school and was an amalgamation of two elementary schools. Students were coming to a new, unfamiliar building with spaces still under construction, seeing adult faces that were unfamiliar, traveling on buses for the first time, or traveling unfamiliar bus routes. Student's alarm systems were quite activated, and at any given moment, there were students running away, yelling and screaming, or immobilized in some part of the building. It was a difficult time to introduce a new paradigm for classroom management.

There was no way to fix the reality of the situation. Emotional safety and support were all we could offer. We worked to name and organize the experience for the teachers, who could then name and organize for the students the challenge of coming to a new place. The provision of safe relationships in the school community helped to ensure that nobody felt isolated and that everyone was working together with shared intention to provide a safe school environment for teachers and children. The playfulness component of PACE was used as much as possible with staff. At meetings administrators facilitated ways to play. Admittedly, there were often stories that communicated black humor, but making sure there were regular opportunities to have good belly laughs helped everyone keep going. In all three school communities, the relationships between staff are close. There is the feeling of being in something together, and, as we learned in part one of this book, we can do so much more when we are sharing brains.

In the spirit of sharing brains, we have asked each school community to nominate staff who are "champions" of the model. The hope is that this group will meet regularly, deepening their own practice and serving as mentors to their colleagues. Sian and Deni will meet with the group, again facilitating the sharing of experiences and the knowledge of how to deepen the practice of DDP. One of the goals for this group will be to identify areas of knowledge that staff would like to know more about and then plan four two-hour workshops that any interested staff can attend. In this way, we will continue to build both safety and support for school communities.

PRINCIPAL AND STAFF PERSPECTIVES

Below are the voices of three of our principals;

Supporting Staff was key. During our three-year journey to embed trauma-informed practices in our school and classrooms, it became very clear that I would need to pay close attention to how I was supporting staff in their work. Adjusting how we support students and behavior management approaches school-wide is a challenging endeavor and required thoughtful approaches to staff learning and support. It was not enough to simply provide staff with information and then to monitor the implementation of PACE and trauma-informed approaches. This journey of learning would have an emotional impact on the adults as well, and it would create many tensions and opportunities along the way. I needed to create the space and time for staff to have open and honest dialogue about their experiences. I began to set aside significant time for staff to share their successes (big and small!), unpack their challenges, and notice/name the strategies they were using with students. It needed to be okay for staff, including me, to grapple with this approach and be vulnerable enough to share their struggles without judgment. Over time, staff began to authentically support one another and be comfortable to question, challenge, celebrate, and push one another in their practice. Individual conversations about students became rooted in what we were beginning to understand about how trauma was impacting our students, and how PACE and trauma-informed practices could impact their success. I remember vividly at one meeting when a staff member was commenting on the small steps forward she had observed with her student and she commented, "This is a long journey and it's really hard." My response, which became a common thread in supporting staff, was that "It is really hard . . . that's how we know it's important!"

Principal

We use PACE at our school to support students and support each other, and we know that you use PACE with us too and it calms our brains. When we are PACE-ful there is laughter, creativity, collaboration, and a sense that our school is a special place where students are loved and accepted, and that no one is alone through their struggles. Things can be loud and hectic, but people are smiling, laughter comes easily, and staff don't hesitate to do something funny to show their care and connections to students: an impromptu game of tag on the front lawn, a secret handshake, some fancy dance moves, some creative snack making, 20 stickers on a cheek, and the list could go on and on.

It is the third week of September, and it seemed that both staff and students were on edge today and there was not much room for play or laughter or curiosity. I am reflecting on the day wondering what made the day feel not very PACEful. I felt the stress of administrative tasks not yet completed, too many morning meetings, the pressure of preparing for a staff meeting after school, and, most pressing, that we did not "have enough healthy brains to share." We were just triaging and were not really meeting students' needs, and it felt hectic and unsettled. I have learned over my six years as principal here that there will be days that will feel like this, and that I need to trust that tomorrow will be a better day, tomorrow we will feel more PACEful. I know that the connections we make with students, our belief that if students could do better they would, and our sense of community at our school will give us the strength to continue. Truly it was the morning phone call with a trusted friend, a hug from the Grade 1 teacher, and a belly laugh with my VP that gave me strength.

I feel so fortunate to have the opportunity to learn about PACE and to help the staff here use this framework to understand and connect with our children and families. Connection and love grows brains. The following story illustrates this point beautifully; Connection preceded compliance, co-regulation before the expectation for self-regulation and a year of PACE.

Five-year-old Robbie's mother was evicted from their home, and Robbie and his two siblings were sent to live with their grandmother and her boyfriend. Robbie's mom struggles with addictions, has lost contact with the children and with Robbie's dad, and has been in and out of jail for domestic assault charges. Robbie came to school every day seeking support and comfort, and he attached to an ECE in his classroom, calling her mommy, staying in physical contact with her for the whole day, and responding in violent ways when other students interacted with the her. Robbie often had meltdowns at school, and he sometimes ran from school property and refused to leave school at the end of the day. When we called Robbie's grandmother to come and support us at the school, she would often arrive to pick him up and would yell at him. Those situations felt out of control. Grandma was overwhelmed, and expressed concerns that we were "babying" the kids by the way we interacted with them. We were being PACEful, and this involved lots of care and attention. We were PACEful with grandma, and we worked with our local family and children's services to help Robbie feel safe and advocated that the family remain with us even though they moved out of area.

This year, Robbie has not had any outbursts and he has been engaging in learning in his classroom. He waves hello to the ECE to whom he was literally attached to last year and then goes off and plays with his friends. On Friday, grandma came to pick up Robbie's older brother Jack for a doctor's appointment. Robbie came to the office and saw Grandma leaving with Jack. He instantly fell to the ground and begged his grandma to take him with her. His whole body was tense and I thought we were heading for a meltdown. Then something beautiful happened. Grandma didn't yell or shame him. She named his feelings, looked for something of hers to give him, and gave him five big hugs and reassured him she would see him at home. Jack hugged his brother and said, *"Remember you're safe at school, it's ok buddy, we will see you soon."* It was a heartwarming moment, and Robbie came into my office to calm down and was back in class not long after leaving his grandma.

Principal

The recognition of the harmful impact of trauma on the lives of children, parents, and educators evolved from many years of struggling to meet the needs of all stakeholders in communities where poverty and trauma go hand in hand, and are experienced day after day. Our school teams are often overwhelmed by the volume of students experiencing extreme stress responses. We identified a real and pressing need to find more impactful ways of supporting children and staff through these difficult times. As an administrator, PACE offered a framework that enabled focused professional development and storytelling during staff meetings. (Acronyms in education are often the best way to shut down a conversation in many staff rooms, and I must say that there has been a broad acceptance of the use and understanding of PACE among staff). Emphasizing the importance of observing some children through a trauma-informed lens has raised awareness and curiosity among staff, the ability to reserve judgment in the moment, and to mostly be empathetic as the first response. We have more staff asking questions like *"What has happened to that child?*" rather than "*What is wrong with that child?*" Staff are more likely to accept that while experiencing a stress response, the child simply can't change their behavior. Most staff understand the importance of making meaningful, proactive connections with students in order to have credit in the emotional bank for times of need.

I have discovered that PACE meets the needs of all children, not just those who have experienced trauma. Our goal is to make all students, parents, and staff feel safe. At our site, we had the privilege of sharing time with parents who told stories of their intergenerational struggles with trauma. Staff sat and listened. One parent stated,

> *People with resources manage their emotions and actions better than we do. Our children can see that we are frustrated with all of the barriers that we are facing. We need stability and compassion from schools and care providers, it's as if we don't matter, agencies don't want to build relationships with us, we have to tell our story so many times to so many different workers.*

Parents let us know that when an educator asks "*What is going on at home?*," the result is shame, anxiety, a sense of inadequacy, and defensiveness. We have become better at inviting parents to share with us their knowledge of their children so that we can better meet their needs. Staff call parents to let them know their child is "*not themselves today*" and we wonder together how to support the child in school. We know that to judge creates a barrier for all of us. We have become better at listening and providing empathy, and we have noticed that there is much less tension between school and home.

I thank my colleagues, Sian, and her team for helping me to keep my sanity. Our learning has relieved the pressure of having to "fix" kids or "to make them stop." We have also learned the necessity to look after our own brains. Most days we experience harrowing moments of deeply sad, traumatic, and at times violent events. We have had to learn to be PACEful with ourselves, to treat ourselves with the compassion that we treat our students and families. The idea that students struggling emotionally respond best to well-regulated adults who are gentle, calm, and curious has helped me to become better regulated when I feel my own fight or flight responses kicking in. Having PACE as our framework helps me step back emotionally and remember to make the moment about the child, parent, or staff member in distress. Sometimes I wonder how some of the children manage to get themselves to school, how they adapt to survive, and I wonder how I can fulfill my responsibility to improve the life chances of those who make such an effort to bring forward their best self, given the complexity of their lives. I am reminded to use my privileged position to draw upon whatever I can to achieve this goal. PACE has been a helpful and flexible approach to becoming a truly trauma-informed community.

Vice-principal

The voices of these three administrators underscore how forming attachments is a long game, is hard work, and requires a great deal of support from each other. PACE provides a framework to keep us going. When we can stay the course, the reward for both staff, families and students is rich.

A teacher from one of our schools articulated that understanding how trauma impacted children's brains and the PACE framework was transformative, and was the most valuable and applicable professional development opportunity she had had in her 15 years of teaching. She felt that she had always been an educator that was respectful of student's dignity and was curious by nature but that Dyadic Developmental Practice and PACE helped her find more patience and develop better skills to help children learn. She stated, "*It's good to have the PACE framework in my head. What I might want to say when I am frustrated is not what I should say. PACE helps me know how I want to respond. It is a framework that is bolstered by science and helps me not be stressed.*" In further conversation, she reflected:

> I remember about 10 or 11 years into my career, I felt that I was reaching my used-by date and feeling disappointment in myself. Everyone around me was saying that there was definitely a time that educators were *done* teaching *these* students and I wondered am I here at that point? Then I started on this project. I was suddenly so much more hopeful about what we are doing. I remember saying, "We are all really in something together that feels bigger and more hopeful. We are going to get somewhere." It's hard but it's always been hard. I didn't feel part of it before and felt I carried so much on my shoulders. There was nothing connecting us. Now I feel connected in this work and I feel empowered, energized and hopeful, so hopeful. I come to work and can be tired, but I never feel hopeless anymore.

Another teacher reflected about her construction of a PACEful classroom:

> PACE has made me truly enjoy coming here. I don't have to spend all day listening to stories that revolve around kids and their bad behavior. To learn that trauma created physiological responses that hijacked kids was a game changer. You can look at it self-ishly—your day can be so much better. Your whole teaching experience can be so much better by using PACE and by being curious. It makes my job so much more pleasant. I can focus on where I want to go with my students. There will always be blips through-out the day but I use them as an opportunity to notice my students upset and to teach them how to "Goldilocks." How to find what feels just right. It may take some tries and some mistakes but we all have something that makes us feel just right. If kids are angry and upset, we talk about it and find our way through it. We have big colourful P, A, C, E on our walls to remind us all how to be with one another. I even see the students PACEing sometimes!

Both of these teachers remark on the incredible support and expertise of their educational assistants who are able to develop powerful relationships with students. They reflected on the change in culture of the school over the past four years and feel that PACE has permeated into the practice of most educators. Children feel calmer, and educators are more confident in moving away from prioritizing compliance to prioritizing understanding and creating opportunities for success.

One's staff's understanding of being trauma-informed was communicated in a poster she adapted from one she read in a blog from a special education teacher (see figure 16.1) (https://exceptionalelementary.com). This stands in a frame in the administrator's office for all staff and parents to see.

In this School

We are Trauma Informed

We CONNECT before we correct

We understand that behaviour is **communication**

We teach self-regulation
We allow "Do-Overs"

We think "can't" not "won't"

We empathize when someone is "flipping their lid"

We practice c**o-regulation**

We believe in restoration not punishment

We know healing happens in relationships

Figure 16.1   A Credo Adapted by One of Our Teachers from Special Educator Kelsey Herald. "Exceptional Elementary." Posted by Kelsey Herald: Exceptional Elementary, August 17, 2019. https://exceptionalelementary.com/.

HIGH SCHOOL

This book has concentrated on the work being done in elementary schools with children from junior kindergarten to grade eight. We have begun to explore what the framework might look like with adolescents in high school. We have an alternative program in our area that offers opportunities for adolescents and adults to work toward their Ontario Secondary School diploma. Most of the students at this site have struggled in mainstream high schools, given mental health issues, learning difficulties, and behavioral challenges that reflect developmental trauma. Some students are young parents who can take advantage of the childcare program. The team offer flexible programing, allowing students to work individually or in groups, in school, online, and in the community. Learning plans are developed with each student to reflect their needs and abilities.

Much like for the elementary schools that we described, secondary staff were also aware of their students' relentless outside-of-school-struggles that made inside school learning so very challenging. Given their age and increased ability to exercise rights and responsibilities, teenagers can be more difficult to influence. They often don't come to school, so it's harder to form relationships with them. Even if they do come to school physically, they may be absent emotionally. They may be high, inebriated, sleeping, or protecting their fears in other ways—disinterest, lack of motivation, and defiance. Teenagers are often less "cute" than their elementary-aged selves or more frightening, which can make it harder for staff to be persistent in forming relationships. What peers think matters more than what adults think or want in adolescence. This is especially true for those teens who have not had the opportunity to have a safe and caring adult relationship. How then to become a safe, caring adult? And how could staff provide education when it felt like time for teaching was running out?

The impetus to adopt Dyadic Developmental Practice as a trauma-informed framework came in part from the strong indigenous programming that was being offered at our alternative learning site. The Focus program is offered to First Nation, Metis, and Inuit youth. In Canada, the impact of colonization, the horrendous legacy of the Residential School System, and ongoing discrimination has meant that every aboriginal person has suffered trauma directly or indirectly. As for many nations with an aboriginal population, non-aboriginal people have done little to secure a sense of safety for aboriginal individuals or communities. Aboriginal youth are overrepresented in the criminal justice system and child-welfare systems, and underrepresented in postsecondary education programs and government positions.

Most indigenous youth, therefore, come to our education systems with a deep sense of mistrust that reflects both historical injustices and trauma as well as the immediate impact from intergenerational transmission of that trauma. Most of our First Nation youth will have immediate or extended family members who struggle with mental health, substance abuse issues, and interpersonal violence. We must be trauma-informed and provide a better sense of belonging if we are to provide equal opportunity for learning for our First Nation youth.

The high school team wanted to develop their trauma-informed practice in a way that reflected indigenous values. They felt that Dyadic Developmental Practice mirrored the aboriginal values of wisdom, love, respect, bravery, honesty, humility, and truth. Although the indigenous program is a small part of the alternative high school, many of its practices and philosophies extend through other programs at the school. The Dyadic Developmental Practice model was felt to be essential for both indigenous and non-indigenous students. The hope was that a theoretically and clinically sound model could lessen the divide between indigenous and non-indigenous students, helping staff understand and respond to each child's unique experience as well as developing a culture in the school that was more tolerant, compassionate, and inclusive.

As with the elementary schools, the team were already using many trauma-informed strategies and policies. The majority of their students have more than four ACEs. The team were already very skilled in developing relationships with their students and being flexible and creative in teaching curriculum. Students can say that it is the relationships with caring teachers that brings them to school. However, staff were still looking for ways to better understand their students, develop deeper relationships, and provide more safety for students who were enrolled but not coming to school. In late 2018, we began to meet to explore how staff could use PACE as a way to inform their conversations with students. Together we explored the possible meaning behind the child's behavior, discussed how we might address that behavior in conversation with the student using A/R dialogue, were reflective about the impact on our own brains when students' behavior was frightening or avoidant, and also how staff can support each other. This work is new, but it builds on the existing literature that communicates the imperative for caring relationships with adolescents.

WHERE ARE WE IN OUR JOURNEY?

At the time of writing, we are in the fourth year of this project. The tensions that were identified at the beginning of our journey are still present, but no longer seem impossible to resolve. Staff are beginning to embed PACE into their practice. Empathy and playfulness are perhaps the most accessible part of the model. When staff are together, curiosity is becoming a natural way to begin the process of planning for a child. It is more difficult for staff to remember to use curiosity with a child to help them build an understanding of their experiences. This may be related to time. There is often another dysregulated child waiting for the same support, and it is not always possible to go back to a child and make sense of what happened. For some teachers, there is still some tension about "opening a can of worms" and feeling that they don't have the training to deal with a child's emotions. Now that we have layers of support, we look at how these conversations can be developed without anyone feeling anxious.

Principals continue to hold steady to the original goal of helping children with developmental trauma change their brains so they can access education. They provide the compass for their staff. We have many outstanding teachers, educational assistants, and support staff who work tirelessly to create safety through relationships. They can say that Dyadic Developmental Practice has offered them a framework to come back to when they feel challenged by a student. We have two other school boards that have committed to using Dyadic Developmental Practice as a framework to develop safe relationships. We have set the structure for better support, and we look forward to deepening our understanding of what it means to be trauma-informed using Dyadic Developmental Practice. Chapter 19 outlines in more detail what we have learned and our hopes for the future.

In our next chapter, we explore the tensions that continue to challenge educators and provide examples—successful and not so successful—of how staff have managed them.

17

PACE and A/R Dialogues in a Regular Classroom Setting

There have been many discussions of how to use PACE or A/R dialogues when faced with the tensions that we outlined earlier. Let's look at each concern in turn and how teachers were able to navigate them. We will then provide you with examples of how school staff used PACE rather than traditional behavior management strategies in their interactions with students.

TENSIONS FOR EDUCATORS WITHIN THE CLASSROOM

1. Acceptance and empathy allows the child to get away with misbehavior, creating a loss of authority with that child and with other students observing.

Feeling out of control is a painful experience. It tends to make us feel scared, anxious, inadequate, angry, and embarrassed. For teachers, being in control of their classroom may feel like an expectation from their administration teams as well as a personal expectation, and to lose control may invoke shame in the anticipation of, or very real, critical judgment. When we feel out of control, most of us try to regain equilibrium by becoming controlling. We tighten up schedules, policies, procedures, and start insisting on compliance until things run smoothly again. Acceptance and empathy when you don't feel safe may feel like you are exacerbating chaos rather than reigning it in.

Some staff really struggled with the belief that you either had control *or* you were empathic and accepting. They felt it was binary. In all four schools, we had staff who were insistent that the administrators instill more discipline and were unhappy that behavior did not result in strong enough consequences to stop it. In discussions, teachers were encouraged to reflect upon their own experience with needing control. What did it feel like when a child didn't comply with requests? How did that connect with their own experiences growing up? What were the responses from their parents, coaches, teachers, and mentors when they didn't follow rules? Why did they follow rules? Why did they not comply in particular incidences? Administrators or student support counselors then helped them understand why a student might not be able to comply with a request. Securely attached children are willing to comply and please the adults in their world. Why were some students not able to do so? The hope was that through such discussion, teachers could come back to an understanding stance rather than a controlling one.

When we are set on having control, we lose the ability to be attuned and to be mutually responsive. The interpersonal bridge is washed away, the other person disappears, and connection seems impossible to find. We move away from our social engagement system and start to communicate signals of danger rather than safety. For some children, this makes it impossible to comply or compliance reflects underlying fear. For children with developmental trauma, allowing someone else to control them is terrifying, and resistance is a survival strategy. Since these children believe that their safety comes from being in control, having a teacher insist that they are the one who is in control is a great threat to their sense of safety, and it initiates a greater need for control on their part. It becomes a strong invitation for a power struggle! When either the child or the teacher wins, they both lose!

Having your own oxygen mask on is always the first step. Increasing awareness of our own thoughts, feelings, and reactions makes it less likely that we will "flip our lid" (Siegel & Hartzell, 2004). Together, staff reviewed the Dyadic Developmental Practice model to understand that acceptance and empathy did not preclude giving limits and consequences. In fact, limits and consequences were a necessary part of providing safety in the classroom, as were predictability of routines and responses. Acceptance and empathy allow us to keep that interpersonal bridge and stay *with* our students while we communicate what behavior is acceptable or not. It is the underlying emotional experience that is accepted without judgment. When we keep our understanding lens, we know that the behavior is an adaptive response to a neuroception of danger or life threat—it's just not adaptive behavior for the classroom. Empathy communicates that we understand. Empathy does not mean that there will be no limits or consequences. As we have talked about before, until we understand, we don't know how to respond. In staff meetings or consultation meetings, we role-played how to provide those limits or consequences using PACE.

Staff were encouraged to notice how students responded to them when they were set on control or when they were able to experiment more with using acceptance and empathy. Insisting on having control tended to result in power struggles and escalation of behavior. The following story illustrates the dissolution of vertical and horizontal bridges for both teacher and student as well as the loss of the interpersonal bridge when the teacher was set on having control.

Matias was a grade three student who on paper would have met all the criteria for oppositional defiant disorder. He needed so much control over his relationships and environment. This need for control stemmed from finding a way to manage a chaotic family life with parents who struggled with substance abuse and had a conflictual relationship, a father who was in and out of jail, limited food for him and his four younger siblings, and frequent evictions from their home. In school, Matias would enter his classroom in the morning, grab an apple and a granola bar, and wander around the classroom dropping crumbs and garbage, saying mean things to his classmates, and making annoying sounds that disrupted the teacher's attempts to speak to the rest of the class. His teacher would issue a directive to sit down and be quiet. Such a directive was a met with a complete lack of acknowledgment by Matias. His teacher then raised her voice and issued the directive again, adding *"Did you hear me?"* Matias would again ignore her. The third time the teacher issued the directive with a threat that a failure to comply would result in him going to the principal's office. The annoyance in her voice was very clear, her voice was loud, her face looked angry, and her body posture stiff. Matias would then start swearing, pull books from the shelf, or throw whatever was near him on his way out of the classroom. His teacher would then angrily direct him to the principal's office where he would typically spend the rest of that day, refusing to go back to class.

The teacher in this example was set on control and was not able to wonder why Matias was not able to sit at his desk or tolerate that he needed to walk around the classroom. She had placed his desk right beside hers at the front of the room believing that she could influence him better if he was near her. Although well-meaning, she failed to understand that, given his early experience, he was constantly expecting danger. Being that close to an adult and having his back to the rest of his classmates was just too dangerous for him. The more his teacher would insist, the more terrifying the prospect became, and eventually Matias would fight then flee in his attempt to manage the perceived danger.

His teacher's arousal level each morning was high, and she alternated between anger at Matias and anger at herself for not managing better. Both she and Matias met each morning expecting conflict and very quickly didn't like each other, which meant that interactions between them didn't get better.

A student support teacher approached this teacher with empathy and asked her if she would be willing to try PACE as an experiment. They explored together why Matias couldn't sit as asked or what his constant noises might be about. There didn't need to be an answer, just possibilities. These were written on Post-it Notes and placed on the teacher's desk. They explored the possibility of creating a safe space within the classroom. The teacher was initially frightened that if she allowed Matias to wander or not sit as his desk all the other students would do the same and she would have complete chaos. This fear was met with PACE. They went back to the supposition that if a child could do better, he or she would. Some students may want to do the same initially, but if they were ready to learn, they would find it boring to not participate in lessons and be motivated to sit at their desk. When the teacher felt ready, the student support teacher facilitated a repair in the relationship with Matias:

Teacher: "Matias, I have to apologize to you. I have been expecting you to sit at your desk and listen to me and have not realized that that is just too difficult for you. I have been getting cross with you rather than helping you and I'm sorry. Mrs. F has been helping me understand that your brain is not at all ready for what I am asking, it's too worried about things going wrong and you have to be on watch all the time for bad things that might happen. No wonder you get so mad at me! I have just not been understanding how hard it is for your brain to relax and know it's safe to sit still and listen. I wonder if you would be willing to try something with me?"
Matias: fiddling with a toy looked up briefly.
Teacher: "I think we need to make you a safe place to be in the classroom until you feel ready to sit at a desk. I thought maybe the back of the room where the books are, but you may have another idea?"
Matias: looked more interested but still didn't join the conversation
Teacher: "We could start with my idea and if it doesn't work we can change it. Any time it doesn't feel safe you can go to Ms. T.'s (principal) office as I know that feels better for you there. I am sorry that I haven't realized before how hard it is for you in class. I think I just wanted you in here so you could learn and I've been doing it all wrong!"
Matias: "Yes, you have!"
Teacher: "Thanks for being so honest! I feel better that you and I are going to figure this out. I may still get it wrong sometimes, but I trust that you will tell me when I do! Deal?"

To meet Matias's opposition with PACE, his teacher had to change her understanding of what it meant to have authority. She came to understand that she would actually influence him more successfully when she focused on understanding, accepting *his* need for control, and providing empathy for his experience. When she provided signals of safety in this way, Matias was more likely to take the risk to give up some of his own need to control and allow her to direct him. He had to trust her to begin to comply.

Matias did start staying longer in the classroom. There were still times where his behavior was distracting to the rest of the class and his teacher needed to set a limit. She practiced with her colleagues how to set limits with PACE and reminded herself that there would be consequences, but not to their relationship.

Teacher: "Matias it seems like you are really having a hard time being in class this morning. Your brain is saying no way, it's not safe here! I would like you to take a break to see if we could calm that brain of yours. You can go to your spot at the back of class or I could ask Ms. T. if you could go to her office for a bit."
Matias: "NO! I'm not going!"
Teacher: (matching his affect) "Oh boy! So hard to listen to what I ask when you are not feeling safe! You are saying 'No way! No way! I have to be in charge! I'm not going to listen!' Tell you what, I'll give you a few minutes to think about what is best for you and I'll take a few minutes to help the others get started on their math and then we will decide what your brain needs the most this morning. Here, I'll put a snack in the back of the room in case you need some additional brain fuel to decide."

Matias continued to be distracting for a minute or two but because he hadn't been met with angry direction he didn't escalate into aggressive behavior. He wandered to his spot in the back of the room, unwrapped his granola bar, and took a book from the shelf to look at the pictures. Once his teacher had introduced the lesson she went to Matias.

Teacher: with delight "I knew we could figure this out!" Do you think this is the right place for now or do you want to go to Ms. T.'s office?"

Matias: "No, here."

Teacher: "I really like that book. Shall I read a page or two to you while the other kids are quiet?"

Matias: Nodded.

Eventually, as Matias developed trust and his teacher developed confidence in the model, she might introduce some curiosity around what made it difficult for him that morning and to offer her own guesses to help Matias become more aware of his underlying experiences and how they were linked to his behavior. That might have sounded something like . . .

Teacher: "Matias do you have any ideas about what was bothering you this morning?"

Matias: "No!"

Teacher: with energy "Lets figure it out! We need to know!" I wonder if you have something hard on your mind. Your body tends to have much more difficulty being still when you are worried about something. Did something happen at home or before you came to school this morning that was hard and got stuck on your mind?"

Matias is free to offer something or not. Matias will experience that his teacher wants to understand and accepts a response or lack of one. She is no longer focused on an authoritarian form of control, but on a reciprocal relationship. Her authority is now coming from a confidence that they can work it out. that Matias has to learn to trust her in order to comply. and that help from her colleagues is there should she need to separate Matias from the class for anyone's safety. She was also able to experience that she didn't lose authority with her other students when she could use PACE with Matias. In fact, the other students became more tolerant of him, and eventually came to use the same language with him: "*Matias it doesn't seem like you feel safe right now. Do you need some space?*"

Ms. T. noted that at the beginning of the journey with Dyadic Developmental Practice there were many children who just couldn't be in class and that there would frequently be five children in the office or a continuous rotating stream of students angry with their teachers. Toward the end of the third year of the project, she realized that there were many fewer children out of class and she was less occupied with co-regulating heightened affect. Her staff were providing the necessary safety signals for the students to stay with them in class.

2. The use of acceptance and empathy meant that there could be no "expectation" for that child's behavior or learning.

The push for students to meet learning expectations is such an integral part of education. Federally, provincially, and at the board, school, classroom, and individual level, there are expectations about learning and behavior. As we introduced Dyadic Developmental Practice to our schools, there was some worry that acceptance meant letting go of these expectations.

We went back to what is meant by acceptance in Dyadic Developmental Practice. Just as acceptance is not antithetical to limit setting, it is not antithetical to setting expectations. Dyadic Developmental Practice, we believe, promotes high expectation for increased learning when we have access to safe healthy relationships. Science tells us that we can do more together than we can on our own. We may not know where the ceiling is for our students, but we know we are most likely to reach it or stretch it when we can develop relational safety and can build those vertical, horizontal, and limbic system bridges we discussed in the first part of this book. Not having expectations is also a way that schools perpetuate inequity. If we remove or lower our expectations too much, we are communicating implicitly that the student is not capable of learning. We may create a sense of inadequacy or reinforce the already existing sense of defectiveness. Coming back to our lessons from intersubjectivity, we may come to believe in our abilities—or lack of them—because we first see them reflected in the eyes of our teachers.

Re-visiting the need to understand what a child's behavior is communicating also helped us resolve this tension. As a team, we would go back to the brain science and see that a child who could not meet learning expectations may be blocked further down his or her brain. He or she did not yet have the safety and or the neural integration necessary to manage the frustrations, reasoning, executive function, memory functions, sensory integration, or other skills that were pre-requisites to learning. As we puzzled about where obstacles for learning might lie, we developed plans for reasonable expectations. For some students that meant that academic learning was postponed. Other students were ready for academic tasks, and it was that learning that provided them with self-esteem and confidence. Knowing where to start and how to proceed was only possible when we made understanding each child a priority.

A teacher in one of our schools felt strongly that high expectations for her students' learning was the way to ensure that they would have success in other areas of their life. Many of her students rose to the challenge and took great pride in their work accomplishments. Josey, however, refused to complete work. Power struggles would often ensue, with her teacher keeping her in for recess if work wasn't completed. One morning, the teacher was annoyed and said firmly, "*Josey! You need to do your math.*" Josey's response was to get up from her desk tipping over the table and swearing. She left the classroom and was pacing back and forth in the hallway. Another teacher who was walking down the hallway approached her saying, "*Josey my friend, what's going on?*" She put her arm around her shoulders, saying, "*Come walk with me.*" Five minutes later, Josey was able to return to class completely regulated. She didn't complete her math but was able to have a conversation about what was hard for her about math. She needed the expectations to be modified but not discarded. She had missed a great deal of the basic concepts, given changes in school, and needed to have more practice with basic math concepts before she could feel confident and ready to take the risk to learn more complicated math.

Some teachers motivate students to reach goals by using token economies. This can be very effective with highly motivated students who have well developed self-regulation skills. Seeing a visual progression toward a goal can be very satisfying. For students whose brains cannot yet provide the necessary neural integration for self-regulation, token economies have limited success. Often a student may be engaged with the system for a morning or a day or two, but quickly loses interest. Carter, in contrast, was a young grade one student who became fixated on earning stickers, and in no time, the teacher's intent to motivate positive behavior became another way for Carter to control the adults in the room. He wanted to know when he was going to earn his reward, asking multiple times a day. No answer satisfied him, and he would negotiate for half rewards, early rewards, and different rewards. An additional goal was put on his sticker chart: do not ask staff about rewards. As you can imagine, he never achieved his sticker for this goal and rarely for others. The frustration and shame that he experienced when he couldn't live up to expectations would cause him to rage and destroy the classroom. Carter didn't have the insight or the capacity to regulate his emotions to behave in the expected ways.

Token economies, level systems, or rewards often direct students with developmental trauma toward an opportunistic approach to life. They behave in a particular way to get the reward, but if no reward is forthcoming, they return to antisocial behavior or are angry at the person they see to be withholding the reward. Or the student may decide that since the teacher wants them to achieve the reward, the easiest way to upset the teacher is to reject it. Behavior may be managed but not changed, and the individuals don't learn about why they behave in the ways they do. Nor do they learn the value of reciprocal relationships and how to develop them. Inadvertently, such strategies may reinforce the shame that is driving the behaviors that are problematic. Several years ago, Sian was consulting to a school program that used behavioral principles as its primary philosophy. They were interested in learning more about trauma-informed practice. There was a young boy who had made himself a fort, and he would spend the majority of his time there. His teachers reported that he rarely participated in class activities. On the wall above his fort was a sticker chart with all the children's names and a number of stickers beside each name. This young boy had a handful of stickers while his classmates were on their second or third row. Although the intent was to motivate him to behave appropriately, it did the opposite. Every day, he was visually reminded that he couldn't meet expectations, so he stopped trying. While Sian was there that day, he did come out of his fort to join another student who had become frustrated with not receiving his sticker for good behavior. Together the two of them destroyed the classroom.

How might PACE have helped this situation? Acceptance: this student was doing the best he could. Curiosity: What made it difficult for him to participate in class? Figure 18.1—What Lies beneath Behavior—in chapter 18 offers some common reasons for behavior to guide our wonderings. Empathy: the provision of empathy for how hard it was for him to be with his peers and learn in class. A staff member might have entered the fort if allowed or sat outside it. They might have chatted about something they knew he liked or been quiet, but either way communicated that there was acceptance of his being in the fort and there would be no expectation to come out. Playfulness if appropriate: could a staff have joined with him in building the fort, delighting in his creativity or choice of objects to fortify his space? We have observed that when staff crawl under the desk or into the safe space the child has created and just been with them and waited, the child becomes regulated quite quickly. Obviously, if a child doesn't yet want you in their space, you might need to find the appropriate distance, so the child doesn't stay agitated. Or if you don't fit, you can invite the child to help you build your own fort! Acceptance and empathy very often are enough to help the child regulate and be ready for a conversation about what needs to happen next.

The balance between having expectations for work completion and acceptance/empathy for the child's struggle was something the staff at all four school sites grappled with. There were teachers too far on either side of the scale. Those focusing on meeting curriculum expectations without attention to their relationship were often frustrated and discouraged by students' seeming lack of initiative, drive, ability, etc. They placed the responsibility for learning on the student and found it difficult to be curious about the many obstacles—including the belief that learning is the student's responsibility—that interfere with being open to learning. Other teachers fell on the opposite scale where many hours of their day were taken up with listening to student problems. Teachers were drawn in to the child's experience of being overwhelmed and they became worried that additional pressures to learn would be too much for them. Staff meetings and consultation times were used to wonder about each staff member's experience of this conflict and ways of responding with PACE were explored and role-played.

A teacher on the limited expectation end of the scale had the following conversation with her high school student.

Teacher: "I have to apologize to you."
Brooke: looked surprised
Teacher: "Yes, I have not been communicating well enough to you that, despite all the big things going on in your life, you are a smart kid and capable of getting your credits. Instead of giving you encouragement, I think I have been holding you back."
Brooke: "I don't think so."
Teacher: That's the problem! I think I have been contributing to you feeling you can't learn. I love spending time with you and I definitely think you need someone to listen to all the hard things you have going on but you also need a teacher who says you can do this girl! From now on, we are going to find a way to do both. I will listen *and* teach! I know you can learn and I will remind you every day, so you know that I am right!"

The teacher would check in with Brooke at the beginning of class and ask her how her day was. She would present her with work that she knew she could be successful with. There were some days where Brooke was dysregulated and not able to do the work, but her teacher used her acceptance and empathy "*I'm so sorry you are having such a hard day today*" but did not lose sight of the expectation. Curiosity was used to wonder about what would help her, "*I wonder if you need a break for 5 minutes or a chat with Mrs. M? You can come back to this when your brain feels a little less scattered? Let me know what kind of break feels best for you right now."* Staff who place priority on expectation at the expense of the relationship often have a more difficult time accepting Dyadic Developmental Practice as a framework. Administrators help these staff members reflect on the underlying reasons for imbalance with the use of PACE. Educators may have avoidant attachment patterns where it feels safer for them to focus on behavior rather than the development of relationships. Some staff remained adamant that the use of such a framework was not helpful and sometimes transferred from the school. Some were willing to work with a colleague to stretch into new ways of relating with students. For these teachers, PACE was just as necessary to learn as it is for our vulnerable students.

3. The additional time and resources directed at a child who presented with challenging behavior was taking time away from children who wanted to learn.

Children who are not yet settled to learn, certainly require additional resources. In our current political climate, the human resources that support vulnerable children seem to always be in jeopardy. We know students do better when they can borrow a regulated, safe adult's brain. Unfortunately, those adult brains are too few. It is true children with developmental trauma require more resources. It is also true that we are morally obligated to provide some of our most vulnerable children with education and social supports. What does that mean for children at all different stages of readiness to learn and how can Dyadic Developmental Practice be helpful?

In our four schools, this tension is always there in some form. Approximately two thirds of the population in these schools have more than four ACE's as well as experience other traumatic experiences such as poverty, racism, homophobia, or other injustices. Parents can increase the tension when they become upset that their child has been hurt by another child or is being prevented from learning. Staff can become stuck between their desire to help the child with difficulties and help the students who are ready to learn. This reality is named regularly. It is not a tension that is going to be fixed. The challenge is to accept it, have empathy for the very real struggle, and stay regulated ourselves. We also strive toward the belief that if we can create an environment of safety, then everyone will fare better. We believe Dyadic Developmental Practice to be essential for some but good for all students. As our vulnerable populations feel safer, they will become better able to regulate their behavior and emotions, and it will be easier for everyone to stay in or move toward a social engagement system.

In the absence of enough regulated adult brains, a staff member may at times have to make the difficult choice to attend to the child with a high need for resources and to another child or children who are more regulated and open to learning. What we decide to do may change given our level of fatigue, mood, beliefs, or judgment. Often this is a difficult choice as it places the staff member in a position where they feel one child wins and another loses. Staff grappled with other possibilities. Did it always have to be a win–lose situation? If we consistently choose one child's needs over another, then it probably is and we will not be able to build toward an inclusive model of education. Sometimes staff felt that other children in the class benefited from observing how the adults communicated caring and desire to help everyone in the school community as well as watching how adults set limits around the ability to meet needs. They found that making the tension explicit helped. A teacher may communicate to the class that he or she must attend to a particular classmate at that moment and that the scheduled activities must change or the class must wait. She can do that with empathy and can later return to a discussion where the class can express safely their feelings about being asked to wait.

There may also be times where the child with high needs must wait. This again can be done with PACE: "*Ryder I can really see that you are very frustrated right now and I would love to be able to help you with that. I am going to call the principal to come and help because right now I need to be with the other kids. As soon as I get a chance I will come to see if we can figure out what is upsetting you.*"

We found that this tension was reduced when a child's well-being was seen as the responsibility of the whole school staff rather than of one individual. Teachers were able to suggest to a student who was having difficulty that they seek out some help from another trusted adult. This could provide the win-win option: the child was able to receive support and the teacher was able to attend to teaching the rest of the class.

4. Aggressive or intimidating behavior was making other students frightened and what was their responsibility to the other children in the class.

Aggressive behavior can be very frightening. Staff really struggle when they think that one child's behavior is traumatizing the other children in the class. They again experience being stuck between two seemingly opposite tasks: help the child who is being aggressive or help the children who are fearful.

Staying regulated ourselves was a crucial first step for both the aggressor and those students observing. That doesn't mean you have to be calm, as that might be misattuned for the student whose affect is dysregulated. You probably need to match the vitality of that affect—be more animated to match the student's energy but not become agitated yourself—to communicate that you are *with* the upset student. Being regulated is essential. Teachers were aware that their students were keenly watching how they responded. If a staff member moves into mobilization or immobilization in the face of the aggression, then the other students will be left alone in their experience and will be more likely to be scared. If a staff member could stay in their social engagement system and provide a regulated response to the aggressor, then children recognized that they would be kept safe by that relationship even if the incident was still frightening.

Sometimes a student will be very anxious or fearful despite all best efforts to create safety. Many of the children in our three schools have witnessed domestic violence and may become dysregulated by conflict. Watching the staff member stay regulated was important, but it was also important to organize the child's experience with PACE. A conversation might sound something like:

> Joey I really see how scared you were by Jordon's anger today. It was hard wasn't it? (said more with empathy than curiosity). I wonder if your brain thought you were going to get hurt by him. I think sometimes that happens at home. You get scared because mum and dad fight and hurt each other. Jordon was having a hard day, wasn't he. I think he also has big things on his mind and his body explodes sometimes. Then he feels bad, but I don't think he knows how to control it yet. What do you think?

If the staff was not sure of the child's home experience a conversation could still occur based on what they noticed about the child's demeanor. For example:

> Joey, you seem really scared by Jorden's aggression today. I'm sorry you were scared, that's not a nice feeling. I wonder if your mind was telling you that he was going to hurt you and you'd better get out the way! Sometimes when we are scared our bodies want to fight back or run out of the room or sometimes you might feel frozen to the ground and can't do anything. It seemed like you were a bit frozen. Did I notice that right?

Just being with a child trying to understand their experience will help them know that they are not alone and will build trust in the relationship with you.

The third component of the response to address this tension was to talk with the class as a whole about stress responses. Sometimes the information was given through a science class or a specific book read to a class or social studies. In all the schools in this project, they discovered that when students understood their classmate's behavior—and their own—they were less worried by it. Sometimes teachers worried about confidentiality and were concerned about telling the class about a particular student's home life. Certainly, details can't be shared without that child or family's permission, but generalities such as *"Jorden is having a hard time keeping his lid on at the moment because there is lots of hard things on his mind."* or *"Stress can make us all flip our lids. When we are stressed some things that help us are being kind to one another and asking what we can do to help"* can be useful.

5. The struggle to balance a child's need for safety with the need to teach him or her curriculum.

This tension is similar to the one about expectation versus acceptance/empathy. An educator's job is to teach and make sure that students have the relevant information to participate fully in life. The pressure to ensure literacy standards are met can be high. However, we know that without a sense of emotional safety our brains are not open to learning. Safety must be our first priority. The difficulty for most educators is knowing when to encourage a student to complete work and when to allow the child to play or work at a level that is perhaps below what the teacher knows that child can do.

We have learned in our six years in the Belong program that students show the desire to learn as soon as they feel safe. It was not easy for Deni, our teacher, to learn to wait for that moment, but it came invariably. Any attempts to push curriculum before that child felt ready was met with resistance. Teachers in our project schools are beginning to develop the same confidence. In a public school, a teacher may only have the child for a year. In our alternative high school, teachers feel keenly the need to prepare students for the work force and that there is never enough time. The pressure to "teach" can feel overwhelming. The administration team work hard to reinforce that learning is essential, but curriculum can be modified or delayed based on the child's ability to access it. Accessibility may change from moment to moment and from day to day, or may not develop for a year or two. The administrators play an important role in helping teachers know that they are preparing a child for learning when they can create a safe place for them in the classroom and develop a trusting relationship with a student. For Jacob in chapter 16, that took from kindergarten to grade three. What he received from his teachers in junior kindergarten and every subsequent grade was essential for him to learn to read and write.

Crystal came to the alternative high school in February of grade 9 after being expelled from her regular high school. She was angry, reactive, and defensive. She often didn't come to class and was typically disruptive when she did. Any attempts to direct or influence her were met with opposition. It would have been so easy not to like her given her many defensive strategies. Mrs. W was her English teacher. She felt a stubborn resolve to get to know Crystal. She would bring in magazines and put them on her desk with a note about a picture or article she thought Crystal might like. When Crystal threw them off her desk with disgust, Mrs. W accepted the rejection and understood that she needed more time. She tried hard to smile at Crystal every time she came to class, and when Crystal avoided her eye contact, she would use her voice in a way that communicated delight and compassion. She continued to put things on Crystal's desk that she thought she would enjoy: a cartoon, joke, cute picture, a cup of tea. After about two months, Crystal could sit in class without disrupting others or leaving. Mrs. W still did not put any expectations on her to produce work. After two weeks of settled behavior, Mrs. W placed a note on her desk that said "I think if we work together you could get your credit. Want to try?" It took Crystal another week, but she stayed after class one day and gruffly said, "*What do you want me to do? Don't expect it to be good!*" Mrs. W with delight replied, "*I have some ideas for books and projects. I can't wait to hear what you think about my ideas. You may have a better one and that would be ok too. Let's meet tomorrow and I'll tell you what I have been thinking and what I think you will be good at.*" Crystal was able to choose a project that she was interested in and through Mrs. W's belief in her abilities started to be more confident. Although she tried hard to show that she didn't care one way or another, Crystal was proud of her ability to work and earn her English credit.

Sometimes we try to introduce something, and the time is right, and sometimes we get it wrong. One of the common experiences of a child with developmental trauma is inconsistency; of knowing, trying, or behaving in a socially acceptable way. The Dyadic Developmental Practice framework allowed us to accept that the student wasn't able that day to know or take a risk to learn, not because they were not trying, but because there was insufficient safety. Staff could then be curious as to why that might be and have empathy for the child's confusion about why he or she might not be able to do what they did yesterday. If we have pushed incorrectly and the child becomes upset, we can apologize and repair the relationship. We might say something like:

> *I'm so sorry that I asked you to complete this today when it feels too hard. I am sure that it will feel easier at another time and we will try then. I think sometimes it's hard for you and for me to know when your brain is ready for learning isn't it? I'll try to get better at recognizing when it's ready and when it's not! We will be detectives together!*

When we can stay well ourselves and stay in our social engagement system, we will more able to find the win-win solutions and stay away from binary thinking. We must have both safety and learning to be truly trauma informed.

It has been the struggling to understand and work with these tensions that has helped us learn to translate knowledge into practice. The strong leadership of the administrative teams kept the compass true, and the persistence and dedication of staff teams permitted exploration and creation of a different possibility. The tensions will continue to exist. We can name them and can recognize there is no one or no easy answer.

EXAMPLES OF PACE AND A/R DIALOGUES

The following illustrate the use of PACE and A/R dialogues with students in our four schools:

In a grade four classroom, there were a number of students who would become dysregulated quickly; the classroom had the luxury of having two educational assistants. One morning, one child was starting to get upset. His voice was starting to get loud and he was beginning to pace around the classroom. One educational assistant grabbed a vase from the window sill, transforming it into her CB radio.

"Papa Bear! Papa Bear! Come in! I have a kid in distress." The other educational assistant grabbed a marker and replied "Mama Bear, I hear you! What is going on?"
"Papa Bear, I'm not sure! Should I ask?"
"Mama Bear, you should certainly ask! A kid in distress needs help!"
"Papa Bear, you are wise. Give me a moment and I'll ask." The staff member turned to the student who was now listening with a smile on his face and says, "Papa Bear wants to know if you need help?"
The student grabs the vase and says "Papa Bear, it's Little Bear! I'm good. Over and Out!"

A grade two classroom was a very busy classroom and the teacher struggled to get everyone listening to her math instruction. Rather than get into power struggles, she terminated the lesson and then next day turned the classroom into a pirate ship. She brought in some eye-patches and hats and gave each student a treasure map. They had to leave the ship (carpet) and use the map to explore the classroom for treasure (information). The students had to find cards with symbols on them and bring them back to the ship. On the back of each card was a number and color. The class then had to sort them into patterns and discover the rule for each pattern. When all patterns were identified, there was a pirate feast of grog (juice) and cookies. Later in the year when they were learning about animal habitats, the classroom became a jungle.

As relationships develop, staff are able to tease students and use a sense of humor to turn moods around. When staff can approach a child with a smile, it communicates that they are not afraid of the child's behavior, and power struggles are often averted. Jackson, a grade seven student, came to class with his hood up and ear plugs in, and flung his backpack down beside his desk rather than hang it up on a peg at the back of the room. Mr. D noticed and said, *"Hey Jackson, looks like you are having a rough day!"* Jackson stuck up his middle finger and muttered some curse words. Rather than get upset Mr. D was delighted and said, *"Jackson, you have the most expressive middle finger ever! I love how you are able to use it to tell me how you feel! I'm sorry you are grumpy. Let me know when you are ready for one of my jokes. I know they will cheer you up!"* He left Jackson at his desk without asking him to take his ear phones out, take his hood down, or hang up his back pack. To do so would have caused an escalation in his behavior. About 10 minutes later, he wrote a joke on a piece of paper and put it on his desk. *"Let me know if you can't figure out the answer and for $5 I'll tell you. I bet you can't manage the suspense!"* Mr. D didn't lose any authority with Jackson or with the other children. Jackson needed some acceptance of his mood and some space rather than direction.

Rachel in grade 10 was becoming discouraged with her work and starting to shut down. Her teacher said with some urgency *"Quick! Do a handstand against the wall. I'll do one too. I've heard its really good for brains when they are stuck!"* The two did handstands against the classroom wall and started to chat about Rachel's gymnastic abilities while they spent some time upside down. Then they did an experiment to see whether it had helped. Because Rachel was in better humor, she was able to get her work done with some support from her teacher.

The aforementioned examples also illustrate acceptance of the emotional experience that underlies behavior. Staff did not use force to push a student to comply rather they used their relationship and playfulness to co-regulate their affect. Students were then better able to comply. Acceptance of our underlying experiences tends to immediately make us feel better.

Michelle and Emma were best of friends. One day they had an argument that resulted in mean things being said by both of them. They came into the classroom crying and angry, and refused to sit together. The teacher's impulse was to problem solve and to help them through their argument. Instead, she communicated that she understood that they were both so upset with one another and how that would certainly make it hard to want to sit together! She gave them permission to sit in different parts of the classroom. It wasn't long before Emma and Michelle gravitated back to working together.

Matt was a grade four student who had a chaotic family life. This was his fourth school in five years. He was oppositional and reactive when things didn't go his way. One day he lost his temper and started to rip up his work and throw whatever he could find. His teacher with energy approached him saying:

> *Matt! You are so so upset! So angry! I wonder what could be causing you to be this upset? We need to figure that out because it sure doesn't look comfortable for you right now. Walk with me to a quieter space so you don't throw more things or rip up more of your work. Once we figure out what upsetting you, you and I can clean up together.*

The teacher was able to accept that he was angry and upset while also communicating that his behavior wasn't appropriate. Turning too quickly to limits and consequences would have increased his dysregulation. Once he was calm, the teacher was able to offer him more empathy for how hard it was for him when he got upset and could engage him in cleaning up the classroom.

Neveah was a grade eleven student who struggled with addictions and was involved in a volatile relationship. One day she came to school with a black eye and bruises on her arms. She seemed to make light of her injuries and was saying to the other students that it wouldn't have happened if she hadn't been drunk and made her boyfriend angry. Her teacher recognized that she wanted to immediately launch into an impassioned speech about how violence was never warranted, and that the incident should be reported to the police. She checked herself, however and reminded herself to be curious about why Neveah would make light of being hurt. Rather than speak to her during class time, she asked Neveah to come see her during lunch time. She started the conversation by saying, *"Neveah, I have spent the morning being curious about why I feel so angry that you have been hurt and you don't seem to have any anger at all! I can't really figure it out and wondered if you could help me understand?"* Neveah predictably minimized her experience: *"Oh Miss, it's no big deal, it doesn't hurt. I just have to learn not to make him mad that's all."* Again, the teacher recognized her desire to argue with Neveah and tell her she was wrong! She took a deep breath and said, *"We may have to agree to disagree on that Neveah. Help me understand why you think its ok for him to hurt you."* Neveah shrugged, *"I shouldn't have made him mad."* It's easy to see how a conversation like this can get into an argument quickly, and no amount of logic or evidence will change Neveah's mind. Instead, her teacher became curious about where she had learned to make pain go away:

I really see how much you can make pain go away! How did you learn to do that? I worry that you must have had a lot of pain in your life if you are that practiced at it. Now you don't even notice when people hurt you! I really hope Neveah that you can find relationships where you don't have to have armor like that. It must be heavy to wear every day. I know you think it's not a big deal but are you ok with me thinking that it is a big deal? I don't want you to be hurt. You have clearly had enough of that in your life. Do you have a safety plan for getting out of the way when your boyfriend is angry? Can I give you numbers to call if you are scared or needing some help? You may think I am over-reacting, but it would make me feel better to know you have some numbers in your phone if you need them. Can I program them in?

In this example, there would be no benefit to arguing. Empathy and curiosity about what made it hard for Neveah to experience the violation to her body could begin the possibility of her thinking differently while also communicating her teacher's concern and caring for her.

Dayton (17 years) came to school high most days. Sometimes he fell asleep at the back of the class, and sometimes he was more disruptive. Sending him home or lectures would not have changed the behavior. The staff had to be curious with one another and then with Dayton about what being high meant to him. The staff had noticed that Dayton did make it to school most days, so figured it was important to him at some level. He also participated most fully in cooking class. He seemed to enjoy preparing food and suggesting to others that they try what the class had made that day. They wondered if learning made him anxious and whether cannabis was a way to manage that anxiety. They knew that Dayton lived with his grandparents and that their health was not good. Dayton had a younger brother who also lived with them. Dayton at 17 years had a lot of responsibility in his family. Perhaps he felt that getting high was easy and that family and school expectations were hard? The staff started by just naming what they saw, "*Dayton its' great to see you at school! I see that you are high today, I wonder if being high makes it easier to be here?*" They didn't expect an answer, just wanted to Dayton to know that they noticed and invite him into being curious about what his drug use was about. They continued to wonder with him, "*I have been thinking that you are most confident in cooking class. I wonder what it is about that class that makes you more comfortable? Any guesses?*" and "*I've been thinking about how to help you feel more confident about your learning when you come to school. I would like to figure that out with you. Let me know if you have any guesses for me!' In the meantime, I will continue to work on it.*" In this example, we have to be curious about what is underneath the behavior if we are to have any hope of changing it. Tackling the drug use head on would result in Dayton tuning us out. Of course, if his drug use placed him or others in danger, we would have had to limit him being at school or involved the police before being curious. However, in this case, there were no safety issues and staff could engage Dayton with acceptance, curiosity, and empathy. As the relationship developed, they were able to state their concern about how the drug use was a short-term coping measure, but was jeopardizing long-term tasks such as graduating or getting a job.

Empathy is perhaps the easiest part of PACE for most people starting their journey with Dyadic Developmental Practice, and this is evident in the examples given earlier. In all four schools, staff have worked hard to meet their student's dysregulated behavior with empathy. Some of what you may hear as you walk down the halls are statements like:

> "I'm so sorry that we are having a hard time agreeing right now.
> It's hard when we don't see things the same way isn't it?"
> "I'm sorry you are so upset. You are having a hard day!"
> "It seems too hard for us to talk right now. I really would like to help."
> "I am sad that today is such a struggle"
> "Oh Boy! You are yelling so loudly, something must be
> making it a very hard day for you. I'm sorry"

In Chapter 18, you will find a tip-sheet on how to match the vitality of the student's affect. We often think of empathy being given in a soft, gentle tone, but remember that can feel misattuned to a child who is having big feelings. What do we do with students who reject our empathy? Sometimes students will experience our empathy as condescending or "fake" and accuse of using an annoying voice. We must first accept their experience. We can then be curious about why the child can't accept caring in this way and what can we do to communicate that we understand in a way that works for them. Often anger at an adult who is expressing empathy is about fear of vulnerability. A student may be terrified of wanting or needing comfort and must avoid it at all costs. Not giving a student compassion or empathy will not be good for them but we must find creative and playful ways of sneaking it in in ways that they can tolerate. Slipping notes into agendas, texts for teenagers, or warning that an empathic voice is about to come out of you so the student may want to cover their ears, communicates that you understand their fear, but will be persistent with what is ultimately good for them.

18

Two R's

Relationship and Resources

RELATIONSHIPS

One of the most important things we have learned during the last four years is that to transfer knowledge to practice requires a relationship. Not surprising really, since primacy of safe relationships is the core tenet of DDP and Dyadic Developmental Practice. We had the luxury of working with Wendy Fisher, who has been supporting our three elementary schools for a number of years and has been involved with the trauma-informed project from the start. She has additional DDP training, and for her Bachelor of Child and Youth Care placement she explored the question of how she, as a consultant, could help educators embed Dyadic Developmental Practice into their teaching practice and classroom culture.

In one school, Wendy worked with three staff who worked together in a kindergarten classroom. There were a number of challenging students in this classroom, and the staff were struggling to know how to meet their needs. In another school, who were not involved directly in the trauma-informed project, Wendy worked with four staff who had different roles within the school. This team had hoped to increase their learning so that they could support the other staff with trauma-informed practice.

To start, each team had to find joint intention—to come together over a period of twelve weeks to learn more about Dyadic Developmental Practice as a framework for trauma-informed practice. Everyone also had to agree to meet after school hours and to reschedule the meeting if any one member of the group were not able to be present. Each staff member was asked to complete a questionnaire designed to determine what they already knew about trauma-informed practice and what they would like to know more about or improve (see Appendix C). The same questionnaire was completed at the conclusion of sessions. Each session was guided by a time for reflection and the introduction of resources to augment existing knowledge. Dan Siegel and Tina Payne Bryson's book *The Whole Brain Child*, Kim Golding's book *Observing Children with Attachment Difficulties in School*, Kim and Dan's book *Creating Loving Attachments*, and Sarah Naish's book *The A–Z of Therapeutic Parenting* were excellent sources of information for teachers.

To help focus the learning, each staff were asked to identify one child that they wanted to know better and with whom they could be more successful in developing a relationship. In Wendy's group, who had not had previous Dyadic Developmental Practice training, she provided additional focus by asking them to complete the Thinking About Your Child Questionnaire (Granger, 2009) at the beginning of her work with them. At the time of writing, this group had not yet finished their work with Wendy, but the intent was to ask them to complete the questionnaire at the end of their sessions together.

Conversations with the participants in both groups highlighted the importance of having regular meetings where they could be reflective about their own experiences as well as be curious about their student's underlying experience. The group who had had previous training were able to delve more deeply and more quickly into practice than the group from a school who were at the beginning stages of learning.

Team members, Amelia, Hannah, and Ella, articulated, "*Dyadic Developmental Practice has become more a part of us, of who we are rather than a technique. The key for us was that it became a natural part of our being and who we are—we use it now without thinking. It is a way of being rather than a teaching strategy. Needs to be a part of you.*" The team was able to see that their new way of being was so much more helpful to children. "*They can trust how you are going to be. They know that their teacher is going to be interested in their feelings, will talk to them in a particular way, give them some options to choose from, notice when things aren't working . . . it's about creating expectations.*" The educators beautifully articulate and illustrate how developing attuned, repetitive, and intrinsic interactions can create the sense of safety that will lead to learning.

Amelia, Hannah, and Ella talked about how they practiced and practiced a particular component of Dyadic Developmental Practice (e.g., matching affect or storytelling) until it became easy. They would notice for each other when they saw the other use a the principle and felt that the commitment to coming together, both with Wendy each week and with each other every day, was an important ingredient of deeper learning.

Amelia told a story of a child who was new to her class at the beginning of the subsequent year. She had taught his older brother, who had a number of flight and fight behaviors that made being in the classroom difficult. On the first day of school, the two brothers were in the bathroom causing havoc. Amelia approached the younger child with empathy. She knew his brother well and saw similar traits such as not wanting to be seen when he was upset, running away, and defiance. She said she started using her storytelling voice right away and narrated how she saw that he must be scared on his first day at school, how everything must feel so unfamiliar. She felt she understood him and prioritized the building of a relationship rather than attempt stop his behavior. She offered him a hiding spot in the classroom, telling him it wasn't very big but she could put some cushions on the floor of a closet for him where he could be safe when he was upset. She recounted how the very next day at school, it was easier for this child to come to her. He wanted to eat his snack in the closet. Amelia had responded *"absolutely!"*, and he had taken himself there with no fuss. Amelia could recognize that prioritizing the relationship in this way had not always been who she was as a teacher. As a new teacher, she felt she would have expected him to eat at the snack table with everyone else and sent him to the principal if he had made a fuss. All three team members recognized how much better they felt as teachers—and as people—when they could use PACE and prioritize safety in relationships. Amelia reported that she also felt that she had become a much better parent since learning PACE and A/R dialogue and was being less focused on her children's behavior and more focused on their emotional experiences.

The importance of *"knowing"* was something both Amelia and Ella stressed— knowing a child, knowing a parent, knowing when something wasn't working, and knowing when to shift expectations. Ella also stressed the importance of knowing when she and her team teachers were doing something well. In a classroom, it can feel like adults are moving constantly from one student crisis to another. Again, the ability to come together in reflection each day or during quiet self-reflection times outside the classroom was seen as crucial. It is also important to know when *not* knowing is okay. It took so much courage for the team to suspend knowledge for periods of time: to tolerate discovery rather than knowing. Amelia, Hannah, and Ella could point to Wendy's steadfast acceptance and empathy as experiences that helped them at these times. All three are experienced teachers and could say that prior to this initiative, they knew what they were doing was important. They now all say that they have much more confidence that what they are doing is making a difference in their young students' lives and have garnered a stronger sense of purpose.

The ability to have Wendy work with teams to embed the principles of PACE and A/R dialogue into practice requires team members to be open to new learning. Both teams had members who were already sensitive to their students' experiences, believed in the importance of relationships, and were intuitively incorporating many trauma-informed practices into their work. When introduced to Dyadic Developmental Practice, these educators were excited by the opportunity to learn more about trauma and about how to build effective relationships with their challenging students. The additional opportunity to work with Wendy, who herself embodies PACE, allowed them to move knowledge into practice. Although they were asked for an additional commitment in busy schedules, all team members reported that they were refueled by the meetings. As we reflect on what this team has articulated, it reminds us of Dan Siegel's acronym FACES as a description of healthy brain functions. Amelia, Hannah, and Ella have highlighted that it is flexibility, adaptability, coherence (being open, harmonious with one another, reflective, and honest), energy, and stability that are ingredients of a good trauma-informed kindergarten classroom. They want also to communicate: "Have a sense of humour and always dig deeper."

Wendy felt she too benefited from coming together with these two school teams. She felt more confident in her Dyadic Developmental Practice skills as well as her group facilitation skills. She outlined some factors that she felt contributed to their success as groups.

- **Observation:** First, Wendy took some time to observe life in the classroom. The team of three felt relieved that she could see the challenge certain children were bringing to the classroom and didn't have to convince Wendy that things were difficult.
- **Flexibility:** Meetings were scheduled in a way that respected the team's time and level of energy. For example, at busy times of the year, the team may not meet for three weeks. At other times, they may have weekly meetings. Time of sessions also varied based on what the team wanted to learn, their energy level, or competing commitments.
- **Acceptance:** All team members come to the table with different levels of experience, and there was no judgment about what members knew or didn't know.
- **Attunement:** Learning and information giving was guided by the needs of group members. In this way, learning was co-constructed through reciprocal dialogues. What the group wanted to learn was dictated by the conversations that developed rather than by a particular curriculum or template.
- **Process versus Content:** Similarly, to what administration teams noted about learning, Wendy recognized that it was the coming together to discuss, reflect, and grapple with tensions that was working to embed the learning not the giving of information. The safety that developed in the group allowed each member to be open to exploration of their student's experiences as well as their own and to be receptive to new ways of responding.

The next pages contain some resources and exercises that the group found helpful.

RESOURCES

PACE

Teachers often make their own summary of PACE for themselves or for the classroom. Below is a summary of PACE for you to use or adapt.

TEXTBOX 18.1

PACE is an attitude and a way to communicate to others that they can be close to us without fear. When we can provide these safety signals to children, it is a way to co-regulate their affect, help them find emotional equilibrium, and gradually make sense of their lives. They are not tools to be applied in a linear or template fashion. We do not apply one cup of Playfulness followed by two teaspoons of Acceptance, one tablespoon of Curiosity, and two cups of Empathy. Acceptance of underlying experience must be a constant. Empathy can be used liberally, but may not always be tolerated. Sometimes curiosity and playfulness must wait until the child is more regulated.

Playfulness: When we play with another we experience enjoyment. The mirror neurons in our brains help us experience ourselves the way that other people see us, so when an adult enjoys a child, the child feels enjoyable. For children who have been hurt, this is a new experience, as abuse and neglect inherently cause shame and their experience of themselves is typically one of being unlovable, a nuisance, disgusting, and unwanted. It's really hard to play with someone you don't like, so when we can be playful with hurt children, we are communicating that they are enjoyable and likeable. Being playful with hurt children also communicates that you are confident and hopeful that their lives will improve. Play is also a crucial component of learning how to get along with others. Without play in their lives, hurt children are further isolated from others and from learning opportunities. Learning how to play is a really important step toward healing. With your students, think of ways to gently tease, joke, and delight in them.

Acceptance: Acceptance is of the child's underlying emotional experience that leads to behavior. Acceptance makes us feel safe. It communicates that our support is unconditional and that the behavior is less important than the relationship. For children with developmental trauma, it can be difficult to accept their underlying deep sense of self-loathing, rage, or despair. As parents or teachers, we like to argue with, reassure, minimize, or distract children from painful feelings. We need to challenge ourselves to accept all parts and all experiences of our students so that they can begin to integrate those parts themselves and begin to heal. If we can accept the child underneath the behavior, then their self-acceptance will increase and it will help them be ready to address their behavior.

Curiosity: Helps us stay in our understanding stance and explore what might be causing the challenging behavior. Children with developmental trauma don't typically have any idea why they do what they do or why adults to what they do. The story they make up is usually that they are bad kids or adults are mean. Wondering out loud invites the child to be more reflective, bridging the right and left hemispheres, and helps organize their experiences so that they can be less confusing. When we really want to understand a child, intersubjectively, we communicate that the child is worth understanding.

Use "I wonder" liberally. "I wonder how come . . . ? Lets figure it out!" Be sure your curiosity is also nonjudgmental and it communicates interest in the child you are discovering.

Empathy: Helps us feel "felt." It is not sympathy, pity, or reassurance. It can communicate that we understand and are "with" the student. When we feel others are with us in our experience we can do more and feel braver or stronger. We can express empathy for any emotional experience, not just sadness. We communicate our empathy verbally and nonverbally through our tone, intensity and rhythm of our voice, our soft gaze and open body posture, and, when safe, touch. Having empathy for a child's experience does not mean that there will be an absence of consequence or limits. Consequences and limits can be delivered with empathy.

"It's so hard right now." . . . "I'm so sorry this is tricky." . . . "Oh boy, you really wished you could."

CURIOSITY: WHAT LIES UNDERNEATH BEHAVIOR?

In training therapists and teachers, we often use this exercise (table 18.1). We write as many challenging behaviors as we can think of on the top of flip-chart paper and ask small groups to list what might cause a child to behave in this way, with particular emphasis on emotional experiences. You will see that fear, shame, need for control, desire for connection, anger, and sadness are common to a wide range of behaviors. Knowing this helps us stay away from being reactive with consequences— How do we consequence fear or shame?—and have empathy and compassion for our student's painful emotional experiences.

Following are examples of tip sheets presented to the team to help them learn specific A/R dialogue skills.

Table 18.1   What Lies Underneath Behavior?

Aggression	Stealing	Lying	Substance Abuse	Defiance
Fear	Fear	Fear – to avoid	Shame	Need for
Terror	Jealousy	trouble	Anxiety	control
Sensory	Blocked	Blocked	Fear	Shame
integration	empathy	empathy	Loss	Fear
difficulties	Shame	Shame	Sadness	Anger
Embarrassment	Impulsivity	Anger	Sleep issues	Sadness
Misperception	Anger	Need for control	Genetic	Loneliness
of intent	Need	Dissociation	predisposition	Mistrust
Shame	Desire	Attempt at	Poor social	Poor
Anger	Need for control	connection/	supports	frustration
Need to	Lack of	desire to	Desire to belong	tolerance
control	understanding	belong	Poor self-esteem	Poor self-
Anxiety	Mistrust	Lack of	Poor coping	regulation
Hunger		understanding		Sense of
Lack of sleep		Poor self-esteem		inadequacy
Impulsivity		Mistrust		Sensory
Blocked				integration
empathy				difficulties
Way to belong				Fatigue
(e.g., gang)				

Toileting issues	Running Away	Suicidal Ideation	Hoarding	Self harm
Fear	Fear	Sadness	Anxiety	Shame
Shame	Shame	Despair	Fear	Anger
Anger	Anger	Loneliness	Impulsivity	Sadness
Poor ability to	Loneliness	Substance use	Need for	Despair
recognize	Terror	Depression	comfort	Need for
body cues	Need to avoid	Anger	Compulsive	connection
Loss	intimacy/	Need for	Loss	Loneliness
	demands	connection		
	Mistrust of			
	parents or			
	authority			
	Embarrassment			
	Peer pressure			

School Refusal	Inattention	Sleep problems	Impulsivity
Fear	Depression	Fear	Fear
Anxiety	Lack of sleep	Hunger	Anger
Shame	Hunger	Self-regulation	Sensory
Responsibility for parent's	Fear	difficulties	integration
well-being	Language processing	Substance use	difficulties
Lack of sleep	difficulties	Shame	Desire for
Sensory issues that make	Anxiety	Depression	connection
bus rides difficult	Second language	Dissociation	Social anxiety
Victimization at school	Sensory integration		
Substance use	difficulties		
Fatigue			

There may be other things that you can think of that might be causing a child—or parent—to behave in a particular way. Poverty, victimization of any sort, and discrimination may also a big part of what makes our students struggle to learn. We cannot change these powerful influences of behavior through consequences. Although consequences may be part of our response, they are not what are going to change the underlying source of the behavior. Our goal is to increase our student's felt sense of safety so that such big behaviors will no longer be necessary. When consequences are of value, they need to be given with PACE. When we can communicate that there are consequences for a behavior but no consequence to our relationship, we can increase the child's sense of safety and trust that you are acting in a way that holds their best interest in mind. The consequences of increased structure and supervision are two examples.

TEXTBOX 18.2   MATCHING AFFECT–EMPATHY–TIP SHEET

What Is Matching Affect?

"The core of empathy is attunement and the non-verbal matching of affective expression" (Golding & Hughes, 2012, p. 196).

- Affect is the outward expression of the emotion being experienced.
- A student expresses his or her emotions through affect; the educator expresses his or her understanding of and empathy for this experience by matching the student's affect.
- This is how understanding of the student's inner experience is conveyed by the educator.

How do educators set the emotional tone for students?

- When a student is becoming dysregulated, it is important for the adult to stay regulated and nurturing (Golding, 2013, p. 80).
- The adult remaining calm does not mean being quiet. If an educator uses an intense but regulated tone that matches the intensity of the student's feelings, this will support the student in becoming regulated (Golding, 2013, p. 80). For example, if the student is sad, the educator should be softer and quieter. If the student is angry, the educator needs to use a more intense tone without becoming angry himself/herself (Golding, 2013, p. 80).

Intensity is perceived in the loudness of the sound.

When a student's voice is slow, the educator's voice is slow. When a student's voice is agitated, the educator's voice is animated, matching the rhythm and intensity of the student's voice (Golding & Hughes, 2012, p. 196).

TEXTBOX 18.3   STORYTELLING & WONDERING ALOUD–TIP SHEET

Stories are used as a means of communication

- Educators use stories to teach, to build relationships, and for understanding.
- Stories can be a gentle way to connect with students and make sense of the experience being explored.
- Stories emerge formally or informally.

Coherent narrative: (Siegel, 2015, Golding, 2008, Hughes & Baylin, 2016)

- It helps us to heal and move on by integrating new information with what we already know.
- It helps us to understand our life experiences.
- It is a dynamic story that changes as we experience and learn, and develop a deeper understanding of our past.
- Creating a coherent narrative helps promote emotion regulation.

Intersubjectivity: "Storytelling is at the heart of an intersubjective approach" (Golding, 2013).

- Refers to the common sense and shared meanings constructed by people in their interactions with each other.

Wonder aloud: (Golding, 2013).

- An adult can help children make sense of their experience and inner emotional life by wondering aloud.
- Consider how parents link behavior being displayed by their infants by talking to them and wondering about what he or she is feeling.
- Wonder aloud to make sense of behavior.
- "To accomplish this an adult has to appropriate, 'mentality-taking,' the perspective of the child in order to understand how the child is feeling underneath the behavior which is an expression of these feelings."

Examples:

"I wonder if Dillan is feeling very angry because he had to leave the playground. He was really enjoying playing and he is mad that he has to come inside."
"I think you might be feeling a bit angry because it is time to clean up."
"I know this is hard for you . . . I am wondering if you are feeling . . ."

REFLECTIONS AND ROLE-PLAYS

Some of the reflections that were used with these two teams included the following;

- What does control mean to you?
- How did your parents influence you to comply?
- What do you notice about your thinking and emotions when you feel out of control?
- What does matching the vitality of affect mean to you? Do you see value in using it to co-regulate a student's emotions? What does it feel like when you try matching affect?
- Where to you think you could increase storytelling with student to help them understand their behavior or what is happening in the classroom?
- What does success mean to you and how do you measure it?

Role-Plays

Using PACE of A/R dialogue can feel right and intuitive, but the conversation you have in your head does not always come out the way you would like it to when you most need it. Most of us are uncomfortable with role-play, but it is a powerful way to practice the PACE language. With a colleague or in your small group, you can role-play interactions or situations you encounter in your classroom or can use the following examples to guide you. Remember to first wonder what the behavior might be communicating. How might you use a playful, curious or empathic response? How might matching the vitality of affect sound? You might want to write your responses down before you role-play. You may also want to compare a non-PACEful approach with a PACEful one, and ask your colleague how each interaction felt to them. The purpose of role-plays is to allow us to play with ideas, make mistakes, and receive feedback from your colleagues. Allow yourself to experiment.

Suggested role-plays:

(1) Shannon, a grade four student, is typically a quiet student who tries hard to please and do her work well. You inform the class that this afternoon's schedule changed to accommodate a presentation to the school from the community police officer. A few minutes later, you ask Shannon and two other students to hand out books. Shannon doesn't seem to have heard so you ask again. Shannon jumps up, yells "*I heard you! I'm not doing it! I hate you!*", and runs from the class.

(2) Reggie is a grade seven student who is often absent. When he does attend class, he frequently falls asleep at his desk. He doesn't complete much work, but the work he does hand in suggests that he is bright and creative. Your attempts to encourage him to do his work typically result in opposition. You approach

him one day and say, "Reggie how can we help you get your work done?" He responds with "I don't care!"

(3) Jaycee enters her grade two classroom yelling at her friend *"I hate you! You are not coming to my birthday party!"*

(4) Sixteen-year-old Justin is clearly high. He is not being disruptive, but the other students are giggling and pointing to him.

(5) Emma (seventeen years) is furious at another student in her class. She is swearing and intimidating. *"I'm going to f_____ kill you! You had better watch out you B____. Don't think you are going to get away from this!"*

Becoming PACEful is like learning a new language. You don't become fluent immediately. It takes determination and practice. Please don't give up! You will find that you can access specific phrases and moments when it "sounds" right. It may be a word or two, then a phrase, then a sentence, and then a story. One day, you will find that you don't have to think so hard about PACE and that it has become more embedded and integrated with your existing skills.

It can also be really hard to practice on your most challenging students. Practice with your children, spouses, and nieces and nephews first. They will likely respond faster and give you confidence that you are on the right path with PACE. The most important advice, however, is to find someone to learn with. It will be so much harder on your own.

19

What Have We Learned?

Four years ago, when we set out to have Dyadic Developmental Practice be our framework for trauma-informed education, we were not quite sure what that would look like. All of the existing literature talked about the importance of relationships and that a child's degree of current relational health is a strong predictor of almost every aspect of neurodevelopmental function (Hambrick, Brawner, & Perry, 2018). However, there was little to help teachers know how to respond to students who could not trust relationships and who were invested in rejecting them, controlling them, or avoiding them. DDP, as we mentioned, was first developed as a family therapy for children with developmental trauma. It made sense that the lessons from attachment theory, intersubjectivity theory, and interpersonal neurobiology, which informed how we created safety and change in the therapy office should have similar implications for the classroom. Improving relationships can help buffer developmental risk (Hambrick et al., 2019). In our journey we discovered a number of ingredients that helped, or hindered, the development of those relationships. We outline those ingredients below.

LEADERSHIP

The culture of a school is highly dependent on its leaders. The leaders of our four schools are passionate about and committed to creating a culture where all students can learn. Given the demographics of each school, administrators recognized the need to understand and respond differently to their students. They were no longer satisfied with managing behavior and they wanted to find ways to change it. They recognized both the difficulties and potential of becoming explicitly trauma-informed, and had the courage and confidence to lead their staff in the journey. Leaders were in classrooms and hallways demonstrating PACE and supporting teachers. That meant that administrative tasks were attended to after school hours, making for long days and a tolerance for things not being done. Leaders also recognized the need for joint intent and collaboration. Although there were many times they would have liked to take over or tell people what to do, they were able to create a safe environment for their staff to experiment, fail, disagree, have successes, laugh, cry, fall down, pick themselves up, and keep going. Dyadic Developmental Practice for them gave them a language or framework to hone what was already intuitive. All have an excellent sense of humor, have vision, patience to reach it, a large capacity for acceptance and empathy, and an insatiable curiosity about their students and profession. They are strong advocates for their staff and students and they embody the two hands of parenting: nurture, warmth and empathy with provision of limits, guidance, and knowledge. It has truly been an honor to work with such strong, innovative leaders.

Each administrator will be the first to say that they would not have been able to achieve shifts in culture alone. They too needed relationships to nurture and guide them. Strong relationships between the three elementary schools as well as the development of teams within each school was essential. The regular coming together of the teams with Sian—an outside resource—was important, as was learning from other community agencies and partners. A true reflection of the term Ubuntu, which in the Xhosa culture means "I am because we are."

LOOKING AFTER TEACHER'S BRAINS

The first goal of our project was to disseminate information, teach everyone about how trauma impacts our student's brains, and introduce them to Dyadic Developmental Practice as a way to offer the safety required to engage students in learning. It became clear very quickly that looking after staff's brains needed to precede or accompany any new learning. It is a parallel process to preparing our student with trauma to learn. Safety in the workplace was a priority. Unfortunately, we could not eliminate violent outbursts. We were able to support staff by advocating for additional educational assistants and coordinate community resources. Support teams were given further training in Dyadic Developmental Practice so they could provide additional consultation and support. Sian and Deni were available for consultation or attendance at staff meetings. We wanted to ensure that nobody felt alone with the problem.

In addition to the provision of knowledge and consultation, administrators insisted on teachers taking breaks as needed, whether it be an hour or some days away from school. Teachers were given permission, explicitly and implicitly, to make decisions about reducing curriculum expectations or about what response they felt best suited the child, themselves, or their class in that moment. If the staff member's action was not optimal, they were met with PACE and helped to understand the incident, explore different possibilities, and importantly, how to initiate a repair in the relationship with the student(s). The message was that we were in this together and support was unwavering. Food and humor were also plentiful!

We would like to do more. Our current goal is to advocate for additional professional development days for schools who work with large populations of vulnerable students and families. Extra time is needed for connection, reflection, and play. Days can involve moving from crisis to crisis, with little time to pause and get the support from colleagues. Often teachers are with their students all day with limited or no opportunities to connect with other staff members. After the school day, there are family commitments and then preparation for the next day. It can be lonely. In Ontario, we have a set number of professional development days with specified agendas for learning. There is not enough time for staff in these specialized schools to reflect on their experiences, learn from each other, grapple with tensions, and continue to co-construct what it means to be a trauma-informed school and, importantly, play with one another.

Some schools in the United States have adopted a four-day week, mostly as a cost-cutting measure. Critics have highlighted the disadvantage for students who rely on school for two meals a day, parents who cannot afford additional child care, and the increased isolation for students in rural areas. Research seems to be limited and inconclusive about the impact on students (Anderson & Walker, 2015, Davey & Hall, 2015, Hill & Hayward, 2015). One school adopted a four-day work-week for a different reason: looking after their teacher brains.

The director of a K–12 Charter School close to Philadelphia observed a difficulty retaining young teachers. Her team adopted a four-day week for teachers and instructional staff while students continued to attend school for five days. The hope was to encourage teachers to pay more attention to self-care and promote a more nurturing culture for staff. Teachers could choose to work Monday to Thursday or Tuesday to Friday. Instructional time for students, therefore, remained the same. Assessments or other activities were moved to days were the regular teacher was not there to ensure the most consistency with relationships. The school also experimented with team teaching and smaller classrooms to support teachers.

Some school boards in the United States and Canada have experimented with year-round school programs for both elementary and secondary students. Students still attend the same number of days at school, but vacation time is redistributed so that there are more frequent breaks and a shorter break in the summer. Year-round calendars (single-track or multitrack) are typically implemented for reasons other than teacher well-being (Graves, 2011). Research is limited on how well they address issues surrounding student achievement (Graves, 2018), and there is even less research that looks at the impact on educator's well-being.

An initiative in New Zealand seems to be targeting both the issue of student achievement and teacher well-being. A professional development program called Te Kotahitanga was developed by Bishop (2001) and other researchers from the University of Waikato, specifically to target the poor educational experiences of their indigenous, Maori, population. Like with Canadian and the American indigenous populations, there was a consistent disparity between Maori and non-Maori students. Bishop and Berryman (2014) saw that most teachers wanted to improve learning opportunities for their indigenous youth, but saw the reasons for lack of student engagement as deficiencies within the student, family or indigenous community. Because of the "deficit" narrative, teachers believed that solutions lay outside of their control. Students, in contrast, unanimously identified that it was the quality of their relationships with their teachers that determined their educational achievement (Bishop & Berryman, 2014). Students provided recommendations to the project that focused on the need to develop and adopt a relationship-based pedagogy in the classroom. Teachers needed to change their perceptions, beliefs, and interactions if change was to occur (Bishop & Berryman, 2014).

Educators in target schools were, consequently, offered an 18-month Blended Learning course that allowed teachers to connect online and face-to-face. The researchers wanted a learning experience that allowed for more reflection and reflexivity rather than offer short-term, limited professional development and to move educators from a deficit to agentic practice. A recent article in the Toronto Star Atkinson Series that explores Education Without Oppression, quoted "[The program seems to be allowing educators to move from] powerlessness to confidence and fatigue to vitality" (Paradkar, 2019). Administration teams facilitate regular meetings with teachers and students to evaluate how teachers are learning. The administration team is trained to facilitate these meetings in ways that communicate that teachers have value. The knowledge that the program is firmly rooted in research and evidence-based practice provided a stable framework that guided learning. One teacher felt, "the more that our teachers engage, the more that our teachers make connections, the more they explore their own thoughts and feelings and experiences and knowledge and skills, the more open and alive and better teachers they become" (Paradkar, 2019).

The Te Kotahitanga initiative mirrors some of what we have learned from exploring how Dyadic Developmental Practice can be integrated into a classroom: the importance of relationships to provide safety, understanding before reacting, and the time for ongoing dialogue and reflection with consultants and in small learning groups that guide our conversations and practice with vulnerable students. It may be that when teachers feel supported, have access to knowledge, and develop relationships with students, well-being is fostered more than when given additional or more frequent breaks from work.

THE POWER OF RELATIONSHIP

The development of deeper relationships benefited both the teacher and the student. A study that compared the practice of platooning (the practice of teachers specializing in particular subjects) and looping (students keep the same teacher for two years in a row) confirms the importance of relationships. Platooning as a practice arose from the notion that teachers with a particular expertise could help more students achieve better on standardized tests than a teacher who had more general knowledge.

Fryer (2018) from Harvard University asked 23 elementary schools in Houston, Texas, to adopt platooning for a period of two years, and then compared reading and math scores to students from traditional schools where a main classroom teacher continued to teach most subjects. Test scores were the same at the beginning of the two-year period. After two years, Fryer found that both reading and math scores of students taught by specialists were worse than those who had been taught by one teacher. Suspensions and absences were suddenly higher in schools who used specialist teachers. Vulnerable students scored three times worse on reading and math scores. Interestingly, specialist teachers reported less job satisfaction. Hill and Jones (2018) in their examination of students around the world found that when people know each other well, it's a better classroom environment for learning, but especially so for minority students.

Some teachers worry that developing a longer or deeper relationship with students encourages an attachment that will cause further harm. Such a belief is not supported by what we understand from resiliency or child development literature. Teachers are powerful attachment figures for children, even if only with them for a school year. If that relationship can be extended, the opportunities for safety and moving from mistrust to trust is extended. Anecdotally, we observe that the children in the Belong program develop the trust required after two years to be ready for a transition to a home school and different teacher. They have learned that adults can be asked for help and are proud of being ready to transition to their home school. Given the practice of split-grades, it is often possible for students to have the same teacher for two years. Of course, this works only when the teacher and student get along. It will not be ideal to have a student for two years with a teacher who does not like them. There must be flexibility in the system to prioritize relationships that will create safety for a student.

NEED TO INCLUDE PARENTS

The other clear learning from our journey is that we need to include parents in our work. In the Belong program, this is easier to manage. We have a small program, and parents agree to participate in parent workshops prior to acceptance of their child. In the larger school, this is obviously not as easy. It is notoriously difficult to engage parents in school events. The parents of our students with developmental trauma are often themselves mistrusting and struggling with a variety of mental health or life challenges. It can be so discouraging for our staff who have used PACE to help a child manage a difficult time in school and then see a parent yell, shame, and blame their child once they are advised of the problem. How can we make it safer for parents to engage, how can we be thoughtful about other barriers to engagement, and what sorts of knowledge and support can we offer?

Dyadic Developmental Practice offers us a framework for our interactions with parents also. When we stay in our social engagement systems and communicate an intention to understand and be helpful, parents have more opportunity to move away from fight or flight behavior. It is not as easy to be open and engaged when responding to adult behavior, but reminding ourselves that action is often different from intent and having a framework to guide our responses helps to convey acceptance of the parent, while we address the behavior about which we are concerned. Our acceptance greatly helps the parent not to become defensive. Safety is also communicated in other ways. Having parents drop in at times for tea or coffee and chats is one way. Displaying art work and pictures of students having fun at the entrance to the school is another way our schools have tried to communicate that school is a safe place. All three elementary schools offer opportunities throughout the school year to come together. Such events typically involve food. Schools have organized barbecues, movie nights, dance evenings, and spaghetti suppers with the very purposeful intent of providing nurturing and communicating acceptance and playfulness—and empathy and curiosity when needed. Many of our parents have not had positive experiences with the education system, and we want to ensure that we can offer them new learning. In one of our schools, grant money was used to provide money for parent volunteers to get police checks so that they could volunteer at school. Schools also work with community partners to provide families with extra food, transportation, or clothing as needed. Student support counselors make efforts to form relationships with parents or caregivers outside of the school building. The Te Kotahitanga program in New Zealand also underscores how engaging with family is an essential aspect of transforming education. Many schools open up to their communities for events, encourage their teachers to be outside interacting with parents during drop offs, pick-ups, or school events.

We are just getting ready to offer Kim Golding's (2008) Nurturing Attachment Workshop for parents. Nurturing Attachments is an 18-week group that offers information about child development from an attachment perspective and offers parents DDP-informed strategies to meet their children's needs. The group also provides a community for parents to make friendships and learn how to support one another. This group will be led by student support counselors and is offered first to parents who have been identified by the principal as parents who would be most likely to engage in such a support. Our hope is that if this group of parents becomes champions of the model, they will help other parents feel safe enough to participate.

In the 2019/2020 school year we hope to identify parents who could join our team of teacher champions who will meet regularly and identify what is helpful or not helpful in our trauma-informed practice. Input from parents is crucial in so many ways. Their voices need to be part of our way forward.

Our alternative high school is starting an education program for parents at one of our elementary schools. They have recognized that there are many adults in that community who would like to finish their high school diploma, but do not feel comfortable in a high school setting. It was hoped that a classroom at the community school could offer parents and other adults a familiar space. If successful, this program may be a way to offer parents some additional programs around parenting and improving relationships.

NEED TO INCLUDE STUDENTS

So often our vulnerable students feel invisible and powerless. Being trauma-informed requires us to give our students a voice. Many of our students who have developmental trauma have no idea what they think and feel. Dyadic Developmental Practice allows us to speak for a child in a way that helps them organize their experiences and discover what they think and feel. Our goal then is to empower the child to assertively address their views to their teachers and peers. We cannot ask children to "use your words" until they first have words to use.

One of the principals recounted a story about a young boy who at the beginning of the school year would quickly become reactive around transition times. When asked to line up, he invariably would hit the teacher or his surrounding peers. His teacher would use acceptance and empathy and provide an organizing narrative for the student: "*It is so hard when I ask you to line up! You find it difficult to stop what you are doing, especially when you like what you are doing in the moment! I am sorry this is so hard.*" After many repetitions of this story, the student one day came up to her and said, "*It would really help me if I could line up with you and you would hold my hand.*" He was now able to articulate what he needed.

We have to be open to noticing and listening to what students have to say whether they are saying it nonverbally or verbally. We also have to have a readiness to respond that shows acceptance. It was crucial important that in that moment when the student articulated what he needed that his teacher hold his hand and allow him to line up beside her. It can be so easy to get lost in our beliefs that this student needs to be more independent, that we need to "teach" him to line up so that he can manage classroom expectations better or worries that if we show one child preference then others will be upset.

Although our intent may be positive, when we worry in this way, we lose the opportunity to listen to the child's voice.

SYSTEM ISSUES: EDUCATIONAL
POLICIES AND PROCEDURES

We have realized that our learning to be trauma-informed is limited by the structure of our education system. There are many things that we don't have control over that contribute to some students' lack of safety.

Transportation is frequently a challenge for many students. Bus rides can be long and noisy, and some students will arrive to school with their nervous systems fully prepared for fight, flight, and freeze responses. Some four- and five-year-olds are on a bus for over an hour to get to school. The personality of bus drivers can also make or break a child's day. Ideally, training in trauma-informed practice needs to include all support staff and creativity is called for about how to minimize bus journeys for young and vulnerable students.

Transportation also impacts when we start and end the school day. We often wish that we could start the school day later for our teenagers and end earlier for our students who can manage only a morning at school before they become overwhelmed. A consistent half day a week would also allow for our staff to have times to meet as teams to reflect, connect, and play, or to have extra time to plan for students. This may not be ideal for parents who work. We may need to experiment with offering flexibility within our existing school schedules so that staff teams can have a half day on a rotating basis.

On our wish list is the opportunity to develop an alternative school for children with developmental trauma. We could then construct our curriculum, our days, bus schedules, and holiday times to meet the needs of our students and teachers.

Curriculum

Increasingly, curriculum is focused on improving academic skills that are then measured by standardized tests. Students with healthy brains may be able to manage an academic focus. Students whose brains are compromised by trauma, developmental disabilities, or neurological disorders need more time and support to learn. Teachers may need to be creative in the timing or structure of curriculum expectations. If students are not ready to learn, attempts to teach and expectations for compliance will result in power struggles. For Jacob in chapter 16, ministry-dictated curriculum was deferred for over three years. The staff had to grapple with what education could look like for him. They had to become comfortable with seeing play as his curriculum. When he was ready, he was then introduced to academic learning. Some students will require a curriculum that targets and strengthens neural connections in lower brain regions to prepare for academic learning that requires connectivity to higher brain regions. Such a program will require educators to manage the anxiety that fuels the belief that they are failing a child if they do not produce academic results. We want to hold our expectation that children can and will learn when we prepare them to do so. We would argue that a failure to be flexible in our curriculum is exacerbating inequality.

Some students require modifications to the curriculum and accommodations that acknowledge difficulties in cognitive processes. In much the same way that we support students with learning disabilities, we might modify the breadth or depth of an assignment and provide scaffolding to manage weaker attention, working memory, executive function, language, numeracy, or writing abilities.

Sometimes those modifications reflect social or emotional sensitivities. In the younger grades, so many activities are organized around holidays or special days such as Father's Day or Mother's Day. Such times can often be times of anxiety for children with developmental trauma and even result in increased behavioral dysregulation. Making something for a father who is in jail or who is feared or for a mother who has not been seen for months can bring feelings of shame, anxiety, anger, or embarrassment. Drawing a family tree and statements about being thankful or grateful at Thanksgiving are other activities that may elicit emotional reactions that prohibit the meeting of curriculum objectives. Differentiating, or providing options, may be one way to be sensitive to this possibility. Making a Mother's Day card or drawing a family tree may be a positive experience for some, but others may prefer to develop art and writing skills in other ways. Some students hate to be seen as different from their classmates and don't want to be given alternative assignments. The key again is to notice what your student is communicating nonverbally and verbally about classroom activities. There are many reasons why a child may become dysregulated, but it is important to wonder about whether it is something about the task or activity. We encourage you to have conversations with the student about how they feel about what they are being asked to do. If they don't know, you can use PACE and A/R dialogue to discover what they think and feel.

Lack of safety is not the same as discomfort. It is neither possible nor advisable to teach in ways that don't cause discomfort to someone. We need to become increasingly tolerant of discomfort in order to build resilience rather then reduce it. But when we can have safe, open, and honest dialogues, we can make implicit biases explicit, and then they are open to change. Naming, organizing, and developing compassion for differences and commonalities will help us develop resilience in our students.

We talked in part II about our feelings about the use of technology with children with developmental trauma. Technology is an integral part of our world, and we need to teach our students how to use it safely and effectively. However, for children who cannot yet regulate or form relationships, technology often seems to cause more difficulties than benefits. We encourage you, especially for students in early grades, to limit the use of tablets for learning as well as for rewards and consequences. Students need to borrow your brain while theirs is developing. You will be able to provide many opportunities for intersubjective experience and co-regulation of affect that will strengthen neural connections that prepare that student for self-regulation and learning. iPads cannot do that.

Implications for Different Cultures and Races

When becoming a trauma-informed school, we also need to understand how experiences of racism, poverty, homophobia, or any kind of discrimination can decrease a student's ability to learn. We have talked in this book mostly about children with developmental trauma, but this hardship often exists within experiences that are not captured by ACE scores. We cannot be truly trauma-informed if we do not pay attention to these inequities.

We may not understand how culture or inequities are experienced by students, but the attunement, acceptance, and curiosity that is integral to Dyadic Developmental Practice offers us a way to wonder about it and talk to the student about how they experience us, relationships and their world.

One of the hardest things for teachers and clinicians to navigate has been how to work with parents whose culture prioritizes obedience to authority figures, offers different opportunities based on gender, or condones the use of physical discipline. PACE is so foreign to some parents, and they are not open to establishing joint intent. Staying in our own social engagement system when we disagree or don't understand other's beliefs or practices is our first goal. Remember, most parenting practices are in the service of teaching what the parent believes are skills necessary for a good life. PACE helps us stay out of a power struggle between cultures. We can agree to disagree. Such a conversation may sound like:

> *Teacher:* "Thank you for coming to speak to me about you son."
> *Parent:* In a hostile tone, "You people are too soft with him, no wonder he doesn't listen to authority in school. He has no respect for you!"
> *Teacher:* "I think your son is struggling to figure out how to behave in school. Help me understand how you help him at home."
> *Parent:* "If he doesn't listen, he gets punished. He gets a smack and sent to his room for the rest of the day."
> *Teacher:* I think you are wondering why we at school don't do the same thing? Our cultures are different in the way they view physical punishment. We are not allowed by law to use physical discipline. We also know that punishing kids in this way is not the best way to learn. Are you OK that we disagree in a big way about discipline? I imagine there are many differences between our cultures that can make it hard for your son and your family at times. Even us speaking in this way is probably very different. I think what is the same is that you and I both want your son to do well in school and have a good life!"

If you find out that parents from any cultural background are using physical discipline, then we are obligated by law in Canada to contact child protective services. Laws may differ in different parts of the world, although most communities will have laws against excessive physical discipline. The requirement to report can also be communicated with PACE.

> I have to by law connect with child protective services because you have let me know that you use physical discipline at home. My hope is that someone will help you be more aware of different ways of influencing your children that doesn't bring you into conflict with the law here. You may be angry with me now?

Being open and honest and communicating the intent to understand and be helpful can help us stay connected with students and parents no matter what the difference is between us. Naming it, making the difference explicit, and ensuring that there is safety to talk and explore how that difference impacts each of us individually and together offers a way forward. Just as it is important to be able to intersubjectively experience and communicate the positive strength and qualities of the child, so too must we experience the positive intentions and strengths of the parents. We must discover that these parents—in spite of behaviors that we may think are not in their child's best interests—are themselves good people, are doing the best they can, and are parents who love their child and show it in the best way that they can. If that is our experience of the parents we meet that they are likely to feel safe with us, even if we disagree about behaviors.

Working with Community Systems

Many of our students have complex needs that require connection with a variety of community services. Sometimes the collaboration between services is excellent. Sometimes it is harder, given difficulties with communication or fundamental differences in philosophy. Our trauma-informed schools have worked hard to provide information to community agencies about how they are working and inviting others to work with them using Dyadic Developmental Practice. Written information is available on the use of PACE. Kingston is a small community, so over the years we have been able to build capacity in our school boards and community organizations so that there is increased knowledge about trauma and Dyadic Developmental Practice as a model to work with. Inevitably, there are differences in practice that can cause conflict. In the same way we handle conflict with parents or between cultures, we must stay open to understand others' perspectives and have the safety to agree to disagree. PACE is needed in interagency meetings as much as it is in individual parent-child-teacher relationships.

Working in Collaboration with Other Models

Working from a Dyadic Developmental Practice framework does not preclude working with other models. The practice of restorative justice is utilized successfully in both the elementary schools and high school. Dyadic Developmental Practice beautifully provides a way for adults to co-regulate students' affect and to help them stay regulated enough to have safe conversations with one another. It helps students integrate their shame and, consequently, to have empathy. Without that preparation, we find students resistant to having conversations with adults or peers.

Stuart Shanker's (2012) work on the zones of regulation is also widely used in our schools. Many students have been introduced to the concept of arousal levels being in the red, yellow or green zones. The traffic light metaphor is a wonderful tool to help students understand how thinking and behavior is linked to arousal levels. We have again found that Dyadic Developmental Practice is an important tool to prepare children for the use of this aspect of Shanker's model. Unfortunately, many teachers teach zones of regulation cognitively and give children the message that they need to change zones when misbehavior occurs. Although Shanker speaks strongly about the need for co-regulation, we see that some people who use this strategy expect students to self-regulate before they have had the support of co-regulation of their arousal levels. Students with healthy brains will be able to self-regulate. Our students with developmental trauma will not be able to change their zone without a great deal of help from trusted adults. For these students, arousal levels can change quickly and without warning in response to unconscious experiences of danger or life threat. They move so rapidly from green to red that they don't have time to be aware of rising feelings or plan to do something about them. They also have poor ability to read somatic cues so don't get the warning that they are approaching the yellow or red zone. Dyadic Developmental Practice and zones of regulation can work well together. With an adult's support, a student may become more able to link his thoughts, feelings, and actions with the red, yellow, or green zone, and it can be a lovely way of developing a non-shame-based narrative about what happens in his body to prepare him for fight, flight, or freeze and eventually what he might be able to do to control his arousal.

EVALUATION AND RESEARCH FINDINGS

In our Belong program, strong leadership, the regular attention to and caring of our team's brains, the power of relationships between adults and with children, the inclusion of parents in our program, and the ongoing listening to the student's voices were ingredients that seemed to promote successful learning and emotional development in our students. Our evaluation data consistently shows significant change in executive function and interpersonal skills. During the first year of our elementary school project, we wanted to see if students in our elementary schools who had received training and support to implement Dyadic Developmental Practice were faring differently than students in a school where staff had not had this training. Two of our three project schools agreed to participate in our survey. Another elementary school who served similar children and families agreed to be a wait-list control group. Based on our evaluation data for children in the Belong program, we expected to see changes in executive function as measured by the BRIEF and improvement in interpersonal functioning and affective strength, two subscales of the BERS in students enrolled in schools where staff had received training. Interested teachers from our project schools and control school were asked to complete the two questionnaires on randomly selected students from their classroom at the end of October (allowing for eight weeks of getting to know a student) and again at the beginning of June. Additional measures of attendance, learning categories on fall and spring report cards, and reading levels were recorded. Eighty-two students representing junior kindergarten to grade eight participated from the two DDP-informed schools, and 87 from the school representing the control group.

We did not find the difference that we expected. Analysis indicated that there was no difference between the schools who had had training and the school which had not received training. At first, the conclusion might be that the training was ineffective or not being used by the project schools. Yet any visitor to the school would have been witness to staff experimenting with PACE and would have heard very different conversations with students in the hallways. Why was the training not translating into change as measured by the BRIEF and BERS as it did in the Belong classroom?

Timing

Our evaluation took place early in the implementation of Dyadic Developmental Practice training. Staff may not yet have had enough experience or confidence with the model. The majority of respondents were from a brand new school. The integration of two schools into one meant a significantly larger school, a new geographic location, and new teachers and administrators. Students took the first year to become familiar with all the changes. We saw a qualitative reduction in dysregulated behavior during our second and third years of the project.

Dose Dependency

We have repeatedly stressed the importance of playing the long game. Our survey snap-shot may have been too small a window to register change. Six months during a stressful year may not have been a long enough period to see the impact of this model. At the Belong program, students have the advantage of having many adults who notice, organize, and provide safety signals from the moment they get off the bus to the moment they leave school. Within a regular classroom, there are many more students and fewer staff to provide the necessary safety signals. It may just take longer for students in a larger classroom to move from mistrust to trust.

Qualitatively, some teachers could articulate that using PACE was impactful as a way to co-regulate students arousal levels and "felt" like a better way to have interactions. Some other teachers believed that students required more traditional discipline, and that acceptance and empathy reinforced poor behavior. Administrators would say that the majority of their staff, however, have committed to PACE as a way to influence their student's felt sense of safety, and that they are now, three years later, seeing more confidence with the model and more settled students. It may be that this settling occurred independently of the use of Dyadic Developmental Practice. Further evaluation is certainly required, but it is our sense that the model is helping some teachers respond to children differently.

Wendy's qualitative evaluation of her teams' experience indicates that the perception of their students changed, even when there were no immediate changes in their behavior. They were able to have more empathy and compassion for students. They were also better able to de-personalize challenging behavior, which allowed them to feel less stressed. They had more confidence with their ability to co-regulate their student's affect and more knowledge about what was happening in the brains and bodies of students when they couldn't comply with requests or classroom expectations. The additional consultation and support was instrumental in helping these educators feel more confident. In our evaluation study, none of the teachers or educational assistants had the opportunity for this deeper learning.

The lack of change in children's behavior, despite positive experiences of intervention, have been also been discussed in the evaluation of a DDP-informed parenting group. Kim Golding's Nurturing Attachments is a group intervention that uses social learning and attachment theory to help foster and adoptive parents understand and respond to their children more effectively. The program uses some Dyadic Developmental Practice and Dyadic Developmental Parenting interventions and promotes reflections and use of role-play. Several evaluations of this program find that satisfaction of the intervention is consistently high. However, despite improvements in parent confidence, sense of competence, and perception of their child's behavior, there were no observable differences in test measurements of the children's behavior or well-being (Golding & Picken, 2004, Gurney-Smith, Granger, Randle, & Fletcher, 2011). What we may expect from a program that is designed to improve teacher or parent insight into behavior is that changes in children's relationships and behaviors would be expected months and years after the program as children learn to trust their parent's acceptance and responsiveness (Everson-Hock et al., 2011). The same effects may occur in our trauma-informed schools.

We certainly need more evaluation. Administration of questionnaires in our fourth year of the project may show the behavioral improvements that some teachers are noticing. We would also like to delve more into how teacher's perceptions of their student's behavior translates into professional satisfaction and personal well-being. We would also like to more formally explore what, anecdotally, we have discovered helps us do this work. How do we ensure strong leadership? How do we cultivate and nurture strong relationships with colleagues? What is needed by educators so that they can have less reactive relationships with children and parents? How do we continue to provide knowledge about trauma-informed practices? How do we continue to build a web of supportive partnerships with community resources? How do we creatively get around school structures and policies that limit our ability to be trauma-informed?

We will continue to be curious about these questions, with large doses of playfulness, steady acceptance, and empathy for one another as we continue on our journey. When Dan first developed DDP over twenty years ago, he didn't imagine that the model would travel beyond the therapy office. Educators can be powerful attachment figures for children. When a teacher can see what a child can't yet see, can experience her value, they can invite that student into a whole new world of possibility. In the words of Dan's poem:

> *If you can accept what you find in me and believe it to be of value*
> *I may learn to do the same.*
> *If you join me inside*
> *And help me to arrange the parts in side—*
> *Name, understand, and*
> *Even be proud of them—*
> *We will know why I do what I do*
> *And we will discover what*
> *I now can begin to do.*

We hope that what we have offered you in our book are new ideas about *how* to develop relationships with children who have been hurt by them, and through connection create the felt sense of safety they so desperately need to learn.

20

Alarmed

We will leave you with a story written by Sian about Eli, a child who experienced developmental trauma. Our hope is that it will tie together the concepts we have introduced in this book and will be another way for you to understand some of your students' experiences.

Sometimes things don't work as they should.
And when things don't work as they should we might get

Frustrated
Mad
Sad
Enraged
Give up
Blame others
Worried
Confused
Frightened
Scared

Sometimes we might think that things will never get fixed.
Eli is a boy whose fire alarm was broken.
As you know, fire alarms are designed to go off to alert us to danger;
We even have special people who fight fires and then reset the alarm in case it is needed again.
When the fire alarm at school goes off, all the students stop what they are doing and go out to the school yard where they wait with their teacher for the fire truck

to come. The firemen and women check if there is a fire, and if there isn't one then they turn the alarm off so that all the kids can go back to learning.

But what if that fire alarm was broken and no matter what those fire people did they could not make the fire alarm be quiet?

Can you imagine trying to learn math or listen to your teacher with all that racket? No sir! All you would get is a headache!

We have a fire alarm in our brain. It's called the amygdala and it's a small part of our brain that has a very huge and important job. It's so important that it starts working before you are even born.

The amygdala is the part of the brain that alerts us to anything that might be a problem for our survival. It rings the alarm when we are

Hungry
Thirsty
Hurt
Scared
Sick

Its job is to make us pay attention and fix the problem.

Once the problem is fixed and our amygdala is satisfied that we aren't in any trouble, the fire alarm is switched off and we can go back to playing or thinking about fun things.

Sometimes for some kids, the amygdala stays on and can't switch off. This is what happened to Eli.

When Eli was a baby, he had a mom who had the same trouble: her fire alarm was always on because she had a boyfriend who would often yell at her and sometimes even push her around so she would get bruises. Her fire alarm kept telling her "This is no good for you!," but she kept thinking it would get better. Her fire alarm told her that staying was no good, but leaving and being alone with a baby was no good either! It seemed like there was nothing for her to do. So, her fire alarm stayed on because the problem of being hurt didn't get fixed and her worries could not go away.

When fire alarms in our brain go off they produce stress hormones. The most powerful stress hormone is cortisol, and it races all around our bodies making sure we are paying attention to the danger.

When babies are growing inside their mom's uterus, everything that their moms eat, drink, smoke, or feel effects the baby—for good or bad—because babies and mom's share a circulatory system. They are joined together for nine whole months.

So baby Eli's brain was starting to get an inkling that he might not be safe and there were things to be worried about. His fire alarm was starting to get a work out and was building muscles that would help him be on the lookout for danger.

It was a good thing, because once Eli was born his world was indeed a dangerous one. His fire alarm was always on!

His mom's boyfriend didn't stop hurting his mom. He just now did in front of Eli. When moms are hurt, this is a huge problem for babies as babies need moms to survive.

Eli was often hungry because his mom was either busy trying to make her boy-friend happy so he wouldn't be mad at them or she was busy taking care of cuts and bruises. She spent a lot of time in her room crying.

Which meant that Eli spent a lot of time in his room crying.

Crying is how babies tell us that something is wrong so fix it!

Eli's first days and months had long periods of time when he was left on his own with no one talking to him or knowing when he was hungry or when his diaper needed to be changed.

Every once in a while, his mom would pick him up and smile at him and would sometimes even sing to him. These were times where his amygdala got to rest a bit and he was filled with joy.

But then she would put him down and things would get quiet again. Or sometimes there would be fights:

Loud voices
Harsh faces
Objects flying
Sounds of faces being slapped
Tastes in his mouth that tasted like fear

These fights were super scary, and Eli's fire alarm would scream at him "DANGER! DANGER!" But what could he do to fix the problem? He was just a baby.

Eli's fire alarm also went off in those long hours without his mom. You see babies are not safe when they are left on their own. They need adults to cuddle them, sing to them, delight in them, and feed and change them. Babies need that for their brains to grow. They can't do those things for themselves. They are just babies for goodness sake!

Eli's world was either too quiet or too loud. His fire alarm was always telling him he was in trouble.

Thankfully, Eli was a smart kid, so he figured out a strategy to drown out the clanging of his fire alarm. He learned how to ignore the loud sounds while always keeping one eye open for trouble.

He learned how to forget how hurt he was when his mom didn't come for him.

He learned how not to feel his tummy saying it was hungry.

He learned to ignore anything that made his body uncomfortable.

He learned how to not care about himself.

He learned that adults can't be trusted and he should just figure things out himself.

He was pretty smart that way, because the noise from his fire alarm was deafening and he would have gone crazy if he didn't figure out how to ignore it.

While other babies were learning how to crawl or talk or were figuring out how toys worked, Eli's days were spent learning how to manage the pain in his head and his heart.

One day he noticed that his mom was crying more than usual. He wondered about it, but not for long because by that time he had learned to not pay attention to anything that required him to think too much or anything that made him feel uncomfortable. He had a place he would go inside his head that gave him some shelter from his fear.

He would just go there anytime he noticed the sound of his fire alarm, and everything would be quiet and hard things just seemed to be far away then. He liked that quiet.

Wait a minute! What was happening! His fire alarm was really, really loud and it was getting hard to ignore! At first, he was irritated because it meant he couldn't stay in that quiet place, but then he started to feel scared. What was happening? Maybe he better try to figure it out!

A strange pair of hands was picking him up. A voice was saying, "Hey baby, everything is going to be alright now." WHAT?! Everything was certainly not alright. Who was this person? Why was she picking him up? Why was his mom crying? Why wasn't it his mom who was picking him up?

Why was he now in a car?
Why was he now at a new house?
Why were there unfamiliar people all around him?
Why didn't anything smell the same?

What was going on????!!!!

What Eli didn't know yet was that someone in his neighborhood had noticed that Eli's world was very frightening and told someone. Big people had decided that Eli needed a home where things were not too quiet or too loud. He had been given different parents!

You may think that this was a good thing, but Eli certainly didn't. He wanted his own mom. She may not have been perfect, but he was used to the sound of her voice and her smell. He wanted her!

Every time his new mom or dad would pick him up, it didn't feel right. His fire alarm screamed at him: this isn't right, danger danger! Eli would then either scream and yell or, sometimes when that didn't work, he just got really, really quiet and would look at the ceiling and go far, far away in his mind to that quiet place he could create. Even though he didn't have big fights around him anymore, and even though he had enough to eat and clean diapers when he needed them, his world still seemed too loud or too quiet. It was just now that he was making it too loud by screaming or too quiet by staying in his quiet place. Strange, he thought to himself.

Soon, Eli had learned to walk and talk. His new parents would get so excited when he took steps or learned new words. Eli wondered why. Didn't all babies learn to walk and talk?

One day he overheard them whispering about him. They were wondering why Eli had such a hard time letting them be excited or letting them comfort him when he bumped into the table or fell over the dog. They were wondering why he didn't want to listen to them and why he would scream and scream when things were not as he expected them to be. They wondered if they were not the right parents for Eli. They looked sad.

Eli suddenly felt an awful feeling. It spread from his heart all around his body and he thought "There is something wrong with me." His fire alarm rang loudly at that because the feeling was such a yucky one. Eli pushed the thought aside and just went on with playing with his new truck.

But he began to notice the sadness in his new mom's eyes when she smiled at him and he couldn't smile back. Or when she tried to show him new things and all he wanted to do was visit the quiet place in his head. Or the irritability in her eyes when she couldn't help him on those days where all he could do was cry.

Then one day, he had new parents. New people, new smells, new things. No! Eli screamed. No! No! No! This is not what he wanted. He was getting used to the old parents. Why hadn't they wanted him? That's right he remembered, there was something wrong with him.

And because there was something wrong with him, he was pretty sure that these new parents wouldn't want him either. He decided there and then that it was better for him to not count on them for ANYTHING. And moreover, he would prove to them that they didn't want a rotten kid.

So, he made it a point to not listen to anything they had to say. He wouldn't go to bed when they told him to or brush his teeth. He broke his toys and those of that other kid they called his brother. He scratched himself until it bled and then wiped it on the couch. Sometimes he would pee in their closet! Every time they tried to be nice to him, his fire alarm would go off telling him "don't trust adults!" So he stopped them somehow. That felt great; in fact at those times his fire alarm would sound very far away. He liked it when his fire alarm was far away because it didn't hurt his head as much. Eli thought they were going to get rid of him at some point, let's get it over with. Better to know where danger was and not let it sneak up on him.

Just as he had predicted there came a day where his things were packed in a box and his parents' eyes were full of tears.

By the time Eli was eight years old, he had had five different sets of parents, five different moms, five different dads, four different dogs, three different cats, three different schools, and the same one feeling that there must be something wrong with him.

Although he was pretty good at ignoring his fire alarm, it was constantly alerting him to the possibility that other people would leave him or hurt him or make fun of him. He would sometimes get really angry and attack people and would sometimes get really quiet and far away. He was so tired of his fire alarm. He wished it would just give him some peace and quiet.

It made it so hard for him to learn to read or to do math puzzles. Then other kids would call him stupid, which would make him roar! Then his teachers would give him trouble and call his parents to come take him home and he would roar some more.

One day, his new foster mom, Susan, said to him, "Eli, I am so sorry that your world feels so frightening and lonely. I think your fire-alarm is broken. It's on and can't go off. That makes it so hard for you to trust that you are safe with other people as your fire-alarm keeps telling you other people are going to hurt you. They are dangerous. I've been doing some reading and thinking, and I think I have found some people who know how to fix broken fire alarms and who might help us. I'm pretty excited about it because I think for eight years you have struggled to fix a problem that is too much for a kid. It's pretty exhausting living with a loud fire alarm in your head. It's time for a rest."

Now Eli, as we know, is a smart kid. He knew that living with a broken fire alarm was a problem. Living with a permanent headache and heartache was definitely tiring. Besides, he secretly longed to do what other boys and girls were doing: having fun, learning in school, and making people happy. He had just learned not to let anyone know that he wanted that.

Could he trust this mom? Did she know what she was talking about? She certainly didn't seem to get so mad at him when he didn't listen or look sad when he didn't want to do anything with her. Her eyes seemed different; he didn't really have a word for it, it just felt different. He kind of liked how he felt when he looked at him with those eyes and used her soft voice.

What Eli didn't know yet was that there was a beginning of a hope that things could be different for him. His fire alarm, however, seemed to scream at him every time he wanted to look into this mom's eyes or wished that she would talk to him in that soothing way. How messed up is that?! Why would a fire alarm go off when he felt good for goodness sake? How could feeling good be dangerous?

Eli was asking a really good question. Why do fire alarms go off when kids are actually safe, having fun, or feeling comfortable? You see when kids have been hurt a lot when they were really young, their brain decides that they couldn't trust anything. Everything could be harmful. When Eli heard that soft voice and wanted to look into those kind eyes, his brain was telling him it was a trick, that if he let his guard down for a minute that she would take advantage and let him down or hurt him in another way. Sometimes his brain told him, "You better not let her close kid, she will see what a rotten-no-good-pathetic kid you really are and she won't want to be your mom any more."

Poor Eli was in such a bind. Should he listen to his fire alarm or should he trust this new feeling that said this could be different? As you might know if your fire-alarm doesn't work very well, sometimes he listened to his fire alarm and some days he listened to his new feeling. The days he listened to his fire alarm, he tried everything possible to push this mom away. He called her names, yelled that he hated her, and that he didn't have to listen because "She wasn't his mum anyway!" He would refuse to eat what she made him, would kick the dog, and some days scream and scream and scream until he thought his lungs might burst.

To his surprise, on those roaring days, the look in Susan's eyes didn't change. Her voice did sometimes as she was quick to let him know that it wasn't ok in this house to hurt the dog or to hurt anyone else, but then her voice would go back to that gentle way of telling him that she was sorry that he was having such a hard time and how hard it must be for him to trust that things could be ok after so many moms and dads and hurts. It was almost like she was talking to herself and she would wonder out loud what he might be thinking and feeling, and how yelling and screaming made so much sense when a boy couldn't be sure whether others could keep him safe. She was even talking about his fire alarm. How did she know these things?

"I wonder if Eli is having a hard time right now because his fire-alarm is working really hard to keep him safe. His fire alarm is telling him everyone is dangerous so keep them away. How lonely that must be for him. How smart though! He doesn't really know me yet. He doesn't know the power of my love and how good we are at fixing fire alarms. He also doesn't know how patient we can be. I hope one day he realizes that he's been doing a job that is way too much for a kid and let us help him."

Eli didn't let Susan know that he loved these words; he pretended that he didn't hear. But boy these words made him feel so different in his tummy. It was just like she said, there was one voice that said "WATCH OUT! ARE YOU CRAZY?!!" but there was also another voice that said "THIS IS GOOD FOR YOU!"

Back and forth and back and forth he went, and Susan waited patiently.

On the good days, Eli's fire alarm would not be so loud and would allow him to do things with Susan. Those days were wonderful; tingly butterflies seemed to float between his stomach and heart. A little bit like worry but not the same. They laughed together while they baked cookies or walked the dog. Sometimes she would just read book after book to him in that lovely voice.

Eli was beginning to wonder if he had had it wrong all this time. When he looked at Susan's eyes, he didn't see a reflection of a rotten kid. He thought maybe he was a likeable kid because Susan's eyes seemed to sparkle when she looked at him and when they laughed together. Could he be causing this feeling in her? He was so used to making people look angry or sad, he wasn't sure that he was capable of making other people happy or delighted.

He tucked this new possibility away for later thinking.

As Susan had promised, the day came for him to go to a new school, Belong. What kind of a name was that for a school he thought. I'm going to hate it and all the other kids are dumb! You may recognize this as a way to manage worry. When Eli was worried, he tried to make himself feel better by putting other people down and pretending he didn't care about anything. He was definitely worried about going to a new school and meeting new people. His fire alarm was clanging!

Amidst the noise of his fire alarm, Eli was surprised about a feeling that popped up, "I want to stay with Susan, I don't want to go to a new school." Mmmm, he hadn't had the feeling of wanting to stay with anyone since he was a baby with his first mom. "Interesting," he thought, "and confusing."

Susan let him know that she would be coming with him. Again, those two opposite thoughts: "I'm not a baby! I don't need anyone for anything!" Right next to "Phew! I'm glad to have her."

For his first visit, he just met with the teachers. His fire alarm was so loud in his ears and he felt very far away from all that was going on. He thought he would just let Susan do all the talking.

Susan was telling the three teachers that she has an amazing boy whose fire alarm is broken and how she really feels that he is going to get the help he needs from Belong. She told them that he had been with them for a few months, and even though he doesn't know it yet, he is a boy who is incredibly brave and kind and strong. Although Eli was in his far-away place, he heard what she was saying and his butterflies started again. Was it possible that she was right that he was brave, kind and strong?

His new teachers also seemed to have sparkly eyes and kind voices. They talked to Susan and said, "You must have a brave and strong boy as coming to a new school is not easy. He must be very worried about whether we will be adults who keep him safe and whether we will make sure that other kids aren't unkind to him. He doesn't know yet that this is a safe place for him."

Eli felt himself be a little more interested in what these new adults were saying.

One of the teachers was explaining that there were other boys and girls in this class who had problems with their fire alarms. Luckily, they were expert fire alarm fixers, and Eli wouldn't be expected to do anything himself at first because their job was to look out for danger and stop it before it came anywhere close to Eli. They said what Susan had sometimes said, how exhausting it must be for a young boy to always be in charge of danger.

They didn't stay very long that first time. All he remembered when they got home was the teacher who told him a joke and that all of them had kind eyes. Pretty good things to remember!

The next week, it was time for him to go to school. Susan drove him and one of his teachers met him at her car. She smiled at him and said, "You must be very nervous, how brave of you to come today!" Eli looked at his feet, but he allowed her to take his hand and lead him into the classroom. When he walked in, the other kids jumped up from what they were playing and met them at the door all saying

"Hi Eli! Want to play LEGO?"
"Hi Eli! Want to paint with me?"
"Hi Eli! Can you play baseball?"
"Hi Eli! I like your shoes!"

Eli thought for the first time, maybe this will be ok. He looked up from his shoes and saw a big sign that said "WELCOME TO BELONG ELI!"

Some butterflies fluttered between his stomach and heart. . . .

His teachers stayed very close to him all day. It didn't seem much like the school he was used to. They played outside a lot that day, and the teachers did everything with the kids and there was lots of laughing. He didn't do much playing, just watched, and that seemed to be ok too. One time a girl spilled her juice and nobody got upset! Another boy got mad and knocked over a chair. Eli froze. Now there was going to be trouble, he was sure. But no! One teacher went over to the boy and wondered what might have happened to make him so upset and how might he help him with his big feelings. Another teacher came over to Eli and sat beside him. She said, "I noticed that when Jacob got really angry then that it was scary for you. Susan let me know that you have seen lots of big anger in your life. I'm sorry you were scared so much of the time, that's a lot for a little kid. I think Jacob was really frustrated because he couldn't get his LEGO just right, and when it doesn't go right he feels like a stupid kid. He's learning that when things go wrong it's not because he's a bad or stupid kid. We will help him with that. And we will help you with that as I'm guessing that is something you feel sometimes too." Then she just sat near him until he could come back from that far-away place.

A few weeks in, everyone was sitting on the carpet chatting after listening to a story. His teacher was asking about what everyone worried about as one of the characters in the story had been a big worrier. One of his new friends Julie said that she worried that she would see her birth mother. She wasn't allowed to see her until she was older, but she worried that she would just bump into her in the street. The teacher commented that she could understand how she would be worried about that and then asked what did she think she would do if she did bump into her? Eli didn't like to admit it, but that was something he worried about too! He hadn't seen his mom in such a long time and he worried that she wouldn't recognize him. Another of his new friends said to Julie, "You know when I was scared of my parents, I asked for visits where there could be an adult supervising. That made me feel safe. If you wanted to see your mom you could ask for that too."

Eli's mind was buzzing. It hadn't occurred to him that he might let people know about his worries and could ask for help like these kids were doing. The kids went on to math class, but Eli couldn't concentrate. His teacher noticed that there was something on his mind because she came over and said, "Hey, I need some help with something would you come help me?"

Eli went over and his teacher handed him a pile of books to bring back to the library. On the way over, she said to Eli "Hey, I noticed that you were thinking about something a lot after our story. Is it something I can help with?" Eli's fire alarm got loud all of a sudden. But something different happened too. Eli could feel a different feeling in his chest, he wasn't sure what it was but it felt strong, maybe it was courage. He took a deep breath and quickly said "I haven't seen my mom in a very long time. I don't know if she is ok and I don't know if she would even recognize me if I bumped into her on the street."

He'd said it! His teacher knelt down and put her books on the ground and said "Eli, how brave of you to tell me that worry. It sure is a big one! I have a feeling you have kept that one inside for a very long time." Eli took another deep breath and looked at his teacher's eyes. They were full of something that looked like kindness. They certainly weren't mad eyes. He liked them. His teacher took his hand and said, "I don't know anything about your mom, but I do know the right people to ask. Would you like me to do that for you?" Eli nodded.

Then he noticed a funny thing. His fire alarm had a different sound. It was softer and further away. He liked that too! "I wonder why?" he thought to himself? I wonder if it's because I told my teacher my worry and she is going to help me with it?

We have said before how smart Eli is and he was exactly right. He was beginning to trust adults, and the more he trusted adults, the quieter his alarm bells were becoming. Susan, his teachers, and even some of the kids didn't make him so scared. What Eli didn't know then is that when the amygdala begins to feel safe, it does not set off the fire alarm, but instead says, "You can get close to that person now if you want. It will feel good if you do."

Eli smiled to himself and then he revisited that thought he had tucked away after he had moved to Susan's house. "Maybe I got this wrong" he thought, "maybe I'm not such a bad kid." He was met with silence inside his head. No alarm bells at all!

Now in case you are wondering whether his fire alarm was fixed, it wasn't yet. Some days and some moments it rang really loudly and he couldn't concentrate, and he was grumpy or went to the far-away place that was quiet. But it didn't seem to stay stuck anymore.

Eli's fire alarm was beginning to work as it should: on and off, on and off—not just on. It was still more sensitive than other kids' fire alarms and would sometimes go on when there wasn't any danger. Sometimes when that happened, Susan and his teachers could help turn it off, but every once in a while he could do it himself! He was learning to figure out whether it was really dangerous or whether his amygdala was being tricked and lying to him. His amygdala certainly needed some more help to tell the difference between who and what was safe and who or what was dangerous.

Eli was learning so much. He was even growing taller to make room for all this new learning! Susan had had to buy him five pairs of new pants the other day and two new pairs of sneakers. Eli was becoming the kid he was meant to be before all that danger turned his fire alarm on permanently. He was starting to believe what others were saying, that he was

Smart,
Kind,
Courageous,
Funny and
. . . a GOOD KID!

None of what had happened to him as a baby or in his first foster homes was his fault. Now that was important learning.

"Late Fragment
And did you get what
you wanted from this life, even so?
I did.
And what did you want?
To call myself beloved, to feel myself
beloved on the earth."
       —Raymond Carver, *A New Path to the Waterfall*

Appendix A

SAMPLE–TERM 2 ALTERNATIVE REPORT CARD

This sample is based on a student in his second year, final term, in Belong. Given the need for confidentiality, the student in this report is fictitious. It is provided to give you an idea of how we communicate progress with our Belong students and what information is articulated to staff when a child transitions back to their home school.

Student:	Principal:
OEN:	Teacher:
Grade:	School:
Reporting Period:	Address:
	Phone:
Days Absent:	
Times Late:	

Strengths	Alternative Program Areas (included in this report)
• Artistic ability • Auditory learner • Intellectual curiosity • Receptive language skills – reading • Visual learner • Kinesthetic learner • Tactile learner • Sense of humor • Willing to take more academic and social risks	1. Executive Function 2. Social Competence 3. Affect Regulation (emotional regulation)
	Ontario Curriculum (reported in the Provincial Report Card)
	Language Math Health and Physical Education Art Science

ALTERNATIVE PROGRAM AREAS

This assessment is based on achievement of alternative learning expectations specified in the IEP, which are not based on the Ontario curriculum.

EXECUTIVE FUNCTION: Jake will continue to develop executive function skills, specifically problem-solving (recognize that he has an academic challenge, be able to think flexibly about the problem, and try to solve the problem) and emotional control (manage his emotions in order to complete tasks). Impulse control and task initiation will continue to be monitored to ensure maintenance of learned skills.

Comments

Problem-solving: Jake has worked hard to understand and experience the benefits of compromising and working collaboratively with partners to accomplish a task. He needs direct instruction about his role at the outset of the task, a quick review of the task, and what to do if he gets stuck. When Jake knows these things, he is far more successful and confident in starting and finishing his work. When too many things are presented at one time (i.e., expectations, new lesson content, lengthy work period, etc.), Jake can become overwhelmed, which then impacts his willingness to attempt the task. When it is a new concept, it is helpful to pre-teach vocabulary or give him a quick overview, linking it to previously taught concepts if possible. If he has some familiarity with the topic, this is often enough for him to attempt the task. He does best when working with partners who are not easily distracted or who do not easily respond to off-topic conversations that Jake may start. A simple checklist of the task expectations is also helpful to keep him on task and gives him an idea of how much is expected.

Jake now responds positively to verbal cues when he is attempting to control a partner or group, or when he is being rigid in his thinking. He often shares his thoughts about why he has shifted his approach or thinking, and allows staff to help him co-regulate his emotions and navigate toward more successful partnerships. Earlier in the year, Jake would typically chose to work on his own rather than a partner. As his understanding of partner and group work has developed, along with multiple opportunities to practice, he has demonstrated more success working collaboratively. Jake now adjusts his efforts and responses to continue working with a partner/group. He may not always like the way things are going, but he will now attempt to problem solve more independently rather than get angry or flee from the task.

Emotional control: Jake still shows signs of frustration. He can still become anxious about academic tasks and will cry or make self-disparaging comments. Frustration and anxiety can stem from something simple like not having an item needed for the task to something more complex like not understanding the task. When any situation arises, Jake is cued to think about what is really going on for him in that moment and whether it's something he can independently manage or something he needs help with (i.e., if he doesn't have a pencil, he can definitely manage that on his own, but if he doesn't understand an instruction, he can ask for help). Jake is more aware of the different sizes of his challenges, and when to act independently and when to ask for help. Staff no longer respond to past strategies of learned helplessness. Empathy continues to be an effective strategy rather than reassurance. He recognizes that staff will approach him with PACE to help him understand why he is struggling in that moment. When he is regulated, he is far more willing to do things more independently and is quite proud of himself when he completes them. For example, when he feels that a task is going to take too long, staff acknowledges this by saying something like "Jake, I know you're worried that this is going to take a long time and you want to get outside and practice soccer. What can you do to get started? Is there anything you need to help you get started?"

Sustained attention: Jake reviews the class schedule daily to make things more predictable and to determine how much time he thinks he'll need to dedicate to different subjects. He tolerates group lessons when they are of interest to him, and he offers on-topic comments and asks clarifying questions. It is important to cue Jake when a lesson is starting and to provide the purpose of the lesson. A general timeframe is helpful to keep him focused, and giving cues to important information during the lesson helps to refocus his attention if it starts to fade (i.e., "Wow, Jake, that's important!"). He can become distracted by others, but has developed his own strategies for sustaining attention. Jake now chooses his seating to build distance between himself and those he knows can be distracting. He attempts to respond to questions early in the lesson and when praised for his efforts and thoughtful responses, he is better regulated to continue listening and participating. Sometimes, it is helpful to let Jake know the question that will be asked of him so that he has time to think about and form his response. Jake has practiced waiting to speak, and now raises his hand more frequently to comment or ask a question. Jake previously offered off-topic comments, and staff have started to ask him if his comments are on topic or not. By asking him the question and telling him he needs to save off-topic comments and conversations for after the lesson, Jake has decreased off-topic comments and has increased on-topic ones. He has learned that during group instruction, the lesson can move faster when he listens and participates, and that he is in a far better position to understand the follow-up task and its instructions. This understanding has considerably cut down on his worry around work completion. Jake is able to sustain attention for longer periods of time if he has the opportunity for body movement prior to the task and if he has a break between tasks that require sustained attention.

SOCIAL COMPETENCE: Jake will continue to build social competence skills to help him participate successfully in a variety of social interactions and build peer relationships. He will begin to use self-advocacy strategies and engage in more reciprocal conversations with staff and peers.

Comments

Self-advocacy skills: Jake has developed a growing set of self-advocacy skills. He is more willing to allow staff to discuss situations with him in order to unravel his perspective, the possible perspectives of others, and the impact his responses can have on his relationships. Jake typically responds in two ways; he either walks away or responds verbally/physically (i.e., takes away an item the peer needs or uses nonverbal gestures). Jake is more direct with staff now and explains what he is thinking. For example, he may want to do something on his own and has difficulty telling a peer. Jake will ask for some staff support to help explain that he just wants space and that it doesn't mean they aren't friends anymore. At other times, Jake wants to control a peer and what they are doing together, and it becomes more about him getting his way than self-advocacy. It is most effective to clearly label what Jake is doing (i.e., "Jake, I think you want Sam to play the game your way and he doesn't seem like he's having too much fun. He walked away because you're trying to control him, not because he's being mean to you. I wonder why you want to have all that control right now."). Ignoring Jake's crying or pouting in these situations is more effective than engaging in long discussions. These strategies and assuming a more helpless position have worked in the past, but he has been consistently encouraged to consider the reasons he uses these strategies.

AFFECT REGULATION: Jake will continue to regulate his affect through identification, modulation, and expression of his emotions through a variety of activities.

Comments

Identifying emotions: Jake has worked very hard to identify his emotions in different situations. It's important to be clear and honest with Jake so that he does not retreat into past strategies that allowed him to distract adults or avoid a situation or task. For example, when Jake stops an academic task and seems frustrated, it is more effective to label that for him (i.e., "Jake, you seem frustrated") and then encourage him to take a moment and decide what he needs to do himself or what he needs from staff before starting the task again. Socially, staff name what is seen (or suspected) and provide perspective. Jake then makes the decision on how to proceed. Jake can still let staff to do all his problem-solving for him. Being playful and calling him on his attempt to get out of hard work is helpful. Staff then let him know that they are certain he can figure it out and that they are there for help if he gets stuck. For more emotionally complex situations, he still requires more direct guidance. Staff consistently communicate with PACE, allowing Jake to navigate challenging emotions and situations in a way that feels safe for him.

Affect modulation: Jake recognizes his emotional states more accurately now and makes attempts to shift states independently (i.e., from tired to alert and from frustrated to calm). He often needs a few minutes to himself to determine what he needs to make the shift. Sometimes he just needs to sit on his own, take a short walk, get a drink, or draw a quick picture. He will often tell staff what he is feeling and what he thinks he could do to shift states.

Affect expression: Jake verbally expresses his emotions with staff most of the time and with peers some of the time. He will usually say "It's just because I. . . ." and then give the reason. He is willing to listen to staff ideas and is less likely to keep his thoughts hidden now. It has been very important to establish safety. Jake has flourished in this area, as he has come to trust and rely on the caring adults in his life and confident in knowing that home and school are working closely together. Jake has worked very hard on establishing home morning routines so that he attends school each day. The more consistent his attendance, the better Jake does socially, emotionally, and academically. He is more relaxed, confident, and open to learning when he has consistent attendance and is incredibly proud of himself. Jake recognizes that he is not expected to carry the stress or anxiety of any adults or peers. This has been an area of personal growth for Jake.

Final comments: As Jake prepares to transition to another school in September, he should look back on his time in this class with pride. He has grown and developed in all areas, and although he will likely face situations that continue to elicit strong emotions, he is able to acknowledge them, identify them more accurately, and analyze possible responses. Jake will ask for help when needed and is open to so many more things than when he started. He is a curious, clever, and very funny boy! He brings joy and smiles to all who interact with him. Jake is sometimes wise beyond his years and other times seems so young. Finding the magical balance between the two has been an important journey for Jake.

Teacher Signature: _____ Date: _____

Principal Signature: _____ Date: _____

Appendix B

Family Workshop

Topics: PACE (playfulness, acceptance, curiosity, and empathy)

SUMMARY

* Review of PACE
* Our kids generally reflect the emotional state that we are in (if we're anxious, our kids will be anxious; if we're aggressive, our kids will be aggressive—or frightened of us); our regulation is crucial—check your own state and put your own oxygen mask on first.
* *Acceptance review*: We don't get to judge how our kids feel, but you don't have to accept behavior that is getting in the way of your relationship (i.e., don't accept hitting, but accept the feeling that they *want* to hit); acceptance tends to calm people; as soon as we start to argue, we stay in a heightened state; problem

solving doesn't need to be immediate; the cortex/thinking is not ready to be talked to yet, so allow both of you to take time to calm the nervous system. Remember, stress hormones take 20 minutes to recede. If you direct or expect too soon, your child is likely to escalate again.

- *Curiosity review:* What's going on? Why is this behavior here right now? When we are curious, we ask "What's going on? You seem frustrated" versus "Get that attitude out of the way!"; curiosity communicates "I'm not interested in the behavior, I'm interested in you and what you are experiencing." When children feel that, it tends to calm them, so the behavior is no longer necessary. If we just operate at the level of behavior, we have no opportunity to understand. Threatening of consequences will rarely work to change the behavior, and we won't know what to do until we understand why your child is having that behavior.

- *Empathy review:* Not sympathy, not pity; we can't give empathy when we're in self-protection mode; our kids have lots of empathy, but not when they feel like they're in trouble or are afraid; they will go right into self-protection; empathy doesn't leave them alone in their feeling. When they are not alone, they are less likely to need their self-defense system. Connection calms their arousal and makes it less likely that challenging behavior is necessary and more likely that the child can keep connected to their cortex where they can access skills that allow them to negotiate or discuss the struggle.

- Our kids will make up their own stories to defend themselves against the shame; this is generated when they make a mistake or are in trouble; "I'm bad, tired, etc." When kids say they are bad, it is our instinct to say "No, you're not!" From a PACE framework, we would need to *accept* first that this is what they are feeling right now and that to argue would be to discount their experience. Then we would use *empathy*, "I'm sorry you feel that way. How hard to carry that around with you!" If you say they are not bad, you will show that you don't understand them in that moment and will likely enter into a power struggle; you need to gently lead them to the possibility that they are not bad; challenge the story they tell themselves, "I know you see yourself as a bad kid. I don't see it that way. Is it ok if we agree to disagree?"

HOW DO WE USE A PACEFUL APPROACH?

- First, check where your arousal levels are—try not to discipline when you're angry; if your child is having a meltdown, it's a meltdown. Adding our own meltdown means that we now have two people operating from the limbic system and there is no way out until one is more frightening or another gets more tired. You need to figure out what your strategy is to take care of yourself and prioritize that before you head into thinking about how to influence your child's behavior. Obviously, if the child is in immediate danger, that takes priority, but most of the time consequences rarely need to be dealt with in the moment.

- Use time-in versus time-out; when our kids are dysregulated they need us the most, sending them on their own to a time-out is not helpful; adults can have time-outs (whatever works for you to manage your own emotions); you will not be able to use PACE if your own arousal levels are too high.
- Start with acceptance: If my child could do better right now, they would. Kids don't like being in trouble or making adults upset; they'd rather be compliant and feel loved, and not have adults be angry with them.
- Then perhaps curiosity: What is going on with my child right now? What might have precipitated their anger/sadness/opposition? You might start offering some guesses. If your regulation is good that process is often enough to interrupt the upset. Even if you don't have correct guesses, your intent to understand will be felt and start the process of calming.
- Empathy for our child's struggle can be communicated at any time in the process. Sometimes our children don't want to hear it if their arousal level is too high, and we may need to match their energy with our empathy; in a louder more energetic voice you might say something like "Boy we are having a struggle here! Such a struggle and I can see it really doesn't feel good!" Then we might drop our voice and communicate empathy in a more gentle way "so hard."
- Playfulness might be added in at any time also. It depends on your child's state, but the use of humor can be an excellent way of communicating connection and shifting emotional state. It is important to make sure you are not using playfulness as a way to "jolly" your child out of their bad mood. The child will experience that as nonaccepting, and it risks that they feel that love is conditional on them being happy and well behaved. Once your child is calm again, then you can decide whether there will be a consequence or can discuss together what happened and what needs to happen now. PACE does not mean there are no consequences; for example, if homework is a struggle you can say something like "I know you don't love to do homework. School all day and then homework. I get it. My worry for you is that you won't get to go to the park tomorrow and I know you love the park. How can we get this done?" versus "Get your homework done or you aren't going to the park"; somehow we have decided in North America that discipline means our kids must feel the hurt/pain—PACE is an approach that creates emotional safety so that self-regulation and compliance skills can be built.
- PACE takes a lot of repetition; it gives you a framework; each of the ingredients can be used alone or together—not sequentialy, and not equal percentages all the time
- Families shared some challenges experienced at home
  - Connection before compliance/correction.
  - Name it to tame it. (Notice)
  - Co-regulation before self-regulation.

Appendix C

PRE-QUESTIONNAIRE
Wendy Fisher and Sian Phillips

Name: _____

Date: _____

Current position: _____

Have you attended training on the attitude of PACE and Dyadic Developmental Practice _____

This questionnaire is designed to determine what you already know about trauma-informed practice. I will ask you to complete a similar questionnaire at the end of our time together so I can assess what you have learned and how I, as support staff, can improve my delivery. Please complete all questions to the best of your ability. To what extent do you understand the following topics?

	Not Very Well			Very Well	
Implications of trauma on a student's brain and attachment	1	2	3	4	5
Emotional implications	1	2	3	4	5
Behavioral implications	1	2	3	4	5
Cognitive implications	1	2	3	4	5
Self-concept implications	1	2	3	4	5
Relationship implications	1	2	3	4	5
Developmental trauma	1	2	3	4	5
The therapeutic attitude of PACE for emotional safety					
Playfulness	1	2	3	4	5
Acceptance	1	2	3	4	5

	Not Very Well			Very Well	
Curiosity	1	2	3	4	5
Empathy	1	2	3	4	5
Strategies that are less likely to work for students with trauma	1	2	3	4	5

How comfortable are you using the following strategies?

	Not at all		Quite	Very	
Being playful	1	2	3	4	5
Displaying acceptance	1	2	3	4	5
Being empathic	1	2	3	4	5
Being curious	1	2	3	4	5
Being a storyteller	1	2	3	4	5
Using time-ins and physical presence	1	2	3	4	5
Connecting before redirecting	1	2	3	4	5
Using "Name it to tame it"	1	2	3	4	5
Matching affect	1	2	3	4	5
Linking behavior to student's experience	1	2	3	4	5

What area would you like to focus on to become more skilled at displaying an attitude of PACE in the classroom?

Would you be comfortable using videotaping as a learning tool and as an opportunity for self-reflection? Videotapes will not be stored nor shared with anyone else. Yes___ No ___

What do you do to take care of yourself when dealing with difficult students and parents?

References

Ainsworth, M. D. S., Bell, S. M., & Stayton, D. J. (1971). Individual differences in strange-situation behavior of one-year-olds. In Schaffer, H. R. (Eds.), *The origins of human social relations* (pp. 17–57). London: Academic Press.

Ainsworth, M. D. S., Blehar, M. C., Waters, E., & Wall, S. (1978). *Patterns of attachment: A psychological study of the strange situation.* Hillsdale, NJ: Erlbaum.

Anderson, D. M., & Walker, M. B. M. (2015). Does shortening the school week impact student performance? Evidence from the four-day school week. *Education Finance and Policy, 10*(3), 314–349.

Badenoch, B. (2017). Safety is the treatment. In Porges, S. & Dana, D. (Eds.), *Clinical applications of the polyvagal theory: The emergence of polyvagal-informed therapies* (pp. 73–89). New York: W.W. Norton & Company.

Baylin, J., & Hughes, D. A. (2016). *The neurobiology of attachment-focused therapy: Enhancing connection & trust in the treatment of children & adolescents.* New York, NY: W.W. Norton and Company.

Bishop, R. (2001). Changing power relations in education: Kaupapa Maori messages for mainstream institutions. In *Professional practices of teaching* (pp. 201–220). Palmerston North, New Zealand: Dunmore Press.

Bishop, R., Berryman, M., Cavanagh, T., & Teddy, L. (2009). Te kotahitanga: Addressing educational disparities facing Maori students in New Zealand. *Elsevier Ltd, 25*(5), 734–742.

Bishop, R., Berryman, M., & Wearmouth, J. (2014). *Te kotahitanga: Towards effective education reform for indigenous and other minoritised students.* NZCER Press.

Bus, A. G., Takacs, Z. K., & Kegel, C. A. (2015). Affordances and limitations of electronic storybooks for young children's emergent literacy. *Developmental Review, 35,* 79–97.

Chiong, C., & Shuler, C. (2010). *Learning: Is there an app for that? Investigations of young children's usage and learning with mobile devices and apps.* New York: The Joan Ganz Cooney Center at Sesame Workshop.

Coan, J. A. (2016). Toward a neuroscience of attachment. In Cassidy, J. & Shaver, P. R. (Eds.), *Handbook of attachment: Theory, research, and clinical applications* (3rd ed., pp. 242–269). New York: Guilford Press.

313

Coan, J. A. (2018). Toward a neuroscience of attachment. In Cassidy, J. & Shaver, P. R. (Eds.), *Handbook of attachment: Theory, research, and clinical applications* (pp. 242–269). New York: The Guilford Press.

Coan, J. A., Beckes, L., Gonzalez, M. Z., Maresh, E. L., Brown, C. L., & Hasselmo, K. (2017). Relationship status and perceived support in the social regulation of neural responses to threat. *Social Cognitive and Affective Neuroscience, 12*(10), 1574–1583. https://doi.org/10.1093/scan/nsx091.

Cohn, J. A., Campbell, S., & Ross, S. (1991). Infant response in the still-face paradigm at 6 months predicts avoidant and secure attachments at 12 months. In Beebe, B., Cohen, P., & Lachmann, F. (Eds.), *The mother-infant interaction picture book: Origins of attachment* (pp. 15–23). New York: W. W. Norton & Company.

Conner, O. L., Siegle, G. J., Mcfarland, A. M., Silk, J. S., Ladouceur, C. D., Dahl, R. E., Coan, J. A., & Ryan, N. D. (2012, July). Mom—it helps when you're right here! Attenuation of neural stress markers in anxious youths whose caregivers are present during FMRI. *PLoS ONE, 7*(12). https://doi.org/10.1371/journal.pone.0050680.

Cook, A., Spinazzola, J., Ford, J., Lanktree, C., Blaustein, M., Cloitre, M., & Van der Kolk, B. (2005). Complex Trauma in Children and adolescents. *Psychiatric Annals, 35,* 390–398.

Cox, R., Skouteris, H., Rutherford, L., Fuller-Tyszkiewicz, M., Dell' Aquila, D., & Hardy, L. L. (2012). Television viewing, television content, food intake, physical activity and body mass index: A cross-sectional study of preschool children aged 2–6 years. *Health Promotion Journal of Australia, 23*(1), 58–62.

Davy, W. L., & Hall, P. R. (2015). *Four-day school week literature review. Analysis of available literature on the impact of a four-day school week.* Peoria, IL: Peoria Unified School District.

Dawson, G., Frey, K., Panagiotides, H., Yamanda, E., Hessl, D., & Osterling, J. (1999) . Infants of depressed mothers exhibit atypical frontal brain activity during interactions with mother and with a familiar, nondepressed adult. *Child Development, 70*(5), 1058–1066.

Dozier, M., Meade, E., & Bernard, K. (2014, September). Attachment and biobehavioral catch-up: An intervention for parents at risk of maltreating their infants and toddlers. In Timmer, S. & Urquiza, A. (Eds), *Evidence-based approaches for the treatment of maltreated children* (pp. 43–59).

Everson-Hock, E. S., Jones, R., Guillaume, L., Clapton, J., Goyder, E., Chilcott, J., Payne, N., Duenas, A., Sheppard, L. M., & Swann, C. (2011). The effectiveness of training and support for carers and other professionals on the physical and emotional health and well-being of looked-after children and young people: A systematic review. *Child: Care, Health and Development, 38*(2), 162–174.

Exceptional elementary. Posted by Kelsey Herald: *Exceptional Elementary*, August 17, 2019. https://exceptionalelementary.com/.

Felitti, V. J., Anda, R. F., Nordenberg, D., Williamson, M. S., Spitz, A. M., Edwards, V., Koss, M. P., & Marks, J. S. (1998). Relationship of childhood abuse and household dysfunction to many of the leading causes of death in adults. *American Journal of Preventative Medicine, 14*(4), 245–258.

Felt, L. J., & Robb, M. B. Common sense research: Common sense media. *Common Sense Media: Ratings, Reviews, and Advice,* August 13, 2019. https://www.commonsensemedia.org/research/technology-addiction-concern-controversy-and-finding-balance.

Fryer, R. G. (2018). The "pupil" factory: Specialization and the production of human capital in schools. *American Economic Review, 108*(3), 616–656.

Fukkink, R. G., & Tavecchio, L. W. C. (2010). Effects of video interaction guidance on early childhood teachers. *Teaching and Teacher Education, 26*(8), 1652–1659.

Golding, K. S. (2008). *Nurturing attachments training resource: Running parenting groups for adoptive parents and foster or kinship carers.* London: Jessica Kingsley Publishers.

Golding, K. S., & Picken, W. (2004). Group work for foster carers caring for children with complex problems. *Adoption & Fostering, 28*(1), 25–37.

Government of Ontario. *Suspension stats: Safe schools.* Untitled Document. Government of Ontario. Accessed September 21, 2019. http://www.edu.gov.on.ca/eng/safeschools/fact s1617.html.

Graves, J. (2011). Effects of year-round schooling on disadvantaged students and the distribution of standardized test performance. *Economics of Education Review, 30,* 1281–1305.

Graves, J., McMullen, S., & Rouse, K. (2018). Teacher turnover, composition and qualifications in the year-round school setting. *The B.E. Journal of Economic Analysis & Policy, 18*(3), 27.

Guangheng, D., Devito, E., Du, X., & Cui, Z. (2012). Impaired inhibitory control in "internet addiction disorder": A functional magnetic resonance imaging study. *Psychiatry Research, 203*(2, 3), 153–158.

Guernsey, L., & Levine, M. H. (2015). *Tap click read: Growing readers in a world of screens.* San Francisco, CA: Jossey-Bass.

Gurney-Smith, B., Granger, C., Randle, A., & Fletcher, J. (2011). "In time and in tune"—the fostering attachments group capturing sustained change in both caregiver and child. *Adoption & Fostering, 34*(4), 50–60.

Haifeng, H., Jia, S., Hu, S., Fan, R., Sun, W., Sun, T., & Zhang, H. (2012). Reduced striatal dopamine transporters in people with internet addiction disorder. *Journal of Biomedicine & Biotechnology, 2012,* 1–5, article id: 854524.

Hambrick, E. P., Brawner, T. W., Perry, B. D., Brand, K., Hofmeister, C., & Collins, J. O. (2019). Beyond the ACE score: Examining relationships between timing of developmental adversity, relational health and developmental outcomes in children. *Archives of Psychiatric Nursing, 33*(3), 238–247.

Hambrick, E. P., Brawner, T. W., & Perry, B. D. (2018). Examining developmental adversity and connectedness in child welfare-involved children. *Children Australia, 43*(2), 105–115.

Hatzinikolaou, K. (2015). Intersubjectivity research and theory: Contributions to the domains of developmental psychopathology and early intervention. *Eleftherna – Scientific Journal of the Department of Psychology, University of Crete, 7,* 264–286.

Hill, P. T., & Heyward, G. (2015). *The four-day school week in rural Idaho schools.* http://www.rociidaho.org/wp-content/uploads/2015/07/ROCI_4DayWeek_Final.pdf.

Hill, P. T., & Jones, D. B. (2018). A teacher who knows me: The academic benefits of repeat student-teacher matches. *Economics of Education Review, 64,* 1–12.

Hinkley, T., Verbestel, V., Ahrens, W., Lissner, L., Molnar, D., Moreno, L. A., Pigeot, I., Pohlabeln, H., Reisch, L., Russo, P., Veidebaum, T., Tornaritis, M., Williams, G., De Henauw, S., De Bourdeaudhuij, I., & for the IDEFICS Consortium. (2014). Early childhood electronic media use as a predictor of poorer well-being: A prospective cohort study. *JAMA Pediatrics, 168*(5), 485–492.

Hourcade, J. P., Mascher, S. L., Wu, D., & Pantoja, L. (2015). Look, my baby is using an IPad! An analysis of YouTube videos of infants and toddlers using tablets. *Proceedings of the 33rd annual ACM conference on human factors in computing systems – CHI 15,* 2015. https://doi.org/10.1145/2702123.2702266.

Howard, J. A. (2013). *Distressed or deliberately defiant?: Managing challenging student behaviour due to trauma and disorganised attachment.* Toowong, QLD, Australia: Australian Academic Press.

Hughes, D. (2012). *It was that one moment.* Worth Publishers.

Hughes, D. A., & Baylin, J. (2012). *Brain-based parenting: How neuroscience can foster healthy relationships with kids.* New York, NY: Norton.

Is too much screen time harming children's vision? *ScienceDaily,* August 6, 2018. http://www.sciencedaily.com/releases/2018/08/180806162718.htm.

Jones, N. A., Field, T., & Davalos, M. (2000). Right frontal EEG asymmetry and lack of empathy in preschool children of depressed mothers. *Child Psychiatry and Human Development, 30*(3), 189–204.

Jung, S. I., Lee, N. K., Kang, K. W., Kim, K., & Lee, D. Y. (2016). The effect of smartphone usage time on posture and respiratory function. *Journal of Physical Therapy Science, 28*(1), 186–189.

Kabali, H. K., Irigoyen, M. M., Nunez-Davis, R., Budacki, J. G., Mohanty, S. H., Leister, K. P., & Bonner, R. L. (2015). Exposure and use of mobile devices by young children. *Pediatrics, 136*(6), 1044–1050.

Kennedy, H., Landor, M., & Todd, L. (2011). *Video interaction guidance: A relationship-based intervention to promote attunement, empathy and well-being.* London: Jessica Kingsley Publishers.

Kim, S. H., Baik, S.-H., Park, C. S., Kim, S. J., Choi, S. W., & Kim, S. E. (2011). Reduced striatal dopamine D2 receptors in people with internet addiction. *Neuroreport, 22*(8), 407–411.

Learning: Is there an app for that? Investigations of young children's usage of learning with mobile devices and apps. September 16, 2019. http://dmlcentral.net/wp-content/uploads/files/learningapps_final_110410.pdf.

Lindsay, G., & Strand, S. (2013). Evaluation of the national roll-out of parenting programmes across England: The parenting early intervention programme (PEIP). *BMC Public Health, 13,* 972.

MacLean, P. D. (1990). *The triune brain in evolution: Role in paleocerebral functions.* New York: Plenum.

Main, M., & Solomon, J. (1990). Procedures for identifying infants as disorganized/disoriented during the Ainsworth Strange Situation. In Greenberg, M. T., Cicchetti, D., & Cummings, M. E. (Eds.), *Attachment in the preschool years: Theory, research, and intervention* (pp. 121–160). Chicago: University of Chicago Press.

Michelle Garcia winner – superflex poser. https://www.socialthinking.com/Products/superflex-unthinkables-poster.

Naish, S. (2018). *The A–Z of therapeutic parenting, strategies and solutions.* Jessica Kingsley Publishers.

Nathanson, A. I., Aladé, F., Sharp, M. L., Rasmussen, E. E., & Christy, K. (2014). The relation between television exposure and executive function among preschoolers. *Developmental Psychology, 50*(5), 1497–1506.

Panksepp, J. (1998). *Affective neuroscience: The foundations of human and animal emotions.* New York: Oxford University Press.

Panksepp, J., & Biven, L. (2012). *The archaeology of mind: Neuroevolutionary origins of human emotion.* New York, NY: W. W. Norton & Company.

Panksepp, J., Normansell, L., Cox, J. F., & Siviy, S. M. (1994). Effects of neonatal decortication on the social play of juvenile rats. *Physiology & Behavior, 56,* 429–443.

Paradkar, S. (2019, September 13). "No one is ashamed to be who they are." This simple Maori idea is revolutionizing teaching in New Zealand. *thestar.com.* https://www.thestar.com/news/atkinsonseries/2019/09/13/no-one-is-ashamed-to-be-who-they-are-this-simple-maori-idea-is-revolutionizing-teaching-in-new-zealand.html.

Porges, S. W. (2004). *Neuroception: A subconscious system for detecting threats and safety.* Washington, DC: Zero to Three.

Porges, S. W. (2011). *The polyvagal theory: Neurophysiological foundations of emotions, attachment, communication, and self-regulation.* New York: Norton.

Porges, S. W., & Dana, D. (2018). *Clinical applications of the polyvagal theory: The emergence of polyvagal-informed therapies.* New York: W. W. Norton & Company.

Powel, B., Cooper, G., Hoffman, K., & Marvin, B. (2014). *The circle of security intervention: Enhancing attachment in early parent-child relationships.* New York: The Guildford Press 72 Spring Street.

Radesky, J., MD, FAAP, & Christakis, D., MD, MPH, FAA. (2016). Media and young minds. *Pediatrics, 138*(5), e20162591.

Rideout, V. J., Foehr, U. G., & Roberts, D. F. (2010, January 1). Generation M2: Media in the lives of 8- to 18-year-olds. *The Henry J. Kaiser Family Foundation.* http://kff.org/other/poll-finding/report-generation-m2-media-in-the-lives/.

Salverson, J. (2018). *Presentation at DDP international conference.* Cobourg, Ontario, October 2018.

Sanders, M. R., Kirby, J. N., Tellegen, C. L., & Day, J. J. (2014). The triple P-positive parenting program: A systematic review and meta-analysis of a multi-level system of parenting support. *Clinical Psychology Review, 34*(4), 337–357.

Scheff, T. J., Phillips, B. S., & Kincaid, H. (2006). *Goffman Unbound! A new paradigm for social science (The sociological imagination).* Paradigm Publishers.

Schore, A. N. (2017). Modern attachment theory. In Gold, S. N. (Ed.), *APA handbooks in psychology. APA handbook of trauma psychology: Foundations in knowledge* (pp. 389–406). Washington, DC: American Psychological Association.

Shanker, S. (2012). *Calm, alert and learning: Classroom strategies for self-regulation.* Don Mills, OT: Pearson Education Canada.

Siegel, D. J. (2012). *Developing mind: How relationships and the brain interact to shape who we are* (2nd ed.). S.l.: Guilford.

Siegel, D. J. (2012). *Pocket guide to interpersonal neurobiology: An integrative handbook of the mind.* New York: W.W. Norton.

Siegel, D. J. (2007). *The mindful brain: Reflection and attunement in the cultivation of well-being.* New York: W.W. Norton.

Siegel, D. J., & Payne, T. B. (2011). *The whole brain child: 12 revolutionary strategies to nurture your child's developing mind.* Bantam Books.

Silani, C. (2013). I'm ok, you're not ok: Right supramarginal gyrus plays an important role in empathy. *ScienceDaily.*

Silani, G., Lamm, C., Ruff, C. C., & Singer, T. (2013). Right supramarginal gyrus is crucial to overcome emotional egocentricity bias in social judgments. *The Journal of Neuroscience, 33*(39), 15466–15476. https://doi.org/10.1523/jneurosci.1488-13.2013.

Soon-Beom, H., Kim, J. W., Choi, E.-J., Kim, H.-H., Suh, J.-E., Kim, C.-D., et al. (2013). Reduced orbitofrontal cortical thickness in male adolescents with internet addiction. *Behavioral and Brain Functions, 9*(1), 11.

Soon-Beom, H., Zalesky, A., Cocchi, L., Fornito, A., Choi, E., Kim, H.-H., Suh, J.-E., Kim, C.-D., Kim, J.-W., & Yi, S.-H. (2013). Decreased functional brain connectivity in adolescents with internet addiction. *PLoS ONE, 8*(2), e57831.

Stern, D. (1998). *Interpersonal world of the infant: A view from psychoanalysis and developmental psychology.* New York, NY: Basic Books.

Stern, D. (2004). *The present moment in psychotherapy and everyday life.* New York, NY: W.W. Norton & Company.

Strouse, G. A., O'Doherty, K., & Troseth, G. L. (2013). Effective co-viewing: Preschoolers' learning from video after a dialogic questioning intervention. *Developmental Psychology, 49* (12), 2368–2382.

Superflex takes on the unthinkables! (Poster). *Socialthinking.* Accessed September 24, 2019. https://www.socialthinking.com/Products/superflex-unthinkables-poster.

Thomas, R., & Zimmer-Gembeck, M. J. (2007). Behavioural outcomes of parent-child interaction therapy & Triple positive parenting program: A review and a meta-analysis. *Journal of Abnormal Child Psychology, 35,* 475–495.

Totsika, V., Mandair, D., & Lindsay, G. (2017). Comparing the effectiveness of evidence-based programs in families of children with and without special educational needs: Short-term & long-term gains. *Frontieres in Education, 2,* 1–14.

Trevarthen, C. (2013). Born for art and the joyful companionship of fiction. In Narvaez, D., Panksepp, J., Schore, A. N., & Geason, T. R. (Eds.), *Evolution, early experience and human development* (pp. 202–220). New York, NY: Oxford Press.

Trevarthen, C., & Aitken, K. L. (2001). Infant intersubjectivity: Research, theory, and clinical applications. *Journal of Child Psychology and Psychiatry, 42* (I), 3–48.

Tronick, E. (2003). "Of course all relationships are unique": How co-creative processes generate unique mother–infant and patient–therapist relationships and change other relationships. *Psychological Inquiry, 23,* 473–491.

Tronick, E. (2007). *The neurobehavioural and social-emotional development of infants and children.* New York, NY: Norton.

Twenge, J. M., & Campbell, W. K. (2019, November). Media use is linked to lower psychological well-being: Evidence from three datasets. *Psychiatric Quarterly, 90*(2), 311–331. https://doi.org/10.1007/s11126-019-09630-7.

Van der Kolk, B. (2005). Developmental trauma disorder: Toward a rational diagnosis for children with complex trauma histories. *Psychiatric Annals, 35,* 401–408.

Vijakkhana, N., Wilaisakditipakorn, T., Rudekhajorn, K., Pruksananonda, C., & Chonchaiya, W. (2015). Evening media exposure reduces night-time sleep. *Acta Paediatrics, 104*(3), 306–312.

Vijakkhana, N., Wilaisakditipakorn, T., Ruedeekhajorn, K., Pruksananonda, C., Chonchaiya, W., Vik, K., & Hafting, M. (2006). Video interaction guidance offered to mothers with postnatal depression: Experiences from a pilot study. *Nordic Journal of Psychiatry, 60*(3), 234–238.

Wang, H., Jin, C., Yuan, K., Shakir, T. M., Mao, C., Niu, X., et al. (2015). The alteration of gray matter volume and cognitive control in adolescents with Internet gaming disorder. *Frontiers in Behavioural Neuroscience, 9,* 64.

Weng, C. B., Qian, R. B., Fu, X. M., Lin, B., Han, X. P., Niu, C. S., et al. (2013). Gray matter and white matter abnormalities in online game addiction. *European Journal of Radiology, 82*(8), 1308.

Zero to eight: Children's media use in America 2013: Common sense media. *Common Sense Media: Ratings, Reviews, and Advice,* October 28, 2013. https://www.commonsensemedia.org/research/zero-to-eight-childrens-media-use-in-america-2013/key-finding-2:-kids'-time-on-mobile-devices-triples.

Zhou, Y., Lin, F. C., Du, Y. S., Qin, L. D., Zhao, Z. M., Xu, J. R., et al. (2011). Gray matter abnormalities in internet addiction: A voxel-based morphometry study. *European Journal of Radiology, 79*(1), 92–95.

Index

About the Authors

Sian Phillips, PhD, Cpsych, is a clinical psychologist in Kingston, Ontario. She is a certified DDP therapist, consultant, and trainer, providing training internationally. She also has a private practice, specializing in the assessment and treatment of children who have experienced developmental trauma.

Deni Melim is an elementary teacher in Kingston, Ontario. She collaborates with school boards, mental health organizations across the province, and community partners to support students with developmental trauma.

Daniel Hughes, PhD, is a clinical psychologist and a member of the American Psychological Association and the Dyadic Developmental Psychotherapy Institute. Dr. Hughes is the author of many professional books and has been the keynote speaker at many conferences. His website is danielhughes.org.

Printed in Great Britain
by Amazon

61702579R00208